ARCHITECTURES OF FESTI\
MODERN EURO!

This fourth volume in the European Festival Studies, 1450–1700 series breaks with precedent in stemming from a joint conference (Venice, 2013) between the Society for European Festivals Research and the PALATIUM project supported by the European Science Foundation. The volume draws on up-to-date research by a Europe-wide group of academic scholars and museum and gallery curators to provide a unique, intellectually-stimulating and beautifully-illustrated account of temporary architecture created for festivals of the sixteenth and seventeenth centuries, together with permanent architecture pressed into service for festival occasions across major European locations including Italian, French, Austrian, Scottish and German. Appealing and vigorous in style, the essays look towards classical sources while evoking political and practical circumstances and intellectual concerns – from re-shaping and re-conceptualizing early sixteenth-century Rome, through providing for the well-being and political allegiance of Medici-era Florentines and exploring the teasing aesthetics of performance at Versailles to accommodating players and spectators in seventeenth-century Paris and at royal and ducal events for the Habsburg, French and English crowns. The volume is unique in its field in the diversity of its topics and the range of its scholarship and fascinating in its account of the intellectual and political life of Early Modern Europe.

J.R. (Ronnie) Mulryne is Professor Emeritus at the University of Warwick, UK.

Krista De Jonge is Professor of Architectural History at the University of Leuven.

Pieter Martens is a Postdoctoral Research Fellow at the University of Leuven and the Université catholique de Louvain.

R.L.M. (Richard) Morris was elected a Senior Scholar of Trinity College, Cambridge, in 2011 and is now completing doctoral research there.

European Festival Studies: 1450–1700

Series Editors

This series, in association with the Society for European Festivals Research, builds on the current surge in interest in the circumstances of European Festivals – their political, religious, social, economic and cultural implications as well as the detailed analysis of their performance (including ephemeral architecture, scenography, scripts, music and soundscape, dance, costumes, processions and fireworks) in both indoor and outdoor locations.

Festivals were interdisciplinary and, on occasion, international in scope. They drew on a rich classical heritage and developed a shared pan-European iconography as well as exploiting regional and site-specific features. They played an important part in local politics and the local economy, as well as international negotiations and the conscious presentation of power, sophistication and national identity.

The series, including both essay collections and monographs, seeks to analyse the characteristics of individual festivals as well as to explore generic themes. It draws on a wealth of archival documentary evidence, alongside the resources of galleries and museums, to study the historical, literary, performance and material culture of these extravagant occasions of state.

Architectures of Festival in Early Modern Europe

Fashioning and Re-fashioning Urban and Courtly Space

EDITED BY
J.R. MULRYNE, KRISTA DE JONGE,
PIETER MARTENS, AND R.L.M. MORRIS

First published 2018
by Routledge
2 Park Square, Milton Park, Abingdon, Oxon OX14 4RN

and by Routledge
605 Third Avenue, New York, NY 10017

First issued in paperback 2022

Routledge is an imprint of the Taylor & Francis Group, an informa business

Publisher's Note
The publisher has gone to great lengths to ensure the quality of this reprint but points out that some imperfections in the original copies may be apparent.

British Library Cataloguing-in-Publication Data
A catalogue record for this book is available from the British Library

Library of Congress Cataloging-in-Publication Data
A catalog record for this title has been requested

ISBN 13: 978-1-03-240208-6 (pbk)
ISBN 13: 978-1-4724-3200-1 (hbk)
ISBN 13: 978-1-315-56780-8 (ebk)

DOI: 10.4324/9781315567808

Typeset in Times New Roman
by Apex CoVantage, LLC

Contents

Figures

Tables

Plates

Contributors

Sydney Anglo (FBA, FSA, FLSW) is Emeritus Professor in the History of Ideas, University of Wales. He has published widely on the history of tournament and chivalry, including the following books: *The Great Tournament Roll of Westminster* (Oxford and London: Oxford University Press, 1968); *Chivalry in the Renaissance* (Woodbridge: Boydell, 1990); *The Martial Arts of Renaissance Europe* (New Haven and London: Yale University Press, 2000); and *L'Escrime, la danse, et l'art de la guerre* (Paris: Bibliothèque nationale de France, 2011). His many books also include: *Spectacle, Pageantry and Early Tudor Policy* (Oxford: Oxford University Press, 1969, 2nd ed., 1997); *Images of Early Tudor Kingship* (Seaby, 1992); and *Machiavelli – the First Century* (Oxford: Oxford University Press, 2005). Recent chapters on Renaissance festivals include: 'The Thames *en Fête*' in Margaret Shewring (ed.), *Waterborne Pageants and Festivities in the Renaissance: Essays in Honour of J.R. Mulryne* (Farnham UK and Burlington VT: Ashgate, 2013), pp. 265–73.

Katharina Bedenbender studied art history, classical archaeology and cultural management at the universities of Marburg, Berlin and Karlsruhe. In 2010 she was awarded a Master of Arts for a thesis on 'Architecture and Decoration of the Staircase of the Scuola Grande di San Rocco in Venice'. Since April 2010 she has been working on her PhD project 'Stairs and Ceremonies in Early Modern Venice' under the direction of Prof. Dr. Hans Aurenhammer and Prof. Dr. Alessandro Nova. From April 2010 to December 2012 she was supported by PhD scholarships at the Bibliotheca Hertziana, Max Planck Institute for Art History, Rome, and from April 2013 until March 2014 at the Centro Tedesco di Studi Veneziani (German Institute for Venetian Studies) in Venice. From 2014 until 2015 she worked as assistant professor for art history at the Goethe University in Frankfurt. More recently she has been preparing a post-doctoral project on Apulian architecture.

Marie-Claude Canova-Green is Professor of French and Comparative Literature at Goldsmiths, University of London. She has research interests in European court entertainments and has edited a four-volume collection of seventeenth-century ballet *libretti*. Recent chapters on festivals include 'Ambivalent Fictions: The Bordeaux Celebrations of the Wedding of Louis XIII and Anne d'Autriche', in Margaret M. McGowan (ed.), *Dynastic Marriages 1612/1615. A Celebration of the Habsburg and Bourbon Unions* (Farnham UK and Burlington VT: Ashgate, 2013), pp. 179–99; 'Lepanto Revisited: Water-fights and the Turkish Threat in Early Modern Europe (1571–1656)', in Margaret Shewring (ed.), *Waterborne Pageants and Festivities in the Renaissance: Essays in Honour of J.R. Mulryne*

(Farnham UK and Burlington VT: Ashgate, 2013), pp. 177–98; and 'Warrior King or King of War? Louis XIII's Entries into his *Bonnes Villes* (1620-1629)', in J.R. Mulryne, with Maria Ines Aliverti and Anna Maria Testaverde (eds), *Ceremonial Entries in Early Modern Europe: The Iconography of Power* (Farnham UK and Burlington VT: Ashgate, 2015), pp. 77–98. She has also published monographs on Molière and early modern French drama as well as an edited collection, *Writing Royal Entries in Early Modern Europe* (Turnhout: Brepols, 2013). A further edited collection on celebrations for the wedding of Charles I and Henrietta-Maria is forthcoming (Abingdon UK and New York: Routledge, 2017).

Richard Cooper is Emeritus Professor of French and Fellow and former Vice-Principal of Brasenose College, University of Oxford. His publications include *Maurice Scève, The Entry of Henri II into Lyon, September 1548*, text with an introduction and notes (Tempe: Arizona Medieval and Renaissance Texts and Studies, 1997); *Marguerite de Navarre, Chrétiens et mondains, poèmes épars*, vol. 8 of *Œuvres complètes de Marguerite de Navarre* (Paris: H. Champion, 2007); [Jean Maugin], *Le Premier Livre de l'histoire et ancienne cronique de Gérard d'Euphrate, duc de Bourgogne* (Paris: Classiques Garnier, 2012); *Roman Antiquities in Renaissance France (1515–65)* (Farnham UK and Burlington VT: Ashgate, 2013). Recent chapters on Renaissance Festivals include: 'Legate's Luxury: The Entries of Cardinal Alessandro Farnese to Avignon and Carpentras, 1553', in H. Visentin and N. Russell (eds), *French Ceremonial Entries in the Sixteenth Century: Event, Image, Text* (Toronto: Centre for Renaissance and Reformation Studies, 2007), pp. 133–61; 'French Renaissance Entries and the Antique', in Marie-Claude Canova-Green and Jean Andrews with Marie-France Wagner (eds), *Writing Royal Entries in Early Modern Europe (1500–1800)* (Turnhout: Brepols, 2012), pp. 153–76; 'French Renaissance Waterborne Festivals in the Sixteenth Century', in Margaret Shewring (ed.), *Waterborne Pageants and Festivities in the Renaissance: Essays in Honour of J.R. Mulryne* (Farnham UK and Burlington VT: Ashgate, 2013), pp. 9–36; and 'The Theme of War in French Renaissance Entries', in J.R. Mulryne, with Maria Ines Aliverti and Anna Maria Testaverde (eds), *Ceremonial Entries in Early Modern Europe: The Iconography of Power* (Farnham UK and Burlington VT: Ashgate, 2015), pp. 15–35.

Lucinda H.S. Dean (Lucy) is a Lecturer in History at the University of Highlands and Islands. Her doctoral thesis (University of Stirling, 2013) bridges the gap between medieval and early modern to provide the first long-term study of Scottish inaugurations/coronations, funerals and weddings (including consort coronations) across four centuries, placing these ceremonies within the complexities of their political context. This research is currently being revised as the basis for a monograph, *Death and the Royal Succession: Scottish Funerals, Coronations and Weddings, c. 1214–1543* (*St. Andrews Scottish History Series*, Boydell and Brewer). She has recently published chapters in E. Woodacre and S. McGlyn (eds), *The Image and Perception of Monarchy in Medieval and Early*

Modern Europe (Cambridge Scholar Publishing, September 2014) and in J.R. Mulryne, with Maria Ines Aliverti and Anna Maria Testaverde (eds), *Ceremonial Entries in Early Modern Europe. The Iconography of Power* (Farnham UK and Burlington VT: Ashgate, 2015) as well as a co-edited volume on *Medieval and Early Modern Representation of Authority in Scotland, England and Ireland* (Abingdon UK and New York: Routledge, 2016). Her new project explores ideas of manhood, masculinity and coming of age, comparing the later Stewart kings. She is also working on collaborative projects in public history in Perth and other locations.

Felicia M. Else is Associate Professor of Art History at Gettysburg College, Pennsylvania. She has published on Bartolomeo Ammannati's architecture and sculpture in the *Burlington Magazine* and the *Sixteenth Century Journal* as well as interdisciplinary studies on water, cartography and science in *Imago Mundi* and *Medicea: Rivista interdisciplinare di studi Medicei*. She has completed work on a forthcoming book in conjunction with the Society for European Festivals Research entitled *The Politics of Water in the Art and Festivals of Medici Florence: From Neptune Fountain to Naumachia* (Abingdon UK and New York: Routledge, 2017).

Martina Frank is Professor of History of Architecture at the Università Ca' Foscari in Venice. Previous academic appointments led her to teaching and research at several European and North American institutions including Lecturer at the Universities of Padua, Udine, Graz and Vienna, Visiting Professor at the Université de Montréal and research scholar at the Canadian Centre for Architecture. She has published books on the patronage of the Manin family, *Virtù e Fortuna. Il mecenatismo e le committenze artistiche della famiglia Manin* (Venice: Istituto Veneto di Scienze, Lettere ed Arti, 1996); on *Baldassare Longhena* (Venice: Istituto Veneto di Scienze, Lettere ed Arti, 2004) and recent work on the representation of gardens in painting from the Middle Ages to the twentieth century, *Giardini dipinti. Il giardino nella pittura europea dal medioevo al primo Novecento* (Verona: Banca Popolare di Verona/Arsenale Editore EBS, 2008). A particular focus of interest in her research has related to architecture, art patronage and art collecting in the Republic of Venice from the fifteenth to eighteenth centuries, to Venetian baroque palaces, villas and gardens in relation to the European cultural background, to academies of art in the nineteenth century, and to theatrical and architectural drawings by the Galli Bibiena workshop in North American collections.

Pauline Lemaigre-Gaffier is a graduate of the École Normale Supérieure and the University of Paris 1 (Panthéon-Sorbonne). She is Associate Professor in Early Modern History at the University of Versailles-Saint-Quentin-en-Yvelines. Her PhD dissertation (Paris 1, 2011) has been published under the title *Administrer les Menus Plaisirs du Roi. La cour, l'État et les spectacles dans la France des Lumières* (Ceyzérieu: Champ Vallon, 2016).

Francesca Mattei obtained her BA and MA at the IUAV University of Venice in 2006, her Master in Architectural History at the University of Rome 3 in 2008, and her PhD in Architectural History in IUAV University of Venice in 2012. In 2013 she won a two-year post-doc research grant at the Polytechnic University of Milan, Mantua campus, focusing on the topic 'Gonzaga's Residences in the Early 16th Century'. In 2016, she won the Alexander von Humboldt Fellowship on 'The drawings by Anonymous Mantovanus A in European Renaissance Architectural Culture'. She has published *Eterodossia e vitruvianesimo. Palazzo Naselli a Ferrara (1527–1538)* (Rome: Campisano, 2013) and many articles dealing with early modern and contemporary architecture; she is the editor of *Federico II Gonzaga e le arti* (Rome: Bulzoni, 2016).

Mikael Bøgh Rasmussen took his PhD in Art History in 2001 in Copenhagen. He is currently H.M. The Queen's Reference Librarian, The Royal Danish Collection. His former employments include Curator at the Museum of National History, Frederiksborg Castle, Hillerød (Denmark); External Lecturer in Art History and Renaissance Studies at the University of Copenhagen; and Academic Staff Member and Local Editor of the RIHA Journal, Danish National Art Library, Copenhagen. His publications include: with Erik Fischer and Ernst Jonas Bencard, *Melchior Lorck*, Vols I–V, Copenhagen 2009– ; '*Maiestatis regiae pictor*. Pieter Isaacsz, portrait painter by appointment to His Majesty', in Badeloch Noldus and Juliette Roding (eds), *Pieter Isaacsz. Court Painter, Art Dealer and Spy* (Turnhout: Brepols, 2007), pp. 139–49; 'Defining dominance: Abraham Wuchters versus Karel van Mander III', in Gerson Digital: *Denmark*, Dutch and Flemish art in European perspective 1500–1900, Part II (The Hague: RKD, 2015), Chapter 6 (http://gersondenmark.rkdmonographs.nl/6.-defining-dominance).

Veronika Sandbichler was from 1992 to 2010 Curator and Vice-Director of the Kunsthistorisches Museum, Schloss Ambras Innsbruck, and has been Director there since 2010. Her duties involve devising and organizing exhibitions, which have included *Wir sind Helden: Habsburgische Feste der Renaissance* (2005), and *Die Hochzeit Erzherzog Ferdinands II: Eine Bildreportage* (2010). Her research topics centre on Habsburg court festivals, museology and the history of collecting. Her recent publications include: '"souil schonen, kostlichen und verwunderlichen zeugs . . ." Die Kunst- und Wunderkammer Erzherzog Ferdinands II auf Schloss Ambras', in Sabine Haag et al. (eds), *Das Haus Habsburg und die Welt der fürstlichen Kunstkammern im 16. und 17. Jahrhundert* (Vienna, 2015), pp. 167–193; 'Torneos y Fiestas de corte de los Habsburgoen los siglos XV y XVI', in Krista De Jonge, Bernardo J. García García and Alicia Esteban Estringana (eds), *El Legado de Borgoña: Fiesta y Ceremonia Cortesana en la Europa de los Austrias (1454–1648)* (Madrid: Fondación Carlos de Amberes, 2010), pp. 607–24; and 'Elements of Power in Court Festivals of Habsburg Emperors in the Sixteenth Century', in J.R. Mulryne, with Maria Ines Aliverti and Anna Maria Testaverde

Introduction: making space for festival

J.R. Mulryne

Architecture and festival have much in common. In the early modern period both speak an international language of symbol and allusion rooted in the classics or the Bible. Both are trans-temporal, reaching back to an established or imagined history in order to create contemporary meaning. Both have aims that are on the one hand political – to boost the self-image of a state – on the other, aesthetic. The interplay between the two forms of creative expression is wide-reaching, whether one thinks of ephemeral architecture constructed to enhance a festival occasion, or permanent architecture adapted or pressed into service to house it. Architecture and festival are, that is to say, typically allied or interactive across sixteenth- and seventeenth-century Europe in a search for expression in the service of dynasty or family, city or state.

This alliance of architecture and festival took many forms. At one extreme, it could involve destruction, as in Pope Paul III's clearances to accommodate the entry of Charles V to Rome in 1535. It could be multiply allusive in, for example, the repeated re-interpretation of an ancient building such as the Colosseum, when religious and cultural change led to a re-conceptualisation of the building's meaning. The alliance could be one of opposites. Festival by its nature is theatre-like, of the moment and occasional. It therefore sits at the opposite end of the spectrum from architecture, which – as normally conceived – looks towards permanence. Yet festival has frequently offered architecture a voice, in the interests of church, state or polis. The ephemeral architecture of festival, like its permanent cousin, has found itself subject to a technical and regulatory context which has shaped and constrained what it has to say – or can say. There are further points of contact. Public architecture and festival have on occasion come together to contribute to the health and well-being of a city, as well as to enhance its ceremonial life – as in the high art and public utility of fountains in Medici Florence. Each of these cross-overs between architecture and festival is among those summarised in this introduction. Taken together, the book and its chapters illustrate the richly-diverse, creative inter-dependence of the two associated art forms.

The book's origins

A growing interest among academic teachers and curator-archivists in the interaction of festival and architecture led, as the Preface to this book explains, to the Society for European Festivals Research and the European Science Foundation's PALATIUM project,[1] convening a joint conference, which took place in March 2013 in the University of Warwick's base in Venice, the Palazzo Pesaro Papafava. The conference, under the title *Making Space for Festival: Interactions between Architecture and Performance*, together with subsequent collaboration between the two organisations,[2] was suggested and then supported by the ESF, and has proved exceptionally fruitful, drawing together researchers with expertise across a wide range of disciplines centred on the interplay of late medieval and early modern architecture with the historical, political and performance concerns of students of festival. In Venice, social and political historians met with and heard papers by museum curators; teachers and practitioners of theatre discussed common interests with students of history of art; and students of literature shared insights with teachers and practitioners of music. The outcome was a set of conference papers judged sufficiently rich to serve as the basis of two volumes in the 'European Festival Studies 1450–1700' series, not the one volume we initially envisaged. The first of these is the present volume. The second, under the working title 'Occasions of State', will appear shortly and will emphasise festivals and architecture as agents of political image-building and state control. In both cases, conference papers delivered at Venice have been re-thought and further researched and illustrated, as a result of discussion at the conference and/or stimulated by editorial questions and comment.

Architecture and festival: the creation and transmission of meaning

The present collection begins with two essays, from Mårten Snickare and Richard Cooper, which complement each other by adopting, in Snickare's case, a historically and culturally wide-angled discussion of the meanings in early modern imagination and thought attributed to the Roman Colosseum; and in Cooper's case, by a thoroughly-researched, more tightly-focused discussion of the 1535 entry of Charles V into the Imperial city. For Snickare, writing under the title 'A Productive Conflict', the monumental Colosseum, already in ruins by the sixteenth century, became 'the site where the two grand narratives of Antiquity and Christianity clashed', most evidently when the ancient building was appropriated as an element in the papal *possessi* (ceremonial entries) of the sixteenth and seventeenth centuries. In the modern world, Snickare points out, the Colosseum came to provide a stage for grand public spectacles, including Easter Passion plays, consciously and

[1] The full title of the PALATIUM project's research was 'Court Residences as Places of Exchange in Late Medieval and Early Modern Europe, 1400–1700 (PALATIUM)'. The project was conducted under the leadership of Professor Krista De Jonge of the Katholieke Universiteit, Leuven, and concluded its investigations in 2016.

[2] This collaboration has included a conference held by invitation in Mons in 2016 as part of the city's European City of Culture celebrations.

inversely reminiscent of the pagan games of antiquity during which Christians were slaughtered. This was a role which allowed the building to serve as a marker for the triumph of Christianity over paganism, specifically when papal processions took it in as they claimed the city for a new pope: an act of reconceptualization by which architecture became imaginatively reassigned as an element of festival.

Richard Cooper's 'A New Sack of Rome?' discusses a more specific yet equally potent reassignment. The aim of Paul III was to recover a Roman *via triumphalis* in order to secure, in visual and imaginative terms, the transformation of an impoverished city, haunted by recollection of its sack eight years earlier by the forces of Charles V, into a city with, once more, a claim to be seen – by Charles and the rest of Europe – as the unchallenged capital of the Roman world. The means were unsparing: the demolition of more than 200 houses and at least eleven churches in order to create a processional route that evoked the inherited grandeur of the city's past. The re-made cityscape thus took on a role, like the conceptual transformations of the Colosseum, in forging Rome's present and future identity out of its past.

Mikael Bøgh Rasmussen's study of the 1563 entry of Maximilian II into Vienna follows and partners these studies by showing how the Habsburg authorities in Vienna sought to boost their city's self-image by linking it with a classical past. Innovative use of ephemeral architecture in the classical style provided the means; Bøgh Rasmussen analyses this architecture in detail. Remarkably, the event also involved an impressive proportion of the city's entire population. Something of the order of 6,000 residents participated to create – through sheer numbers – a living form of temporary architecture. Theatrically costumed and rehearsed, the performers were accompanied by a soundscape typified by cannon fire, and by a *coup de théâtre* featuring an artificial eagle descending vertiginously from the spire of St Stephan's cathedral. This was festal street theatre used to transform the cityscape, however briefly – and without destruction – into an a-historical domain of the mind, by way of an alliance between temporary architecture and the suasive power of festival.

The interface of the festal and the social-political

In one of its many facets, architecture may express aesthetic and cultural meaning. In another, it is practical in intent and effect. Felicia M. Else's chapter, 'Fountains of Wine and Water', takes in both. She notes how a festival, in this case the entry of Joanna of Austria to Florence in 1565, seeks in familiar fashion to enhance the city's prestige. Her study centres, however, on an architectural feature that had a directly practical effect on civic life. Water fountains in the second half of the sixteenth century not only enhanced the Florentine streetscape, but contributed in addition to public health and the city's modernisation, and so played a part in the tightening hold of the Medici on popular allegiance. Fountains had a further role when water turned to wine. The wine-fountain known as the Arch of Happiness, with its inscription *Hilaritas P.P. Florent*,[3] offered, like wine fountains in cities across Europe, to promote public *joie de vivre* and a sense of communal well-being – for one festal day. As Else shows, this is a teasing web of inter-related roles that finds its most high-level expression in Bartolomeo Ammannati's Neptune fountain, an incontestably major work of street architecture which in itself incorporates dynastic, community and festal elements in a complex fusion.

Architecture, festival and the natural environment

If we think of architecture in a wider sense we may turn to the natural as well as the built environment. Two chapters, by Lucinda Dean and Marie-Claude Canova-Green, consider the relationship between festivals and their natural and man-made settings, in order to show the synergies between them. Lucinda H.S. Dean's chapter 'Making the Best of What They Had' discusses how festal occasions such as coronations, weddings and funerals may contribute to 'sacring' the space in which they're performed, or through which they move. Scotland in the thirteenth to the seventeenth centuries, she shows, was distinctive in employing a deceased monarch's funeral procession to connect him with his former land and, in so doing, to confer status on the towns through which the royal corpse passed or which were chosen as resting-places. The more simply politic aim of impressing an incoming royal or élite person by selecting, for his or her first impressions, localities where cultural achievement was greatest led, for example, to St Andrews being chosen to represent Scotland's 'advanced Renaissance culture and learning' when Marie de Guise arrived in 1538. If the motive was commonplace, this ordinary tactic reflects an appreciation of the reciprocal relationship between high ceremony and the natural or the built environment, in the St Andrews instance the environment of university, castle and cathedral.

For Marie-Claude Canova-Green in 'Transformed Gardens', the fascination of garden architecture when set alongside the Versailles festivals of 1664 to 1674 rests on how sophisticated and playful the interaction may become between stage and garden in the hands – in both cases – of expert designers. She writes: 'the royal gardens turned out to be just as artificial as the ones that were painted on the stage sets devised by Vigarani or Torelli' and 'the natural settings of the festivals were, just like Vigarani's stage, the realm of *trompe-l'oeil*'. These are perceptions which would during performance tease an audience's mind as well as its sight, and were meant to do so. Gardens may serve as a designed continuation of the stage set; and the stage set may serve as a continuation of the gardens, although Canova-Green cautions against taking this to be invariable practice. The built auditorium and its audience may, as she shows, itself become the stage in a spatial conceit of almost dizzying complexity, where the *ensemble* of building (the early palace at

[3] 'The Happiness of the Florentine People'.

as Lemaigre-Gaffier demonstrates, with the *Menus Plaisirs* expanding over the period of study (1660–1700) to take on responsibilities in the day-to-day as well as the festival-day conduct of court life. This is perhaps the closest our collection comes to mapping the inter-engaged activities of finance, festival, architecture and the organisation of court culture within, in this case, a rigidly prescribed ritual of behaviour.

Making space for festival

As this brief set of summaries of, and introduction to, the essays in this book has shown, the ways in which the relationship between architecture and festival can be construed – and were construed at the 2013 conference in Venice – are multiple and diverse. In many ways, architecture is the mistress of festival, providing venues and influencing and enhancing or restricting the type of festival which can be presented. This is true of both indoor and exterior space, especially when one thinks of courtyard and park, as well as great hall and purpose-built permanent or semi-permanent locations. Equally important, the architectural spaces for performance carry with them dynastic and historic associations which exert an influence on, and introduce meanings to, the festivals performed within them. They also speak to the achievements of human skill and enterprise. Artificial and natural landscapes, great gardens and open vistas exert their own influence, speaking on various occasions to the wildness of nature on the one hand and to its enrichment by human ingenuity on the other. The chosen location for performance may draw attention to the architecture of cityscape with its implications for historic roots, civic dignity and public well-being. The built environment, widely understood, serves as an active voice in the meanings of festival.

Ephemeral architecture represents in many ways how festival answers back. The elaborate iconographies of ephemeral arches and monuments and obelisks, familiar to every student of festival, represent acts of the mind to stand for, or against, the implicit language of the built environment within which a festival is set or through which a festival procession moves. The processional route followed may offer, in itself, a mute commentary declaring the antiquity of dynasty or city, or the current social and religious hierarchies they embrace. The order of the procession constructs a rigid order of precedence which ideally conforms to, or may on occasion be at variance with, the realities of social and political influence, wealth and power in the society it offers to reflect and the architecture which otherwise expresses these realities. The involvement of militias and liveried retainers tells a story about that society and its power structures which may or may not be true to its actual relationships. The attendance of the common people as audience, and their responsiveness, is, as with every form of theatre, essential to festival's meaning and functioning. In this regard, festival offers a further version of temporary architecture, built out of audience, performers, costume, soundscape and rehearsed behaviours and routines.

The interaction between architecture and festival and the space – imaginative as well as actual – which negotiates between them and which they negotiate, has not often been studied in depth or from multiple angles in one place. We are glad to offer the essays in this book as a map which others may wish to follow and use as an introduction to the diverse perspectives from which the two art forms, and the synergies between them, may be explored.

Chapter 1

A productive conflict

The Colosseum and early modern religious performance

Mårten Snickare

The importance of Antiquity for the political and cultural life of early modern Rome can hardly be overestimated. Scholars, antiquarians, collectors, dealers and forgers were absorbed in the textual and material remains of ancient Rome; artists and architects turned to the ancient sculptures and buildings as models and touchstones; aristocrats looked at Roman Caesars and commanders as role models; people from all over Europe travelled to Rome to experience the ancient marvels.[1]

However, this intense preoccupation with Antiquity was not without tensions. After all, the Caesars and citizens of ancient Rome had been heathens, worshipping false gods. While on the one hand admiring, and building on, the splendour of ancient Rome, on the other hand the early modern papal city also felt a need to display its triumph over the pagan past. Ancient buildings and other remains were not only revered and admired, they also became subject to reconceptualization and physical transformation. The Pantheon, originally a temple to all the Roman gods, had already been converted into a Christian church in the seventh century. Next to the Pantheon, the gothic church of S Maria Sopra Minerva by its very name called attention to the fact that it was built directly on the foundations of a temple to Minerva – thus both supported by, and triumphing over, the Ancient heritage. A similar case is Trajan's column, one of the most admired and well-preserved ancient monuments in the city. In 1588 Pope Sixtus V commissioned a colossal statue of St Peter to be placed on top of the column, in the place where there was originally a statue of the triumphant emperor.[2] Still in its place, the statue of the

---

[1] Richard Krautheimer, *The Rome of Alexander VII* (Princeton, NJ: Princeton University Press, 1985); Leon Barkan, *Unearthing the Past: Archaeology and Aesthetics in the Making of Renaissance Culture* (New Haven, CT: Yale University Press, 1999); David Karmon, *The Ruin of the Eternal City: Antiquity and Preservation in Renaissance Rome* (New York: Oxford University Press, 2011).

[2] Giovanni Augusti and Vincenzo Farinella, 'Nuove ricerche sulla Colonna Traiana nel Rinascimento', in Salvatore Settis (ed.), *La Colonna Traiana* (Turin: Einaudi, 1988), pp. 549–89; Bruno Brizzi, 'The Forum and Column of Trajan After the Fall of the Empire', in Filippo Coarelli (ed.), *The Column of Trajan* (Rome: Editore Colombo, 2000), pp. 229–43.

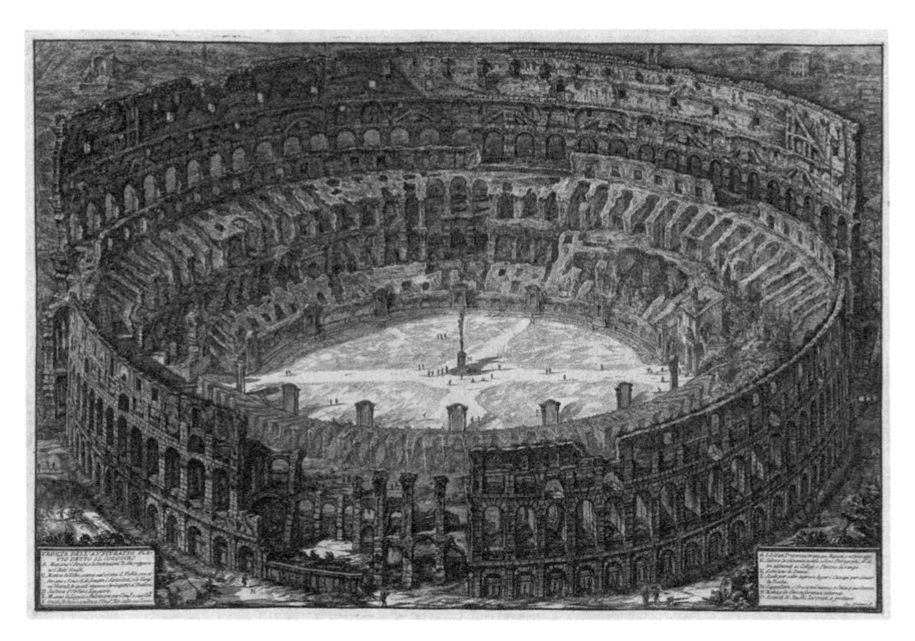

Figure 1.1 Giovanni Battista Piranesi, 'Veduta dell'Anfiteatro Flavio detto il Colosseo', etching in *Vedute di Roma*, 1776 (© and photo: National Library of Sweden)

first pope is thus literally exalted by the firm foundation of Antiquity while, at the same time, triumphing over it.

Matters were brought to a head at the Flavian Amphitheatre, or Colosseum (Figure 1.1). On the one hand it was the most remarkable remnant of ancient grandeur, the foremost landmark of the city and the obvious architectural model to imitate and emulate. On the other hand it was the stage for the most brutal persecution and execution of early Christian martyrs.[3] The Colosseum could thus be described as the site where the two grand narratives of Antiquity and Christianity clashed.

This chapter shows how the ambivalent status of the Colosseum in early-modern Christian Rome made it a most striking and productive stage for religious ceremonial; how the emotional intensity of the religious performances was heightened by the sublime ruin and the gory narratives it evoked; and how the Colosseum in its turn was transformed, physically as well as conceptually, by the performances. I will further show how the productive conflict between Antiquity and Christianity was dramatized in a ritual interplay – or kind of *paragone* – between the Colosseum and St Peter's, centre of the Catholic Church.

---

[3] Donald G. Kyle, *Spectacles of Death in Ancient Rome* (London: Routledge, 1998), pp. 242–8.

The Colosseum, the largest amphitheatre of the Roman Empire, was constructed between 72 and 80 AD, under the emperors Vespasian and Titus.[4] With room for 50,000 seated spectators it was a stage for gladiator and animal fights as well as other public spectacles, such as mock sea battles, mythological dramas, and executions. In the sixth century, after five centuries of use, it was closed to the public due to disrepair. The collapse of the outer walls of the southern part in the eighth century gave the ruin more or less its present shape.

Already in the Middle Ages, papal interest in the Colosseum can be observed.[5] The still-standing northern façade provided a magnificent backdrop along the main papal processional route between St Peter's and the Lateran, its preservation thus becoming a concern for the popes. At the same time, the very same popes made use of the ruined southern part as a stone quarry for the erection of new churches and palaces. Long regarded by scholars as an act of disrespect for the ancient monument, this practice might instead be understood – as art historian David Karmon has recently suggested – as an expression of the great value that came to be attached to it. Stones from the Colosseum were treated as relics which carried with them the grandeur of Ancient Rome as well as the blood of Christian martyrs. An interesting example is the papal Benediction Loggia, built in front of the old St Peter's in the mid fifteenth century. Pius II explicitly ordered stone from the Colosseum for the construction of three superimposed arcades, stylistically recalling the shape of the amphitheatre. Karmon suggests that we interpret this as a way of resurrecting the fallen arcades of the Colosseum in a prominent new location.[6] Arguably, a link was thus created between the ancient amphitheatre and St Peter's, the centre of the Catholic Church. This link would be further elaborated and strengthened in seventeenth-century papal ceremonial.

Passion plays

In the late fifteenth century, almost a thousand years after the last gladiator fights, the Colosseum again became a stage for grand public spectacles, as the Confraternity of the Gonfalone received papal permission to use the ruin for Passion

---

4 On the history of the Colosseum, see P. Colagrossi, *L'Anfiteatro Flavio: nei suoi venti secoli di storia* (Florence: Libreria editrice fiorentina, 1913); Michela di Macco, *Il Colosseo: funzione simbolica, storica, urbana* (Rome: Bulzoni editore, 1971); Jean-Claude Golvin, *L'amphithéâtre romain: essai sur la théorisation de sa forme et de ses fonctions*, 2 vols (Paris: Boccard, 1988); Rosella Rea, 'The Colosseum Through the Centuries', in Ada Gabucci (ed.), *The Colosseum* (Los Angeles, CA: The J Paul Getty Museum, 2000), pp. 161–229; Keith Hopkins and Mary Beard, *The Colosseum* (Cambridge, MA: Harvard University Press, 2005).

5 Karmon, *The Ruin of the Eternal City*, pp. 125ff.

6 Ibid., p. 134.

plays in Easter week.[7] From 1490 to 1539 the Confraternity regularly staged lavish plays with elaborate stage settings and numerous actors and musicians, attracting large audiences. The revival of the Colosseum as a performance venue had direct repercussions on the physical shape of the monument: a new circuit wall around the arena replaced the vanishing traces of the original wall, and new seating was installed. In that way, the adaptation of the ancient ruin to fit the religious performances also involved a partial reconstruction of its original shape.[8]

The Confraternity's choice of venue for the Passion plays was anything but arbitrary. The legends of Christian martyrs who had been brutally butchered in the arena served to heighten the emotional effect of the performance of Christ's suffering and death, while the staging of Christ's Resurrection against the backdrop of the ruinous building formed a strong image of the triumph of Christianity over the pagan past.[9] That an early modern audience was sensitive to this interplay between Antiquity and Christianity is suggested by the following quotation from the travel journal of the German pilgrim Arnold von Harff in 1497:

> *Item in dieser stat lijcht eyn gar schoyn alt pallais ad coliseum geheysschen, is van en buyssen ront off gemmuyrt mit vil kleynen ghewulfften eyn boeuen deme anderen ind bynnen is eyn wijdt ront playtz dae maich man an allen eynden off dit pallais gayn myt steynen trappen. Man saicht uns dat vurtzijden die heren eyn boeuen deme anderen gestanden weren off den trappen, dae hetten sij zo geseyn off dem platz triumpheren strijden vechten ind wylt gedeirs sich zo samen Kempten. Item off desem playtz in dem alden pallays saegen wir off den guden vrijdach unsers heren Ihu passie spleen ind dat gynck allet zo mit leuendichen luden, as dat geysselen crucigen ind wye sich Judas erhangen hatte.*[10]

---

[7] On the Confraternity of the Gonfalone, see Barbara Wisch, 'The Passion of Christ in the Art, Theater, and Penitential Rituals of the Roman Confraternity of the Gonfalone', in Konrad Eisenbichler (ed.), *Crossing the Boundaries: Christian Piety and the Arts in Medieval and Renaissance Confraternities* (Kalamazoo, MI: Medieval Institute Publications, Western Michigan University, 1991), pp. 237–62. On the Passion plays, see Barbara Wisch, 'The Colosseum as a Site for Sacred Theatre: A Prehistory of Carlo Fontana's Project', in Henry A. Millon and Susan Scott Munshower (eds), *An Architectural Progress in the Renaissance and Baroque: Sojourns in and Out of Italy* (University Park, PA: Dept. of Art History, Pennsylvania State University, 1992), pp. 95–111; Nerida Newbigin, 'The Decorum of the Passion: The Plays of the Confraternity of the Gonfalone in the Roman Colosseum, 1490–1539', in Barbara Wisch and Diane Cole Ahl (eds), *Confraternities and the Visual Arts in Renaissance Italy: Ritual, Spectacle, Image* (Cambridge: Cambridge University Press, 2000), pp. 173–202.

[8] Karmon, *The Ruin of the Eternal City*, p. 137.

[9] See also Newbigin, 'The Decorum of the Passion', p. 173.

[10] Arnold von Harff, *Die Pilgerfahrt des Ritters Arnold von Harff* (Cologne: J.M. Heberle, 1860), p. 31.

the suffering and death of Christ (the pavilions are clearly indicated in the etching by Piranesi, see Figure 1.1).[34] Once again recollection of the martyrs was thus mobilised to enhance the emotional effect of the religious ceremony.

In the course of the nineteenth century, the Colosseum was gradually reconceptualised as first and foremost an archaeological site.[35] In our time it has become a site for mass tourism, and for popular cultural projections, such as the blockbuster film *Gladiator* (2000).[36] However, an echo of early modern ceremonial practice lingers in the Good Friday torch light procession from the Colosseum to the Palatine, led by the pope. Flagellants no longer form part of the procession but one might see participants carrying thorny crowns or crosses.

Performative meaning

At its most fundamental level, a performance consists of two elements: space and moving bodies. These two elements are engaged in a constant interplay, affecting, and transforming, each other. Space directs, or choreographs, movement. It places limits, offers possibilities and encourages certain motions rather than others, depending on its physical form as well as its history and previous use. The moving bodies, on the other hand, enhance the space, incorporate it into the whole of the performance and lend it new meaning. They might even bring about physical transformation of space, adjustment to it being made to better suit the choreography of the performance.

Regarded in its interplay with performances and other kinds of bodily movements, a building like the Colosseum appears less stable and invariable than we often tend to think. It is the object of constant renegotiation and transformation, conceptually as well as physically. The meaning of the building becomes not fixed but, rather, performative. It is the meaning performed by and through movements, gestures, and speech acts. However, that is not to say that the meaning of the Colosseum is arbitrary, that it changes with any random action or statement. The performative meaning is governed and limited by the authority of tradition, by conventions, and by the knowledge, authority and social status of the performer(s). In this, it bears a certain resemblance to Judith Butler's definition of performative acts as processes of repetition and citation that necessarily evoke a whole baggage of history and tradition:

> If a performative [action] provisionally succeeds (and I will suggest that 'success' is always and only provisional) then it is not because an intention successfully

34 Hager, 'Carlo Fontana's Project for a Church', p. 336.

35 Hopkins and Beard, *The Colosseum*, pp. 171–3.

36 *Gladiator*, DreamWorks Pictures, 2000; produced by Douglas Wick, David Franzoni and Branko Lustig, directed by Ridley Scott.

> governs the action of speech, but only because that action echoes prior actions, and *accumulates the force of authority through the repetition or citation of a prior and authoritative set of practices*.[37]

This chapter has given examples of acts performed at, and in relation to, the Colosseum in the early modern period. Some of the performers carried authority, such as the pope or Carlo Fontana. Others were less prominent, such as the anonymous pilgrims or the performers and spectators of Passion plays. All of them were engaged in the negotiation of the Colosseum's meaning. However, in this process, all were bound by tradition – or 'prior actions' – and, in particular, by the two authoritative grand narratives of Antiquity and Christianity.

Bibliography

Primary sources

Bonelli de Rasori, Giorgio Maria, *Copioso e compito racconto della cavalcata e cerimonie fatte nell'andare à prendere il possesso in S. Giovanni Laterano N. S. Innocentio X* (Rome, 1644).

Cancellieri, Francesco, *Storia de' solenni possessi de' sommi pontefici* (Rome: Luigi Lazzarini, 1802).

Fontana, Carlo, *Il tempio Vaticano e sua origine* (Rome: Francesco Buagni, 1694).

Fontana, Carlo, *L'Anfiteatro Flavio descritto e delineato* (L'Haja, 1725).

Harff, Arnold von, *Die Pilgerfahrt des Ritters Arnold von Harff* (Cologne: J. M. Heberle, 1860).

Piranesi, Giovanni Battista, *Vedute di Roma* (Rome, 1776).

Secondary sources

Augusti, Giovanni and Vincenzo Farinella, 'Nuove ricerche sulla Colonna Traiana nel Rinascimento', in Salvatore Settis (ed.), *La Colonna Traiana* (Turin: Einaudi, 1988), pp. 549–89.

Barkan, Leon, *Unearthing the Past: Archaeology and Aesthetics in the Making of Renaissance Culture* (New Haven, CT and London: Yale University Press, 1999).

Brizzi, Bruno, 'The Forum and Column of Trajan After the Fall of the Empire', in Filippo Coarelli (ed.), *The Column of Trajan* (Rome: Editore Colombo, 2000), pp. 229–43.

---

[37] Judith Butler, *Bodies that Matter: On the Discursive Limits of Sex* (New York: Routledge, 1993), pp. 226–7.

Butler, Judith, *Bodies That Matter: On the Discursive Limits of Sex* (New York: Routledge, 1993).

Colagrossi, P., *L'Anfiteatro Flavio: nei suoi venti secoli di storia* (Florence: Libreria editrice fiorentina, 1913).

Golvin, Jean-Claude, *L'amphithéâtre romain: essai sur la théorisation de sa forme et de ses fonctions*, 2 vols (Paris: Boccard, 1988).

Hager, Helmut, 'Carlo Fontana's Project for a Church in Honour of the "*Ecclesia Triumphans*" in the Colosseum, Rome', *Journal of the Warburg and Courtauld Institutes*, 36 (1973), 319–37.

Hopkins, Keith and Mary Beard, *The Colosseum* (Cambridge, MA: Harvard University Press, 2005).

Ingersoll, Richard Joseph, *The Ritual Use of Public Space in Renaissance Rome* (unpublished diss., University of California, Berkeley, CA, 1985).

Karmon, David, *The Ruin of the Eternal City: Antiquity and Preservation in Renaissance Rome* (Oxford and New York: Oxford University Press, 2011).

Krautheimer, Richard, *The Rome of Alexander VII* (Princeton, NJ: Princeton University Press, 1985).

Kyle, Donald G., *Spectacles of Death in Ancient Rome* (London: Routledge, 1998).

Macco, Michela di, *Il Colosseo: funzione simbolica, storica, urbana* (Rome: Bulzoni editore, 1971).

Newbigin, Nerida, 'The Decorum if the Passion: The Plays of the Confraternity of the Gonfalone in the Roman Colosseum, 1490–1539', in Barbara Wisch and Diane Cole Ahl (eds), *Confraternities and the Visual Arts in Renaissance Italy: Ritual, Spectacle, Image* (Cambridge: Cambridge University Press, 2000), pp. 173–202.

Rea, Rosella, 'The Colosseum through the Centuries', in Ada Gabucci (ed.), *The Colosseum* (Los Angeles, CA: The J Paul Getty Museum, 2000), pp. 161–229.

Snickare, Mårten, 'Performing Papal Authority. Procession as a Commonplace in 17th Century Rome', in Cathryn Banks and Philiep Bossier (eds), *Commonplace Culture in Western Europe in the Early Modern Period, II: Consolidation of God-Given Power*, Groningen Studies in Cultural Change vol. XL (Leuven, Paris and Walpole, MA: Peeters Publishers, 2011), pp. 143–58.

Wisch, Barbara, 'The Passion of Christ in the Art, Theater, and Penitential Rituals of the Roman Confraternity of the Gonfalone', in Konrad Eisenbichler (ed.), *Crossing the Boundaries: Christian Piety and the Arts in Medieval and Renaissance Confraternities* (Kalamazoo, MI: Medieval Institute Publications, Western Michigan University, 1991), pp. 237–62.

Wisch, Barbara, 'The Colosseum as a Site for Sacred Theatre: A Prehistory of Carlo Fontana's Project', in Henry A. Millon and Susan Scott Munshower (eds), *An Architectural Progress in the Renaissance and Baroque: Sojourns in and Out of Italy* (University Park, PA: Dept. of Art History, Pennsylvania State University, 1992), pp. 95–111.

Chapter 2

A new sack of Rome? Making space for Charles V in 1536

Richard Cooper

In July 1535, Emperor Charles V was triumphant in Tunis, and a series of newsletters, and then etchings by Jan Cornelisz Vermeyen, record the victory of his fleet and army over the Moslems, and his capture of the city and the port of Goletta.[1] There followed a stately triumphal progress across his territories in the south from Sicily through the Kingdom of Naples,[2] with entries to Messina[3] and Naples[4] rapidly immortalised in festival books, collected by diplomats and forwarded to their rulers in November and early December. No doubt as a consequence of the French invasion of Piedmont, Charles then decided to go north, heading for Siena, Lucca and Florence, where his reception was to be recorded in festival books in French, Italian and German in an international campaign of imperial propaganda. But to arrive in Florence, he had to pass through Rome, where he had never been.

---

[1] See Hendrick J. Horn, *Jan Cornelisz Vermeyen, Painter of Charles V and His Conquest of Tunis*, 2 vols (Doornspijk: Davaco, 1989).

[2] See his itinerary in Jean de Vandenesse, *Journal des voyages de Charles-Quint, de 1514 à 1551*, ed. Louis Prosper Gachard (Brussels: Académie Royale de Belgique, 1874); also in Manuel de Foronda y Aguilera, *Estancias y viajes del Emperador Carlos V* ([Madrid], 1914); additional information in his correspondence, see Otto Looz-Corswaren, 'Die römische Korrispondenz Karls V in Madrid und Simancas', *Nachrichten von der Gesellschaft der Wissenschaften zu Göttingen, Mittlere und neuere Geschichte*, 1 (1934–36), 109–90; Maria Antonietta Visceglia, 'Il viaggio cerimoniale di Carlo V dopo Tunisi', in José Martínez Millán (ed.), *Carlos V y la quiebra del humanismo politico en Europa (1530–1558)*, 4 vols (Madrid: Sociedad estatal para la conmemoración de los centenarios de Felipe II y Carlos V, 2001), vol. 2, pp. 133–72.

[3] For his entry to Messina on 21 October 1535 see the albums: Andrea Sala, *La triomphale entrata di Carlo V Imperadore Augusto, in la inclita citta di Napoli et di Messina con il significato delli Archi Triomphali et delle Figure antiche in Prosa et Versi Latini* ([Rome: A. Blado], 1535); *Copia de una lettera della particularità dell'ordine con il quale la Maestà Cesarea intrò in Messina, et del Triompho et sumptuosi apparati gli forono fatti, carri et Archi Triomphali richissimi con alcuni versi et prosa latini in honore de Sua Maestà* (Rome: A. Blado, 30 October 1535).

[4] For his entry to Naples on 25 November 1535 see the albums by Andrea Sala, *Il triomphale apparato per la entrata de la cesarea maestà in Napoli* (Venice: P. Danza, 1535); and Sala, *La triomphale entrata*.

What kind of welcome would the Eternal City prepare for him, so soon after the last calamitous visit of his army, sharply etched into the Roman memory? Following the Sack of 1527 and the disastrous Tiber floods of 1530, the city remained very poor, its population reduced to some 30,000, its inhabitants fearing a renewed spate of rape and pillage from protestant troops. As the Mantuan ambassador wrote to the Duke: '*perché in effetto la città è povera, consumata dal sacco, et de Diluvii d'acque*' ('because in fact the city is poor, worn down by the Sack and the floods').[5] Other diplomats are unanimous in reporting both the terror of the Roman people and the Pope's own suspicion that Charles has '*quelque maulvaise fantaisie*' ('some evil intention'):[6] '*È 'l vero che Cittadini Romani alcuni però rimangono sospesi et sospetti con qualche ricordo del Sacco che hebbero che non si facci alle volte disordini*' ('The truth is however that some Roman citizens, with memories of the Sack they endured, are anxious and suspicious that there may be outbreaks of disorder').[7]

> *Ancor non sonno asciutte le lachrime dalli occhi che vennero per il sacco ne seppulte ne scordate le ingiurie ch'ha recevuta questa Città di Roma, qual' di qua a cent'anni non è per possere ritornare nel stato et nel essere che era dianzi: chi offende facilmente si scorda, et non l'offeso.*
>
> [The tears shed over the Sack are not yet dry from their eyes, nor are the memories buried or forgotten of the harm suffered by this City of Rome, which for the next hundred years will not be able to return to its former state, nor be as it once was: the offender easily forgets, but not the offended party].[8]

And they confirm the abject poverty of the city: '*Et veramente questa republica è poverissima, ne si ritrova più de ducati 1500 de intrata, tutta però impegnata, et li cittadini sono molto pochi, molto poveri, et con pochissima industria*' ('This city truly is very poor, and its income is no more than 1,500 ducats, which is all pledged, and there are very few citizens, all of them very poor and unproductive').[9]

The prospect of thousands of imperial troops descending on Rome filled with apprehension the city fathers, who were relying on their Roman Pope for help,

---

[5] Dispatch of Pellegrino to the Duke of Mantua, 22 January 1536, in Archivio di Stato, Mantua, ms *Gonzaga* 886.

[6] Dispatch of Jean Du Bellay to François Ier, 23 September 1535, in Jean Du Bellay, *Correspondance*, ed. R. Scheurer, 2 vols (Paris: Société de l'Histoire de France, 1969, 1973), vol. 2, p. 108; he adds that the supporters of the Emperor like the Colonna '*commancent fort à fourbir leurs harnois et faire provision de bastons de guerre*' ('are busily starting to polish their armour and stock up with firearms').

[7] Pellegrino dispatch, 20 November 1535, ms *Gonzaga* 885.

[8] Pellegrino dispatch, 23 November 1535, ms *Gonzaga* 885.

[9] Dispatch of Bragadin to the Venetian Signoria, 5 December 1535, in Archivio di Stato, Venice, *Arch. Propr. Roma*, 5, no. 22.

'*vedendo che per loro si potrà far molto piciola dimostratione verso Sua Maestà se non sono aiutati*' ('seeing that, without help, they themselves could only put on a very poor show for His Majesty').[10] Even as late as March, just before the Emperor finally arrived, many Romans were fleeing the city: '*perchè ognuno voria portare via le sue robe . . ., et assai di questi Romani vano fuori di Roma et fuggino le lor donne per timore che hano*' ('Because everyone would wish to take their possessions away . . ., and many of these Romans are going out of Rome, and their women are fleeing in fear').[11]

A Roman by birth, Paul III was determined to restore his city, to protect it from the depredations of the lime kilns, and to revive the Medici festivals of Leo X.[12] Great celebrations were held for his *possesso* in 1534,[13] which gave a foretaste of the future style, and a sense of the city recovering from a long illness. Within a month of his election, he had appointed Latino Giovenale Manetti to the new post of commissioner for antiquity, responsible for the preservation of the ancient city, working alongside the three *conservatori*[14] and the *maestri delle strade*. Manetti was a humanist,[15] knowledgeable on classical inscriptions, associated with the Roman Accademie dei Vignuaoli and dei Virtuosi, together with Paolo Giovio, Giovanni Gaddi and his secretary Annibale Caro, all passionate antiquarians and collectors.[16] Their pride in their city was soon to be put to its sternest test, faced with the advancing imperial army, the hostility of the citizens, empty municipal and papal coffers, however anxious they were to put on a brave show for their illustrious guest. The ambiguity of attitudes is revealed in a famous letter of Paolo

---

[10] Bragadin dispatch, 5 December 1535.

[11] Rodi, dispatch to the Duke of Ferrara, 31 March 1536, in Archivio di Stato, Modena, *Serie Ambasciatori, Roma*, busta 35, ms 233, III.

[12] See Vincenzo Forcella, *Tornei e giostre, ingressi trionfali e feste carnevalesche in Roma sotto Paolo III* (Rome: Artigianelli, 1885); also Filippo Clementi, *Il Carnevale romano nelle cronache contemporanee* (Rome: F. Settii, 1899), pp. 143–71, 178–84.

[13] *La Coronatione de Papa Paulo Terzo* (Bologna: J. da Rubiera, 1534?).

[14] Emmanuel Rodocanachi, *Institutions communales de Rome sous la papauté* (Paris: A. Picard, 1901), p. 233.

[15] Ludwig Pastor, *The History of the Popes*, vols 11–12, trans. R.F. Kerr (London: Kegan Paul, Trench, Trübner & Co, 1912), vol. 12, pp. 563–6; Léon Dorez, *La Cour du Pape Paul II*, 2 vols (Paris: E. Leroux, 1932), vol. 1, pp. 115–40; Cesare d'Onofrio, *Renovatio Romæ* (Rome: Edizioni Mediterranee, 1973), pp. 138–42; Ronald T. Ridley, 'To Protect the Monuments: The Papal Antiquarian (1534–1870)', *Xenia Antiqua*, 1 (1992), 117–21; Angela Quattrocchi, 'Latino Giovenale de' Manetti: un diplomatico "umanista" nella Curia pontificia', in Armand Jamme and Olivier Poncet (eds), *Offices et Papauté (XIVe–*XVIIe siècles). *Charges, hommes, destins. Actes du Colloque (2001–02)* (Rome: École française de Rome, 2005), pp. 829–40; David Karmon, *The Ruin of the Eternal City: Antiquity and Preservation in Renaissance Rome* (Oxford: Oxford University Press, 2011), pp. 26–7.

[16] Michele Maylender, *Storia delle accademie d'Italia*, 5 vols (Bologna: L. Cappelli, 1926–30), vol. 5, pp. 466–7, 478; Richard A. Cooper, *Litteræ in tempore belli* (Geneva: Droz, 1997), pp. 234–6.

Giovio, who speaks of Rome awaiting Charles '*in publica lætitia et privato luctu*' ('with public joy and private sorrow').[17]

Paul and his advisers put together a very ambitious programme, for which abundant sources have survived,[18] whether in diplomatic dispatches, papal and municipal archives, artists' drawings, or the festival books published in various languages as evidence of the rebirth of Rome.[19] The 1536 entry is also appropriate to the present volume, because it involved wholesale destruction to make space for the imperial triumphal route, in what was the largest programme of demolition in Rome before Sixtus V, making it almost unique in Renaissance festivals for its combination of archæology, scenography and town planning.

The preparations were greatly complicated by the lack of a firm date for the imperial entry, originally expected for New Year 1536[20] (and so leaving little time

---

17 Paolo Giovio, *Lettere*, ed. G.G. Ferrero, 2 vols (Rome: Istituto Poligrafico dello Stato, 1956–58), vol. 1, p. 171, 28 December 1535.

18 Bartolomeo Podestà, 'Carlo V a Roma nell'anno 1536', *Archivio della Società Romana di Storia Patria*, 1 (1877), 303–44; Marialuisa Madonna, 'L'Ingresso di Carlo V a Roma', in Marcello Fagiolo (ed.), *La Città effimera e l'universo artificiale del giardino* (Rome: Officina, 1980), pp. 63–8; Marialuisa Madonna, 'L'Ingresso di Carlo V a Roma', in Marcello Fagiolo (ed.), *La Festa a Roma dal Rinascimento al 1870*, 2 vols (Rome and Turin: U. Allemandi, 1997), vol. 1, pp. 50–65; Marialuisa Madonna, 'Il revival del trionfo classico: Da Alessandro VI alla sfilata dei rioni', in Marcello Fagiolo (ed.), *La Festa a Roma dal Rinascimento al 1870*, 2 vols (Rome and Turin: U. Allemandi, 1997), vol. 1, pp. 34–41, 36; Bonner Mitchell, 'Charles V Triumphator', in James V. Mehl (ed.), *In Laudem Caroli: Renaissance and Reformation Studies for Charles G. Nauert Jr* (Kirksville: Thomas Jefferson University Press, 1998), pp. 95–112. For the decorations made for Charles, see André Chastel, 'Les Entrées de Charles Quint en Italie', in Jean Jacquot (ed.), *Fêtes et cérémonies au temps de Charles Quint. IIe Congrès de l'Association internationale des historiens de la Renaissance (2e section)* (Paris: Éditions du Centre national de la Recherche scientifique, 1960), pp. 197–206; Bonner Mitchell, 'The S.P.Q.R. in Two Roman Festivals of the Early and Mid-Cinquecento', *Sixteenth Century Journal*, 9 (1978) 4, 95–102, 99–100; Bonner Mitchell, *Italian Civic Pageantry in the High Renaissance* (Florence: Olschki, 1979), pp. 125–9; Bonner Mitchell, *The Majesty of the State: Triumphal Progresses of Foreign Sovereigns in Renaissance Italy, 1494–1600* (Florence: Olschki, 1986), pp. 151–66; Vincenzo Saletta, 'Il Viaggio di Carlo V in Italia', *Studi meridionali*, 10 (1977), 268–92; Fabrizio Cruciani, *Teatro nel Rinascimento. Roma 1450–1550* (Rome: Bulzoni, 1983), pp. 568–85; Karmon, *The Ruin*, pp. 101–10.

19 Albums of the entries: [Andrea Sala], *Ordine, pompe, apparati, et cerimonie, delle solenne intrate, di Carlo V Imp. sempre Aug. nella citta di Roma, Siena, et Fiorenza* (Rome: [A. Blado, 1536]); [Sala, Andrea], *Ordine, pompe, apparati e ceremonie della solenne intrata di Carlo Quinto Imp. nella città di Roma* (Bologna: V. Bonardo, [1536]); and that of Zanobio Ceffino for the Duke of Florence, *La Triumphante Entrata di Carlo V Imperatore Augusto in l'alma Citta de Roma Con el significato delli archi triomphali & delle Figure antiche In prosa & versi Latini* (n.p., [1536]).

20 He intended to make a short stay, call a council of Kingdom, then leave for Rome: see the dispatch of Bragadin, 11 December, 1535, in Archivio di Stato, Venice, *Arch. Propr.*

for preparations), then repeatedly put off until Carnival. This delay gave Paul the chance to imitate Medicean festivals when, in expectation of Charles coming in late winter, he and Manetti planned to welcome him with a programme of parades and masquerades for the Carnival of 1536,[21] which had not been celebrated in Rome since the death of Leo X. Manetti and his *maestri delle strade* were keen to give a central position to the Navona festival on *giovedì grasso*, 24 February 1536: to celebrate Charles's victories they recreated Æmilius Paulus's defeat of Perseus and subsequent triumph in 167 BC after the Battle of Pydna in the third Macedonian War. Under Leo X this particular triumph had already been enacted for the *Festa di Agone* in 1514 by Cardinal Tommaso Inghirami, but the choice in 1536 of Paulus's triumph was as much a compliment to the eponymous Pope as to the imperial victor. The thirteen triumphal cars processed from the Capitol, along Via Papale, over Ponte Sant'Angelo to the Vatican, then back to Piazza Navona. On the Friday and Saturday bulls were sent around the city, and jousts were staged.[22] To bring greater prestige to the city, two accounts of the festival were printed and circulated, a new initiative in Rome.[23] Tradition was again renewed on the Carnival Sunday, when the *Festa di Testaccio* was revived, with the usual slaughter of pigs and oxen.[24]

These ceremonies, which required no demolition, took place in the west and south of the city, a different area from that finally planned for Charles's entry, which the Pope and his team had been planning since early December, and on a much bigger scale than the Carnival. To mark the victory in Tunis, they sought to recreate the ancient Via Triumphalis, but starting from the south: a classical *triumphator* would normally have entered from the West in Trastevere, crossed the river on the Pons Triumphalis, then passed the Circus Flaminius, Theatre of Marcellus, Circus Maximus, around the Palatine and the Colosseum, then the Forum, finally

Roma, 5, no. 24: '*La venuta de lo Imperator in questa Citta si aspetta habbi ad esser molto presta*'; Pellegrino wrote on both 3 and 27 November that Charles would be in Rome for Epiphany, ms *Gonzaga* 885.

[21] See Marcello Alberini, *I Ricordi*, ed. D. Orano (Rome: Forzani, 1901), pp. 461–2: '*credendosi che Sua Maestà dovesse venire per el carnesciale*' ('believing that His Majesty would be coming for Carnival'); Giovio also thought Charles would arrive in time for the Testaccio festival, *Lettere*, vol. 1, p. 171, 28 December 1535. It was agreed with the city that the Pope would pay for the Carnival, '*perchè in honorar S.M. saria forse conveniente tutta la pompa della festa di Nagone*' ('because all the pomp of the Navona festival might pehaps be appropriate to honour His Majesty'), see Rodolfo Lanciani, 'La Via del Corso dirizzata et abbellita nel 1538 da Paolo III', *Bulletino della Commissione archeologica comunale di Roma*, 30 (1902), 232–3.

[22] Forcella, *Tornei*, pp. 20–9.

[23] See the album *Li triomphi fatti a Roma il giovedì grasso per la festa di Agone* (reprinted in Rome, 1887); see also the account by E. Carro Ro[mano] sent to Ieronimo Orsino d'Aragona, *L'Ordine della Festa celebrata in Roma, per Carnevale, nella piazza d'Agone & di S Pietro, con la dechiaratione et significato delli carri* (n.p., n.d.).

[24] See Forcella, *Tornei*, pp. 29–31, 39; Clementi, *Carnevale*, p. 179; Cruciani, *Teatro*, pp. 537–48.

ascending the Capitol.[25] Paul III's plan was to welcome the Emperor from the south through the Porta San Sebastiano, picking up the ancient route by the Circus Maximus, and following it accurately, to the Forum, but then, instead of ending at the Capitol, processing to the Vatican. Along this route his team would be able to expose to view the finest antiquities, so that '*le gioie, l'ornamenti, la grandezza, le reputazione e fede delle istorie di questa cittade si mostrasse attraverso le antiquitate et le ruine*' ('the very jewels and ornaments, the greatness, the fame and the truth of this city's history can be displayed through its antiquities and ruins').[26]

The original plan was to embellish the route with a series of richly ornamented triumphal arches, perhaps as many as nine, as suggested in the drawings of Sangallo[27] and in others attributed to Peruzzi,[28] all under the command of Giovanni Gaddi, who would organise the '*archi triomphali et altri ornamenti*' ('triumphal arches and other decorations'), and would enlist Giovio and his humanist friends to do inscriptions: '*dicono che farano 9 archi trionfali che costarano da 15 milla scudi . . . El Iovio è sopra a trovar le invention de le inscription de li archi con altri literati, e così chi a le cure tendano e soleciteno di far presto*' ('They say that nine triumphal arches will be erected costing 15,000 *scudi* . . . . Giovio is busy with other humanists inventing the inscriptions for the arches, and so those responsible are aiming, and encouraging others, to be quick').[29]

The Pope had entrusted other more courtly entertainments to his son, Pierluigi Farnese: '*El s^or^ Pier Louise dà ordine de Caccie e de preparar comedie s'el si sarà a tempo*' ('Pierluigi is organising hunts and commissioning comedies, if time allows').[30] It is not clear if any of these comedies were performed, even though Giovanni Gaddi was associated with the foremost Italian theatre troupe, the Compagnia della Cazzuola. Indeed, compared with other imperial entries through Italy in 1535–1536, the celebrations in Rome were rather low key, focusing almost entirely on the spectacular triumphal progress. Messages coming from

---

25 See the itinerary in Madonna, 'L'Ingresso' (1997), p. 52.

26 Alberini, *I Ricordi*, vol. 1, p. 470.

27 See Christoph L. Frommel and Nicholas Adams (eds), *The Architectural Drawings of Antonio da Sangallo the Younger and His Circle*, vol. 1: *Fortifications, Machines, and Festival Architecture* (Cambridge, MA: MIT Press, 1994).

28 Guglielmo De Angelis d'Ossat, 'Gli archi trionfali ideate dal Peruzzi per la venuta a Roma di Carlo V', *Capitolium*, 18 (1943), 287–94; Mircea Toca, 'Osservazioni sul cosidetto taccuino senese di Baldassare Peruzzi', *Annali della Scuola Normale Superiore di Pisa, classe di lettere e fiolosofia*, ser. III, 1 (1971), 161–79; Heinrich Wurm, *Baldassarre Peruzzi, Architekturzeichnungen* (Tübingen: E. Wasmuth, 1984); Marcello Fagiolo and Marialuisa Madonna (eds), *Baldassarre Peruzzi: pittura, scena, e architettura nel Cinquecento* (Rome: Istituto della Enciclopedia italiana, 1987). Reproduced in Madonna, 'L'Ingresso' (1997), figs 1, 41–3.

29 Dispatch of Conte Campeggio to the Duke of Mantua, 24 December 1535, ms *Gonzaga* 884.

30 Conte Campeggio, dispatch of 24 December 1535.

the imperial court tended to discourage any lavish expenditure, Charles being keen to ingratiate himself with the Roman people, and to avoid any negative propaganda about a possible second Sack: '*Sua Maestà non vole Archi Triomphali, ne Pompe, ne spesa ne brochati ne altro che venghi al danno del detto Populo*' ('His Majesty does not want triumphal arches or pomp or expense or brocade, or anything else which might be detrimental to the Roman people').[31] But the Pope and his commissioner had different ideas, and were determined to take the opportunity to restore the city of Rome to its ancient glory, as Giovio mused ironically: '*Qua si pensa in archi e statue e in addrizzar strade innenelenchissime per l'entrata di Cesare, qual sarà quando Dio vorrà*') ('They are thinking here of arches and statues, and of straightening out innumerable roads for Caesar's entry, which will take place God knows when').[32] Giovio's correspondence traces the stages in the planning, the scaling down of the number of arches: '*Noi qui faremo archi di carta bellissimi, e sono per farsi di marmi*' ('We here will erect magnificent paper arches, which will later be built of marble');[33] and the reluctance of the Roman people to pay for such magnificence: '*Il Popolo Romano in Capitolio ha tratto alla staffa, e non vorrebbe contribuire a gli archi e colossi*' ('On the Capitol the Roman people have resisted and do not want to contribute to the arches and statues').[34] Finally the Pope ended up bearing most of the costs, taking a loan with the Strozzi, dividing some expenditure with the city,[35] and imposing a tax on the curia, on artisans' guilds, and on *forestieri* (foreigners),[36] trying to avoid the Roman people having to contribute.[37] An ambassador like Pellegrino wondered how foreigners could afford to pay, '*siamo a tal foggio assassinate*' ('this is how we are being assassinated').[38]

---

[31] Dispatch of Pellegrino, 5 January 1536, ms *Gonzaga* 886, confirmed by letter of Hieronimo Negro, see Marc'Antonio Michele, 17 January 1536: '*sua Maestà non vol dar spesa alcuna a questo popolo*' ('His Majesty does not want to involve the Roman people in any expenditure'), in *Lettere di Principi*, ed. G. Ruscelli (Venice: G. Ziletti, 1564–77), vol. 3, fol. 150–150v.

[32] Giovio, *Lettere*, vol. 1, p. 180, 29 January 1536.

[33] Ibid., p. 183, 6 February 1536.

[34] Ibid., p. 171, 28 December 1535.

[35] Lanciani, as published in 'La Via del Corso', pp. 231–3, the document sharing expenditure with the city; Rome, Archivio Storico Capitolino, *Decreti di Consigli, Magistrati e Cittadini Romani*, Credenzone 1, vol. 30, 10 December 1535.

[36] Recorded in the *Libro di esazzione dell'imposizione fatta da Bindo Altoviti per la venuta dell'imperatore a Roma* (22 January–29 May 1536), in Archivio di Stato, Rome, Camerale I, *Viaggi dei pontefici sovrani esteri*, busta 1563–64, 112/20. The tax on the courtiers was 14,000 *scudi* according to Guido da Crema in his dispatch of 20 December 1535, ms *Gonzaga* 884.

[37] According to Pellegrino's dispatch, 22 December 1535, ms *Gonzaga* 885, the Pope will pay 2,000 *scudi*, the Cardinals 2,000, and a tax will be imposed on the curia, '*artisani e pover huomini forastieri*' ('artisans and poor foreigners'), but he does not want the Romans to have to pay.

[38] Pellegrino dispatch of 22 December 1535, ms *Gonzaga* 885.

The preparations remained on the drawing board, awaiting firmer news of the Emperor's movements: '*di qua si fa preparamenti grandi per sua venuta, sino a qui di disegni, indugiando l'opera più tarda*' ('major preparations are being made for his arrival, just plans for now, the construction comes later').[39] Once it was clear Charles would not arrive till Carnival,[40] there was more time for Paul III's grand plan: '*alle ruine et a l'arco tutavia se solecitano più*' ('they keep pressing on ever more with the demolitions and the arch').[41] Gaddi hired artists,[42] and spent 23,101 ducats on decoration, while the programme of demolitions was rolled out.[43] Fifty thousand ducats were raised,[44] and in fifteen weeks, three miles of highway were cleared, under the supervision of Gaddi and the two *maestri delle strade*, Manetti and Angelo del Bufalo de' Cancellieri. Rabelais, who was hostile, writes of over 200 houses being demolished and three or four churches: this is in fact an understatement, as there are records of eleven churches being dismantled.[45] The

39 Archivio di Stato, Lucca, Anziani al tempo della Libertà, 619, dispatch to the Anziani of Orsucci and Dalportico, 15 December 1535.

40 See Jean Du Bellay's letter to Claude Dodieu, 25 December 1535, where he thinks it will be later than originally expected, probably not before the end of February: see Du Bellay, *Correspondance*, vol. 2, p. 220. This is confirmed in the correspondence of the nuncio in Venice, Girolamo Verallo, on 3 January 1536, where Charles is expected at the end of February, '*dove un'altra volta par che si voglia coronare*' ('where it seems he wants to be crowned again'), *Nunziature di Venezia*, vols 1–2, ed. F. Gaeta (Rome: Istituto storico italiano per l'età moderna e contemporanea, 1958), vol. 2, p. 36; Pier Giovanni Baroni (ed.), *La Nunziatura in Francia di Rodolfo Pio, 1535–1537* (Bologna: arti grafiche Tamari, 1962), p. 360, 18 January 1536. Pellegrino hears on 5 January 1536 that he will leave Naples on 20 January, ms *Gonzaga* 886.

41 Conte Campeggio wrote on 12 February 1536 that he was not expected till mid-Lent, ms *Gonzaga* 886.

42 See Giovanni Gaddi's register in the Archivio di Stato, Rome, Camerale I, *Viaggi dei pontefici sovrani esteri*, busta 1563–64, which lists his expenditure on the Arch of San Marco, Porta di San Pietro, Porta di Palazzo, Ponte Sant'Angelo and the Porta di San Sebastiano.

43 See Francesco Cancellieri, *Storia de' solenni possessi de' sommi pontefici* (Rome: L. Lazzarini, 1802), p. 94; Rodolfo Lanciani, *Storia degli scavi di Roma*, 4 vols (Rome: E. Loescher & Co, 1902–12), vol. 2, pp. 63–74; Antonino Bertolotti, 'Speserie segrete e pubbliche di Paolo III', *Atti della Deputazione di Storia patria per le Provincie dell'Emilia*, n.s. III.1 (1878), pp. 169–212; Lanciani, 'La Via del Corso', pp. 229–55; Madonna, 'L'Ingresso' (1997), pp. 50–67; Maria Antonietta Visceglia, *La città rituale: Roma e le sue cerimonie in età moderna* (Rome: Viella, 2002), pp. 53–197.

44 Bertolotti, 'Speserie', pp. 175–7, expenditure of Gaddi is 33,113 scudi.

45 See the list in Biblioteca Apostolica Vaticana [BAV], *Cod. Vat. Lat.* 8468, fol. 208, *Memoria delle chiese ruvinate in Roma doppo la venuta dell'Imperatore Carlo V*; also printed in Pastor, *History*, vol. 12, p. 654. The churches listed are: San Lorenzo delli Spetiali [=San Lorenzo in Miranda]; Santa Margarita verso il Coliseo; Santa Maria verso Torre del Contil [=Santa Maria in Cambiatoribus or Magnanapoli?]; San Biagio ai Monti sotto San Pietro in Vincula; San Nicola alla Colonna Traiana; Sant'Andrea alla Colonna

maestri worked with such ruthless vigour, as a diarist reported in a key phrase, '*tal che in molti lochi la cittate ha mutato forma*' ('that in many places the city has changed shape').[46] The ambassador Pellegrino shows the Pope at work making space: '*N^re^ Sig fa rovinar case e luoghi in Roma per alargar le strade et far piazze acciò che meglio si possa honorar la M^ta^ Cesarea come sua Sta intende di fare*' ('His Holiness is demolishing houses and other places in Rome to widen the streets and open up squares, resolved to honour Caesar as best he can').[47] The widening of streets and squares was not just for show: it had to accommodate the passage of the very large and imposing retinue of troops which the Emperor planned to bring with him,[48] for whom lodgings had also to be found by Cardinal Uberto Gambara.[49]

The first stage of the entry was from the basilica of San Paolo fuori le Mura to the Capitol, and was to be paid for by the city.[50] Along the southern approach on the Via Appia, '*la via trionfale antica*' ('the ancient triumphal way'),[51] major roadworks had improved the route to the Porta di San Sebastiano, '*et da S. Paolo fino alla detta porta è fatta di nuovo una spianata larga et agevole à cavalcare*'

---

di Antonino; another '*sotto Montecavallo*', near Frangipani; another near the Palazzo of Cardinale Rimini; the Spedaletto della Rotonda; '*una chiesa per far la strada alla venuta dell'Imperatore da San Marco alle case delli Madaleni*' ('a church to clear the route for the imperial entry from San Marco to the Madaleni properities'); another [=San Salvatore in Julia?] '*per far la strada dalli Madaleni in Campidoglio*' ('to clear the route from the Madaleni to the Capitol'); another, not on this list, was San Leonardo de Albis, in Piazza Giudea.

[46] Alberini, *I Ricordi*, p. 467.

[47] Dispatch of Pellegrino, 22 January 1536, ms *Gonzaga* 886.

[48] Dispatch of Guido da Crema, 20 December 1535, ms *Gonzaga* 884: '*s'intende che sua Maestà viene colla maggior pompa che facesse mai nell'entrata d'alcun altro luogo*' ('they say that His Majesty is coming with greater pomp than ever for the entry to any other place'). Jean Du Bellay wrote on 6 December 1535 that Charles was expected to bring 2,500 of his own guard and 4,000–5,000 of the Colonna faction. See Du Bellay, *Correspondance*, vol. 2, p. 186.

[49] Pellegrino wrote on 23 November 1535, ms *Gonzaga* 885: '*et si truova che non solamente male ma pessimamente se alloggiarà, et se dubbia che per questa cagione non gli naschi qualche disordine*' ('and it turns out that they will not just be lodged badly, but very badly, which raises fears of possible disorder').

[50] Authorised in the decree of 12 January 1536, Archivio Segreto Vaticano [ASV], Camera Apostolica, Div. Cam. 98, fol. 89v–90v: '*In primis fare spianar et reimpir et levar le acque dove faccia de bisogno in la strada de la scola Greca per in sino alla chiesa di S. Paulo. . . . Item rassettare la strada da San Paolo fine al fino delli Prati ad canto all'ultime vigne della via Appia fuor de la porta di S. Sebastiano*' ('Firstly to level and fill and drain where necessary on the road from the Schola Græca up to the Basilica of San Paolo. . . . Also to repair the road from San Paolo up to where the meadows end by the last vineyards of Via Appia outside the Porta di San Sebastiano').

[51] See the album, [Sala], *Ordine, pompe, apparati,* fol. Aiii v.

('and from San Paolo to that gate a broad esplanade has been newly built, easy to ride along'),[52] arriving at the former Porta Appia, for which Antonio da Sangallo had designed chiaroscuro decorations of which a drawing survives,[53] painted on a triumphal arch of wood and canvas, representing Scipio's triumph in Africa.[54] The imperial party would then pass under the adjacent Arch of Drusus, before following the Via San Sebastiano to San Sisto Vecchio, '*per via dritta*' ('along a straight road'), thanks to major roadworks,[55] and admiring en route the Baths of Caracalla, before arriving at the Circus Maximus, and turning right on to Via San Gregorio by the magnificent Septizonium.[56] Expenditure is recorded on expropriation and compensation, but also on attempts to avoid too much demolition by going through *vigne* (vineyards). The effects of Paul III's roadworks here are clearly seen in Bufalini's 1550 map of the city.[57]

From this point the route could have gone straight on through the Circus Maximus along the Via dei Cerchi. The planners rejected this more direct itinerary[58]

---

[52] [Sala], *Ordine, pompe, apparati*, f. Aiii v; Ceffino, *La Triumphante Entrata*, f. A v: '*per una amplissima et bella via, che molti giorni prima per tale effetto era stata ordinata*' ('along a very wide and fine road, which had been constructed many days before for this very purpose').

[53] Frommel and Adams, *The Architectural Drawings*, vol. 1, pp. 181, 368, U 1014Ar; Lanciani, *Storia degli scavi*, vol. 2, p. 59.

[54] Detailed description in [Sala], *Ordine, pompe, apparati*, f. Aiii v–Aiv v; Ceffino, *La Triumphante Entrata*, fol. Aii v–Aiii.

[55] [Sala], *Ordine, pompe, apparati*, fol. B.

[56] See the decree of 12 January 1536, ASV, Cam. Ap., Div. Cam. 98, fol. 89v–90v: '*Item far rasettare nel medesimo modo, et spianar la strata predetta dalla porta sopradetta fino che se ha da rivoltare a Septisolio, facendo aprire la vigna di Maphfei, qual incomincia a dicta rivolta et che essa ad Septem Solio damnificandola quanto mancho si possa*' ('Also to have the said road repaired and levelled in the same way from the gate [of San Sebastiano] till it turns for the Septizonium, cutting through the Maffei vineyard, which begins at the turn and ends at Septizonium, damaging it as little as possible'); Gaddi's register in the Roman Archivio di Stato cited by Podestà, 'Carlo V', p. 313, records expenditure of '*400 ducati per far spianare le strade dalla porta di S Sebastiano all'arco di San Marco*' ('400 ducats to level the roads from the Porta San Sebastiano to the Arch of San Marco'). The album [Sala], *Ordine, pompe, apparati*, fol. B, specifies that Charles was met at the gate, then escorted '*per via dritta . . . per insino à presso à Cerco massimo*' ('along a straight road up to near the Circius Maximus').

[57] Francesco Ehrle, *Roma al tempo di Giulio III: La pianta di Roma del 1551* (Rome: Danesi, 1911).

[58] Alberini, *I Ricordi*, p. 467–9: '*prima slargando alquanto la strada dalla porta Appia a S. Sisto, et da San Sisto alli Benzoni, et perchè li non si poteva tirare a filo senza grandissimo danno de privati, tenendosi su la mano dritta rincontro alli Benzoni . . . hanno tagliato alcune vigne, et se si fosse sequitato dritto per Cerchi a piazza Montanara, volendo che Sua Maestate vedesse la maraviglia della antiquitate, non le haverebbe viste*' ('firstly widening the road from the Porta Appia to San Sisto Vecchio, and from San Sisto to the vineyard of the Benzoni family, and because they could not trace a straight route without major damage

for a longer, but much more impressive one, which would show off more picturesque monuments, exposing the classical antiquities to the admiration of their visitors, as the diarist Alberini writes: '*caminato per la cittate più habitata, benchè questa facesse [sembrare] la via più longa et per consequentia la cittate più ampia et onorata*' ('riding through the more populated part of the city, even if this made the route seem longer, and as a result the city seem more extensive and distinguished').[59] The new vistas and perspectives opened up for the imperial party around the Septizonium are recorded in a famous contemporary panorama by Maarten Van Heemskerck,[60] who was an eye-witness to the preparations in 1535–1536.

Turning right from the Septizonium therefore, a major new road had been cut through various properties between the Palatine and the Celio,[61] giving an unencumbered view of the full height of the Severan monument, '*per una amplissima strada solo per tale entrata fatta giunse a quel tanto degno simulacro di settem solio, dove era una bellissima fontana che di acqua rosa ne bagnava tutti che per ditta strada passavano*' ('along a very broad street constructed specially for this entry, he arrived at that most worthy monument of the Septizonium, where there was a very fine fountain which sprayed with rose water all who passed along it').[62] Since one of the expropriated properties was not bought till February, it is clear that the planners were working right up to the deadline.[63] The diarist Alberini describes what the Emperor could see as he rode along this new road: '*dall'una mano, il Settisolio con le antiquitati de palazzo Maggiore e, dall'altra, li aquedutti et altre antique ruine del Monte Celio, et in fronte o capo di questa strada lo arco di Constantino composto di diverse spoglie o ruine, come anchora ve si conoscano le effigie di Cesare et Traiano*' ('on one side the Septizonium with the antiquities

---

to private property, they cut through some vineyards, keeping the Benzoni property on the right; and suppose they had kept straight on through Piazza and Via dei Cerchi to Piazza Montanara [by the Theatre of Marcellus], if they wanted His Majesty to see the wonderful ruins, he would not have seen any').

[59] Alberini, *I Ricordi*, p. 469.

[60] Christian Hülsen, *Die römischen Skizzenbücher von Marten van Heemskerck*, 2 vols (Soest: Davaco, 1975), vol. 2, pp. 113, 116, 127; Elena Filippi, *Maarten van Heemskerck: Inventio Urbis* (Milan: Berenice, 1990), p. 24 and tav. 14–15; see also Étienne Dupérac, *Vestigi delle antichità di Roma* (Rome: L. della Vaccheria, 1575), pl. 13.

[61] Conte Campeggio reports on 1 February 1536, ms *Gonzaga* 886, how from San Gregorio '*è fata una via nova*', and '*è fato tanto larga la via*' ('a new road has been made'; 'the road has been made very wide'); the album [Sala], *Ordine, pompe, apparati*, f. B records how, after the Circus Maximus, '*per una spianata fatta di nuovo si volse al Settizonio di Severo, da questo fino all'arco di Costantino, s'è fatta una strada di nuovo*' ('passing along a newly built esplanade, he turned at the Septizonium of Severus, and from there a new road has been made to the Arch of Constantine').

[62] Ceffino, *La triomphante entrata*, fol. Aiii.

[63] The Vineyard of Hieronimo Maffei near the Septizonium, bought on 4 February 1536: see Lanciani, *Storia degli Scavi*, vol. 2, p. 38.

of the Palatine, and on the other side the aqueducts [of Claudius] and the other ancient ruins of the Coelian, and at the far end of this street the Arch of Constantine, composed of various spolia, of which the images of Caesar and Trajan can still be made out').[64]

To embellish this newly cleared road, the planners had erected the fountain at the Septizonium, and by the aqueduct of Claudius an Arco di Verdura designed by Sangallo, the first modern arch built on the route.[65] Ahead could be seen the Arch of Constantine, under which the Emperor was to pass, and behind it the Colosseum. The walls around had been demolished to open up this perspective:'*s'è fatta una strada di nuovo: cioè rotte da ogni banda le mura, che v'erano, in modo che la vista percuote subito nell'arco, et in quella mirabil mole del Coliseo*' ('a road has been newly built, by demolishing the existing walls on each side, allowing the gaze to fall directly on the arch and on that wondrous bulk of the Colosseum').[66] Similarly, the space around the Arch of Constantine had been cleared, as wide as the arch itself, to open it up to view.[67] Charles was reported to be very impressed by this monument to imperial triumph: '*si dilettava di guardare la gloriosa memoria del suo si famoso Antecessore*' ('he looked with pleasure at the glorious memorial of so famous a predecessor').[68] Passing under the central arch, he was to turn left at the Meta Sudans, and climb the Via Sacra, which had been widened and straightened, cutting through *vigne*,[69] creating a perspective from the Colosseum to the Arch of Titus, with the so-called Templum Pacis on the right,[70] preserved in a drawing by Dosio,[71] and in prints by Dupérac[72] and Lauro.[73] A rumour was spread by the French, as anti-imperial as Rabelais, and recorded by Martin Du Bellay, about how '*entre plusieurs edifices, qui pour luy faire la voye plus large et droicte avoient esté abbatus et demolis, fut aussi abbatu le Temple de Paix*'

64 Alberini, *I Ricordi*, p. 470.

65 Frommel and Adams, *The Architectural Drawings*, vol. 1, pp. 181, 368, U 1014Ar, '*per la volta della strada presso a Setti Soli di verdura*' ('for where the road turns near the Septizonium, an arch of foliage'); Lanciani, *Storia degli Scavi*, vol. 2, p. 59.

66 [Sala], *Ordine, pompe, apparati*, fol. B.

67 The *maestri delle strade* were instructed on 12 January 1536, ASV, Cam. Ap., Div. Cam. 98, fol. 89v–90v: '*Item mettere in insula l'archo di Constantino quanto è largo*' ('Also to create an island around the full width of the Arch of Constantine').

68 Ceffino, *La Triumphante Entrata*, fol. Aiii.

69 The *maestri delle strade* were further instructed on 12 January 1536, ASV, Cam. Ap., Div. Cam. 98, fol. 89–90v: '*Item sequitar, spianar alarghare detta strada procendo all'archo di Tito, et far aprire la Vigna all'incontro di detto archo*' ('Also to prolong, level and widen this road towards the Arch of Titus, and to cut through the vineyard adjacent to this arch').

70 Alberini, *I Ricordi*, p. 471: '*la inestimabile grandezza del tempio della Pace*' ('the incalculable splendour of the Temple of Peace [Basilica di Constantine/Maxentius]').

71 Florence, Uffizi, Gabinetto di Disegni e Stampe, A 2531.

72 Dupérac, *Vestigi*, pl. 15.

73 Giacomo Lauro, *Antiquæ urbis splendor* (Rome, 1612), pl. 138.

('among the many buildings which had been knocked down and demolished to make his route wider and straighter, there was also the Temple of Peace').[74] This was a false rumour, but it made good French propaganda, seeing this demolition as a bad omen for peace in Europe.

Alberini's diary gives details of what the Emperor could see as he rode up to the Arch of Titus, and towards the climax of his progress: '*et de qui venendo all'arco de Titto, lassando su la mano dritta l'amfiteatro che oggi se dice il Culiseo, et il Tempio del Sole nelli orti de Santa Maria Nova et dalla sinistra tuttavia sequitando le ruine del Palatino da questo arco de Tito*' ('and coming from here to the Arch of Titus, leaving behind on his right the amphitheatre known today as the Colosseum, and the Temple of the Sun [Temple of Moon and Sun] in the gardens of Santa Maria Nova [Santa Francesca Romana], and keeping on his left from this Arch of Titus the ruins of the Palatine').[75] He was reportedly delighted to see, in this arch, another monument to imperial triumph,[76] before coming upon the panorama of the whole Forum looking towards the Arch of Septimius Severus and the Capitol, its contemporary state recorded in the famous Heemskerck panoramas.[77] The path through the Campo Vaccino had previously been twisty, before Paul III cleared a straight route through the Forum between the two arches by expropriation and massive demolitions: '*s'è tirato à filo una strada per mezzo il Foro Ro[mano] antico per infino all'arco di Settimio, et buttati intorno quelli edifitii moderni, che impedivano la vista di quelle miracolose ruine, che vi sono*' ('a road has been cut straight through the middle of the ancient Roman Forum right up to the Arch of Septimius Severus, and all the modern buildings have been knocked down which blocked the view of the marvellous ruins to be seen there').[78] This is confirmed in Alberini's diary, where instead of the '*via storta all'arco de Settimio, per più grandezza tagliando la possessione de Iuliano Madaleni, fu tirato da uno arco all'altro una strada deritta*' ('crooked route to the Arch of Septimius Severus, for greater impact a straight road was drawn from one arch to the other, cutting through the property of Giuliano Madaleni').[79] As he rode through the Forum, Charles could admire the monuments which major demolition work had made visible. If we enlarge one of Heemskerck's panoramas of the Forum, we see workers labouring in the foreground with pickaxes, presumably levelling the processional

---

[74] Guillaume and Martin Du Bellay, *Mémoires*, ed. V.-L. Bourrilly and F. Vindry, 4 vols (Paris: Société de l'Histoire de France, 1908–19), vol. 2, p. 341.

[75] Alberini, *I Ricordi*, pp. 470–1.

[76] Ceffino, *La Triumphante Entrata*, fol. Aiii: '*non manco del secondo che del primo prese diletto*' ('he was no less delighted by the second than by the first').

[77] See Heemskerck's view of the Forum through the Arch of Titus, and his general view towards the Capitol: Hülsen, *Die römischen Skizzenbücher*, vol. 2, pp. 75, 105, 125; Filippi, *Maarten van Heemskerck*, tav. 56.

[78] [Sala], *Ordine, pompe, apparati*, fol. B.

[79] Alberini, *I Ricordi*, p. 471.

route of the Via Sacra in preparation for the imperial triumph.[80] A contemporary album describes the sights on each side as Charles passed under the Arch of Titus into the Forum:

li rappresenta dinanzi à gli occhi il Campidoglio et l'Arco di Settimio, à sinistra l'anticaglie del Palatino, à destra le ruine del Tempio della Pace, il Tempio di S. Cosimo et Damiano, creduto da alc[u]ni, il Tempio di Castore et di Polluce, et da altri de gli Dei penati, vedesi il Colonnato tutto scoperto di Antonino et di Faustina, et da ultimo il Tempio di Saturno, ch'hoggi chiamano S. Adriano

[there before his eyes was the Capitol and the Arch of Septimius Severus, to his left the remains of the Palatine, to his right the ruins of the Temple of Peace, the Temple of Santi Cosma e Damiano, which some think was the Temple of Castor and Pollux, and others that of the Penati, and the cleared portico could be seen of [the Temple of] Antoninus and Faustina, and lastly the Temple of Saturn, now called [the church of] Sant'Adriano].[81]

The diarist Alberini specifies that demolitions had taken place outside the church of Santi Cosmo e Damiano, the effects of which are seen in the Heemskerck drawings:[82]

appresso el tempio di Castore et Polluce, altri vogliano di Romolo et Remolo, che hora si dice Santi Cosmo et Damiano, e ne dicano alcuni fosse lo erario el quale era nel tempio di Saturno alle radice di Campidoglio. Al quale, perchè si vedesse la magnifica porta composta di spoglie con colonne et architrave, è stato ruinato un portico alla moderna assai onorevole che impediva la vista di quel tempio et [della] porta

[nearby, the Temple of Castor and Pollux, which others think is that of Romulus and Remus, and is now called Santi Cosma e Damiano, and some say it was the Ærarium which was in the temple of Saturn at the foot of the Capitol. In order to reveal this magnificent *pronaos* made up of *spolia* with columns and architrave, a more modern and not unattractive portico was demolished, because it blocked the view of the temple and *pronaos*].[83]

---

[80] Hülsen, *Die römischen Skizzenbücher*, vol. 1, p. 7; Filippi, *Maarten van Heemskerck*, tav. 7.

[81] [Sala], *Ordine, pompe, apparati*, fol. B.

[82] Hülsen, *Die römischen Skizzenbücher*, vol. 1, p. 10; Filippi, *Maarten van Heemskerck*, tav. 8.

[83] Alberini, *I Ricordi*, pp. 471–3.

The diarist also mentions demolitions outside the Temple of Antoninus and Faustina, probably little chapels demolished between the columns, rather than the whole church of San Lorenzo in Miranda:

> *Appresso vedeasi il portico suntuoso di colonne et di freggio del tempio de Antonio et Faustina, denanzi al quale essendo edificato la chiesa di San Lorenzo della universitate delli speciali che lo occupava, perchè restassi alla vista più libero et più bello fu ruinato et tolto via*
>
> [Nearby could be seen the sumptuous portico made up of columns and frieze of the Temple of Antoninus and Faustina, built in front of which was the Church of San Lorenzo occupied by the Collegio degli Speziali, which was demolished and cleared away to free up and improve the view of the Temple].[84]

This is confirmed in a list of eleven churches destroyed, which reports the demolition of '*S. Lorenzo delli Spetiali in campo, acciò si vedesse le colonne dov'è scrittro Divino Antonino et Deve Faustine*'.[85] Later panoramas, such as that of Lauro from 1612,[86] show the lasting effects of Paul III's slum clearance, opening up views of the Palatine to the Emperor's left, and of isolated temples like the remaining three columns of the Temple of Castor and Pollux:

> *Alla sinistra l'accompagnava tuttavia per la costa del monte le ruine del Palatino et in su el Foro le reliquie delli rostri et del famoso tempio di Vesta et reliquie de colonne et portici che per la strada si veggano; et di mezzo la strada nel Foro, perchè dall'uno arco all'altro fosse la strada più libera per linea diretta, è stato ruinato un torraccio*
>
> [On the heights to his left he still had the ruins of the Palatine, and within the Forum the remains of the Rostra and of the famous Temple of Vesta, and remains of columns and porticos visible along the route; and so as to clear the route straight through the middle of the Forum from one arch to the other, an old tower [torre dell'Inserra] was demolished].[87]

This tower was almost certainly only one of several demolished in this area; the space all around the Arch of Septimius Severus had been cleared, including a medieval tower which obstructed the view, and a wagon repair business,[88] revealing to the imperial gaze the arch in all its splendour:

---

[84] Lanciani, *Storia degli Scavi*, vol. 2, pp. 58, 63.

[85] BAV, *Cod. Vat. Lat.* 8468, fol. 208; Pastor, *History*, vol. 12, p. 654.

[86] Lauro, *Antiquæ urbis splendor*, pl. 136.

[87] Alberini, *I Ricordi*, pp. 473–4.

[88] For instance, the *maestri delle strade* were instructed on 12 January 1536, ASV, Cam. Ap., Div. Cam. 98, fol. 90r–v, to '*levar quella casaccia dishabitata quale sta avanti*

> *per dritta linea pel foro Romano attraversando, et giunto al'altro tanto celebrato arco di Lucio Settimio, sua Maiestà fu constretta dal desio del vedere si degna cosa, et d'intendere quello ne dicevano le littere vi sono scritte per alquanto fermarsi*
>
> [His Majesty, having crossed the Roman Forum in a straight line, and reached that other very famous arch of Lucius Septimius, paused a little, overcome by desire to see such a worthy monument and to learn what the inscriptions said].[89]

Next to the arch lay the reclining (and talking) statue of Marforio, noted by all visitors to Rome, for which Sangallo had designed a special monumental ædicule.[90] It seems that the original plan was to take Charles up from Marforio to the Capitol,[91] which would have been the endpoint of the classical *via triumphalis* and, looking back, would have given a panorama of the monuments of the Forum along Paul III's new route. But the Pope had not had time to put into effect his rebuilding of the Capitol, which he entrusted to Michelangelo, and the hilltop was in a squalid state. In a change of plan, the route turned right by Marforio, '*per una strada tirata nuovamente, che riesce à'l palazzo di S. Marco*' ('along a newly designed road, which led to the Palazzo di San Marco'),[92] past the Column of Trajan freed from the clutter around it, to Piazza San Marco, where houses had

---

al tempio di Bacco' ('to remove that empty rundown building in front of the Temple of Bacchus'); to '*buttar in terra l'hostaria di Cavalier quasi incontro a S. Adriano tanto che si scopra l'archo di Septimio*' ('to knock down the Hostaria di Cavalier almost opposite Sant'Adriano to reveal the Arch of Septimius'); and also to '*far levar quella casaccia la quale è attaccata alla torre dinanzi al detto archo, et levare un pezzo di tecto quale è attaccato alla detta casa ove si fanno sett[are] le caroze*' ('have that rundown building removed up against the tower in front of the arch, and to remove the piece of roof which adjoins that building in which carriages are reparied'). They also knocked down San Niccolò de Columna and Sant'Andrea alla Colonna de Antonino, to free up the Column of Trajan and the Colonna Antonina, see BAV, *Cod. Vat. Lat.* 8468, fol. 208; Pastor, *History*, vol. 12, p. 654; Lanciani, *Storia degli Scavi*, vol. 2, pp. 58, 63.

89 Ceffino, *La Triumphante Entrata*, fol. Aiii.

90 Frommel and Adams, *The Architectural Drawings*, vol. 1, pp. 159, 344, U 859Ar.

91 The Roman people had agreed to decorate Piazza del Campidoglio '*con prospettive et altre cose necessarie insieme con la sallita et scesa di essa piazza*' ('with perspectives and other things necessary, as well as the ascent to and descent from this square'): see Lanciani, 'La Via del Corso', p. 232. This route can be seen in Lauro, *Antiquæ urbis splendor*, pl. 137.

92 [Sala], *Ordine, pompe, apparati*, f. B. The *maestri delle strade* were instructed, ASV, Cam. Ap., Div. Cam. 98, fol. 90v, 12 January 1536, to '*far fornire de ruinar le ruine cominciate da Marforio sino in cima la costa ad man sinistra et dicta costa far sbassar più che si può per agguagliare di qua et dilla la strada*' ('take steps to complete the demolitions begun from Marforio up to the top of the slope on the left, and to have the slope lowered as much as possible to make it level on each side of the road').

been demolished to make the square bigger, and their owners compensated.[93] As the threshold between classical and modern papal Rome,[94] this square was chosen as the site of a major triumphal arch, probably designed by Giovanfrancesco Sangallo, planned as hexagonal and to be sited in the middle, but finally erected at the far end of the square.[95] On 21 January 1536, Paul was shown the design for the arch,[96] which, for lack of time, would be made of wood and canvas, but to be rebuilt later in marble as a memorial to the entry.[97] The design, celebrating the victories in Tunis, reminded observers of the Arch of Constantine,[98] but was seen as new and original, and caused great excitement, being praised by Vasari, and moved diplomats to send drawings and descriptions.[99]

The Emperor passed under this arch, and turned left along a new road, cleared by demolitions,[100] diametrically across to the Palazzo dei Cesarini (on the site

---

[93] Lanciani, *Storia degli Scavi*, vol. 2, p. 61.

[94] Ceffino, *La Triumphante Entrata*, fol. Aiii: '*ma poi da Marforio voltando lasciando il diletto de le anticaglie vedute da banda penso che le moderne non manco li dovessino dilettare, che di continuo alzando gli occhi per tutte le finestre ne poteva a suo beneplacito di bellissme vedere*' ('but then turning from Marforio and leaving behind the pleasure of the antiquities he has seen, I think that the modern sights might delight him no less, and as he kept looking up at all the windows he could see as many splendid sights as he could wish').

[95] [Sala], *Ordine, pompe, apparati*, fol. B: '*in sul canto ultimo della piazza*' ('on the far side of the square'). See Frommel and Adams, *The Architectural Drawings*, vol. 1, p. 352 (U914Ar), pp. 269, 484 (U4015Ar–v), pp. 273, 494 (U4159Ar); see also the reconstruction in Madonna, 'L'Ingresso' (1997), pp. 58–9, figs 24, 31–2.

[96] See Conte Campeggio's dispatch of 22 January 1536, ms *Gonzaga* 886: '*che poi si farà di marmori, al presente di legnami et tella*' ('which will be built in marble, but for the present in wood and canvas').

[97] See Francesco Chieregato's dispatch of 15 January 1536, ms *Gonzaga* 886: '*qual habbi ad esser per segno et archetipo de un marmoreo perpetuo che di subito si ha a fare secondo il modello delli antichi*' ('which is to be a model for a permanent one in marble, which is to be built straightaway in imitation of ancient arches').

[98] Ceffino, *La Triumphante Entrata*, fol. Aiii: '*uno riccho et bellissimo Arco. . ., quasi in sul modello de l'arco di Constantino*' ('an elaborate and very fine Arch . . . almost an imitation of that of Constantine'); described on fol. Aiii r–v.

[99] [Sala], *Ordine, pompe, apparati*, fol. Br–v: '*un'Arco trionfale superbissimo disegnato da Mastro Anton[io] da S. Gallo Architetto eccellentissimo, la forma del quale per essere nuova, et non più usata . . . ve ne mando la pianta col disegno del quadro*' ('a most imposing triumphal arch, designed by the outstanding architect Antonio da Sangallo, whose design is so new and unusual . . . that I am sending you its plan and a drawing a its appearance'); described on fol. Bv–Bii v.

[100] The *maestri delle strade* were instructed, ASV, Cam. Ap., Div. Cam. 98, fol. 90v, 12 January 1536, to '*far la strada per le case di m. Mariano Stalla et vicini in capo al palazzo de s. Marco secondo l'ordine dato et levare el portico di m. Marco Magdaleni*' ('to construct the road through the houses of M. Mariano Stalla and his neighbours behind the Palazzo San Marco as ordered, and to remove the portico from M. Marco Magdaleni's house').

of present-day Largo di Torre Argentina):[101] '*e butano a terra certe case per adrizar ben la via che viene a riferire a Cesarina*' ('and they are knocking down some houses, to make the road which leads to Piazza dei Cesarini completely straight').[102] So demolitions were not just taking place in the ancient city, but also in the more modern part. From there the Pope undertook to pave the traditional processional route, Via Papale, past the Palazzo Massimo, turning left to Campo dei Fiori,[103] opposite Palazzo Farnese,[104] then down Via del Pellegrino,[105] with all the streets widened and cleared of rubbish.[106] In this section, leading to

---

[101] Conte Campeggio's dispatch of 1 February 1536, ms *Gonzag*a 886, records the routre as '*per una ruina novamente [fatta]*' ('through newly demolished buildings') to Palazzo dei Cesarini; confirmed by Chieregato, 15 January 1536, ms *Gonzaga* 886, '*dove si fa una strada nova che tira per diametro alla via del gia card. Della Valle*' ('where a new road is being built leading diametrically to the street of the late Cardinal Andrea della Valle'); [Sala], *Ordine, pompe, apparati*, fol. Bii v, writes that: '*fu menato per il nuovo taglio fatto dall'altro canto di S. Marco, fino alla strada, che riesce à Cesarini, et quindi per la via della Valle fino à Massimi, donde volse à campo di Fiore et per via dritta arrivò al Castello*' ('he was led through a new road cut on the far side of Palazzo San Marco, up to the road which comes out at Palazzo dei Cesarini, then along the Via della Valle up to Palazzo Massimo, where he turned into Campo dei Fiori, and took a straight road to the Castel Sant'Angelo').

[102] From Campeggio's dispatch of 22 January 1536, ms *Gonzag*a 886.

[103] The route is described in the instruction to the *maestri delle strade*, ASV, Cam. Ap., Div. Cam. 98, fol. 90v, 12 January 1536: '*far far la mattonata da casa de Cesarini sino in Campo di Fiore*' ('have the brick paving done from Palazzo dei Cesarini up to Campo dei Fiori').

[104] The diarist Biagio Martinelli, BAV, *Cod. Vat. Lat.* 12277, fol. 273, 25 January 1536, describes how the Pope viewed the route near Palazzo Farnese, '*volens vedere aliam ruinam pro amplianda Platea*' ('wishing to see another demolition for widening the square').

[105] Ceffino, *La Triumphante Entrata*, fol. Aiii v, gives the route as '*via dil Papa*' ('Via Papale'), then '*da Cesarini et da la Valle passando*' ('going by Palazzo Cesarini and Via della Valle'), then '*da casa di Massimi*' ('Palazzo Massimo'), then '*volta da macelli de campo di Fiore, et giunto insu la bella Piaza se adrizò per la via del Pellegrino*' ('turning by the butchers of Campo dei Fiori, and arriving in this square, he headed along the Via del Pellegrino').

[106] See the instructions to the *maestri delle strade*, ASV, Cam. Ap., Div. Cam. 98, fol. 90v, 12 January 1536: '*Item al uscita di Campo di Fiore dove è la Ruina di Maximi per questa intrata della Cesarea maestà allargar la strada in tutto o in parte secondo la volontà et ordine dattaci N. S.; Item comandar per tutte le stradi di Roma dove sta impedimento di monti di sterchi o stabii o di altre cose, si debiano levar et tenerle nette sotto pene gravissime*' ('Also coming out of Campo dei Fiori, where the Massimo family property has been demolished for his Imperial Majesty's entry, to widen either all or part of the street in accordance with His Holiness' instructions to us; also to order, throughout the streets of Rome, where they are blocked by piles of human or animal dung or other things, that they be cleared and kept clean, or risk severe penalties').

Ponte Sant'Angelo, some triumphal arches were planned, but probably not built,[107] although there were further demolitions to open access to this monumental bridge, which was embellished with eight statues, and led to an ornamental gate to the Castello Sant'Angelo, from where a new direct road was cleared leading to the Vatican and hung with tapestries.[108] Drawings by Heemskerck and others record the decorations applied to the façade of the papal palace.[109]

This long triumphal route leading from San Paolo fuori le Mura to the Vatican was cleared in a few weeks to create a latter-day Via Triumphalis for the victor of Tunis and his thousands of troops: Paul III tried it out for himself in January 1536, to see how the demolitions were coming along.[110] The Mantuan ambassador Pellegrino reported how the Pope's workmen were busy on the triumphal arches,

> *a ruinar Case et muraglie, a spianar et addirizar strade, orti, giardini et vigne con tanta ruina hora per questa città che è cosa grande a honorare su M^{ta} per li lochi dove ella dovarà passar, in modo che tucti li Maestri, Ingegnieri, Muratori, Maestri legniami, Pintori et altri simili artifici tutti sono in opera et occupati a chi meglio saprà far*
>
> [demolishing houses and walls, levelling and straightening roads, orchards, gardens and vineyards, with such destruction around this city at present, and such a major effort to honour His Majesty through the places along his route, that all

[107] [Sala], Ordine, pompe, apparati, fol. Bii v, asserts that in this section '*di notabile non viddi altro che la strada da ogni banda accortinata d'arrazerie et di quadri di pitture bellissimi*' ('he saw nothing of note other than the street on both sides hung with tapestries and beautiful pictures'). But Ceffino, *La Triumphante Entrata*, fol. Aiii v–Aiv, mentions large images by the former Cancelleria of Christ, of St Jerome, of Cleopatra and of Lucretia, as well as inscriptions by San Celso in Via del Banco di Santo Spirito.

[108] [Sala], *Ordine, pompe, apparati*, fol. Bii v–Biii; Ceffino, *La Triumphante Entrata*, fol. Aiv.

[109] Burton L. III Dunbar, 'A Rediscovered Sixteenth-Century Drawing of Charles V's Entry to Rome', *Sixteenth Century Journal*, 23 (1992) 2, 195–204; Hülsen, *Die römischen Skizzenbücher*, vol. 2, pp. 70, 130; Filippi, *Maarten van Heemskerck*, p. 25, tav. 36; [Sala], *Ordine, pompe, apparati*, f. Biii r–v; Ceffino, *La Triumphante Entrata*, fol. Aiv v; Madonna, 'L'Ingresso' (1997), p. 63.

[110] See Campeggio's dispatch of 22 January 1536, ms *Gonzaga* 886; and that of Bragadin, 25 January 1536, Archivio di Stato, Venice, *Arch Propr. Roma*, 5, no. 44, describing the route, '*per adreciar della qual non solamente se ruinano case, ma etiam chiese*' ('to straighten which not only houses but also churches are being demolished'); confirmed by the diarist Martinelli, 25 January 1536, BAV, *Cod. Vat. Lat.* 12277, fol. 273, '*per viam quam praeparare fecit in receptione Caesaris. Discurrit totum iter et ruinas quas Latinus Juvenalis exercebat*' ('along the route which he is having prepared to welcome Caesar. He rode along the whole route through the demolitions which Latino Giovenale was superintending').

> the Architects, Engineers, Masons, Carpenters, Painters and other artisans are all hard at work and doing their very best].[111]

His resentment about the financing of this work is apparent, when he writes of an impending second Sack of the city:

> *ma la maggior parte sono alle spese de'povari Cortigiani, Forestieri et officiali, et certamente quasi si può dire un'altra ruina con 'l danno havuto per il passato, ma bisogna bere a questo calice*
>
> [but most of the cost is falling on the Courtiers, on the Foreigners and the Curia officials, which really makes one almost expect a second Sack, with the damage suffered last time, but we have to taste this bitter cup].[112]

Paolo Giovio was characteristically ironical, when he joked about the Emperor coming to see the '*ruinas Urbis antiquas et modernas*' ('the ancient and modern ruins of the city').[113]

Yet all these demolitions can also be viewed – not so much as a *ruina* – but rather as an attempt to modernise a mediæval city, opening up perspectives in the spirit of a new taste for the antiquarian picturesque. This taste is clearly seen in two paintings executed in Rome in 1535–1536, in the years of these feverish preparations. One is Heemskerck's picture of the Abduction of Helen in a landscape of ruins, painted in 1535 during his stay in Rome (Walters Art Gallery); the second is more convincing still, painted in Rome in 1536 by Hermannus Posthumus, *Landscape with Roman Ruins*, now in Liechtenstein, illustrating, from well-known objects in collections, the theme of *Tempus edax rerum*.[114] Both paintings flatter Charles V as a *triumphator* worthy of Scipio Africanus, as seen in the fresco cycle in the Palazzo Caffarelli-Vidoni, Rome, attributed to Pierin del Vaga, echoing the laudatory decorations on the arch of San Marco: Charles as Roman emperor passing under an arch, by the reclining figure of Tiber and the Wolf, with the majestic ruins ahead of him.

---

111 See Pellegrino's dispatch of 28 January 1536, ms *Gonzaga* 886.

112 Ibid., 28 January 1536.

113 Giovio, *Lettere*, vol. 1, p. 171, 28 December 1535.

114 Nicole Dacos, 'Herman Posthumus et l'entrée de Charles Quint à Rome', *Bulletin de l'Association des Historiens de l'Art Italien*, 5 (1999), 2–13; Ruth Rubinstein, '"Tempus edax rerum." A Newly Discovered Painting by Hermannus Posthumus', *The Burlington Magazine*, 127 (1985), 425–33; Nicole Dacos, 'De 'Tempus edax rerum' à "Roma quanta fuit ipsa ruina docet": Hermannus Posthumus, l'Entrée à Rome de Charles Quint et Latino Giovenale Manetti', in Nicole Dacos (ed.), *Roma quanta fuit, ou l'invention du paysage de ruines* (Paris: Somogy; Brussels: Musée de la Maison d'Erasme, 2004), pp. 145–79.

But this entry also asserts the Roman Pope as the protector of Roman imperial patrimony, as the restorer of the monuments of a city sacked by the Imperial army, who has moved heaven, earth and piles of rubble, to make space for the imperial entry. The fresco by the Zuccari brothers in Caprarola makes it quite clear who is the *triumphator* in this festival: the Emperor, on a lower step, is seen paying homage to the Farnese Pope.[115]

Bibliography

Primary sources

MANUSCRIPTS

Bragadin, Lorenzo, dispatches to the Venetian Signoria, Archivio di Stato, Venice, *Arch. Propr. Roma*, 5.

Campeggio, conte, dispatches to the Duke of Mantua, Archivio di Stato, Mantua, ms *Gonzaga* 884.

Crema, Guido da, dispatches to the Duke of Mantua, Archivio di Stato, Mantua, ms *Gonzaga* 884.

Gaddi, Giovanni, register in the Archivio di Stato, Rome, Camerale I, *Viaggi dei pontefici sovrani esteri*, busta 1563–1564.

Libro di esazzione dell'imposizione fatta da Bindo Altoviti per la venuta dell'imperatore a Roma (22 January–29 May 1536), Archivio di Stato, Rome, Camerale I, *Viaggi dei pontefici sovrani esteri*, busta 1563–64, 112/20.

Martinelli, Biagio, *Diaria*, Biblioteca Apostolica Vaticana [BAV], *Cod. Vat. Lat.* 12277.

Memoria delle chiese rovinate in Roma doppo la venuta dell'Imperatore Carlo V, BAV, *Cod. Vat. Lat.* 8468, f. 208.

Orsucci, Niccolò and Dalportico, Girolamo, dispatches to the Anziani, Archivio di Stato, Lucca, *Anziani al tempo della Libertà*, 619.

Pellegrino, Fabrizio, dispatches to the Duke of Mantua, Archivio di Stato, Mantua, ms *Gonzaga* 885–886.

Rodi, Filippo, dispatches to the Duke of Ferrara, Archivio di Stato, Modena, Serie Ambasciatori, *Roma*, busta 35, ms 233.

EARLY PRINTED BOOKS

Carro Ro[mano], E., *L'Ordine della Festa celebrata in Roma, per Carnevale, nella piazza d'Agone & di S Pietro, con la dechiaratione et significato delli carri* (n.p., n.d.) copies in Rome, Biblioteca Angelica; BAV, *Capponi*, IV 814.

[115] In the Anticamera del Concilio of the Villa Farnese at Caprarola; also in a pen drawing in the Louvre.

Ceffino, Zanobio, *La Triumphante Entrata di Carlo V Imperatore Augusto in l'alma Citta de Roma Con el significato delli archi triomphali & delle Figure antiche In prosa & versi Latini* (n.p., [1536]); copies in British Library [BL], 9930.f.71(2) and C.33.h.7; Bibliothèque nationale de France [BnF], R17246 and Rés. OC.1815.

Copia de una lettera della particularità dell'ordine con il quale la Maestà Cesarea intrò in Messina, et del Triompho et sumptuosi apparati gli forono fatti, carri et Archi Triomphali richissimi con alcuni versi et prosa latini in honore de Sua Maestà (Rome: A. Blado, 30 October 1535); copies in BL, 9930.c.4; BAV, *Chigi*, IV 2204, int 13.

Dupérac, Étienne, *Vestigi delle antichità di Roma* (Rome: L. della Vaccheria, 1575).

La Coronatione de Papa Paulo Terzo (Bologna: J. da Rubiera, 1534?); copy in BL, 1071.g.22(4).

Lauro, Giacomo, *Antiquæ urbis splendor* (Rome, 1612).

Lettere di Principi, ed. G. Ruscelli (Venice: G. Ziletti, 1564–77).

Li triomphi fatti a Roma il giovedì grasso per la festa di Agone (reprinted in Rome: Stab. Danesi, 1887), for the Nozze Grampini Stearns (copies in B[iblioteca] A[postolica] V[aticana]).

Sala, Andrea, *Il triomphale apparato per la entrata de la cesarea maestà in Napoli* (Venice: P. Danza, 1535); copies in BL, 1057.h.25(2) and C.33.h.9.

Sala, Andrea, *La triomphale entrata di Carlo V Imperadore Augusto, in la inclita citta di Napoli et di Messina con il significato delli Archi Triomphali et delle Figure antiche in Prosa et Versi Latini* ([Rome: A. Blado], 1535); copies in BL, 1318.c.7(3) and 9930.c.15; BAV, *Chigi*, IV 2204, int 14.

[Sala, Andrea], *Ordine, pompe, apparati, et cerimonie, delle solenne intrate, di Carlo V Imp. sempre Aug. nella citta di Roma, Siena, et Fiorenza* (Rome: [A. Blado, 1536]); copy in BL, 1318.c.7.

[Sala, Andrea], *Ordine, pompe, apparati e ceremonie della solenne intrata di Carlo Quinto Imp. nella città di Roma* (Bologna: V. Bonardo, [1536]); copies in BnF, 8° RA5.914; Rés. K.1341 and Rés. M.371.

SECONDARY SOURCES

Alberini, Marcello, *I Ricordi*, ed. D. Orano (Rome: Forzani, 1901).

Baroni, Pier Giovanni (ed.), *La Nunziatura in Francia di Rodolfo Pio, 1535–1537* (Bologna: arti grafiche Tamari, 1962).

Bertolotti, Antonino, 'Speserie segrete e pubbliche di Paolo III', *Atti della Deputazione di Storia patria per le Provincie dell'Emilia*, n.s. III.1 (1878), pp. 169–212.

Cancellieri, Francesco, *Storia de' solenni possessi de' sommi pontefici* (Rome: L. Lazzarini, 1802).

Chastel, André, 'Les Entrées de Charles Quint en Italie', in Jean Jacquot (ed.), *Fêtes et cérémonies au temps de Charles Quint. IIe Congrès de l'Association internationale des historiens de la Renaissance (2e section)* (Paris: Éditions du Centre national de la Recherche scientifique, 1960), pp. 197–206.

Clementi, Filippo, *Il Carnevale romano nelle cronache contemporanee* (Rome: F. Settii, 1899).

Cooper, Richard A., *Litteræ in tempore belli* (Geneva: Droz, 1997).

Cruciani, Fabrizio, *Teatro nel Rinascimento: Roma 1450–1550* (Rome: Bulzoni, 1983).

Dacos, Nicole, 'Herman Posthumus et l'entrée de Charles Quint à Rome', *Bulletin de l'Association des Historiens de l'Art Italien*, 5 (1999), 2–13.

Dacos, Nicole, 'De 'Tempus edax rerum' à 'Roma quanta fuit ipsa ruina docet': Hermannus Posthumus, l'Entrée à Rome de Charles Quint et Latino Giovenale Manetti', in Nicole Dacos (ed.), *Roma quanta fuit, ou l'invention du paysage de ruines* (Paris: Somogy; Brussels: Musée de la Maison d'Erasme, 2004), pp. 145–79.

De Angelis d'Ossat, Guglielmo, 'Gli archi trionfali ideate dal Peruzzi per la venuta a Roma di Carlo V', *Capitolium*, 18 (1943), 287–94.

Dorez, Léon, *La Cour du Pape Paul II*, 2 vols (Paris: E. Leroux, 1932).

Du Bellay, Guillaume and Martin, *Mémoires*, ed. V.-L. Bourrilly and F. Vindry, 4 vols (Paris: Société de l'Histoire de France, 1908–19).

Du Bellay, Jean, *Correspondance*, ed. R. Scheurer, 2 vols (Paris: Société de l'Histoire de France, 1969, 1973).

Dunbar, Burton L. III, 'A Rediscovered Sixteenth-Century Drawing of Charles V's Entry to Rome', *Sixteenth Century Journal*, 23 (1992) 2, 195–204.

Ehrle, Francesco, *Roma al tempo di Giulio III: La pianta di Roma del 1551* (Rome: Danesi, 1911).

Fagiolo, Marcello and Marialuisa Madonna (eds), *Baldassarre Peruzzi: pittura, scena, e architettura nel Cinquecento* (Rome: Istituto della Enciclopedia italiana, 1987).

Filippi, Elena, *Maarten van Heemskerck: Inventio Urbis* (Milan: Berenice, 1990).

Forcella, Vincenzo, *Tornei e giostre, ingressi trionfali e feste carnevalesche in Roma sotto Paolo III* (Rome: Artigianelli, 1885).

Foronda y Aguilera, Manuel de, *Estancias y viajes del Emperador Carlos V* ([Madrid], 1914).

Frommel, Christoph L. and Nicholas Adams (eds), *The Architectural Drawings of Antonio da Sangallo the Younger and His Circle*, vol. 1: *Fortifications, Machines, and Festival Architecture* (Cambridge, MA: MIT Press, 1994).

Giovio, Paolo, *Lettere*, ed. G.G. Ferrero, 2 vols (Rome: Istituto Poligrafico dello Stato, 1956–1958).

Horn, Hendrick J., *Jan Cornelisz Vermeyen, Painter of Charles V and His Conquest of Tunis, Paintings, Etchings, Drawings, Cartoons and Tapestries*, 2 vols (Doornspijk: Davaco, 1989).

Hülsen, Christian, *Die römischen Skizzenbücher von Marten van Heemskerck*, 2 vols (Soest: Davaco, 1975).

Karmon, David, *The Ruin of the Eternal City: Antiquity and Preservation in Renaissance Rome* (Oxford: Oxford University Press, 2011).

Lanciani, Rodolfo, 'La Via del Corso dirizzata et abbellita nel 1538 da Paolo III', *Bulletino della Commissione archeologica comunale di Roma*, 30 (1902), 232–3.

Lanciani, Rodolfo, *Storia degli scavi di Roma*, 4 vols (Rome: E. Loescher & Co, 1902–12).

Looz-Corswaren, Otto, 'Die römische Korrispondenz Karls V in Madrid und Simancas', *Nachrichten von der Gesellschaft der Wissenschaften zu Göttingen, Mittlere und neuere Geschichte*, 1 (1934–36), 109–90.

Madonna, Marialuisa, 'Il revival del trionfo classico. Da Alessandro VI alla sfilata dei rioni', in Marcello Fagiolo (ed.), *La Festa a Roma dal Rinascimento al 1870*, 2 vols (Rome and Turin: U. Allemandi, 1997), vol. 1, pp. 34–41.

Madonna, Marialuisa, 'L'Ingresso di Carlo V a Roma', in Marcello Fagiolo (ed.), *La Festa a Roma dal Rinascimento al 1870*, 2 vols (Rome and Turin: U. Allemandi, 1997), vol. 1, pp. 50–65.

Maylender, Michele, *Storia delle accademie d'Italia*, 5 vols (Bologna: L. Cappelli, 1926–30).

Mitchell, Bonner, 'The S.P.Q.R. in Two Roman Festivals of the Early and Mid-Cinquecento', *Sixteenth Century Journal*, 9 (1978) 4, 95–102.

Mitchell, Bonner, *Italian Civic Pageantry in the High Renaissance* (Florence: Olschki, 1979).

Mitchell, Bonner, *The Majesty of the State: Triumphal Progresses of Foreign Sovereigns in Renaissance Italy, 1494–1600* (Florence: Olschki, 1986).

Mitchell, Bonner, 'Charles V triumphator', in James V. Mehl (ed.), *In Laudem Caroli: Renaissance and Reformation Studies for Charles G. Nauert Jr* (Kirksville: Thomas Jefferson University Press, 1998), pp. 95–112.

Nunziature di Venezia, vols 1–2, ed. F. Gaeta (Rome: Istituto storico italiano per l'età moderna e contemporanea, 1958).

Onofrio, Cesare d', *Renovatio Romæ* (Rome: Edizioni Mediterranee, 1973).

Pastor, Ludwig, *The History of the Popes*, vols 11–12, trans. R.F. Kerr (London: Kegan Paul, Trench, Trübner & Co, 1912).

Podestà, Bartolomeo, 'Carlo V a Roma nell'anno 1536', *Archivio della Società Romana di Storia Patria*, 1 (1877), 303–44.

Quattrocchi, Angela, 'Latino Giovenale de' Manetti: un diplomatico "umanista" nella Curia pontificia', in Armand Jamme and Olivier Poncet (eds), *Offices et Papauté (XIVe–XVIIe siècles). Charges, hommes, destins. Actes du Colloque (2001–02)* (Rome: École française de Rome, 2005), pp. 829–40.

Ridley, Ronald T., 'To Protect the Monuments: The Papal Antiquarian (1534–1870)', *Xenia Antiqua*, 1 (1992), 117–21.

Rodocanachi, Emmanuel, *Institutions communales de Rome sous la papauté* (Paris: A. Picard, 1901).

Rubinstein, Ruth, '"Tempus edax rerum." A Newly Discovered Painting by Hermannus Posthumus', *The Burlington Magazine*, 127 (1985), 425–33.

Saletta, Vincenzo, 'Il Viaggio di Carlo V in Italia', *Studi meridionali*, 10 (1977), 268–92.

Toca, Mircea, 'Osservazioni sul cosidetto taccuino senese di Baldassare Peruzzi', *Annali della Scuola Normale Superiore di Pisa, classe di lettere e fiolosofia*, ser. III, 1 (1971) 1, 161–79.

Vandenesse, Jean de, *Journal des voyages de Charles-Quint, de 1514 à 1551*, ed. Louis Prosper Gachard (Brussels: Académie Royale de Belgique, 1874).

Visceglia, Maria Antonietta, 'Il viaggio cerimoniale di Carlo V dopo Tunisi', in José Martínez Millán (ed.), *Carlos V y la quiebra del humanismo politico en Europa (1530–1558)*, 4 vols (Madrid: Sociedad estatal para la conmemoración de los centenarios de Felipe II y Carlos V, 2001), vol. 2, pp. 133–72.

Visceglia, Maria Antonietta, *La città rituale: Roma e le sue cerimonie in età moderna* (Rome: Viella, 2002).

Wurm, Heinrich, *Baldassarre Peruzzi, Architekturzeichnungen* (Tübingen: E. Wasmuth, 1984).

Chapter 3
Vienna, a Habsburg capital redecorated in classical style
The entry of Maximilian II as King of the Romans in 1563

Mikael Bøgh Rasmussen

On 16 March 1563, Maximilian of Habsburg entered Vienna in a triumphal entry celebrating his recent election and coronation as King of the Romans, or Emperor-to-be the Holy Roman Empire. For the city of Vienna, this meant elevation to a new position as primary residence of the Empire, and for Austria confirmation of its role as the centre of imperial power of the house of Habsburg. In hindsight it is clear that this new position did not last long, as Maximilian's successor, Rudolph II, would transfer the centre of power to Prague, the capital of the richest and most prestigious of the Habsburg realms. In 1563, however, the Viennese had reason to celebrate their city's new position and the bright prospects that came with it.

What I will put forward here is, firstly, a short discussion of available sources dealing with the planning and unfolding of the entry; secondly, a description of the entry as it emerges from these sources and a presentation of the key messages as they were expressed on the occasion;[1] and thirdly, a comparison with the entries into Prague in 1558 and 1576 of Ferdinand I and Rudolph II, respectively, on the

---

[1] Others have dealt with the entry before, such as Josef Wünsch, 'Der Einzug Kaiser Maximilians II. in Wien 1563', *Berichte und Mitteilungen des Altertums-Vereins in Wien*, 46–7 (Vienna, 1914), 9–34; Werner Kayser, 'Melchior Lorichs' Ehrenpforten und Weinbrunnen zum Einzug Kaiser Maximilians II. in Wien, insbesondere die Ehrenpforte beim Waaghaus', *Philobiblon*, 23 (1979) 4, 279–95; Harriet Rudolph, 'Humanistische Feste? Habsburgische Festkultur in der zweiten Hälfte des16. Jahrhunderts', in Thomas Maissen and Gerrit Walther (eds), *Funktionen des Humanismus: Studien zum Nutzen des Neuen in der humanistischen Kultur* (Göttingen: Wallstein, 2006), pp. 166–90. Howard Louthan has given an overview and interpretation of the entry and its setting, stressing the Catholic and dynastic aspects of Wolfgang Lazius' programme: Howard Louthan, *The Quest for Compromise: Peacemakers in Counter-Reformation Vienna* (Cambridge: Cambridge University Press, 1997), pp. 35–42. A more recent treatment is Nora Höglinger, *Der Adventus Imperatoris in Wien – Ephemere Festarchitektur in der habsburgischen Haupt- und Residenzstadt zwischen 1550 und 1800* (Diss., University of Vienna, 2012).

occasion of their coronations. This short comparison will serve to highlight the unique character of Maximilian's 1563 entry. The uniqueness lies both in the novelty of its design, which showed, for the first time in Vienna, triumphal arches in classical style, and in the stress that was put on the Austrian and Viennese heritage of the Habsburgs and of the imperial office.

The sources

The staging and the literary and vocal aspects of the 1563 entry have come down to us through two descriptions, both published in Vienna, one in Latin in 1563, the other in German in 1566.

The Latin description, under the title *Epitome solenniorum, quae in auspicatum adventum invictiss. ac sacratiss. Rom. Caesaris D. N. Maximiliani, Bohemiae regis et archiducis Austriae . . . respub. Viennen. omnia obsequii ergo supplex . . .*,[2] contains the inscriptions, poems and speeches that the emperor elect and his family would have encountered during the entry.[3] These included speeches by city councillors and some of their offspring representing the city's youth. Among these were Adam Übermann, the son of city council member Johannes Übermann, and Leonard Iglshofer. The largest portion of the book, the *Periphrasis solenniorum*, recounting the entry itself and its setting, was written by court historiographer Wolfgang Lazius, who was responsible for most of the programme. This account was followed by laudatory poems by Paulus Schede, called Melissus, from Franconia, and Caspar Sitnick from Ljubljana (Laibach) in Carniola. Lazius's Latin description is the official account of the entry and was published immediately after the event at the city's cost. As a source, it must therefore be treated more as the image of the entry as it was planned rather than as an account of how it actually unfolded.

The German description that appeared three years later under the title *Gründtliche und khurtze beschreibung des alten und jungen Zugs welche bede zu Einbeleittung . . . Kaiser Maximiliani des Anndern . . . zu Wienn den 16. Martii richtet worden* was published by Caspar Stainhofer, Michael Zimmermann's successor at

---

[2] Wolfgang Lazius, *Epitome solenniorum, quae in auspicatum adventum invictiss: ac sacratiss: Rom: Caesaris D.N. Maximiliani, Bohemiae Regis et Archiducis Austriae etc. una cum quatuor arcuum triumphalium constitutione, eorumque explicatione, Respub: Viennen: omnia obsequii ergo supplex F.F.* (Vienna: Michael Zimmermann, 1563).

[3] The printer Michael Zimmermann was paid 11 guilders and 2 shillings by the city treasurer Hans Übermann on 3 April 1563 for the printing of the description. See Karl Uhlirz, 'Urkunden und Regesten aus dem Archive der K. K. Reichshaupt- und Residenzstadt Wien, II, 1520–1619', *Jahrbuch der kunsthistorischen Sammlungen des allerhöchsten Kaiserhauses*, 18 (Vienna, 1897), 79–85, here p. 82: '*Michael Zimerman, puechdrucker alhie, hat gedruckt 450 exemplar dea einzugs und oration, so vor der Römisch kgl. Maj. Und kunigin gethon; von jedem 6 dn., ut quitt., 11 fl. 2 sh. Dn.*'.

the printing press in the St Annahof in Vienna. It was Stainhofer's first publication, and very likely compiled by the printer himself.[4]

Stainhofer's account is illustrated – rather coarsely – with woodcuts by the Viennese blockcutter Donat Hübschmann. Stainhofer received a payment of 50 guilders from the city council, more than four times the sum the city had paid for Zimmermann's publication, in recognition that Stainhofer had given a copy to each of the city councillors and burgomasters.[5] In the city account book the entry is described as the 'triumph of his Roman imperial majesty', an appropriate title as Maximilian had, since the publication of the Latin version, become emperor on the death of Ferdinand in 1564. Stainhofer's description of the entry was written after the occasion and, while it may be based on the official description by Lazius, was also informed by eyewitness accounts as well as by visual sources in the form of illustrations of most of the ephemeral architecture. It appears to have been published for an audience that had experienced the entry themselves and as such may have been intended to function as a souvenir of the splendid occasion.[6]

These written descriptions are supplemented by further entries in the account books of the city of Vienna, by documents from the government of Lower Austria, and by a woodcut and two drawings by Melchior Lorck, the designer of the visual setting, which may have been made in preparation for yet another publication that never saw the light of day.

The event

The election of Maximilian of Habsburg as King of the Romans had taken place on 24 September 1562, and was followed by his coronation in the church of St Paul

---

[4] Caspar Stainhofer, *Gründtliche und khurtze beschreibung des alten unnd jungen Zugs welche bede zu Einbeleittung . . . Kaiser Maximiliani des Anndern . . . sampt derselben geliebsten Gemahl und Kindern von der Crönung von Franckfurt zu Wienn den 16. Martii richtet worden, sambt aller schönen und zierlichen Ehrenporten Prunnen und anderer Solenniteten warhafftigen angehaenckten Contrafacturn . . .* (Vienna: Caspar Stainhofer, 1566).

[5] This payment was made on 31 October 1566: *Den letzten tag octobris hab ich Caspar Stainhover, puechtrucker alhie, aus bevelch des herrn bürgermaister und rath bezahlt umb destwillen, dass er einen jeden herrn der Römisch kaj. maj. triumpf schön illuminiert uberantwort und presentirt hat macht laut und vermut quitting 50 fl.* See Uhlirz, 'Urkunden und Regesten', p. 89.

[6] The discrepancy between official accounts of entries and festivities and eyewitness descriptions represents a distinction between the event as it was planned and, ideally, would have unfolded and the event as it more or less came to be, is a topic addressed by, among others, Tamar Cholcman, who stresses the political agenda inherent in the official accounts. See Tamar Cholcman, *Art on Paper: Ephemeral Art in the Low Countries: The Triumphal Entry of the Archdukes Albert and Isabella Into Antwerp, 1599* (Turnhout: Brepols, 2013).

in Frankfurt am Main on 20 November.[7] These events resolved the uncertainty which had, for a decade, surrounded the succession plan for the imperial title, with Maximilian having been in constant fear that his cousin Philip II of Spain, the son of the late Emperor Charles V, would be chosen instead of himself, the son of Ferdinand I, Charles's brother and successor. The coronation was thus an affirmation of the Austrian branch of the Habsburgs as the branch that should carry the imperial title and, for Maximilian, the reward for many years of strife and subjugation under his indecisive father.[8]

After his coronation, Maximilian and his entourage travelled for a period of months towards Vienna, both overland and down the Danube, celebrating at every stop along the way. The grand finale was his entry into what was already his home of choice, Vienna, which had been his residence since 1552. He had spent his earliest youth in the city, from 1527 to 1533, but had been sent by his father with his siblings to Innsbruck, away from the Turkish threat that was strongly felt in Vienna in the years after the siege of 1529. In 1541 he had been attached to the court of his uncle, Emperor Charles V, and began his military and political training. He married Charles's daughter Maria and was elected King of Bohemia in 1548, but was sent to Spain to the court of his cousin Philip II, who was the emperor's favoured choice as his successor. However, since 1552 he had spent most of his time in Vienna, where a new residential building was erected for him. While Vienna had been the site of the main imperial residence in earlier centuries, it had been somewhat neglected until Maximilian's father, Ferdinand I, established most of his growing administration there in the 1530s and began renovating and enlarging both the city and the Hofburg. Yet it was only with Maximilian that it was restored to prominence as a courtly residence and, after his crowning as King of the Romans in 1562, and therefore emperor-elect, as an imperial residence.

The 1563 entry was not the first festivity Maximilian celebrated in the city. Apart from his own arrival festivities in 1552, of which we know little, he had arranged an entire month of tournaments in honour of his father in 1560, with splendid costumes and settings, among which were a mock sea-battle (*naumachia*) on the Danube, the appearance of the 2.4 m tall Habsburg house-giant Giovanni Bona (Bartmä Bon von Riva) dressed as a wild man, and pageants and fireworks relating to the overall theme of the tournament: the competition between Venus and Mars.[9] The 1563 entry was only a one-day festival, and as such may not have

[7] The most important treatment of the event is Josef Wünsch, 'Der Einzug Kaiser Maximilians II. in Wien 1563', *Berichte und Mitteilungen des Altertums-Vereins in Wien*, 46–7 (Vienna, 1914), 9–34.

[8] Paula Sutter Fichtner, *Emperor Maximilian II* (New Haven, CT and London: Yale University Press, 2001), pp. 52–60.

[9] This tournament is known through descriptions and depictions in Hans Francolin Burgunder's *Thurnier Buch* from 1561, with engravings by Hans Sebald Lautensack. Cf. Wilfried Seipel (ed.), *Wir sind Helden: Habsburgische Fest in der Renaissance*, Exhibition

matched the 1560 tournament in splendour and sophistication, but it became the most elaborate entry yet to have been performed in Vienna, and the first to show triumphal arches in the Roman manner.[10]

Planning

The planning of the entry into Vienna began in January 1563. The city council entrusted the programme to the learned oversight of the leading figure of Vienna University, Wolfgang Lazius, while the creation of the elaborate setting was given over to those artists living in the city at the time. First and foremost of these was Melchior Lorck, an artist who had only recently returned from Constantinople, where he had been a member of an important Habsburg embassy under Ogier Ghislain de Busbecq. Lorck made a name for himself immediately after his arrival in Vienna in 1559 or 1560 as someone versed in classical learning – *antiquitatis studiosissimus*, as he himself boasted – and emerging as the most capable for the task of all the city's artists.

As the city account books show, numerous artists, citizens of Vienna and foreigners working in the city, were given the aim of executing the designs of Lazius and Lorck. Among them were the printer Michael Zimmermann, who printed designs appropriate to the occasion on the illustrated garments of 600 infantrymen; the blockcutter Georg Wiesensteiger who provided the block from which to print them; the painter Hans Widmer who coloured-in the costumes; the carpenters Hans Dorer, Hans Wudtko and Michel Ringhammer, who made wooden apples, pears and other fruit; the goldsmith Conrad Mair, who crafted golden leaves (*'rausch-oder flindergolt'*); the goldsmith Cristoph Pachmair, who made special gold and silver coins to be distributed during the entry; the painters Heinrich Vogtherr (the Younger), Lorenz Kraler, Joseph Pauenwein, Jan Plundian, Daniel Meldemann, Mert Schmelzer and Wilhelm Wasser, who worked on the larger decorations; and the master builder of St Stephan's Cathedral, Hans Sophoi, who laid out the foundations for the triumphal arches and had made a new gateway through the wall in front of the cathedral to welcome the emperor-to-be. The sculptors Matthias Manmacher (described as the servant of Emperor Ferdinand I), and Leonhart and Caspar Weller, worked on the ephemeral gates of honour, while the silvering of parts of the giants was entrusted to Georg Koller.[11]

Catalogue, Schloss Ambras, Innsbruck, 10 June–31 October 2005 (Vienna: Kunsthistorisches Museum, 2005), pp. 80–82.

[10] Ferdinand I had made an entry into Vienna on 14 March 1558 after his coronation as Holy Roman Emperor which was, as it appears from the descriptions, much less elaborate and entirely lacked the ephemeral architecture that characterised Maximilian's entry five years later. Cf. Joseph Feil, *Kaiser Ferdinand's I. Einzug in Wien, 14. April 1558* (Vienna: Karl Ueberreuter, 1853).

[11] Uhlirz, 'Urkunden und Regesten', pp. 80–82.

The city council, which carried the financial burden, was in close contact with the court's representatives from the government of Lower Austria during the two months of preparation between January and March 1563, in order to ensure Maximilian's acceptance of the programme. By 1 March, Maximilian, who was known for his enjoyment of public celebrations and display, expressed his keen anticipation of his 'joyful entry' as Roman king, no doubt to the relief of the city fathers.[12]

The entry

The overall structure of the entry will be familiar from similar events all over Early Modern Europe. Maximilian, together with his family and entourage, arrived by ship and landed on the banks of the river to the north of the city, outside the Rothenturm gate. Here they were greeted by 300 cavalry and 5,000 infantry from the regional and city militia. They proceeded across the bridge, on which, at a gateway decorated with trees, flowers and fruit, a short poem welcomed the sorely-missed ruler and rejoiced at his good health. At the city gate they were met by the burgomasters, city council members and judges, and by 600 boys dressed in imperial black and yellow or Austrian white and red. More poems were presented here, amongst which was one referring to Marcus Manlius, who had defended his city for a month against overwhelming numbers during the Gallic siege of Rome in 390 BC – probably a reference to hopes that Maximilian would defend Vienna from the Turks.[13] The 85 musicians, militia and a large group of representatives of the city's youth, were also dressed in the same colour scheme, making the spectacle of the pageant a celebration of Empire and Austria together. A baldachin of yellow silk had also been constructed, embroidered with the imperial eagle in black, under which Maximilian and Maria rode after their arrival at the city gate, accompanied by the clangour of the city's church bells.[14]

---

[12] Anton Mayer (ed.), *Quellen zur Geschichte der Stadt Wien, Abt. 1: Regesten aus in- und aus- ländischen Archiven mit Ausnahme des Archives der Stadt Wien, Bd. 2* (Vienna: Verein für Geschichte der Stadt Wien, 1896), No. 1492–95. The organisation of the planning thus followed the well-established pattern typical of this kind of occasion. Cf. Gerrit Jasper Schenck's 'Idealschema' concerning the planning and execution of occasions such as *adventus* and entries, in Gerrit Jasper Schenck, *Zeremoniell und Politik: Herrschereinzüge im spätmittelalterlichen Reich*, Forschungen zur Kaiser- und Papst- geschichte des Mittelalters. Beihefte zu J.F. Böhmer, *Regesta Imperii*, 21 (Cologne, Weimar, Vienna: Böhlau, 2003), Ch. III.A.1.d., pp. 266–78.

[13] Lazius, *Epitome solenniorum*, p. 10.

[14] Uhlirz, 'Urkunden und Regesten', p. 81: '. . . *den 14 januari dises 1563. Jars hab ich zu den fransen and den neuen himel, darunter die Römisch kgl. maj. und die konigin eingeritten, kaft von Christofen Pirkhamer, cramer und burger alhie, drei dock mitlseiden, schwarz, gelb und weis, gewegen 4 phund aindlif lot zwai quintet; das phund per 18 sh. dn., thuet laut geburlicher quittung 9 fl. 6 sh. 14 dn.*'. The baldachin can be seen on the

The entry procession led the emperor-elect through the whole city, from the Rothenturm in the north to the Hofburg in the south, and lasted for some six hours (see Plate 1). As was often the case on such occasions, the entire population was involved in the festivities. In this instance, at least 6,000 residents had been dressed and drilled for their roles in the spectacle, putting a heavy strain on the city's finances.

Along the entire route the streets were lined with trees decorated with large artificial fruits including apples, pears and oranges amongst others, as well as with *Rauschgold* – strips of golden metal foil that glistened and rattled, complementing the salvoes of cannon and the jubilation of the crowd in producing aural effects to supplement the visual staging. On the route there were four major stopping points at which orations and recitations in celebration of the elected king were performed. Two of these main stops, one religious and one political, were the dominant landmarks of the entry: St Stephan's Cathedral and the Hofburg. Along the way, three triumphal arches were erected, while three wine wells spouted red and white wine – an entirely new feature in a Viennese context, and rarely seen anywhere in Austria until then.[15] These temporary features were all to the designs of Melchior Lorck who, according to the city account books, 'worked for two months unceasingly, even at night, on the works, on designing and painting the arches and wells'.[16] The design of the arches and wine wells is known both from the 1566 festival book, where they are illustrated in woodcuts by Donat Hübschmann, and from a woodcut after, and two drawings by, Melchior Lorck which give us a good indication of their structure.[17]

Maximilian was simultaneously Archduke of Austria, King of Bohemia, prospective King of Royal Hungary (the minor part of the former realm still held by the Habsburgs), and Emperor *in spe*. The three arches celebrated his three different

---

first woodcut showing the arrival of the royal couple in Stainhofer's *Gründtliche und khurtze beschreibung*. A similar baldachin was used at Ferdinand's entry 5 years earlier, but appears to have been in need of replacement. Cf. Feil, *Kaiser Ferdinand's I. Einzug*. Stainhofer deals at some length with the honorific connotations of the baldachin as a sign of the ruler as God's vicar on earth, cf. Stainhofer, *Gründtliche und khurtze beschreibung*, fols 5–6.

[15] Herta Blaha, *Österreichische Triumph- und Ehrenpforten der Renaissance und des Barock* (Diss., University of Vienna, 1950), p. 130, mentions that only on two other occasions before Maximilian's entry had triumphal arches been seen in Austria, on the occasion in both instances of Charles V's entries into Innsbruck and Schwaz in 1530.

[16] Uhlirz, 'Urkunden und Regesten', p. 82: [24 March] '*Item dem Melchior Lerchen, kunstreisser, so ertslichen die model zu den dreien ehrenporten gerissen und gemalt und zwai monat lang ohn underlass daran gearbait, gerissen und gemalt hat an den porten und pruennen auch bei nachts unverdrossen gewesen, hab ich für sein arbait und für sein bemuehung zalt vermug quittung 79 fl. 2 sh. 20 dn.*'.

[17] Werner Kayser, 'Melchior Lorichs' Ehrenpforten und Weinbrunnen zum Einzug Kaiser Maximilians II. In Wien, insbesondere die Ehrenpforte beim Waaghaus', *Philobiblon*, 23 (1979) 4, 279–95.

levels of titles, archduke, king and emperor apparent, and at the same time represented a broadening of perspective and influence from local to imperial rule.[18] Throughout the programme, however, a strong emphasis was laid on the Austrian aspect of these levels, whereby Vienna asserted herself as the red and white thread running through the entire iconography of the entry. Yet this was not only a political message which the city of Vienna could embrace. The Austrian theme was also an affirmation of Maximilian's claim to the succession, as opposed to that of his cousin Philip II of Spain who had been the dominant contender for the imperial title until relatively recently.

The three arches were: the Austrian Arch (Porta Austriaca), erected not far from the Rothenturm to the north; the Bohemian Arch, erected immediately after the pageant had exited from St Stephan's, at the turn of the route westwards; and the Roman Arch, erected at the Kohlmarkt, at the final turn of the route to the south and towards the Hofburg.

The Porta Austriaca

The Austrian Arch (see Plate 2 and Figure 3.1) was modelled on a Roman triumphal arch, flanked by two double-sized wooden giants in Roman armour, holding the insignia of the Empire and Vienna. It was dedicated by Emperor Ferdinand and the *senatus populusque viennae*, and saluted the return of the city's son, the archduke, who would also succeed as emperor.

Within the arch, images of members of the Habsburg family flanked the walls, stressing the dynastic succession.[19] Poems by the prominent poet Johannes Seckerwitz celebrated Ferdinand's and Maximilian's roles in the battle against the Turks, with special reference to the city's delivery from the siege of 1529. Importantly, they also expressed trust in Maximilian's anticipated adoption of this role as defender against the infidel. On top of the arch, Charity and Hope flanked a peacock, interpreted in a poem by Claudius Claudianus as the bird of Juno and an omen forecasting the prosperity of Austria. The peacock was also used at this date by the Habsburgs as a means of gathering their many lands under one symbol. Maximilian himself issued a coin after his coronation as Hungarian king in September 1563 featuring three crowns and, on the obverse, an image of the peacock with its tail fanned out to display the many insignia of the lands under its rule.

Vienna and Austria were thus intent on welcoming their ruler, but also stressing his family connection with them, the responsibilities he would carry and the particular hopes vested in him.

---

[18] Louthan, *Quest for Compromise*, pp. 35–42.

[19] Lazius, *Epitome solenniorum*, pp. 10–11; Stainhofer, *Gründtliche und khurtze beschreibung*, fol. 8r.

CLAVDIANVS AD INCLYTAM AVSTRIAM.

Quod picturatas galeæ Iunonia Cristas
Ornet Auis, uel quod pictas uariata per Alas
Rubra per albentem ostendat diuisa Fluentem
Auspicium hæ referunt ueteremq; ab origine Gentem.

Gaudia Siromæ natiq; Patrisq; ferebat.
Laurea, quæ Solymum clade cruenta fuit:
Quam non læticiam tua diua Corona meretur,
Quæ cum patre pio, Pace fideq; redit.

Röm: Kai: Mait: etc. zu Ehren/Sein etliche Arcustriumphales oder Ehrnporten/ Auch Rhorbrunnen vnd dergleichen anderst mehr/Erbawet vnd auffgericht worden/zu Wien in Osterreich/Durch Melchiorn Lorichs/ Im Jar M. D. Lxiij.

Figure 3.1 Melchior Lorck, *Porta Austriaca* (Austrian Arch) (© Staatliche Museen Berlin, Kupferstichkabinett). Photo: SMK)

Wine well

From the Porta Austriaca the pageant moved towards the cathedral. On the way it passed by the first wine well, on the Lugeck, the red and white wine of which was interpreted in inscriptions. The well was also one of the points for distributing bread, nuts and fruit to the populace. It is depicted in a drawing by Melchior Lorck, and in a primitive woodcut by Donat Hübschmann in Stainhofer's book (see Figure 3.2 and Plate 3).[20]

The inscriptions, quoted in Stainhofer, stressed both the colour symbolism of the wine as the beneficence flowing from the house of Austria (associated with its red and white national colours) and, on the side facing the cathedral, its Eucharistic significance as evoking the Sacraments of Baptism and Communion.[21] Here, as at the next stop, the cathedral, the Catholic faith of the heir apparent was thus alluded to, most likely to disperse any doubts about Maximilian's Protestant sympathies, which had made his acceptance as heir to the empire very hard to embrace for both his father and the pope.

St Stephan's Cathedral

When the pageant reached St Stephan's Cathedral it was received by the representatives of the Church and the University. Paulus Schede (Melissus) recited his poem to Maximilian on behalf of the University stressing the newly-empowered ruler's duty fully to embrace and defend the Catholic religion.[22]

A special feature of this event was the appearance on the church spire of standard-waving youths, and of a mechanical eagle flapping its wings, that descended, suspended by a wire, from the top of the spire towards the emperor (Figure 3.3).[23]

---

[20] Lorck's drawing has explanatory inscriptions in the artist's own hand surrounding the framing of the motif (*Rom. Keÿ: Mait. etc. zu Ehren sein etliche Arcustriumphales oder Ehrnporten, auch Rhorbrunnen vnd dergleichen / anderst mehr Erbauhen vnd auffgericht worden, zu Wien in Osterreich, durch Melchiorn Lorichs anno 1563*) and a numbering in another hand that together seem to indicate that Lorck had himself planned the publication of his architectural inventions, which however, became obsolete on the publication of Stainhofer's treatise. See Erik Fischer, Ernst Jonas Bencard and Mikael Bøgh Rasmussen, *Melchior Lorck*, 5 vols (Copenhagen, Royal Library: Vandkunsten, 2009–), vol. 5 (forthcoming), catalogue no. 1563, 1–5.

[21] One of the poems attached to the fountain read: '*Der du nit waist, was Osterreich, / Hat für ein Wappen, Sihe gleich. / Mit was Farben herauss jetzt fleyst, / Aus dem Prunn vnd was er aussgeüst. / Vnderschiedlich Erst Rotten Wein, / Weisser heraus auch fleüsset fein. / Die zaigen, das Wasser vnd Pluet, / Floss auss der seitten Christi Guet. / Mit dem er vnns erlöset hat, / Jhens vns gelassen füern Fluch, ein Pad*'. Stainhofer, *Gründtliche und khurtze beschreibung*, fol. 8v.

[22] Lazius, *Epitome solenniorum*, p. 13.

[23] Stainhofer, *Gründtliche und khurtze beschreibung*, fol. 10r.

Figure 3.2 Drawing by Melchior Lorck of the *Wine Well on the Lugeck*, 1563 (© Statens Museum for Kunst (National Gallery of Denmark). Photo: SMK)

Figure 3.3 Donat Hübschmann, *Adlerflug* (Flight of the Eagle), in Caspar Steinhofer, *Gründtliche und khurtze beschreibung des alten unnd jungen Zugs . . .* (Vienna, 1566) (© Bayerische Staatsbibliothek, under Creative Commons Licence (CC BY-NC-SA 4.0))

The eagle was meant to designate both imperial power and divine sanction of such power, casting Maximilian as chosen and accepted by heaven. Characteristic of the new style of this entry compared to earlier entries in Vienna was its employment, in staging the event, of the formal language of classical antiquity: in this case Jupiter's eagle as a stand-in for divine authority. While classical precedents had played an important role in the image of imperial rule on several earlier occasions, such as the Habsburg entry in Antwerp in 1549 and the tournaments of 1560, the erection of gates of honour in the shape of Roman triumphal arches was a new sight in Vienna.

Porta Bohemica

After Mass and a reception by the bishop inside the Cathedral precincts, the imperial entourage proceeded to the south, only to encounter Porta Bohemica, marking a change in the route's direction (see Plate 4). Maximilian had been crowned Bohemian king in September 1562, and the arch, another triumphal arch in Roman style, elevated the celebrations from the welcome home of an archduke to the praise of the king of another country. In fact, what was celebrated here was the double kingship of both Bohemia and Hungary, marked at the summit of the arch by a lion holding the crests of both realms, and by the prominent 'W' at the keystone, possibly alluding to Wenceslaus IV (1361–1419), king of Bohemia and Holy Roman Emperor, a double role that Maximilian II had himself been elected to enter upon. As Maximilian had not yet been crowned king of Hungary – this would happen on 8 September that year – these allusions were premature. However, the protracted wars in Hungary, a major preoccupation for Maximilian and his father ever since the death of King Louis II of Hungary at the Battle of Mohacs in 1526, ensured that any doubt had to be dispelled about Maximilian's succession to this kingdom, the legitimacy of which had been inherited along the same lines as in Bohemia.[24]

[24] In 1515, Emperor Maximilian I had adopted Louis II, and engaged him to his granddaughter Maria of Austria, while Maximilian I himself became engaged to Louis's sister Anna Jagiellonica with the provision that if Maximilian I died before the marriage could be consummated, then Maximilian's grandson Ferdinand should step into the role as groom instead. This happened in 1521, and Ferdinand of Habsburg thus twice became the brother-in-law of the Hungarian king Louis II. When Louis died, Ferdinand's wife Anna had a claim to the throne that could be transferred to her husband, and Ferdinand's sister Maria, the young dowager queen, pointed to him as the successor. This way of inheritance was confirmed by Ferdinand's election by an electoral council meeting in Stuhlweissenburg (Bratislava). However, another electoral council convened at Székesfehérvár, representing the majority of Hungarian nobles who were not interested in a Habsburg takeover of Hungary, and elected their most prominent lord John Szapolyai. This led to the *de facto* division of Hungary in 1526 and several wars over the next centuries. See Matthias Pfaffenbichler,

The inscriptions alluded to the theme of the crest-holder on the top of the arch, the lion which supported the Bohemian and Hungarian coats of arms. The myth of Hercules and the Nemean lion was evoked as a symbol of the strength expected from Maximilian. Also, the Roman hero Aemilius was cited as an exemplary and ancient predecessor whom Maximilian should emulate in defence of his country.[25] The rhinoceros and elephant at the base of the arch underlined the ideals of strength and steadfastness. Personifications of the lands under the Bohemian and Hungarian crowns were seated in niches and the succession of kings of Bohemia and Hungary was illustrated on the walls inside the arch. Again, the theme of rightful succession was made central to the programme.

Porta Romana

After a further, smaller wine well on the Graben, again known in its layout from a drawing by Melchior Lorck, repeating the colour symbolism of the red and white, and alluding to both Austria and the Eucharist,[26] there came another turn in the route. Here stood the last of the triumphal arches, the Porta Romana (see Plate 5). As with the others, the model was, fittingly, an antique Roman triumphal arch but this arch was more elaborate than the other two and, in celebrating the imperial theme, represented another elevation of the entry's rhetoric.

The virtues of Justice and Faith crowned the upper level, where they flanked the imperial eagle, placed at the centre with wings outstretched. According to the descriptions, this was meant to reflect the joyous welcome by the Empire of the newly-crowned imperial successor. The eagle could both bow and flap its wings to greet him, and turn around to repeat the gesture once he had passed through the gate.[27] On the front, on the lower levels, classical Roman gods and goddesses gathered in a display of Roman tradition and the workings of divine Providence.

'Das andere Reich. Die osmannische Herrschaft unter Süleiman dem Großen', in Willfried Seipel (ed.), *Kaiser Ferdinand I. 1503–1564: Das Werden der Habsburgermonarchie*, Exhibition Catalogue, Kunsthistorisches Museum, Vienna, 15 April–31 October 2003 (Milan: Skira, 2003), pp. 109–15; István Fazekas, 'Ungarns König Ferdinand I', in Seipel, *Kaiser Ferdinand I. 1503–1564*, pp. 117–29; Teréz Oborni, 'Die Herrschaft Ferdinands I. in Ungarn', in Martina Fuchs and Alfred Kohler (eds), *Kaiser Ferdinand I. Aspekte eines Herrscherlebens*, Geschichte in der Epoche Karls V, 2 (Münster: Aschendorff, 2003), pp. 147–66; Rhoads Murphey, *Ottoman Warfare 1500–1700* (New Brunswick, NJ: Rutgers University Press, 1999); Fichtner, *Emperor Maximilian II.*

[25] Lazius, *Epitome solenniorum*, p. 14; Stainhofer, *Gründtliche und khurtze beschreibung*, fol. 10v–12r.

[26] The poem on the well is given in Stainhofer, *Gründtliche und khurtze beschreibung*, fol. 12r.

[27] Lazius, *Epitome solenniorum*, p. 16; Stainhofer, *Gründtliche und khurtze beschreibung*, fol. 13v.

Below were Hercules and Juno, above them Mars and Apollo, and on top of the first level Jupiter and Minerva, referring on the left to strength and on the right to prosperity and wisdom.

The central theme was once again succession, this time in regard to imperial power. Two large depictions on the upper level showed Emperor Ferdinand to the left handing a great globe to Maximilian, who approaches to accept it from the right. The inscriptions on the arch were to be read as father and son in dialogue: the father, Ferdinand, explains that the government given him in his youth was now too difficult to manage and his son must take over, while the son, Maximilian, accepts the challenge, but wishes his father to live long and remain in charge of government.

On the walls inside the arch, below these figures, beneath the keystone crest with the imperial eagle, was crafted a succession of emperors and rulers from the house of Habsburg, among them the immediate family of Maximilian himself, including his rival for the imperial crown, Philip II of Spain, his cousin and brother-in-law. Thus, the arch stresses the imperial succession and the coherence and harmony of the house of Habsburg, both of which had been insecure since the beginning of the 1550s due to religious hostilities and internal rivalry, but which now appeared to be resolved with the conferring of the succession on the family's Austrian branch.[28]

After passing yet another wine well, the layout of which is not known, the Hofburg was reached, where elaborate fireworks were ignited. In the courtyard stood a newly-erected wooden citadel, manned by 'Turks', to be stormed and taken by the combined forces of Austria, Bohemia, Hungary and the Empire, some 1,500 men in total. However, as night was falling and everyone was tired, the show was postponed till the next day. When it was finally performed, it appears that most of the participants lacked enthusiasm, and the drama was somewhat lost on the audience.[29] The theme of this finale, the struggle against the Turks, was a theme central to Habsburg ideology and was often referred to in pageants and entries. In this case, it was also alluded to at the Porta Austriaca at the beginning of the entry route. The placement of this theme at both the beginning and the end of the route could be seen as a reminder of both its actual and symbolic importance for the new ruler and his city. For the city, the Turks were a constant threat, but the Turk acted also as a symbolic substitute for all spiritual challenges to the defender of the 'true' faith, in this case Catholicism. Thus, the Turkish theme had both a general, symbolic meaning, applied on this and on many other occasions to a wide field of reference, signifying both a generalised external enemy and a threat to religion, and carrying in this instance a specific meaning related to the city of Vienna and to its struggle against actual Turks.

If we compare Maximilian II's 1563 entry to the one his father Ferdinand I was given by the same city in 1558, we find clear differences in scale, character

[28] Fichtner, *Maximilian II*, pp. 50–62.

[29] Stainhofer, *Gründtliche und khurtze beschreibung*, fol. 16.

and sophistication. Even if Ferdinand's entry was festive and had cost the city of Vienna a substantial amount of money, Maximilian's outshone it in every respect. Ferdinand's entry has come down to us via the description by the head of Vienna University, Georg Eder, supplemented as a source by the account of the city treasurer presented to the council after the event. Although special emphasis is put on the orations in Eder's account, with less attention devoted to the physical setting and decoration, we nevertheless get an idea of the visual and aural side of the entry.

Five years before Maximilian's *adventus*, Ferdinand entered the city from the same direction, passing through the Rothenthurm gate, processing along the same streets, with a reception and pause at the cathedral to hear a *Te Deum*, and moving via St Michael towards the Hofburg, where the day concluded with jousts and a *melée* in his honour, including the burning down of a wooden castle. Representatives of the city, its youth and the city and rural militia were dressed for the occasion in red and white. Flags decorated the streets, and a baldachin with the imperial eagle embroidered in black and yellow stood inside the city gate to welcome the new emperor. However, neither triumphal arches, nor wine wells, nor artificial eagles flapping down from St Stephan's tower were to be seen. No trees with fruit or rustling gold lined the streets, and the number of participants was significantly smaller than was to be the case for Maximilian. The themes of dynastic succession and of regal and imperial virtues were also given much less prominence.[30]

Conclusion

The three arches that Maximilian and his entourage passed through along the route from the Rothenturm to the Hofburg repeatedly stressed the theme of succession that was so crucial for the would-be emperor himself and for the stability of the realms which his father Ferdinand had taken into his possession on behalf of the Austrian branch of the family. For Vienna, which hosted the celebrations, the recurring theme of the city as the natural home of Habsburg rule was an affirmation and a proud reminder to their new ruler that he must embrace it as such. This message should perhaps be seen in the light of competition with Prague, capital of Bohemia, and the other important residence of the Habsburgs in Ferdinand's realms, which had held a more prominent position in preceding decades. To the benefit of Vienna, their wishes came true: Maximilian kept his base in the city, embellished it and lived there almost exclusively for the next twelve years. The celebration of the entry in the 1566 publication, three years after the event and in the vernacular, could be interpreted as a sign of its general interest and of its importance to the city of Vienna and its people.

Vienna had affirmed itself as the capital, not only of Austria, but *de facto* of the Empire, and the entry of the Roman King in March 1563 could be seen as the

[30] This short description is based on Feil, *Kaiser Ferdinand's I. Einzug*.

inaugural event marking the city's new prominence. For the first time Vienna put on the guise of classical empire, not only in a symbolic sense, as had been the accepted convention for centuries, but materially manifest also in the architectural devices created for the entry. The Roman pantheon was adopted to certify the city's celebration of the Austrian ruler, and the splendour of ancient Rome in the form of arches that adorned the city for a little while, gave it a touch of antique glamour. As the centre of power for the archduke, the king and the emperor, united in the figure of Maximilian II, Vienna could celebrate a new position with bright prospects for the future. Thus, Maximilian's entry, represented in the work of Lazius and Lorck, evoked classical learning and Roman tradition through inscriptions and designs which allowed it to emerge as the first entry into Vienna with a real classical setting.

The character and tone of courtly spectacle in Vienna would, however, change significantly during the 1560s and early 1570s, largely due to what could be termed an Italianisation of courtly culture. Lazius, an historiographer of Austrian origin, and Lorck, the German-Danish artist who had learned to handle the classical languages of art and architecture, were both deeply rooted in a Northern tradition. As Herta Blaha has suggested, their programme had much in common with the great woodcut triumphal arch of Maximilian I, designed by Albrecht Dürer and a group of contemporary artists, and based on the scholarship of Maximilian I's court historiographer Johannes Stabius.[31] Despite the Roman precedents, in iconography and architecture alike, the programme retained a rather traditional character through the stress laid on a genealogical theme, highlighting dynastic succession and the importance of the city of Vienna, which were natural on this particular occasion given the insecurity of Maximilian's claim to the imperial crown and Vienna's uncertain status, up until Maximilian's election, as the centre of imperial rule.

The next large-scale festivities held in Vienna were to be planned and designed by Italians, by the scholar Jacopo Strada and the artist Giuseppe Archimboldo. Strada, who had been appointed to Ferdinand's court in 1560, and Archimboldo, who had been made court painter in 1562, were both of a new breed distinguished by an Italian humanist outlook, and were to become instrumental in changing the cultural setting of the Habsburg court during the 1560s. Strada had engaged in a scholarly dispute with Lazius over antiquarian matters, ancient coins in particular, at the time of the planning of Maximilian's entry, and expressed to Maximilian serious concerns about the validity of Lazius's learning, a view that led to the redirection of the scholarly and artistic outlook of the courts.[32] However, neither Strada nor Archimboldo was available to the city of Vienna at the time of Maximilian's entry, and would only come to the fore in the years that followed.

Lazius and Lorck had made Maximilian's entry into a dynastic, historical, political and religious manifestation of the claim of the Austrian branch of the

[31] Blaha, *Österreichische Ehrenpforten*, p. 14.

[32] Louthan, *Quest for Compromise*, pp. 24–46.

Habsburgs to the title of Emperor, and of the role of the Habsburgs as defenders of the Catholic faith.[33] Strada and Archimboldo, in their designs for the Viennese festivals and tournaments of 1570 and 1572, created hitherto unseen allegorical scenographies and choreographies involving the imperial family, stressing their virtues and universal roles and depicting them in the guise of Olympian gods. These new designs were realised by means of an entirely fanciful antiquarian and allegorical framework, stressing scholarship, innovation and vision, while the themes that had been of utmost importance to Maximilian's Viennese entry – dynastic right, historical precedence and the defence of 'true' religion – were less directly played out.[34]

The entry of Maximilian II in 1563 thus marks a point of transition in the history of Habsburg courtly culture in Vienna, inaugurating at the same time a new era of magnificence in classical style and in the staging of Roman imperial tradition, while bringing to a close the era of dynastic, religious and historiographic arguments referring to the right to rule.

Bibliography

Primary sources

Feil, Joseph, *Kaiser Ferdinand's I. Einzug in Wien 14. April 1558* (Vienna: Karl Ueberreuter, 1853).

Lazius, Wolfgang, *Epitome solenniorum, quae in auspicatum adventum invictiss: ac sacratiss: Rom: Caesaris D.N. Maximiliani, Bohemiae Regis et Archiducis Austriae etc. una cum quatuor arcuum triumphalium constitutione, eorumque explicatione, Respub: Viennen: omnia obsequii ergo supplex F.F.* (Vienna: Michael Zimmermann, 1563).

Mayer, Anton (ed.), *Quellen zur Geschichte der Stadt Wien, Abt. 1: Regesten aus in- und aus-ländischen Archiven mit Ausnahme des Archives der Stadt Wien, Bd. 2* (Vienna: Verein für Geschichte der Stadt Wien, 1896).

Stainhofer, Caspar, *Gründtliche und khurtze beschreibung des alten unnd jungen Zugs welche bede zu Einbeleittung . . . Kaiser Maximiliani des Anndern . . . sampt derselben geliebsten Gemahl und Kindern von der Crönung von Franckfurt zu Wienn den 16. Martii richtet worden, sambt aller schönen*

[33] Ironically, Melchior Lorck had been a strong partisan of Lutheranism in his earlier years. Cf. Erik Fischer, Ernst Jonas Bencard and Mikael Bøgh Rasmussen, *Melchior Lorck*, 5 vols (Copenhagen: Vandkunsten, 2009), vol. 1.

[34] Thomas DaCosta Kaufmann, *Variations on the Imperial Theme in the Age of Maximilian II and Rudolph II: Studies in Ceremonial, Art and Collecting* (New York: Garland, 1978). The themes remained central to the self-image as well as to the propaganda of the Habsburgs for another century, but the staging in elaborate allegories made them less dominant and outspoken.

und zierlichen Ehrenporten Prunnen und anderer Solenniteten warhafftigen angehaenckten Contrafacturn . . . (Vienna: Caspar Stainhofer, 1566).

Uhlirz, Karl, 'Urkunden und Regesten aus dem Archive der K. K. Reichshaupt- und Residenzstadt Wien, II, 1520–1619', *Jahrbuch der kunsthistorischen Sammlungendes allerhöchsten Kaiserhauses*, 18 (Vienna, 1897), 79–85.

Secondary sources

Blaha, Herta, *Österreichische Triumph- und Ehrenpforten der Renaissance und des Barock* (Diss., University of Vienna, 1950).

Cholcman, Tamar, *Art on Paper: Ephemeral Art in the Low Countries. The Triumphal Entry of the Archdukes Albert and Isabella Into Antwerp, 1599* (Turnhout: Brepols, 2013).

Fazekas, István, 'Ungarns König Ferdinand I', in Wilfried Seipel (ed.), *Kaiser Ferdinand I. 1503–1564: das Werden der Habsburgermonarchie*, Exhibition Catalogue, Kunsthistorisches Museum, Vienna, 15 April to 31 August, 2003 (Milan: Skira, 2003), pp. 117–29.

Fichtner, Paula Sutter, *Emperor Maximilian II* (New Haven, CT and London: Yale University Press, 2001).

Fischer, Erik, Ernst Jonas Bencard and Mikael Bøgh Rasmussen (eds), *Melchior Lorck*, 5 vols (Copenhagen, Royal Library: Vandkunsten Publishers, 2009–), vol. 5 (forthcoming).

Höglinger, Nora, *Der Adventus Imperatoris in Wien – Ephemere Festarchitektur in der habsburgischen Haupt- und Residenzstadt zwischen 1550 und 1800* (Diss., University of Vienna, 2012).

Kaufmann, Thomas DaCosta, *Variations on the Imperial Theme in the Age of Maximilian II and Rudolph II: Studies in Ceremonial, Art and Collecting* (New York: Garland, 1978).

Kayser, Werner, 'Melchior Lorichs' Ehrenpforten und Weinbrunnen zum Einzug Kaiser Maximilians II. in Wien, insbesondere die Ehrenpforte beim Waaghaus', *Philobiblon*, 23 (1979) 4, 279–95.

Louthan, Howard, *The Quest for Compromise: Peacemakers in Counter-Reformation Vienna* (Cambridge: Cambridge University Press, 1997).

Murphey, Rhoads, *Ottoman Warfare 1500–1700* (New Brunswick, NJ: Rutgers University Press, 1999).

Oborni, Teréz, 'Die Herrschaft Ferdinands I. in Ungarn', in Martina Fuchs and Alfred Kohler (eds), *Kaiser Ferdinand I. Aspekte eines Herrscherlebens*, Geschichte in der Epoche Karls V, 2 (Münster: Aschendorff, 2003), pp. 147–66.

Pfaffenbichler, Matthias, 'Das andere Reich. Die osmannische Herrschaft unter Süleiman dem Großen', in Willfried Seipel (ed.), *Kaiser Ferdinand I. 1503–1564. Das Werden der Habsburgermonarchie*, Exhibition Catalogue, Kunsthistorisches Museum, Vienna, 15 April to 31 August, 2003 (Milan: Skira, 2003), pp. 109–115.

Rudolph, Harriet, 'Humanistische Feste? Habsburgische Festkultur in der zweiten Hälfte des16. Jahrhunderts', in Thomas Maissen and Gerrit Walther (eds), *Funktionen des Humanismus. Studien zum Nutzen des Neuen in der humanistischen Kultur* (Göttingen: Wallstein, 2006), pp. 166–90.

Schenck, Gerrit Jasper, *Zeremoniell und Politik. Herrschereinzüg im spätmittelalterlichen Reich*, Forschungen zur Kaiser- und Papstgeschichte des Mittelalters. Beihefte zu J.F. Böhmer, Regesta Imperii, 21 (Cologne, Weimar, Vienna: Böhlau, 2003).

Seipel, Wilfried (ed.), *Wir sind Helden. Habsburgische Fest in der Renaissance*, Exhibition Catalogue, Schloss Ambras, Innsbruck, 10 June–31 October 2005 (Vienna: Kunsthistorisches Museum, 2005).

Wünsch, Josef, 'Der Einzug Kaiser Maximilians II. in Wien 1563', *Berichte und Mitteilungen des Altertums-Vereins in Wien*, 46–7 (Vienna, 1914), 9–34.

Chapter 4
Fountains of wine and water and the refashioning of urban space in the 1565 *Entrata* to Florence

Felicia M. Else[1]

In 1565, the *entrata* of Johanna of Austria, bride-to-be of Duke Cosimo I de' Medici's heir, Francesco I, launched a flurry of activity in a city already undergoing changes driven by princely ambitions imposed on the features of an old Republic.[2] For this important alliance between the Medici and the daughter of the late Habsburg emperor Ferdinand I, Cosimo wanted to pull out all the stops. Vincenzo Borghini devised grandiose ephemeral monuments to adorn the streets, replete with painstakingly-researched classical, historical and religious subjects, together with substantial permanent structures, from colossal columns to the reception hall of the Salone dei Cinquecento, that were rushed to completion.[3] Bringing together the permanent and the ephemeral, the scenographic elements of such festivals, as many have noted, informed the development of space in Cinquecento Florence.[4]

---

[1] I would like to thank J.R. Mulryne, Margaret Shewring, Krista De Jonge and Gettysburg College for their advice and collegial support for this chapter.

[2] For an overview of Cosimo's building activities, see Giovanni Fanelli, *Firenze* (Rome and Bari: Laterza, 1980), pp. 94–113 and Henk T. van Veen, *Cosimo I de' Medici and His Self-Representation in Florentine Art and Culture*, trans. Andrew P. McCormick (Cambridge and New York: Cambridge University Press, 2006), pp. 4–27.

[3] On the *entrata*, see Domenico Mellini, *Descrizione dell' entrata della sereniß. Reina Giovanna d'Austria et dell'Apparato, fatto in Firenze nella venuta, & per le felicissime nozze di S. Altezza* (Florence: Giunti, 1566); Giovanni Battista Cini, 'Description of the Festive Preparations for the Nuptials of the Prince Don Francesco of Tuscany', in Giorgio Vasari (ed.), *Lives of the Painters, Sculptors and Architects*, trans. Gaston du C. de Vere, 2 vols (New York: Knopf, 1996), vol. 2, pp. 897–1019; Piero Ginori Conti, *L'apparato per le nozze di Francesco de' Medici e di Giovanna d'Austria* (Florence: Olschki, 1936); Rick Scorza, 'Vincenzo Borghini and *Invenzione*: The Florentine *Apparato* of 1565', *Journal of the Warburg and Courtauld Institutes*, 44 (1981), 57–75; and Randolph Starn and Loren Partridge, *Arts of Power: Three Halls of State, 1300–1600* (Berkeley, CA: University of California Press, 1992), pp. 151–212, whose reconstructions are used in this study.

[4] Fanelli, *Firenze*, pp. 107–10; Anna Maria Testaverde, 'Feste Medicee: la visita, le nozze e il trionfo', in Marcello Fagiolo (ed.), *La città effimera e l'universo artificiale del*

But nothing transforms a space like a fountain, particularly in a place like Florence, which for centuries had no strong tradition of aqueducts or public water supply. This study will explore three fountains that marked the processional route of the *entrata* of 1565, two ephemeral wine fountains and Bartolomeo Ammannati's *Neptune Fountain* (1560–1574) in the Piazza della Signoria (Plate 6).[5] Influences on iconography and visual form will be suggested, looking at contemporary works in villas and the tradition of festival decorations outside Florence, and an analysis offered as to how each fountain engaged problematic aspects of its site and how that affected the *entrata* procession. The focus on fountains bears particular relevance to Cosimo because of the importance the Duke placed on the control of water, devoting considerable resources to building aqueducts, managing riverways, developing a naval force and strengthening coastal areas. These bold initiatives held great political significance, from the needs of local civic government to the broader arena of Mediterranean maritime power.[6]

Fountains of wine: catering to German tastes with Florentine style

Among the many remarkable structures in the *entrata*, the wine and water fountains at the Arch of Maritime Empire and the Arch of Happiness or Public Merriment (*Hilaritas*), would have stood out in Florence, by virtue of being a genre more common in festival traditions north of the Alps. Borghini acknowledged this when he wrote to Cosimo to explain his inclusion of his unusual wine fountains: 'the German nation regards it as a great and very magnificent thing to make

giardino (Rome: Officina, 1980), pp. 82–5; and Antonio Godoli, 'Vasari e Ammannati agli Uffizi: forma e materia', in Cristina Acidini and Giacomo Pirazzoli (eds), *Ammannati e Vasari per la città dei Medici* (Florence: Polistampa, 2011), p. 56.

5 On the Neptune Fountain, see Malcolm Campbell, 'Observations on Ammannati's Neptune Fountain: 1565 and 1575', in Andrew Morrogh, Fiorella Superbi Gioffredi, Piero Morselli and Eve Borsook (eds), *Renaissance Studies in Honor of Craig Hugh Smyth* (Florence: Giunti Barbèra, 1985), pp. 113–36; John Pope-Hennessy, *Italian High Renaissance and Baroque Sculpture* (London: Phaidon, 1996), pp. 220–6 and 481–3; Felicia M. Else, 'Water and Stone: Ammannati's Neptune Fountain as Public Ornament' (PhD Diss., Washington University in St. Louis, 2003); Veen, *Cosimo I de' Medici*, pp. 107–12; and Detlef Heikamp, 'La Fontana di Nettuno: La sua storia nel contesto urbano', in Beatrice Paolozzi Strozzi and Dimitrios Zikos (eds), *L'acqua, la pietra, il fuoco: Bartolomeo Ammannati Scultore* (Florence: Giunti, 2011), pp. 182–261.

6 On Cosimo's water management projects, see Giorgio Spini, 'Introduzione generale', in Giorgio Spini (ed.), *Architettura e politica da Cosimo I a Ferdinando I* (Florence: Olschki, 1976), pp. 32–46; Felicia M. Else, 'Controlling the Waters of Granducal Florence: A New Look at Stefano Bonsignori's View of the City (1584)', *Imago Mundi*, 61 (2009) 2, 168–85; and Emanuela Ferretti, 'Dalle sorgenti alle fontane: Cosimo I e l'aquedotto di Firenze', in Paolozzi Strozzi and Zikos, *L'acqua, la pietra, il fuoco*, pp. 262–75.

fountains that spout wine . . . I see them used often in their festivals'.[7] In this same spirit of welcoming northern guests, views of northeastern Habsburg cities were painted around the courtyard of the Palazzo Vecchio, the penultimate stop of the *entrata*.[8]

Borghini was indeed on to something regarding the popularity of ephemeral wine fountains among the Habsburgs, although their appeal was much broader. Fountains spewing wine had long delighted audiences all over Europe, particularly within the court culture of late Medieval and Renaissance Burgundy.[9] One such fountain at the wedding of Charles the Bold and Margaret of York in Bruges in 1468 had red wine flowing from the drawn arrow of a sculpted Turk and white wine of Rhenish origin appropriately from a German musketeer.[10] Other examples range from a wine-flowing town cross in Scotland to a fountain of wine and beer in Reims to a *tableau vivant* of figures spewing water, wine and milk in Milan.[11] In the case of Borghini, it is possible to pinpoint specific festivals he had investigated, as listed in his preparatory notes for the *entrata*, and many examples appeared in ceremonies for the Holy Roman Emperor Charles V, perhaps leading

---

[7] Author's translation of *'la nazione todesca reputa gran cosa e molto magnifica far fontane che gettino vino e veggole usate assai nelle feste loro* '. See Ginori Conti, *L'apparato*, p. 22 and Rick Scorza, 'Ricerca storica e invenzione: la collaborazione di Borghini con Cosimo I e Fransceco, i suoi rapporti con gli artisti, gli apparati effimeri', in Gino Belloni and Riccardo Drusi (eds), *Vincenzo Borghini: Filologia e invenzione nella Firenze di Cosimo I* (Florence: Olschki, 2002), p. 108.

[8] Cini, 'Description', p. 961; Ettore Allegri and Alessandro Cecchi, *Palazzo Vecchio e i Medici* (Florence: S.P.E.S., 1980), pp. 277–82; and Starn and Partridge, *Arts of Power*, pp. 174–5.

[9] Table fountains of water, some with moving parts, were known in the Medieval period, but scholars point out that table fountains and wine fountains were separate genres, as sediment from wine would have clogged small moving parts. See Stephen N. Fliegel, 'The Cleveland Table Fountain and Gothic Automata', *Cleveland Studies in the History of Art*, 7 (2002), 19–22.

[10] On this fountain and the importance of Burgundy as a shaper of Renaissance culture, see Marina Belozerskaya, *Rethinking the Renaissance: Burgundian Arts Across Europe* (Cambridge: Cambridge University Press, 2002), pp. 135–6, 201–8. My thanks to Krista De Jonge for pointing out this important influence.

[11] Lucinda H.S. Dean, 'Enter the Alien: Foreign Consorts and Their Royal Entries into Scottish Cities, c. 1449–1594', in J.R. Mulryne, Anna Maria Testaverde and Ines Aliverti (eds), *Ceremonial Entries in Early Modern Europe: The Iconography of Power* (Farnham and Burlington, VT: Ashgate, 2015); *Die blijde incoemste en Crooninghe van Coninck Karel die negenste die ghesciet is inde Stadt van Reims* . . . (Antwerp: Jan van Ghelen, [1561]), p. 3 under 'Treasures in Full: Renaissance Festival Books', British Library (hereafter 'Renaissance Festival Books'), http://special-1.bl.uk/treasures/festivalbooks/BookDetails.aspx?strFest=0025; and Silvio Leydi, 'I trionfi dell' "Aquila Imperialissima". Note sugli apparati innalzati a Milano per gli ingressi trionfali di Cristina di Danimarca duchessa di Milano, Carlo V imperatore e Filippo principe di Spagna', *Schifanoia*, 9 (1990), 13.

to his association of them with the 'German nation'.[12] Political symbols abounded in these seemingly frivolous works – the Imperial eagle and lions featured in wine fountains at Aachen and Bologna. An illustration of the fountain at Bologna for Charles's Coronation in 1529 shows two lions on columns with red and white wine pouring from their mouths to a dense and not entirely sober crowd below.[13]

Perhaps more to Borghini's taste would have been the classicising display at Poitiers in 1538 for the Progress of Charles V through France which included a fountain '*ben fatta a l'anticha*' ('well made in the antique manner') with a female figure from whose breasts issued white and red wine, accompanied by two women representing France and Germany.[14]

By contrast, Borghini would have found few examples of great wine fountains around Florence. For the entry of Margaret of Austria into Florence in 1536, six barrels spewing wine were surmounted by a '*grasso nudo*' ('fat nude') at the Porta a Prato.[15] In the Entry of Cosimo into Siena in 1560, wine flowed into a basin from grapes squeezed by the hands of Noah, thus denoting abundance.[16] For the *entrata*, Borghini wanted to go beyond such predecessors to impress his Habsburg audience, drawn to the event by the bride's Austrian origins. Both of the Florentine fountains would need to offer the requisite red and white wine and feature classicising figures in playful and imaginative scenarios. Borghini's fountain at the Arch of Maritime Empire, carried out by sculptor Giovanni dell'Opera, took the form of a beautiful siren seated on a large fish who squeezed red and white wine from her breasts into a large, ornate basin, reconstructed by Randolph Starn and Loren Partridge. Domenico Mellini described how the odour, colour and taste of the wine drew many people, and Borghini added a twist to further enliven this creation.

---

[12] Biblioteca Nazionale Centrale di Firenze (hereafter BNCF), ms. II.X.100, fol. 17r. For transcriptions, see Ginori Conti, *L'apparato*, pp. 124–5; Scorza, 'Vincenzo Borghini', pp. 36–7; and Starn and Partridge, *Arts of Power*, pp. 359–60, n. 190.

[13] Giordano Conti, 'L'incoronazione di Carlo V a Bologna', in Marcello Fagiolo (ed.), *La città effimera e l'universo artificiale del giardino* (Rome: Officina, 1980), p. 44 and Nikolas Hogenberg, *Gratae et laboribus aequae posteritati Caesareas sanctique patris longo ordine et urmas aspice et artifice. . . .* (The Hague: Engelbert Bruning, [1532?]), p. 69 under 'Renaissance Festival Books', http://special-1.bl.uk/treasures/festivalbooks/BookDetails.aspx?strFest=0095. For the fountain at Aachen, see *Römischer Küniglicher Maies: Krönung zu Ach geschehen* (Augsburg: Sigmund Grim and Marx Wirsung, 1520), p. 9 under 'Renaissance Festival Books', http://special-1.bl.uk/treasures/festivalbooks/BookDetails.aspx?strFest=0078.

[14] *La solenne et triomphante entrata dela cesarea maesta, nella Franza, con li superbi apparati, e archi triomphali. . . .* ([n.p.], [1539]), p. 7 under 'Renaissance Festival Books', http://special-1.bl.uk/treasures/festivalbooks/BookDetails.aspx?strFest=0109.

[15] Giorgio Vasari, *Le opere di Giorgio Vasari*, ed. Giovanni Passelli, Part 2 (Florence: David Passigli, 1832–8), p. 1474.

[16] A description of this entry appears among Borghini's notes. See BNCF, II.X.100, f. 32–36v and Anton Francesco Cirni, *La reale entrata dell'Eccellentissimo Signor Duca et Duchessa di Fiorenze in Siena* (Rome: Antonio Blado, 1560), n.p.

In the mouth of the fish was a key that activated a jet of water, which in the way of a 'prank doused those thronging around the wine' taking more than their fair share.[17] Borghini took a similar approach for the fountain at the Arch of Happiness, executed by sculptor Nanni di Stocco. Set on a pedestal, two satyrs poured red and white wine from wineskins on their shoulders. Just as in the Siren Fountain, Borghini planned some comic relief in the form of two *putti* straddling geese (or swans) between their legs. From the beaks of these birds, whom the *putti* held by their necks, water sprayed forcefully and unexpectedly on those who drank too much. A nearby inscription drew cleverly on the words of Catullus, 'Away water, the bane of wine'.[18]

The visual form of these fountains shows Borghini reinterpreting this northern genre by drawing on Florence's ongoing developments in classical revival and in fountain design. Florentine sculptors created fountains for villas and public squares in the sixteenth century, employing designs that emphasised statuary over water effects, partly because of scarcer water supply.[19] Borghini's wine fountains exhibited a playful take on Renaissance naturalism typical of works in garden settings, in which the boundaries of art and nature purposely overlapped. The way real wine flowed from the sculpted Siren's squeezed breasts or satyrs' wineskins conflated the real and the artificial in the same vein as larger-scale permanent works, like Tribolo's *Fountain of Florence* at Cosimo's Villa Castello, whose figure of Florence appears to wring real water out of her bronze tresses (see Plate 7).[20]

But it must have been Borghini's surreptitious sprays of water that made these fountains a hub of activity and amusement, dubbed by Scorza as '*una frivola e quasi buffa*' ('frivolous and almost ridiculous'). These, too, have resonances with the rarefied world of the private courtly villa where water tricks – pranks or games using hidden water sources to unexpectedly douse guests – were enormously popular. Such diversions employed complex hydraulics and automata and, like wine and table fountains, harked back to earlier Burgundian creations, like the remarkable gardens of Hesdin near Arras, where an entire rainstorm could be

---

[17] Author's translation of '*per bagnare con scherzo la gente, che quivi havesse intorno al vino fatto calca*'. Cini characterised them as 'too eager to drink the white and red wine'. On this fountain, see Mellini, *Descrizione*, p. 41; Cini, 'Description', p. 918; Ginori Conti, *L'apparato*, pp. 21–3; and Starn and Partridge, *Arts of Power*, pp. 277 and 219, fig. 68.

[18] Mellini identified the birds as geese, Cini as swans. The translation of the Catullus inscription (from poem 27, lines 5–6) is from Starn and Partridge, *Arts of Power*. See Mellini, *Descrizione*, pp. 89–90; Cini, 'Description', p. 947; Ginori Conti, *L'apparato*, pp. 44–6, 99; Starn and Partridge, *Arts of Power*, pp. 291, 224, fig. 75; and Scorza, 'Ricerca storica', pp. 108–11.

[19] Bertha Wiles, *The Fountains of Florentine Sculptors and Their Followers From Donatello to Bernini* (New York: Hacker, 1975), pp. 17–21 and Pope-Hennessy, *Italian High Renaissance*, pp. 217–33.

[20] Claudia Lazzaro, *The Italian Renaissance Garden* (New Haven, CT and London: Yale University Press, 1990), pp. 131–2 and 174–7.

summoned.[21] Hidden jets that created 'surprise showers', *scherzi d'acqua*, were widespread throughout sixteenth-century villas, often planted in spaces where viewers might stop to admire a work of art, or at enclosures such as Tribolo's Grotto of the Animals at the Villa Castello (Figure 4.1).[22]

Just as these water tricks were noted for their humour and inventiveness, so Borghini's wine fountains must have conveyed a similar sense of light-hearted fun and artful contrivance. Cini's description gives some sense of the spirited atmosphere, noting how the rush of water from the fish under the Siren was met 'not without laughter among the expectant bystanders'.[23]

Each fountain had its own iconographic tradition that drew on sources in and beyond Florence. In his notes regarding the Siren Fountain, Borghini proposed 'a woman who spurts water or wine from her breasts . . . one of those marine nymphs described by the poets'.[24] Such a figure drew from a cast of similarly-sensual female deities, an image of fertility appealing to a male-dominated audience.[25] The wine fountain at Poitiers, mentioned above, bore a similar figure, and Ammannati's nude sculpture of Ceres, planned for a fountain in the Salone dei Cinquecento although never installed, also squeezed water from her breasts.[26] Sirens, the mythical daughters of the sea god Phorcys best known as the tempting enchantresses in Homer's *Odyssey*, adorned various fountains of the Renaissance, including a fifteenth-century fountain in Naples of the Siren Parthenope, the mythical foundress of the city, whose breasts flowed with water.[27] Borghini's Siren might have even been inspired by similar breast-squeezing figures newly-installed by Giambologna along the four corners of his *Fountain of Neptune* in Bologna before his return to Florence for the *Entrata*.[28]

---

[21] Fliegel, 'The Cleveland Table Fountain', p. 16.

[22] Lazzaro, *The Italian Renaissance Garden*, pp. 65–7. My thanks to Claudia Lazzaro and Ralph Lieberman for the photograph of the water trick at the Villa Castello.

[23] Cini, 'Description', p. 918.

[24] Author's translation of '*una donna che getta aqqua o vino per le mammelle . . . una di quelle ninfe marine scritte da'poeti*' from Ginori Conti, *L'apparato*, p. 120.

[25] Lazzaro, *The Italian Renaissance Garden*, p. 144.

[26] Ammannati's sculptures, now in the Bargello, were completed by 1561, and it remains unclear why the fountain was never installed. For recent discussions, see Emanuela Ferretti, 'Bartolomeo Ammannati, la Fontana di Sala Grande e le trasformazioni del Salone dei Cinquecento da Cosimo I a Ferdinando I', in Paolozzi Strozzi and Zikos, *L'acqua, la pietra, il fuoco*, pp. 136–55 and Dimitrios Zikos, '". . . Che accozzamento è stato questo suo"? Sul simbolismo delle statue di Ammannati per il Salone dei Cinquecento', in Paolozzi Strozzi and Zikos, *L'acqua, la pietra, il fuoco*, pp. 156–81.

[27] Lazzaro, *The Italian Renaissance Garden*, p. 144, and Nicholas Richardson, 'Sirens', in Simon Hornblower and Antony Spawforth (eds), *The Oxford Classical Dictionary* (Oxford: Oxford University Press, 2005) (Oxford: Oxford University Press, 2012), 1372.

[28] These figures were installed by January, 1565, and the whole fountain completed in January of 1567. See Pope-Hennessy, *Italian High Renaissance*, p. 488.

Figure 4.1 Water tricks at Niccolò Tribolo, *Grotto of the Animals*, various stones and shells, 1550–1572, Villa Medici, Castello (Photo: Ralph Lieberman)

Among the elaborate spectacles for the Entry of Leonor of Austria into Lisbon in 1521, intended to 'Burgundianize' the Portuguese court, were two Sirens whose breasts offered red and white wine. A Siren adorned part of a fountain topped by a personification of Messina at the Entry of Charles V into that city in 1535, a festival Borghini listed among those he consulted.[29] In these instances, Sirens served to glorify imperial power and maritime supremacy, a message also desired in Borghini's work. The Siren Fountain featured alongside the Arch of the Maritime Empire, a grand tripartite façade teeming with *all'antica* marine deities, geographic personifications and riches of the seas, such as corals, fishes and shells. Two giants represented Oceanus and the Tyrrhenian Sea, accompanied by Tethys, Proteus and Neptune while allegories of Peru and Elba glorified the territorial expansions of the Habsburgs and the Medici.[30] The Siren Fountain was located front and centre of the overall structure, set before a large niche containing the giant figures of Oceanus and the Tyrrhenian Sea. Thus its offerings of wine and *scherzi d'acqua* complemented the language of abundance and prosperity represented in the marine motifs on the arch, the bounties of the waters controlled by the Duke and his imperial kin. Both fountain and arch were ambitious visual statements; however, as Starn and Partridge slyly observe, such juxtapositions of Tuscan and Austrian power 'exposed the pretense of Florentine grandeur in a larger world over which the Medici court had little control except by art and artifice'.[31]

The Siren Fountain and the Arch of the Maritime Empire occupied an important but problematic space, at the foot of the Santa Trinità bridge south of the Piazza Santa Trinità and the Palazzo Spini (see Figure 4.3). It would have been the fourth stop along the route, as the procession made its way in an easterly direction along the right bank of the Arno and marked an important turn northwards towards the core of the city (see Figure 4.2). Starn and Partridge noted that this spot as well as that of the other wine fountain were chosen to 'satisfy the taste of the *popolo* while keeping it at a distance . . . at the southeast and southwest boundaries of the Roman *castrum* . . . marginal to the ancient core of the city'.[32]

That said, those areas surrounding the Santa Trinità bridge had been impressively fitted-out for previous entries. During the Entry of Leo X in 1515, a triumphal arch dedicated to *Fortezza* (Fortitude) marked the foot of the Santa Trinità bridge on the left bank while a replica of the Vatican obelisk greeted the procession

---

[29] On Borghini's list, see note 11. For the Messina fountain, see *Copia di vna lettra della particularita dellordine con il quale la maesta cesarea intro in Messina. . . .* ([n. p.], 1535), p. 9, under 'Renaissance Festival Books', http://special-1.bl.uk/treasures/festivalbooks/BookDetails.aspx?strFest=0101.

[30] Mellini, *Descrizione*, pp. 37–42; Cini, 'Description', pp. 915–9; Ginori Conti, *L'apparato*, pp. 21–3; and Starn and Partridge, *Arts of Power*, pp. 277–8.

[31] Starn and Partridge, *Arts of Power*, p. 171.

[32] Ibid., p. 196.

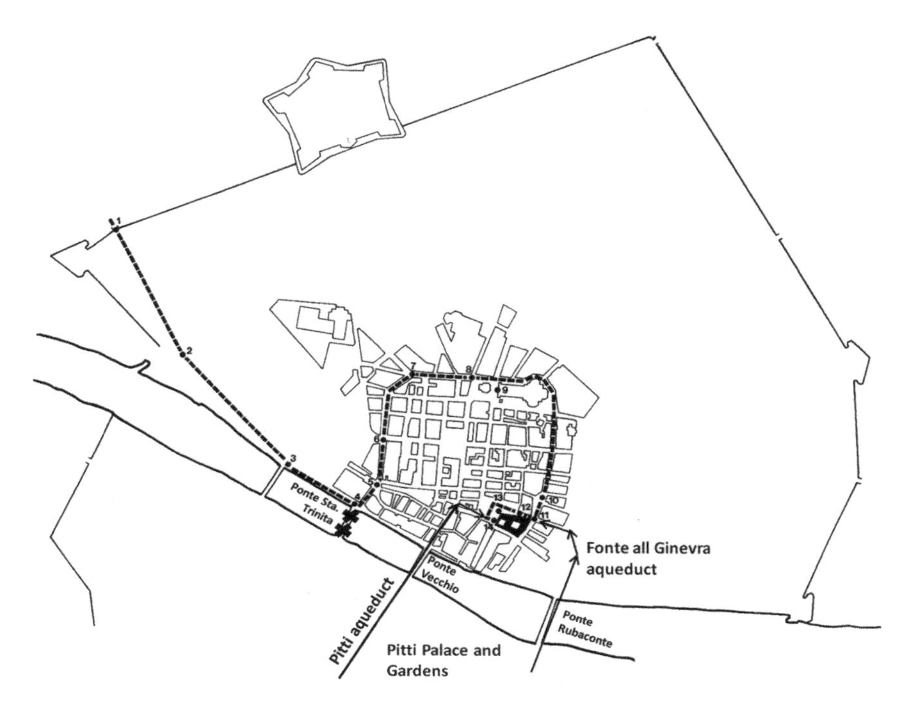

Figure 4.2 Reconstruction of routes of the Pitti and Fonte alla Ginevra aqueducts drawn on Starn and Partridge's map of the 1565 processional route (From Starn and Partridge, *Arts of Power*, ill. 64. Courtesy of University of California Press)

at the opposite side of the river.[33] For the Entry of Charles V into Florence in 1536, the area at the Trinità bridge on the left bank bore colossal river gods of the Arno, Rhine, Danube, Bagrada and Ebro, the rivers of the Emperor's domains.[34] The placement of maritime subjects and hydrographic deities along the riverbank itself makes sense, and Borghini's Arch of the Maritime Empire perhaps expanded on this strategy.

As scholars have noted, Borghini faced one daunting challenge: the Trinità Bridge was still in ruins after the flood of 1557, referred to in his preparatory notes as 'Ponte Rovinato'.[35] The overall form and placement of the Arch suggest a strategy of coverage and diversion. The tripartite façade was situated so that

---

33 Testaverde, 'Feste Medicee', p. 72 and figs. 93 and 96.

34 Bonner Mitchell, *The Majesty of the State: Triumphal Progresses of Foreign Sovereigns in Renaissance Italy (1494–1600)* (Florence: Olschki, 1986), pp. 171–2.

35 Ginori Conti, *L'apparato*, p. 21; Starn and Partridge, *Arts of Power*, p. 169; and BNCF, II.X.100, fol. 45.

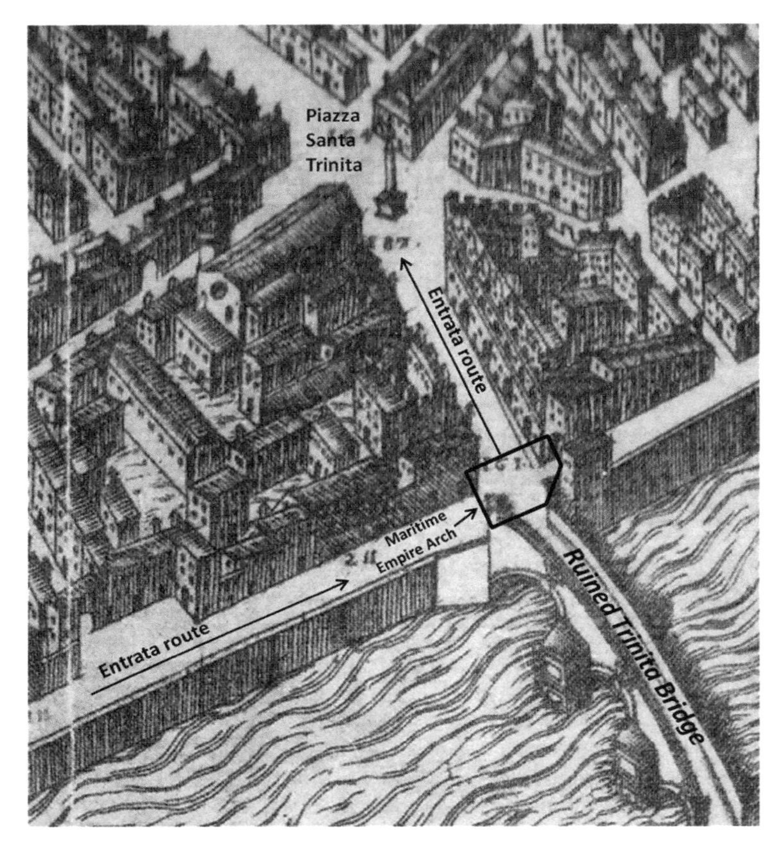

Figure 4.3 Location of the *Arch of Maritime Empire* and the 1565 processional route indicated on Stefano Bonsignori, *Nova pulcherrimae civitatis Florentiae topographia accuratissime delineata*, 1594, engraving by Girolamo Franceschi 1584. Numbering shown refers to Bonsignori's original. (© The British Library Board, MAPS* 23480 (21) 603.1.16 (p. 69))

one end would cover up the view of the ruined bridge to the south, another end faced the oncoming procession from the east with the central section angled to direct the party towards the next stop at the grand Column of Piazza Santa Trinità. Furthermore, Cini noted that the façade employed some kind of optical trick to appear complete from two different vantage points: 'a thing of singular artifice . . . which rendered that street . . . even more imposing and more beautiful than could be believed'.[36] In the centre of all this was the Siren Fountain. Its evocation of the

[36] Cini noted the addition of another facade to hide the scaffolding. See Cini, 'Description', pp. 915–16, 919.

luxuries and pranks of the private villa would have been echoed by an illusionistic grotto portraying Proteus and other sea monsters in a niche behind the Giants. When one considers the crowd that would have gathered to consume the wine and to watch the humorous effects of the water jet, it becomes clear how dramatically this space was re-fashioned. In a city the architectural fabric of which was still predominantly medieval, the sight of a voluptuous Siren, whose breasts the viewer was actually encouraged to approach, would have been as unusual as the free-flowing wine.

The other wine fountain, that of the Arch of Happiness, tells an equally rich story, in this case set among the more terrestrial mythological realm of Bacchus. Here, satyrs, *putti* and geese frolicked among the companions of Bacchus, decorating an enclosed arch topped by a joyous, smiling woman bearing an inscription, 'HILARITAS P.P. FLORENT'. ('Happiness of the Florentine People'). Two preparatory drawings show Borghini developing the arrangement of figures on the fountain with the two satyrs standing above seated *putti*, all set on a larger circular *tazza* (see Figure 4.4 and Figure 4.5).[37] In the second drawing, the figures and jets of wine and water are turned more outwardly, creating a stronger silhouette, and poses are given more liveliness and detail, particularly the grip of the *putti*'s hands around the necks of the geese. Mellini describes the final work as bearing a beautiful, decoratively carved ('*intagliato*') pedestal set on three large steps ('*scaglioni*').[38] With no less than six figures, this wine fountain was more intricate than its counterpart at the Arch of the Maritime Empire.

This subject of public happiness had important precursors in earlier Habsburg-related festivals. The concept was fitting to wedding celebrations, and here spoke also to Cosimo's munificence.[39] Wine fountains further reinforced this notion, as Borghini explained their relevance to the Duke: 'for the entire well-being of a city it is not enough that its citizens be occupied with trades, rich in goods, harmonious among themselves, and at peace with their neighbors, since it is necessary at times to make them happy and to gladden them'.[40] The subject of HILARITAS POPULI FLORENTINI has previously appeared in the Entry of Charles V into Florence in 1536, represented simply by a statue of a joyful woman.[41] The combination of female personification and satyrs featured in a portrayal of *Hilaritas* for the Entry of Phillip II into Mantua in 1549, a festival that Borghini listed among those he had researched. This female figure held a palm and cornucopia, set on a pedestal which bore the inscription PUBLICA HILARITAS on one side, dancing boys on another, nymphs playing instruments on a third and satyrs

[37] The second drawing comes from a different collection of Borghini documents, BNCF, Magliab. VIII, 1393, c. 278r, first published by Scorza. See Ginori Conti, *L'apparato*, p. 45 and Scorza, 'Ricerca storica', p. 108 and Tav. VII.

[38] Mellini, *Descrizione*, p. 89.

[39] Scorza, 'Ricerca storica', p. 109.

[40] Starn and Partridge, *Arts of Power*, p. 170.

[41] Mitchell, *The Majesty*, p. 171.

Figure 4.4 Preparatory sketch for the *Arch of Happiness*, 1565, Biblioteca Nazionale Centrale di Firenze, ms. II.X.100, c. 79v (reproduced by permission of the Ministero dei beni e delle attività culturali e del turismo/BNCF)

Figure 4.5 Preparatory sketch detail for the fountain at the Arch of Happiness, 1565, BNCF, MS Magliabechiano VIII, 1393, c. 278r (reproduced by permission of the Ministero dei beni e delle attività culturali e del turismo/Biblioteca Nazionale Centrale di Firenze)

drinking and eating on the fourth.[42] In Borghini's case, he could take the analogy to a literal conclusion, fusing classical subjects that drink and pour wine with real Florentines consuming the fruits of ducal prosperity.

The visual form of the fountain shows affinities with those by Florentine artists. Scorza suggests the influence of Montorsoli's Orion Fountain in Messina with its statues of pagan deities, elaborate narrative scenes and the use of large, flat circular *tazze*.[43] An even closer example would have been the fountain in the courtyard of the Palazzo Vecchio with Verrocchio's *Putto with Dolphin* on

42 *Descrittione delli archi et dechiaratione delle statoue, [et] apparati publici, fatti alla entrata in Mantoua del serenissimo prencipe di Spagna, a XIII di Gennaro. M. D. XLIX* ([n. p.], [1549?]), p. 7, under 'Renaissance Festival Books', http://special-1.bl.uk/treasures/festivalbooks/BookDetails.aspx?strFest=0114. See note 11 for Borghini's list.

43 Scorza discussed this influence in conjunction with another fountain planned for the stop at the Ponte Carraia but not realised for the *entrata*. See Scorza, 'Ricerca storica', pp. 109–11.

Figure 4.6 Niccolò Tribolo, *Fountain of Hercules and Antaeus* (detail of *putti* with geese), c. 1543, marble, Villa Medici, Castello (© Alinari/Art Resource, NY)

a specially-carved porphyry *tazza* set on *scaglioni*.[44] Satyrs and geese-wielding *putti* adorned fountains by Tribolo at Cosimo's Villa Castello, an elaborate garden complex the planned hydrographic layout and fountain iconography of which presented an idealised vision of Medici-ruled Tuscany. On the Fountain of Florence, satyrs appear as supporting figures below the lower *tazza* and in the reliefs on the upper stem, joyously playing musical instruments.[45] The focal point of the garden, the Fountain of Hercules and Antaeus, bore a remarkable group of *putti* with geese along the lower stem, whose gracefully interlacing forms animate the surface and, in typically Mannerist fashion, led the viewer to enjoy different angles around the structure (see Figure 4.6).[46] Like Borghini's wine fountain, the *putti* grasp the necks of the geese and water spurts out of the birds' beaks, a composition derived

[44] On this cylix fountain type popular throughout the sixteenth century, see Wiles, *The Fountains*, pp. 6–16 and 58–67. On the fountain in the courtyard of the Palazzo Vecchio, see Allegri and Cecchi, *Palazzo Vecchio*, pp. 227–9.

[45] Lazzaro, *The Italian Renaissance Garden*, pp. 167–77.

[46] Wiles, *The Fountains*, p. 84; Pope-Hennessy, *Italian High Renaissance*, p. 220; and Lazzaro, *The Italian Renaissance Garden*, pp. 172–4.

from a Hellenistic type.[47] Altogether, Borghini's concoction had the artistic complexity of a permanent work of art, thus modifying the playfulness of wine, water tricks and a festival atmosphere. One final witty detail centres on the inscription from Catullus mentioned earlier, 'Away water, the bane of wine'. Not only did this ancient verse echo the sentiments of those being doused, but it was also reflected in the arrangement of the jets of water and wine. Borghini gave clear instructions that the water and wine stay separate, declaring that water may be 'very necessary to human life but it gives little joy'.[48]

As remarkable as this fountain must have been, its urban site was just the opposite. The intersection of the Borgo dei Greci and the Via dei Leoni, or Proconsolo, was literally the back end to the city's main civic Piazza (see Figure 4.7). Nestled at the rear of the Palazzo Vecchio's northern side, past the Via dei Gondi, this corner led to the more industrial easterly quarter of Santa Croce, a section of the city that included the Stinche prison and factories for cloth dyeing.[49] Even today, the space, now the south end of the Piazza San Firenze, where the Baroque complex of S. Filippo Neri serves as the Tribunale, is awkward and cramped. In 1565, this section would have had the much older church of San Firenze on the northeast (number 58 on Figure 4.7) and to the south, in lieu of the unified walls visible today forming the back corner of the Palazzo Vecchio, a hodgepodge of irregular structures comprising the former site of a *serraglio* of lions.[50] Borghini himself noted the space to be 'entirely unseemly and badly done' ('*tanto scomodo e mal fatto*') and found it unsuitable for the Arch of Prudence, the monument dedicated to the virtues of Cosimo.

Like the Arch of the Maritime Empire, the Arch of Happiness served as a turning point at the end of a long straight processional route, in this case following

---

47 For variations attributed to Tribolo and his circle, see Wiles, *The Fountains*, pp. 84–5 and Claudio Pizzorusso and Antonia Boström, catalogue entries nos. 89–91 in Cristina Acidini Luchinat et al. (eds), *The Medici, Michelangelo, and the Art of Late Renaissance Florence* (New Haven, CT and London: Yale University Press, 2002), pp. 225–8.

48 Author's translation of '*Ma il fatto sta che l'acqua sebbene è necessarissima alla vita umana, nondimeno dà poca allegrezza*'. See Giovanni Bottari and Stefano Ticozzi (eds), *Raccolta di lettere sulla pittura, scultura ed architettura*, 8 vols (Milan: Silvestri, 1822), vol. 1, p. 206.

49 Fanelli, *Firenze*, pp. 62–3 and Eve Borsook, *The Companion Guide to Florence* (Woodbridge: Boydell and Brewer, 2000), pp. 72–107.

50 On these structures, see Borsook, *The Companion Guide*, p. 77 and Piero Fiorelli and Maria Venturi (eds), *Stradario storico e amministrativo del Comune di Firenze*, 3 vols (3rd ed., Florence: Polistampa, 2004), vol. 1, p. 391. A serraglio of live lions, symbols of the Republic, had been there since the fourteenth century but were moved in 1550. The association, however, was still present, as Mellini described this location as 'where the lions had been'. The present back section of the Palazzo Vecchio was not built until 1588. See Agostino Lapini, *Diario fiorentino di Agostino Lapini dal 252 al 1596*, ed. Giuseppe Odoardo Corazzini (Florence: Sansoni, 1900), p. 108; Mellini, *Descrizione*, p. 88; and Allegri and Cecchi, *Palazzo Vecchio*, pp. 12, 361.

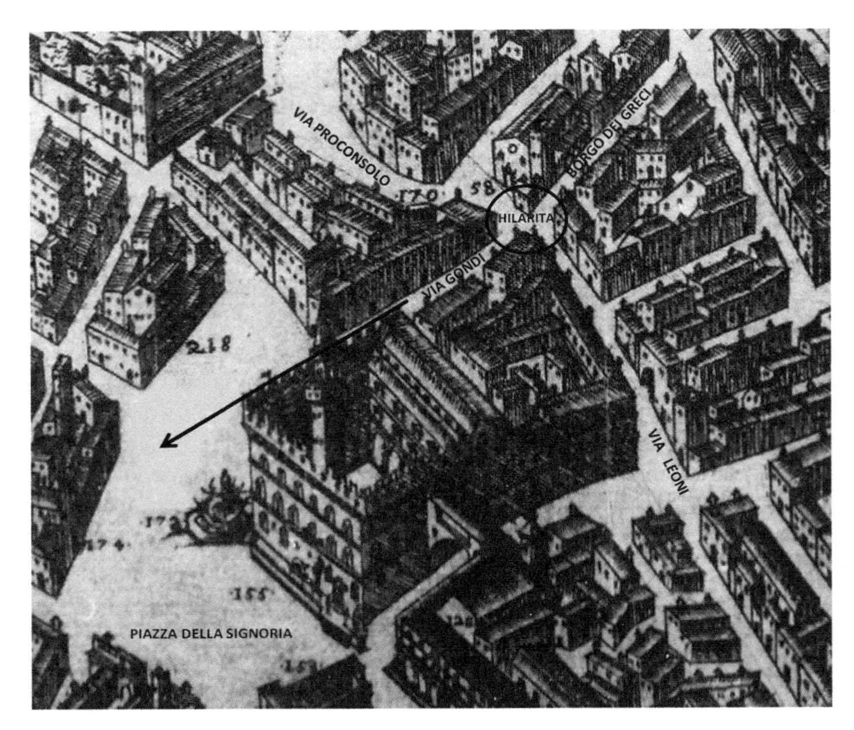

Figure 4.7 Location of the *Arch of Happiness* (*Hilaritas*) indicated on a detail from Stefano Bonsignori, *Nova pulcherrimae civitatis Florentiae topographia accuratissime delineata*, engraving, 1594, reprint by Girolamo Franceschi of the 1584 original. Numbering shown refers to Bonsignori's original. (© The British Library Board, MAPS* 23480 (21) 603.1.16 (p. 69))

the *Entrata's* southern progress down the Via Proconsolo from the Cathedral and directing it westward towards the Piazza della Signoria down the Via dei Gondi (see Figures 4.2 and 4.3). As Ginori Conti suggests, Borghini came up with a plan intended to hide both the Borgo dei Greci and the Via dei Leoni.[51] Unlike the grand open layout of the riverside Arch, this structure presented a more intimate, squared-off enclosure, described as a '*piccoletto*' ('rather small') closed triumphal arch with openings along the side to allow people in this narrow space to exit freely. This small structure evoked a festive spirit in keeping with its theme, bearing paintings of Bacchus, Bacchants and satyrs drinking, dancing and singing 'in a thousand pleasing ways'.[52] Here, too, the wine fountain took a prominent

[51] Ginori Conti, *L'apparato*, p. 44.

[52] A verse from Horace read 'Now is the time to drink and with free foot to beat the earth' (translation from Starn and Partridge). See Mellini, *Descrizione*, pp. 88–90; Cini,

central position, underneath the main figure of Hilaritas and would have appeared a relatively ornate work within a close-knit space. The overall shape of the Arch and the openings along the sides appear specially designed both to obscure the problematic urban site around it and to accommodate the crowds that would have formed around the fountain. With its ancient pastoral characters, water tricks and enclosed decorated surfaces, this Arch re-fashioned the space into a delightful enclave, drawing on the vocabulary of contemporary villas. In this case, the element of actual wine gave it an international appeal, one that Borghini hoped would attract both his Habsburg audience and the local citizenry.

The Neptune Fountain and the approach to the Piazza della Signoria

The grandest fountain of all, Ammannati's Neptune Fountain, awaited the procession as it headed towards the last stop among the public spaces of the city, the Piazza della Signoria (see Plate 6). The fountain depicts the god Neptune atop a chariot pulled by four horses, set within an octagonal basin of purplish *marmo mischio*, the four corners of which each supported a trio of bronze figures, comprising a marine deity flanked by smaller satyrs or fauns. Unlike the wine fountains, the Neptune Fountain was created as a permanent work of art, begun well before plans for the wedding were underway. This important public work featured a colossal block of white Carrara marble as its centrepiece, the prestige of which launched a heated artistic competition.[53] The L-shaped Piazza della Signoria had a history of politically-charged occupation and appropriation since the mediaeval Republican era, reflected in the statuary erected there over the years, including Michelangelo's *David*, Bandinelli's poorly-received *Hercules and Cacus* and, under the firm rule of Cosimo, Cellini's *Perseus and Medusa*, symbolising the Duke's political quelling of Discord through the defeat of his rebellious enemies.[54] In 1540, Cosimo had moved his family from the Medici Palace to the medieval city hall, the Palazzo Vecchio, and proceeded to have Vasari refurbish its interior rooms.[55] By placing the Neptune Fountain against the northwest corner of the

'Description', pp. 946–7; Ginori Conti, *L'apparato*, p. 44; and Starn and Partridge, *Arts of Power*, p. 291.

[53] On the block and the competition see Virginia Bush, *The Colossal Sculpture of the Cinquecento* (New York: Garland, 1976), pp. 145–8; Else, 'Water and Stone', pp. 39–55 and Heikamp, 'La Fontana', pp. 212–33.

[54] On the Piazza della Signoria, see Marvin Trachtenberg, *Dominion of the Eye: Urbanism, Art, and Power in Early Modern Florence* (Cambridge and New York: Cambridge University Press, 1997), pp. 87–148. On the Piazza statuary see Sarah Blake McHam, 'Public Sculpture in Renaissance Florence', in Sarah Blake McHam (ed.), *Looking at Italian Renaissance Sculpture* (Cambridge: Cambridge University Press, 1998), pp. 158–72.

[55] This massive undertaking is documented in Allegri and Cecchi, *Palazzo Vecchio*, pp. 55–352.

Palazzo Vecchio in line with Michelangelo's *David* and Bandinelli's *Hercules and Cacus*, an axis of *all'antica* colossi was formed mounting guard over what had become the Duke's palace.[56]

It was the water, however, that was the truly new element brought to the Piazza, providing Florence with one of its first public fountains since antiquity. The Florence of the Republic was a city of wells and cisterns, with the Neptune Fountain celebrating the Duke's construction of new aqueducts to provide fresh spring water (Figure 4.2). The 'Pitti aqueduct' originated near the Palace and Gardens of the Pitti, which had been acquired as an additional Medici residence. Several fountains were planned for both Medici complexes with the ducal waters of the Pitti symbolically fueling those of the city. For Ammannati's Neptune Fountain, however, a different aqueduct had to be constructed, that of the Fonte alla Ginevra, which traversed the Ponte Rubaconte and reached its destination from an easterly direction along the Borgo dei Greci, the same area where the Arch of Happiness would be placed.[57] Even with both aqueducts, water could not be taken for granted, as demonstrated by Borghini's instructions to provide an extra water reservoir for the fountain at the Arch of Happiness, in case all the aqueduct water would be needed for the Neptune Fountain.[58]

Borghini felt strongly that the Neptune Fountain should feature as the thirteenth element in the *entrata* even though only the colossal Neptune and two bronze figures would be finished in time. He considered this work 'the most beautiful ornament' of all the elements of the *entrata*, because it was 'real and permanent' ('*vero e stabile*').[59] A great deal of the fountain had to be completed in ephemeral materials – a temporary basin was painted to resemble *marmo mischio* and ten of the bronzes were made in stucco. As Campbell and Heikamp have remarked, the fountain at the *entrata* had higher basin walls, since Mellini and Cini describe it as 'gracefully sustained by several satyrs' with the result that the larger marine deities lay along a continuous upper rim as though 'on the shores of the sea'. In 1572, Francesco de' Medici ordered these walls to be lowered so that the water would be more visible. The result compromised Ammannati's original concept of the basin representing the breaking waves caused by Neptune's arrival, and took away the context that explained the poses and gestures of the subsidiary bronzes.[60] Other differences suggest that the fountain unveiled for the *Entrata* was

---

[56] Bush, *The Colossal Sculpture*, p. 150; Trachtenberg, *Dominion of the Eye*, pp. 276–81; and Heikamp, 'La Fontana', pp. 193–4.

[57] On Cosimo's aqueducts, see Allegri and Cecchi, *Palazzo Vecchio*, pp. 221–2; Else, 'Water and Stone', pp. 225–66 and Ferretti, 'Dalle sorgenti', pp. 263–75. On the link between the Pitti and the Palazzo Vecchio, see Lazzaro, *The Italian Renaissance Garden*, p. 191.

[58] Bottari and Ticozzi, *Raccolta di lettere*, p. 206.

[59] Campbell, 'Observations', pp. 114–15.

[60] Translations of Cini and Mellini from Campbell. For discussion and reconstructions, see Campbell, 'Observations', pp. 115–25 and Heikamp, 'La Fontana', pp. 236–7, 253.

slightly more ornate than the finished work. For example, the satyrs held baskets of fruits and chestnuts as opposed to the single motifs, mostly marine-related, held by the finished statues. Some of the marine deities cradled children in their arms, a feature which was not maintained for the final work, and there were more reliefs and festoons interspersed throughout.[61]

The subject of Neptune suited an event like the *entrata*, as the god was an imposing newcomer to the tradition of public sculpture in Florence and part of a politicised vocabulary boasting supremacy over waters and distant lands. Scholars have noted the popularity of the Neptune figure in other fountains, like those of Montorsoli in Messina and Giambologna in Bologna.[62] Neptune also appeared in festival decorations linked to the Habsburgs. For example, an allegorical painting of Neptune with sirens, tritons and marine horses appeared with that of Bacchus for the Coronation of Charles V in Bologna in 1529.[63] A festival we know Cosimo attended was Philip II's entry into Genoa in 1548, where the Duke may have seen a large painted Neptune representing in not too modest terms his rival, the Genoese Admiral Andrea Doria, paired with Jupiter representing Charles V.[64] At Cosimo's own wedding in Florence to Eleonora of Toledo (1539), Neptune appeared on a chariot holding a trident to signify the Emperor's domination of the Western Ocean.[65]

In the *entrata* itself, Neptune was a recurring figure. At the Arch of Maritime Empire, a painting showed Neptune chasing away troublesome winds, a reference to Virgil's *Aeneid* and a metaphor for Cosimo as a ruler who quenches discord.[66] After the procession passed the Neptune Fountain, its image appeared again on a painted oval in the courtyard of the Palazzo Vecchio, described by Cini as representing 'the profit and advantage that will accrue . . . to the city from the waters that the Duke is constantly engaged in bringing to her'.[67] Inside the Salone dei Cinquecento, where the procession culminated, Neptune features among the ceiling paintings of *The Arrival of Eugenius IV at Livorno* and the *Naval Battle between the Florentines and Pisans*, where he ensured safety and victory for

---

[61] Cini, 'Description', pp. 952–3 and Mellini, *Descrizione*, pp. 99–100.

[62] On Neptune as a 'local ruler image', see Luba Freedman, 'Neptune in Classical and Renaissance Visual Art', *International Journal of the Classical Tradition*, 2 (1995) 2, 227–36.

[63] Conti, 'L'incoronazione', p. 41.

[64] Mitchell, *The Majesty*, p. 181.

[65] Andrew Minor and Bonner Mitchell, *A Renaissance Entertainment: Festivities for the Marriage of Cosimo I, Duke of Florence in 1539* (Columbia, MO: University of Missouri Press, 1968), p. 120.

[66] Scorza, 'Vincenzo Borghini', p. 69 and Starn and Partridge, *Arts of Power*, p. 278.

[67] Cini, 'Description', p. 960. The courtyard image is no longer visible but would have been similar to Pietro Paolo Galeotti's medallion of the subject. See Campbell, 'Observations', pp. 116–17 and Phillip Attwood, catalogue entry no. 98 in Acidini Luchinat, *The Medici*, pp. 235–41.

the Florentines and their allies.[68] Finally, Neptune appeared in a lavish Carnival parade following the wedding, the *Mascherata* of the Geneology of the Gods. A '*carro di Nettuno*' showed the Olympian god atop a giant crab on a rocky base adorned with shells, sponges and corals.[69]

Another reason Borghini wanted the Neptune Fountain as part of the *entrata* might have involved space, or to be more precise, a problematic approach to a particular space. The ideal approach to the Piazza della Signoria had always been from the west, where the Palazzo Vecchio, with its imposing bell tower, the Loggia dei Lanzi and the statues on the site could best be viewed. This is the direction, shown by Vasari in the Palazzo Vecchio paintings, as that of the papal procession entering the Piazza for the *entrata* of Leo X in 1515. It was also the approach Borghini had originally planned for the 1565 *entrata*. But, as Starn and Partridge suggest, this plan had to be altered because of Cosimo's insistence that the processional route retrace the city's ancient Roman walls, presumably having to include therefore the Via del Proconsolo and approach the Piazza della Signoria from the east (see Figure 4.7).[70] From this less usual route along the Via dei Gondi, it would be the Neptune Fountain that the processional party would encounter first.

In light of these circumstances, one feature deserves particular attention: Neptune's chariot, where the form and layout would have enhanced the experience of those entering the Piazza. While showing Neptune on a chariot was not unusual in Renaissance art, Ammannati's portrayal would have been one of the first among large-scale permanent works of sculpture to do so.[71] The chariot form echoed the sculptural language of antiquity and the tradition of festival decorations, as exemplified by the *carro di Nettuno* in the *Mascherata* discussed earlier. Ammannati had aligned Neptune's chariot not with the diagonal corner of the Palazzo Vecchio but along an east-to-west trajectory across the Piazza, a positioning that has implications for how this work engaged its space and viewers. Campbell proposed that the chariot implied a moment in which the god is moving across a horizontal seascape, representing 'Neptune's sudden, splendid arrival in the Piazza Ducale'.[72] The chariot also echoed the direction of its aqueduct, the Fonte alla Ginevra, whose waters approached the Piazza from the Borgo dei Greci and Via dei Gondi.[73]

---

[68] Ugo Muccini, *The Salone dei Cinquecento of Palazzo Vecchio* (Florence: Le Lettere, 1990), pp. 111, 117.

[69] Cini, 'Description', pp. 1004–5 and Anna Maria Petrioli, *Mostra di disegni Vasariani: Carri trionfali e costumi per la Genealogia degli Dei (1565)* (Florence: Olschki, 1966), pp. 52–3.

[70] Starn and Partridge, *Arts of Power*, p. 169. On the *entrata* of Leo X, see Testaverde, 'Feste Medicee', pp. 72–3 and Fig. 23.

[71] Felicia M. Else, 'Horses of a Different Colour: *marmo mischio* and Ammannati's Remarkable Chariot of Neptune', *Sculpture Journal*, 21 (2012) 1, 27–31.

[72] Campbell, 'Observations', p. 122.

[73] Else, 'Water and Stone', p. 257.

This orientation mirrored that of the *entrata* procession itself, providing a dynamic entry for what could have seemed an undesirable back route. After turning right at the Arch of Happiness and heading westward along the Via dei Gondi, the *entrata* would have encountered the Arch of Prudence, a grandiose structure dedicated to Cosimo's civic virtues and showing key scenes from the Duke's reign. At its summit, a magnificent *quadriga*, an ancient-style four-horse triumphal chariot, bore two angels supporting a crown of oak and flanked by the tails of a Capricorn, the zodiacal sign of Augustus Caesar, upon whom Cosimo modelled himself. When the procession passed under the arch, the *quadriga* rotated from facing east to facing west and thereby echoed the parade route and anticipated in both form and orientation the chariot of the Neptune Fountain.[74] The procession would then have seen Neptune from the back, directing the procession forward to the Piazza with his chariot facing in the same westerly direction. As the *entrata* passed alongside the fountain, viewers would have been in a perfect position to notice a dynastic pairing described by Cini and Mellini but not retained for the final work: Francesco's sign of Aries on the back of the chariot and Cosimo's sign of Capricorn on the front.[75] As they made their way around the corner of the Palazzo Vecchio, they would have been greeted by the sound, sight and perhaps a sprinkling of Neptune's waters, as they moved into the main area of the Piazza della Signoria. Standing directly before the fountain, they would have seen the full complement of forms comprising the Olympian god's four-horse chariot and retinue of marine deities, fauns and satyrs, echoing subjects from the two earlier wine fountains. Neptune's sidewards gaze led to the procession's next destinations, the portal leading to the courtyard of the Palazzo Vecchio. Given such an entry into this Republican-era Piazza, a northern audience might never have known just how new and unusual public fountains were to this inland city of Florence (see Plate 8).

Fountains of wine and water helped to re-fashion some very different urban spaces during the *entrata* of 1565. In each case examined here, fountains helped to compensate for a problematic area or approach, and a rich dialogue of sources informed the fountains' style and iconography, drawn from contemporary Florentine works and from the broader traditions of festival decoration and northern court cultures. Exactly how these and other elements of the *entrata* impressed their international audiences remains a difficult question, as the majority of sources documenting the event are biased towards Florence and the Medici court. But as one remarkable study makes clear, we can confirm Borghini got things at least partly right when it came to so-called German tastes. M.A. Katritzky has analysed a description of the *entrata* by a member of the Bavarian court, tentatively identified as Johann Jacob Fugger. Instead of praising the triumphal arches, this German account almost dismissed them, stating 'there were many beautiful *Arcus*

---

74 On the Arch of Prudence, see Cini, 'Description', pp. 947–52; Mellini, *Descrizione*, pp. 91–8; and Starn and Partridge, *Arts of Power*, pp. 291–3 and Fig. 76.

75 Mellini, *Descrizione*, p. 100 and Cini, 'Description', p. 953.

Triumphales . . . highly regarded by all who understood such matters . . . nevertheless not particularly rated by those who do not understand such things'. In the end, only three elements Fugger had seen during the celebration elicited his praise: illuminations on the Cathedral, the enormous Column of Santa Trinità and 'several beautiful fountains . . . including one which flowed with red and white wine'.[76]

Bibliography

Primary sources

Biblioteca Nazionale Centrale di Firenze, ms. II.X.100.

Bottari, Giovanni and Stefano Ticozzi (eds), *Raccolta di lettere sulla pittura, scultura ed architettura*, 3 vols (Milan: Silvestri, 1822), vol. 1.

Cini, Giovanni Battista, 'Description of the Festive Preparations for the Nuptials of the Prince Don Francesco of Tuscany', in Giorgio Vasari (ed.), *Lives of the Painters, Sculptors and Architects*, trans. Gaston du C. de Vere, 2 vols (New York: Knopf, 1996), vol. 2, pp. 897–1019.

Cirni, Anton Francesco, *La reale entrata dell'Eccellentissimo Signor Duca et Duchessa di Fiorenze in Siena* (Rome: Antonio Blado, 1560).

Copia de vna lettra della particularita dell ordine con il quale la maesta cesarea intro in Messina, e del triompho [et] sumptuosi apparati gli forono fatti, carri [et] archi triomphali richissimi con alcuni versi [et] prosa Latini in honore de Sua Maesta ([n. p.], 1535), under 'Treasures in Full: Renaissance Festival Books', British Library, http://special-1.bl.uk/treasures/festivalbooks/BookDetails.aspx?strFest=0101.

Descrittione delli archi et dechiaratione delle statoue, [et] apparati publici, fatti alla entrata in Mantoua del serenissimo prencipe di Spagna, a XIII di Gennaro. M. D. XLIX ([n. p.], [1549?]), under 'Treasures in Full: Renaissance Festival Books', British Library, http://special-1.bl.uk/treasures/festivalbooks/BookDetails.aspx?strFest=0114.

Die blijde incoemste en Crooninghe van Coninck Karel die nege[n]ste die ghesciet is inde Stadt va[n] Reims tswoo[n]daechs den xiiii May M.CCCCC. LXI . . . (Antwerp: Jan van Ghelen, [1561]) under 'Treasures in Full: Renaissance Festival Books', British Library, http://special-1.bl.uk/treasures/festivalbooks/BookDetails.aspx?strFest=0025.

Hogenberg, Nikolas, *Gratae et laboribus aequae posteritati Caesareas sanctique patris longo ordine et urmas aspice et artifice inter venerare manum tradere quae potuit rigido mansura metallo nomina magnorum tot generosa virum*

[76] M.A. Katritzky, 'The Florentine *Entrata* of Johanna of Austria and Other *Entrate* Described in a German Diary', *Journal of the Warburg and Courtauld Institutes*, 59 (1996), 148–73, especially 158–9.

pictor Hogenbergus quod per tua (The Hague: Engelbert Bruning, [1532?]), under 'Treasures in Full: Renaissance Festival Books', British Library, http://special-1.bl.uk/treasures/festivalbooks/BookDetails.aspx?strFest=0095.

La solenne et triomphante entrata dela cesarea maesta, nella Franza, con li superbi apparati, [e] archi triomphali, con tutte le historie pitture, [e] motti latini, che in essi erano, con l'ordine de tutte le feste, che sono fatte per tutte le terre de la Franza ([n.p.], [1539]), under 'Treasures in Full: Renaissance Festival Books', British Library, http://special-1.bl.uk/treasures/festivalbooks/BookDetails.aspx?strFest=0109.

Lapini, Agostino, *Diario fiorentino di Agostino Lapini dal 252 al 1596*, ed. Giuseppe Odoardo Corazzini (Florence: Sansoni, 1900).

Mellini, Domenico, *Descrizione dell' entrata della sereniß. Reina Giovanna d'Austria et dell'Apparato, fatto in Firenze nella venuta, & per le felicissime nozze di S. Altezza* (Florence: Giunti, 1566).

Römischer Küniglicher Maies. Krönung zu Ach geschehen (Augsburg: Sigmund Grim and Marx Wirsung, 1520), under 'Treasures in Full: Renaissance Festival Books', British Library, http://special-1.bl.uk/treasures/festivalbooks/BookDetails.aspx?strFest=0078.

Vasari, Giorgio, *Le opere di Giorgio Vasari*, ed. Giovanni Masselli, 2 vols (Florence: David Passigli, 1832–8).

Secondary sources

Allegri, Ettore and Alessandro Cecchi, *Palazzo Vecchio e i Medici* (Florence: S.P.E.S., 1980).

Attwood, Phillip, catalogue entry no. 98, in Cristina Acidini Luchinat et al. (eds), *The Medici, Michelangelo, and the Art of Late Renaissance Florence* (New Haven, CT and London: Yale University Press, 2002), pp. 235–41.

Belozerskaya, Marina, *Rethinking the Renaissance. Burgundian Arts Across Europe* (Cambridge: Cambridge University Press, 2002).

Borsook, Eve, *The Companion Guide to Florence* (Woodbridge: Boydell and Brewer, 2000).

Boström, Antonia, catalogue entry no. 90, in Cristina Acidini Luchinat et al. (eds), *The Medici, Michelangelo, and the Art of Late Renaissance Florence* (New Haven, CT and London: Yale University Press, 2002), pp. 225–6.

Bush, Virginia, *The Colossal Sculpture of the Cinquecento* (New York: Garland, 1976).

Campbell, Malcolm, 'Observations on Ammannati's Neptune Fountain: 1565 and 1575', in Andrew Morrogh, Fiorella Superbi Gioffredi, Piero Morselli and Eve Borsook (eds), *Renaissance Studies in Honor of Craig Hugh Smyth* (Florence: Giunti Barbèra, 1985), vol. 2, pp. 113–36.

Conti, Giordano, 'L'incoronazione di Carlo V a Bologna', in Marcello Fagiolo (ed.), *La città effimera e l'universo artificiale del giardino* (Rome: Officina, 1980), pp. 38–46.

Dean, Lucinda H.S., 'Enter the Alien: Foreign Consorts and Their Royal Entries in to Scottish Cities, c. 1449–1594', in J.R. Mulryne, Anna Maria Testaverde and Ines Aliverti (eds), *The Iconography of Power: Ceremonial Entries in Early Modern Europe* (Farnham and Burlington, VT: Ashgate, 2015).

Else, Felicia M., 'Water and Stone: Ammannati's Neptune Fountain as Public Ornament' (PhD. Dissertation, Washington University in St. Louis, 2003).

Else, Felicia M., 'Controlling the Waters of Granducal Florence: A New Look at Stefano Bonsignori's View of the City (1584)', *Imago Mundi*, 61 (2009) 2, 168–85.

Else, Felicia M., 'Horses of a Different Colour: *marmo mischio* and Ammannati's Remarkable Chariot of Neptune', *Sculpture Journal*, 21 (2012) 1, 27–41.

Fanelli, Giovanni, *Firenze* (Rome and Bari: Laterza, 1980).

Ferretti, Emanuela, 'Bartolomeo Ammannati, la Fontana di Sala Grande e le trasformazioni del Salone dei Cinquecento da Cosimo I a Ferdinando I', in Beatrice Paolozzi Strozzi and Dimitrios Zikos (eds), *L'acqua, la pietra, il fuoco. Bartolomeo Ammannati Scultore* (Florence: Giunti, 2011), pp. 136–55.

Ferretti, Emanuela, 'Dalle sorgenti alle fontane: Cosimo I e l'aquedotto di Firenze', in Beatrice Paolozzi Strozzi and Dimitrios Zikos (eds), *L'acqua, la pietra, il fuoco. Bartolomeo Ammannati Scultore* (Florence: Giunti, 2011), pp. 262–75.

Fiorelli, Piero and Maria Venturi (eds), *Stradario storico e amministrativo del Comune di Firenze*, 3 vols (3rd ed., Florence: Polistampa, 2004), vol. 1.

Fliegel, Stephen N., 'The Cleveland Table Fountain and Gothic Automata', *Cleveland Studies in the History of Art*, 7 (2002), 6–49.

Freedman, Luba, 'Neptune in Classical and Renaissance Visual Art', *International Journal of the Classical Tradition*, 2 (1995) 2, 219–37.

Ginori Conti, Piero, *L'apparato per le nozze di Francesco de'Medici e di Giovanna d'Austria* (Florence: Olschki, 1936).

Godoli, Antonio, 'Vasari e Ammannati agli Uffizi: forma e materia', in Cristina Acidini and Giacomo Pirazzoli (eds), *Ammannati e Vasari per la città dei Medici* (Florence: Polistampa, 2011), pp. 53–9.

Heikamp, Detlef, 'La Fontana di Nettuno. La sua storia nel contesto urbano', in Beatrice Paolozzi Strozzi and Dimitrios Zikos (eds), *L'acqua, la pietra, il fuoco. Bartolomeo Ammannati Scultore* (Florence: Giunti, 2011), pp. 182–261.

Katritzky, M.A., 'The Florentine *entrata* of Johanna of Austria and Other *entrate* Described in a German Diary', *Journal of the Warburg and Courtauld Institutes*, 59 (1996), 148–73.

Lazzaro, Claudia, *The Italian Renaissance Garden* (New Haven, CT and London: Yale University Press, 1990).

Leydi, Silvio, 'I trionfi dell' "Aquila Imperialissima". Note sugli apparati innalzati a Milano per gli ingressi trionfali di Cristina di Danimarca duchessa di Milano, Carlo V imperatore e Filippo principe di Spagna', *Schifanoia*, 9 (1990), 9–55.

McHam, Sarah Blake, 'Public Sculpture in Renaissance Florence', in Sarah Blake McHam (ed.), *Looking at Italian Renaissance Sculpture* (Cambridge: Cambridge University Press, 1998), pp. 158–72.

Minor, Andrew and Bonner Mitchell, *A Renaissance Entertainment: Festivities for the Marriage of Cosimo I, Duke of Florence in 1539* (Columbia, MO: University of Missouri Press, 1968).

Mitchell, Bonner, *The Majesty of the State: Triumphal Progresses of Foreign Sovereigns in Renaissance Italy (1494–1600)* (Florence: Olschki, 1986).

Muccini, Ugo, *The Salone dei Cinquecento of Palazzo Vecchio* (Florence: Le Lettere, 1990).

Petrioli, Anna Maria, *Mostra di disegni Vasariani: arri trionfali e costumi per la Genealogia degli Dei (1565)* (Florence: Olschki, 1966).

Pizzorusso, Claudio, catalog entries no. 89 and 91, in Cristina Acidini Luchinat et al. (eds), *The Medici, Michelangelo, and the Art of Late Renaissance Florence* (New Haven, CT and London: Yale University Press, 2002), pp. 225–8.

Pope-Hennessy, John, *Italian High Renaissance and Baroque Sculpture* (London: Phaidon, 1996).

Richardson, Nicholas, 'Sirens', in Simon Hornblower and Antony Spawforth (eds), *The Oxford Classical Dictionary* (Oxford: Oxford University Press, 2012), 1372.

Scorza, Rick, 'Vincenzo Borghini and Invenzione: The Florentine Apparato of 1565', *Journal of the Warburg and Courtauld Institutes*, 44 (1981), 57–75.

Scorza, Rick, 'Ricerca storica e invenzione: la collaborazione di Borghini con Cosimo I e Fransceco, i suoi rapporti con gli artisti, gli apparati effimeri', in Gino Belloni and Riccardo Drusi (eds), *Vincenzo Borghini: Filologia e invenzione nella Firenze di Cosimo I* (Florence: Olschki, 2002), pp. 61–99.

Spini, Giorgio, 'Introduzione generale', in Giorgio Spini (ed.), *Architettura e politica da Cosimo I a Ferdinando I* (Florence: Olschki, 1976), pp. 32–46.

Starn, Randolph and Loren Partridge, *Arts of Power: Three Halls of State, 1300–1600* (Berkeley, CA: University of California Press, 1992).

Testaverde, Anna Maria, 'Feste Medicee: la visita, le nozze e il trionfo', in Marcello Fagiolo (ed.), *La città effimera e l'universo artificiale del giardino* (Rome: Officina, 1980), pp. 69–100.

Trachtenberg, Marvin, *Dominion of the Eye: Urbanism, Art, and Power in Early Modern Florence* (Cambridge and New York: Cambridge University Press, 1997).

Veen, Henk Th. van, *Cosimo I de' Medici and His Self-Representation in Florentine Art and Culture*, trans. Andrew P. McCormick (Cambridge and New York: Cambridge University Press, 2006).

Wiles, Bertha, *The Fountains of Florentine Sculptors and Their Followers From Donatello to Bernini* (New York: Hacker, 1975).

Zikos, Dimitrios, '" . . . Che accozzamento è stato questo suo"? Sul simbolismo delle statue di Ammannati per il Salone dei Cinquecento', in Beatrice Paolozzi Strozzi and Dimitrios Zikos (eds), *L'acqua, la pietra, il fuoco: Bartolomeo Ammannati Scultore* (Florence: Giunti, 2011), pp. 156–81.

Chapter 5
Making the best of what they had
Adaptations of indoor and outdoor space for royal ceremony in Scotland *c.* 1214–1603

Lucinda H.S. Dean[1]

> this nobill Earle of Atholl gart make ane curious palice to the king and to his mother and to the [papal] ambassadour quhair they war honourabill ludgit . . . ffor thair huntting and pastyme quhilk was buidit in the midis of ane faire medow ane faire palice of griene tymmer [. . .] the space of thrie house hight; the fluir laid with griene cherittis witht sprattis, medwarts and flouris.[2]
>
> [this noble Earl of Atholl made an intricate palace for the king and his mother and the papal ambassador, where they were all honourably lodged . . . for their hunting and pastimes. This was built in the middle of a fair meadow: a fair palace of green birch timber . . . this was three storeys in height; the floor was laid with sods of turf, with rushes, meadow-sweet and flowers.]

In the early years of James V's majority rule (*c.* 1529–1530) Robert Lindesay of Pitscottie records the young king, accompanied by his mother and the papal legate, taking part in a hunting expedition in the highlands of Perthshire. The earl of Atholl,[3] who hosted the event, constructed a richly decorated temporary palace surrounded by a moat said to be 16 feet deep, crossed by a drawbridge. In so doing,

[1] The author offers thanks to both the AHRC (PhD scholarship) and ESF (conference funding). In addition thanks to Michael Penman my primary supervisor; Ronnie Mulryne and Krista De Jonge for their invitation and subsequent support and advice; and to Katherine Buchanan, Anne Dance and Vikki Lewis for their help in the editing stages of this piece. Also, additional thanks to Katherine Buchanan for permission to use maps she created for use as illustrations in this chapter.

[2] Robert Lindesay of Pitscottie, *The Historie and Cronicles of Scotland: From the Slauchter of King James the First to the Ane thousande five hundrieth thrie scoir fyftein zeir*, ed. Æ.J.G. Mackay, 2 vols (Edinburgh and London: William Blackwood and Sons, 1899), vol. 1, pp. 335–6.

[3] John Stewart, third earl of Atholl: see Samuel Cowan, *Three Celtic Earldoms: Atholl, Strathearn and Menteith (Critical and Historical Recital So Far as Know)* (Edinburgh: Norman Macleod, 1909), p. 25.

Atholl provided a notable example of how outdoor spaces were masterfully transformed for Scottish royal ceremony and entertainment. After the three-day visit by King James and his company, the structure was burnt to the ground by the highland men who had provided the finest food and drink for the royal party.[4] The concept of, and the papal legate's reaction to, this 'palace in the wild' – particularly the burning of it – have inspired a collection of essays on literature, humanism and the Renaissance in Scotland.[5] However, the event itself has not been studied in terms of its qualities as an entertainment for royal visitors, or as a transformation of space for ceremonial performance.

The event formed part of my doctoral research, which entailed the first long-term study of continuity and change in the representation of Scottish royal authority through state ceremony between 1214 and 1603.[6] This chapter will address one of a number of topics which remain unstudied, by offering an introductory survey of some of the spaces transformed for Scottish royal ceremonies during this period. Between the two dates, five different sites were used for inaugurations and coronations of Scotland's kings;[7] eight religious buildings became the resting places of Scottish monarchs;[8] and there were nine sites, in Scotland and beyond, used for royal marriages.[9] Moreover, the number of ceremonial sites greatly increases if other major ceremonies – such as the arrival of queens consort, royal baptisms and royal entries – are added. If one widens the scope to include royal progresses, birthdays, annual religious feasts, tournaments and the entertainment of ambassadorial guests, this total climbs still further. Yet relatively few of these sites have been explored specifically in regard to what they offered the monarch in terms of ceremonial space, why they were chosen, and how they shaped the ceremonies they housed.

Like numerous spaces for Scottish royal ceremonies, Pitscottie's sixteenth-century 'palace in the wild' makes a tantalising impression on history rather than a

---

4 Pitscottie, *Historie*, vol. 1, p. 336.

5 L.A.J.R. Houwen, Alasdair A. MacDonald and Sally L. Mapstone (eds), *A Palace in the Wild: Essays on Vernacular Culture and Humanism in Late-Medieval and Renaissance Scotland* (Leuven: Peeters, 2000).

6 Lucinda H.S. Dean, 'Crowns, Rings and Processions: Continuity and Change in the Representations of Scottish Royal Authority through State Ceremony, c.1214–c.1603' (Unpublished PhD thesis, University of Stirling, 2013).

7 Scone Abbey and the Moot Hill (Perthshire); Holyrood Abbey (Edinburgh); Kelso Abbey (Scottish Borders); Stirling Chapel Royal (Stirling); and the Kirk of the Holy Rood (Stirling).

8 Arbroath Abbey (Angus); Melrose Abbey (Scottish Borders); Dunfermline Abbey (Fife); Holyrood Abbey; Scone Abbey; Paisley Abbey (Renfrewshire); Charterhouse (Perth); and Cambuskenneth (near Stirling).

9 York; Roxburgh and Kelso Abbey (Scottish Borders); Jedburgh Abbey (Scottish Borders); Berwick; Winchester House (London); Holyrood Abbey and Palace; Notre Dame (Paris); St Andrews (Fife); and Oslo (Norway).

defined imprint. The actual building erected by the earl of Atholl no longer exists – hardly surprising for an ephemeral structure, even if this one had not been ceremonially burnt down. In addition no drawings, plans or maps showing what this structure may have looked like, or where it may have stood, have been uncovered as yet.[10] The only indication of the palace's location comes from Pitscottie's near-contemporary description. Here he specifically states that the palace was built in a meadow, indicating relatively flat and fertile land in the bottom of a valley. The palace was, however, situated in the 'highland' setting of the earl of Atholl's estate. Glen Tilt, which extends behind the main Atholl residence of Blair Atholl, is likely to have provided a dramatic natural backdrop for the structure.[11] Pitscottie's report also gives some valuable information regarding the ephemeral building itself, such as the fact that it was positioned within a moated area and that it stood three storeys high. Moreover, he draws attention to an interesting paradox: the structure was luxuriously decorated with fabrics, painted ceilings and glass windows, but the floors were made of natural materials including flowers and turf. These readily-available natural products could have been a cheap alternative as insulating floor covering; conversely, the curious combination of disparate materials could also reflect a specific design intention to amalgamate indoor and outdoor spaces. Even where the sources are limited, therefore, an indication may be found of how one Scottish noble made the best of what he had in order to entertain his royal visitors.

The importance of the spaces inhabited and modified by medieval and early modern people is coming ever more under the spotlight, perhaps following the growing number of studies in political geography.[12] The field of castle studies, for example, increasingly focuses on how surrounding landscapes acted as status enhancement, and reflected the distinct 'spatial ideology' of aristocracy and royalty in medieval and early modern Europe.[13] Moreover, the adaptation of space for festivals and leisure activities, as well as the visual and sensory experience of

---

[10] In an extension of the study of this specific event, a fuller investigation of Atholl family papers (housed at Blair Castle) would have to be undertaken; however, in communications with Jane Anderson, the archivist at Blair Castle, it has been confirmed that no financial accounts for this era have survived.

[11] Thanks to Alasdair Ross for his suggestions in this regard.

[12] For a good introduction see Kevin R. Cox, Murray Low and Jennifer Robinson (eds), *The SAGE Handbook of Political Geography* (London: Sage, 2008).

[13] Thanks to Katherine Ann Buchanan for her inspiration and discussions in regards to castles and landscapes, 'The Social, Geographical, and Structural Environments of Minor Noble Castles in Angus, 1449–1542' (Unpublished PhD thesis, University of Stirling, 2014). See also, Oliver H. Creighton, *Castles and Landscapes: Power, Community and Fortification in Medieval England* (London: Equinox, 2005); Robert Liddiard, *Castles in Context: Power, Symbolism and Landscape, 1066–1500* (Macclesfield: Windgather Press, 2005); Martin Hansson, 'Aristocratic Landscape: The Spatial Ideology of the Medieval Aristocracy', *Lund Studies in Historical Archaeology*, 2 (2006), esp. 197–204.

ceremony through performers, scenery and musicians, is one of growing interest. The fields of archaeology, art history and architecture in Scotland have produced (and continue to produce) many significant projects dealing with individual buildings and related works, with the most prominent of recent royal projects being that at Stirling Palace, which has been at the centre of an intensive initiative by Historic Scotland to re-imagine Stirling Castle, together with important archaeological work being undertaken at Scone.[14]

However, only one prominent ceremonial site has received significant attention centred on its function as a place transformed for use as ceremonial space: the city of Edinburgh. The entry route through Edinburgh, starting at the West Port via the Netherbow and various stopping points along the High Street to Holyrood Palace, has been the subject of a number of studies. The most recent of these, by Giovanna Guidicini, focuses specifically on the use of space, including the use of the West Port as the official entry point, the division between public and private space in royal entries, and the manipulation of these elements in certain of the entries.[15] Guidicini's work on the Edinburgh entry route has opened the way to a much broader understanding of how spaces were adapted and utilised for royal entries.[16] However, the study of historic ceremonial use of built and natural sites plays second fiddle to other current projects. This chapter for its part offers a number of examples to illuminate the various settings used as backdrops for Scottish inaugurations and coronations, royal funerals and royal weddings. In particular, it focuses on the itinerant nature of Scottish kingship, the interaction of indoor and outdoor spaces, and the relative poverty of the Scottish monarchy and how this may have limited the choices available to the country's monarchs.

As an ancient site of inauguration (until *c.* 1249), and a meeting place for the dispensing of justice, Scone, Scotland's premier inaugural location, has received more attention than most of the sites discussed here.[17] Most recently it has come

---

[14] For more information on Stirling Palace Project, see *Historic Scotland website*, www.historic-scotland.gov.uk/index/news/mediaresources/stirling-castle-palace-project.htm [Accessed 28 December 2013]. For Scone archaeology project see below.

[15] Giovanna Guidicini, 'Municipal Perspective, Royal Expectations, and the Use of Public Space: The Case of the West Port, Edinburgh, 1503–1633', *Architectural Heritage*, 22 (2011), 37–52; 'European Themes and Local Awareness: The Reconstruction of Charles I's Entry Into Edinburgh in 1633', Online Exhibition on *Re-Creating Early Modern Festivals Project Website*, www.recreatingearlymodernfestivals.com/ exhibition_giovanna.htm [Accessed 28 December 2013]. Also see works by Alasdair A. MacDonald and Douglas Gray listed in the bibliography.

[16] Guidicini's forthcoming book based on her thesis, 'Scotland Triumphant: The Relevance of Stewart Triumphal Celebrations in Shaping Scottish Renaissance Architecture' (Unpublished PhD thesis, Edinburgh, October 2009) will undoubtedly increase such understanding.

[17] For example: Archibald A.M. Duncan, *The Kingship of the Scots, 842–1292: Succession and Independence* (Edinburgh: Edinburgh University Press, 2002), pp. 127–50; R. Welander, D. Breeze and Tom O. Clancy (eds), *The Stone of Destiny: Artefact and Icon*

under the spotlight through geophysical surveys and excavations undertaken by the MASS project headed by Oliver O'Grady and Peter Yeoman (2005–2009), during which 'convincing evidence indicating the location [to the south of Moot Hill] and partial layout of the Augustinian abbey church' was unearthed.[18] Our understanding of this site is set to continue through subsequent projects directed by O'Grady and Richard Oram.[19] Discussions of Scone as an inaugural site in the thirteenth century are relatively rich but, given that the site consistently hosted royal inaugurations and coronations up until the fifteenth century, relatively little scholarship has explored the continued use of this ceremonial space. As a result, the relative prominence of two distinct indoor and outdoor spaces used in these ceremonies, and what this can tell us about tensions between the powers involved, has not been fully investigated.

In or prior to the thirteenth century, ceremonial developments in the inaugural ceremony at Scone saw a purely outdoor ceremony becoming one that combined indoor and outdoor spaces. Walter Bower's description in the *Scotichronicon* (*c.* 1440), discussing the inauguration of Alexander III in 1249, separates the ceremony into two sections.[20] Archie Duncan suggests that the first section of the ceremony, including the girding with the sword by the bishop of St Andrews and the blessing and 'ordination', took place inside the abbey church. From here the king was led outside to his traditional secular enthronement, an act in which the clerical establishment appears not to have been involved.[21] The direct involvement of William I, Alexander III's grandfather, in the ecclesiastically-dominated English ceremony,[22] combined with Scotland's growing connections with the

(Edinburgh: Society of Antiquaries of Scotland, 2003), *passim*; Oliver J.T. O'Grady, 'The Setting and Practice of Open-Air Judicial Assemblies in Medieval Scotland: A Multidisciplinary Study' (Unpublished PhD thesis, University of Glasgow, 2008), *passim*.

[18] Oliver O'Grady, 'Scone Abbey and Moot Hill, Perth and Kinross (Scone Parish), Geophysical Survey', *Discovery Excavation Scotland*, 8 (2007), 167–8.

[19] One such project is *Royal Scone: Parliament, Inauguration and National Symbol* network project, led by Professor Richard Oram and funded by the Royal Society of Edinburgh, which included the *Royal Scone Conference* (December 2014), at which the author spoke on the importance of place in Scottish inaugurations and coronations, and continued work in 2015, in collaboration with Perth and Kinross Council, to increase public engagement with the site and its functions.

[20] Walter Bower, *Scotichronicon*, trans. and ed. D.E.R. Watt et al., 9 vols (Aberdeen and Edinburgh: Aberdeen University Press and Mercat Press, 1987–1998), vol. 5, p. 295.

[21] Duncan, *Kingship of the Scots*, pp. 138–9.

[22] William I took part in Richard I's second coronation at Westminster in 1194 carrying the royal sword: see Roger de Hoveden, *The Annals of Roger de Hoveden Comprising the History of England and Other Countries of Europe From AD 732 to AD 1201*, trans. and ed. Henry T. Riley, 2 vols (London: H.G. Bohn, 1853), vol. 2, pp. 321–2; 'Coronation of Richard I', in Leopold G.W. Legg (ed.), *English Coronation Records* (Westminster: Archibald Constable and Co., 1901), pp. 46–53.

papacy – including the country's 'special daughter' status,[23] papal gifts, and attempts in the reign of Alexander II to gain the right of unction[24] – provide a basis for claiming that it was during the thirteenth century that the move of a more substantial part of the ceremony to within the church itself occurred.[25] However, the fact that the ceremony remained in two distinct parts implies a still-strong secular influence and strengthens parallels to the Irish situation where, as Elizabeth Fitzpatrick has noted, the king exercised control over the ceremony as a whole and the most the church could claim was that part of the ceremony occurring inside the church or on church land.[26]

A closer investigation of the surviving sources for the ceremonies held at Scone after 1249 reveal that the distinct separation of place between secular enthroning and religious ceremony continued in a unique and distinctly Scottish manner up to and including the coronation of James I in 1424. Moreover, such separation may have been restored for the coronation of James IV in 1488, when the ancient inaugural site was revisited in a bid to legitimise the young king's position following the murder of his father at the hands of the rebels who had raised him to power.[27] Recent archaeological work has assisted in visualising the movement from indoor to outdoor space by giving a definite starting point for the procession up a short incline and ending at the Moot Hill. In addition, Bower's descriptions indicate that in 1249 both prominent churchmen and lay nobles led the king from the indoor location and, while the coronation of Robert II and Robert III (1371 and 1390) saw the extension of this combined ceremony over two

[23] The 'special daughter' status provided by the *Cum Universi* bull (*c.* 1192) meant that the jurisdiction of the archbishop of York over Scottish bishops was set aside and Scottish prelates were permitted to deal directly with Rome or a papal representative. Amongst numerous references to this landmark moment see Archibald A.M. Duncan, *Scotland: The Making of the Kingdom* (Edinburgh: Edinburgh University Press, reprint 1996), p. 264.

[24] *Calendar of Entries in the Papal Registers relating to Great Britain and Ireland: Papal Letters*, ed. W.H. Bliss et al., 16 vols (London: H.M. Stationery Office, 1893), vol. 1, p. 83; *Calendar of Documents Relating to Scotland Preserved in Her Majesty's Public Record Office, London*, ed. Joseph Bain et al., 5 vols (Edinburgh: H.M. General Register House, 1881–1986), vol. 1, no. 1798; Duncan, *Kingship of the Scots*, pp. 118–19; Richard Oram, *Alexander II, King of Scots: 1214–1249* (Edinburgh: John Donald, 2012), pp. 66–9.

[25] Duncan has drawn attention to the fact that the abbey church had been erected in the reign of Alexander I (1107–1124) to suggest that an inaugural Mass had occurred much earlier: *Kingship of the Scots*, p. 149.

[26] Elizabeth Fitzpatrick, *Royal Inauguration in Gaelic Ireland, c. 1100–1600: A Cultural Landscape Study* (Woodbridge: Boydell Press, 2004), pp. 155–8.

[27] Prior to James IV's coronation at Scone, James II was crowned at Holyrood in 1437 and in 1460 James III was crowned at Kelso. After 1488 James V and Mary were crowned in the chapel at Stirling (respectively 1513 and 1542) and James VI was crowned at the parish church of the Holy Rood in Stirling in 1567. See Dean, 'Crowns, Wedding Rings and Processions', ch. 2, sections i–iv.

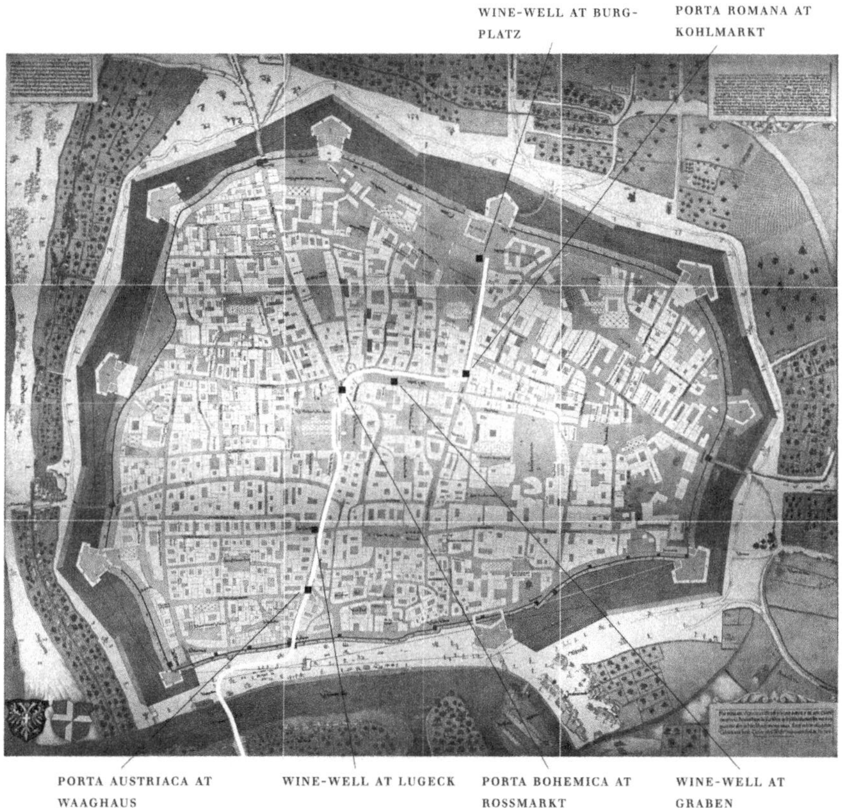

Plate 1 Bonifaz Wolmuet, Plan of Vienna, 1547, lithographic reproduction from 1857/58 by Albert Camesina (Wiener Stadt- und Landesarchiv), with the route of Maximilian's entry into Vienna, 1563, superimposed.

Plate 2 Donat Hübschmann, *Porta Austriaca* (Austrian Arch) in Caspar Steinhofer, *Gründtliche und khurtze beschreibung des alten unnd jungen Zugs . . .* (Vienna, 1566) (© Bayerische Staatsbibliothek, under Creative Commons Licence (CC BY-NC-SA 4.0))

Plate 3 Donat Hübschmann, *Wine Well* in Caspar Steinhofer, *Gründtliche und khurtze beschreibung des alten unnd jungen Zugs . . .* (Vienna, 1566) (© Bayerische Staatsbibliothek, under Creative Commons Licence (CC BY-NC-SA 4.0))

Plate 4 Donat Hübschmann, *Porta Bohemica* (Bohemian Arch) in Caspar Steinhofer, *Gründtliche und khurtze beschreibung des alten unnd jungen Zugs . . .* (Vienna, 1566) (© Bayerische Staatsbibliothek, under Creative Commons Licence (CC BY-NC-SA 4.0))

Plate 5 Donat Hübschmann, *Porta Romana* (Roman Arch).

Plate 6 Bartolomeo Ammannati, *Neptune Fountain*, marble and bronze, 1560–1574, Piazza della Signoria, Florence (photo: Felicia M. Else)

Plate 7 Niccolò Tribolo and Giambologna, *Fountain of Florence*, marble and bronze, 1538–1572, Villa Petraia (originally at Villa Medici, Castello) (photo: Felicia M. Else)

Plate 8 View of Ammannati's *Neptune Fountain* from alongside the Chariot (photo: Felicia M. Else)

and then three days,[28] the leading of the king from one space to the other undoubtedly remained an important element. With the abbey now destroyed and the site greatly altered, fully imagining these spaces may be difficult. Nevertheless, the divide between the inner and outer spaces seems to separate the secular from the religious quite distinctly.

It is possible that the religious ceremony was specifically designed to restrict access to the privileged few, leaving the general public to view only the secular ceremony. However, considering the continued desire of Scottish kings to remain accessible to their people well into the sixteenth century,[29] it is equally possible that for many Scottish nobles, and perhaps even the king, the open-air and accessible nature of the secular enthronement underlined its importance. Yet, when the location of the coronation began to vary in the later fifteenth and sixteenth centuries, the distinction between secular and religious was blurred by the combining of these two elements within an indoor ecclesiastical space.[30] This development was matched by the rise in prominence of the processional arrival and departure of each monarch, beginning with the coronation of the minor James II in 1437, when the young king was led to and from Holyrood Abbey amidst the cheers of the people of Edinburgh.[31] Thus there remained a keen desire for a public element to the coronation proceedings. Nonetheless, by the sixteenth century, a distinct privatising of the most prominent ceremonial elements took place. Was such a development forced by the ever-decreasing age of the monarchs being enthroned? The separation of ceremonial elements may have occurred at Kelso for nine-year-old James III, and seems even more likely on the return to Scone for the fifteen-year-old James IV in 1488. James II was only six years old in 1437 and in the sixteenth century James V, Mary and James VI were all raised to the throne before they were eighteen months old.

Scone's prominence as an inaugural site often masks recognition of its other significant roles, both in regard to ceremony and the more practical business of running the government. It was a frequently-used site for the dispensing of

---

[28] *Records of the Parliament of Scotland* [hereafter *RPS*], 1371/1, Non-parliamentary record: account of the coronation of Robert II (Scone, Coronation Assembly, 26 March 1371); Bower, *Scotichronicon*, vol. 6, pp. 3–4; Andrew Wyntoun, *The Original Chronicles of Andrew of Wyntoun*, ed. F.J Amours, 6 vols (Edinburgh and London: William Blackwood and Sons, 1903–1914), vol. 6, pp. 366–8.

[29] The work at Stirling Palace has uncovered architectural features that suggest that access, while controlled, was comparably less contrived in Scotland even in the sixteenth century: John Harrison, *Rebirth of a Palace: The Royal Court at Stirling Castle* (Edinburgh: Historic Scotland, 2011), for details regarding access to the king specifically see pp. 18–23.

[30] Dean, 'Crowns, Wedding Rings and Processions', ch. 2, sections iii–iv.

[31] *RPS*, 1437/3/2, Procedure: The king's Coronation; John Leslie, *The Historie of Scotland wrytten first in latin by the most reuerrend and worthy Jhone Leslie, Bishop of Ross*, trans. James Dalrymple (1596), ed. E. G. Cody (Edinburgh and London: William Blackwood and Sons, 1890), pp. 56–8.

justice,[32] and rose to prominence as a place for parliament to meet, in conjunction with neighbouring Perth, particularly under the early Stewarts (between 1371 and 1437). For example, in the reign of Robert II, of the seven parliaments and councils with surviving records prior to 1384,[33] five were held at Scone or Perth;[34] and all declarations regarding succession that remain were also promulgated in parliaments at Scone.[35] This tying of the space used for coronation to the space used for the mechanics of government was further strengthened through Robert II's choice of a burial site at Scone Abbey one day before his son's coronation in the same place.[36] The use of this highly-politicised ceremonial space by Robert II demonstrates his understanding of the need to project a façade of stability, even when in 1390 such a thing was far from reality, and emphasises the complex manner in which a choice of setting could shape representations of royal authority.

In relation to funerary arrangements of the medieval and early modern period in Scotland, the indoor site of burial became transformed into a place of mourning by the manner in which it was decorated. From the funeral of Robert I in 1329 to the last burial of a Scottish monarch, James V in January 1543, the extant financial records indicate that the transformation of abbey interiors entailed the use of vast quantities of black cloth, in addition to mourners often being gifted robes of the same colour.[37] Yet, other colours were also employed in these spaces. Elaborately decorated *herses* – temporary structures erected over the deceased – feature from 1329 onwards, when over two pounds weight of gold leaf was provided for the painted structure of a *herse* made of 'boards of Eastland' for Robert I at Dunfermline Abbey.[38] Moreover, these temporary structures and the entire interior were further transformed through the use of flickering light from large numbers of candles. The scale of this lighting could be extraordinary; for example, in 1329 over 8,000 lbs of wax were used.[39] While candles held layers of religious meaning including the apotropaic power of banishing demons and evil spirits, as well

---

32 O'Grady, 'Open-Air Judicial Assemblies', *passim*.

33 John, Earl of Carrick, eldest son and heir, took up role as Lieutenant of the Realm in 1384.

34 *RPS*: 1371 Coronation Assembly, Scone; 1372 Parliament, Scone; 1372 Council, Stirling; 1373 Parliament, Scone; 1378 Parliament, Edinburgh; 1382 Council, Perth; 1382 Parliament, Scone.

35 Ibid., 1371/4, Non-parliamentary record: declaration that John Stewart [. . .] is heir to the throne of Scotland (Scone: Coronation Assembly, March 1371); Ibid., 1373/3, Legislation: [. . .] entailing the Crown on the sons of Robert II (Scone, Parliament, April 1373).

36 Bower, *Scotichronicon*, vol. 6, pp. 3–4; Wyntoun, *Original Chronicles*, vol. 6, pp. 366–8.

37 Dean, 'Crowns, Wedding Rings and Processions', ch. 1, sections ii–v.

38 National Records of Scotland [hereafter NRS], Exchequer Records: Exchequer Rolls, E38/9; *The Exchequer Rolls of Scotland: Rotuli Scaccarii Regum Scotorum* [hereafter *ER*], ed. G. Burnett et al., 23 vols (Edinburgh, 1878–1908), vol. 1, pp. 150, 197, 215.

39 Ibid., pp. 150–1, 193, 232; NRS, E38/9.

as allusion to Christ as the 'light of the world',[40] the effect of this moving form of light as it glinted off the gilt decorations would have been particularly eye-catching in such austere surroundings.

The transformation of abbey interiors used for royal funerals must have been impressive. However, one of the most remarkable uses of space in a Scottish royal funeral, in the context of ceremonial settings and the influence of itinerant kingship on the design of Scottish ceremony, was the manner in which the royal corpse was taken in procession across varying distances towards its final destination, thereby connecting with the very landscapes and townscapes that made up the kingdom. For four hundred years the royal body was accompanied by key members of the royal family and court, as well as members of the poorest levels of society – paid usually to carry torches[41] – between prominent religious and secular sites on the route from the place of death to the place of burial. In many cases, the choice of site carried a particular significance for the royal individual. Robert I's long journey started at Cardross (his favourite residence in Argyll) where his body was displayed in the chapel dedicated to St Serf, while one of the final stopping places on his journey to Dunfermline appears to have been Culross in Fife, central to the cult of the same saint (see Figure 5.1).

Moreover, almost certainly by design, the route took Robert's corpse past the site of his major victory at Bannockburn (24 June 1314); significantly the date of his burial was, it is probable, the anniversary of the same triumph.

The corpse of Robert II also made an extensive journey of between 90 and 100 miles from Dundonald in Ayrshire, in the heart of the Stewart territories of the south west, travelling north and east to the burial site at Scone (see Figure 5.2).[42]

The exact route is not known, but a number of prominent stopping points can be plotted between Dundonald and Scone, including the family mausoleum at Paisley on which Robert II lavished much attention during his lifetime.[43] Each stopping point was made a place of vigil. From the earliest ceremony considered here, the funeral of William I in 1214, the accompanying processions allowed the deceased monarch to be seen amongst his people for the last time (see Figure 5.3).

---

[40] D.R. Dendy, *The Use of Light in Christian Worship* (London: SPCK, 1959), pp. 92–107; Eamon Duffy, *The Stripping of the Altars: Traditional Religion in England 1400–1580* (New Haven, CT and London: Yale University Press, 1993), pp. 361–2.

[41] Certainly the case for James V in 1543: NRS, Exchequer Records, Treasurer's Accounts, E21/40, f. 6r; *Accounts of the Lord High Treasurer of Scotland* [hereafter *TA*], ed. Thomas Dickson and James Balfour Paul, 12 vols (Edinburgh: H.M. Register House, 1877–1916), vol. 8, p. 143. Paupers were also paid for an unspecified task in 1329: *ER*, vol. 1, p. 175. See also: Duffy, *The Stripping of the Altars*, pp. 360–1.

[42] 'Wemyss MS' in Wyntoun, *Original Chronicles*, vol. 6, p. 354; Bower, *Scotichronicon*, vol. 7, pp. 445–7.

[43] *ER*, vol. 2, pp. 503, 622; Ibid., vol. 3, pp. 32, 222; Stephen Boardman, 'Robert II', in Keith Brown and Roland Tanner (eds), *Scottish Kingship 1306–1542: Essays in Honour of Norman Macdougall* (Edinburgh: John Donald, 2008), p. 85.

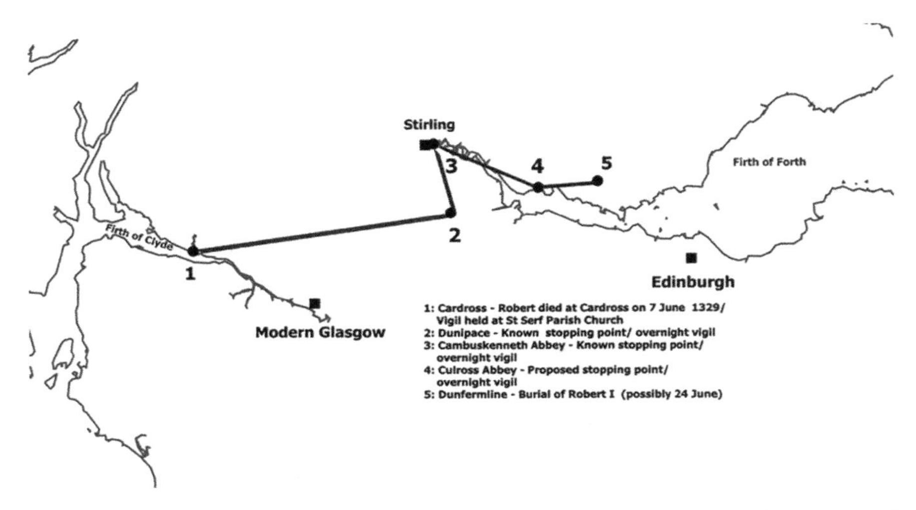

Figure 5.1 Map of the Funeral Procession of Robert I, June 1329 (map created with the assistance of Katherine Buchanan)

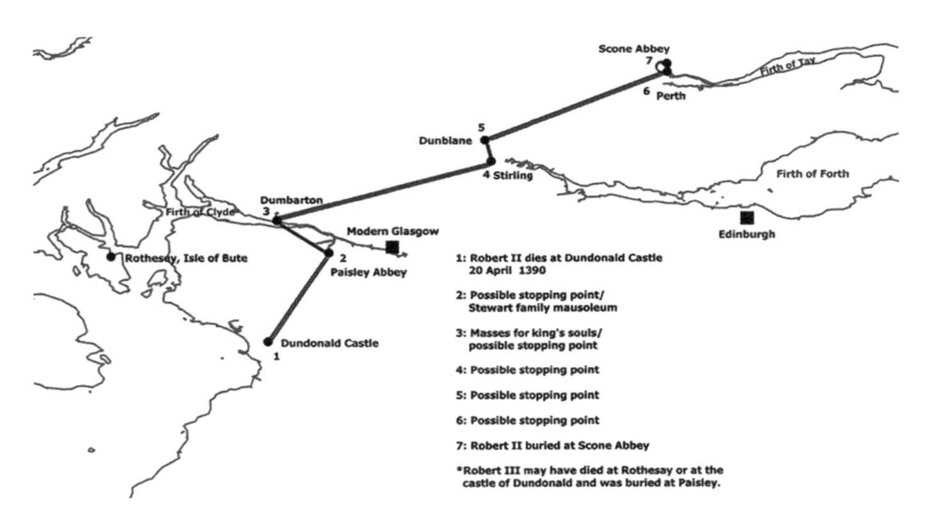

Figure 5.2 Map of the Funeral Procession of Robert II, April 1390 (map created with the assistance of Katherine Buchanan)

From the ceremonies of death to those that held the promise of new life and royal heirs, the sense of place and use of movement were crucial, not only in bidding farewell but in offering first greetings. Both the funeral journey and the arrival journey of a foreign consort involved the public. However, the desire to impress those who attended foreign arrivals was certainly an influence on ceremonial choices. The

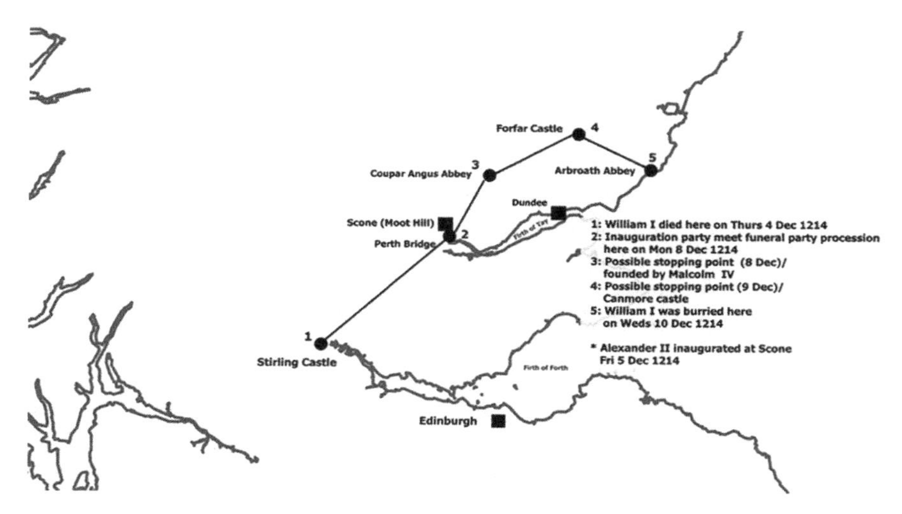

Figure 5.3 Map of the Processional Route for the Funeral of William I, December 1214 (map created with the assistance of Katherine Buchanan)

arrival of the second wives of both Alexander II and Alexander III saw the foreign entourages of their new consorts greeted at Berwick and led respectively through the rich border lands to Roxburgh (1239) and Jedburgh (1286). The distances involved meant stops were required, and in 1286 the journey to Jedburgh would have meant that Coldstream, Kelso and Roxburgh were conveniently-placed stopping points.[44] A glance at the settings for the journey and the marriage gives an immediate impression of the image the Scottish king intended to project. Each of the four sites was well known as featuring among the richest burghs and monastic houses in Scotland; moreover, the abbeys provided some of the grandest Scottish ecclesiastical architecture of the age. These were prime spaces for entertaining foreign guests.[45]

The arrivals of royal consorts remained of great, if not increased, importance. In the case of wives travelling from the continent, the ports at which they landed were particularly prominent in welcoming the large foreign entourages that accompanied the bride. The most commonly-used port of the fifteenth and sixteenth centuries was Leith, undoubtedly due to its proximity to Edinburgh.[46] However, in June 1538 the port and city of St Andrews was transformed to welcome Marie de

[44] It is approximately 35 miles from Berwick to Jedburgh; Berwick to Coldstream (*c.*14 miles), Coldstream to Kelso (*c.*10 miles), and Kelso to Jedburgh (*c.*11 miles).

[45] For more on the abbeys see: Richard Fawcett, *Scottish Abbeys and Priories* (London: Batsford Ltd., 1994), particularly pp. 28–33, 40–2, 135–6; J.H. Lewis, G.J. Ewart et al., *Jedburgh Abbey: The Archaeology and Architecture of a Border Abbey* (Edinburgh: Society of Antiquaries of Scotland, 1995).

[46] Consort arrivals at Leith: Mary Guelders (May/June 1449); Margaret of Denmark (July 1469); Madeleine of France (May/June 1537); Anne of Denmark (May 1590). Also May Queen of Scots returns to Leith (August 1561).

Guise, the French second bride of James V. This choice may have been driven by the influential ambassador, David Beaton, who had recently received the honour of the bishopric of Mirepoix from Francis I and whose ambitious nature led him to become cardinal and archbishop of St Andrews in rapid succession.[47]

As the seat of Scotland's premier archbishop, and home to the country's oldest university and one of Scotland's most eminent cathedrals, St Andrews was probably selected to impress the foreign observers. As Marie disembarked under a 'paill' of royal purple, she was greeted by the sound of trumpets played by splendidly-attired men in Spanish cloaks with ostrich feathers in their hats, as well as a band of nine pages and nine lackeys to attend her, together with the congregated nobles as listed by Pitscottie.[48] The town itself was transformed for her reception, with tapestries decorating buildings and a number of '*pharssis*' (pageants) designed by Sir David Lyndsay, poet and herald, were mounted. The first of these portrayed an angel descending from a mechanical cloud to deliver the keys of the realm to Marie.[49] The following day, the bride and her entourage were taken on a guided tour of all the 'kirkis and colledgis and vniversitie', undoubtedly to build up an image of a king and realm of advanced Renaissance culture and learning. The party remained at St Andrews for a number of weeks amidst feasting, dancing, plays and jousting.[50] By the fifteenth century, the northern ports of the Forth and the grand residences of Fife and Lothian had grown to compensate for the country's loss of the rich border port of Berwick, which had permanently returned into English hands. It was therefore unsurprising that, in a similar fashion to her thirteenth-century counterparts, Marie made a lavish progress, on this occasion via Cowper, Falkland, Stirling and Linlithgow *en route* to Edinburgh for her formal entry.[51]

Holyrood Palace was increasingly favoured as a ceremonial site as the fifteenth and sixteenth centuries progressed, particularly when the palace was extensively developed by James IV and James V.[52] The landscape around Holyrood

---

[47] For more on Beaton, as royal servant and ambassador see Margaret H.B. Sanderson, *Cardinal of Scotland: David Beaton, 1494–1546* (Edinburgh: John Donald, 2001), particularly pp. 45–71.

[48] *TA*, vol. 6, pp. 403–6, 410; Pitscottie, *Historie*, vol. 1, p. 380.

[49] Ibid.; Leslie, *Historie*, vol. 2, pp. 240–1.

[50] Pitscottie, *Historie*, vol. 1, pp. 380–1; NRS, Exchequer Records: 'Libri Domicilli' James V, E31/7, fols 70r–77r.

[51] Ibid., fols 77r–80r. The household accounts show, in the margins each day, the location of the royal household thus verifying the descriptions in Pitscottie, *Historie*, vol. 1, pp. 380–1.

[52] James II was crowned (1437), married (1449) and buried (1460) at Holyrood, and his son James III was also married there (1469); but the most lavish expenses on the fabric of the abbey and its royal lodgings occurred in the sixteenth century: John G. Dunbar, *Scottish Royal Palaces: The Architecture of the Royal Residences During the Late Medieval and Early Renaissance Periods* (East Linton: Tuckwell Press, 1999), pp. 55–73.

played host to a number of ceremonies, including entertainments commissioned by Mary Queen of Scots for the wedding of Lord Fleming in May 1562, attended by the Swedish ambassador on a mission seeking Mary's hand in marriage.[53] The scale and magnificence of the celebrations were clearly designed to impress, with Pitscottie describing a truly spectacular event announced by pyrotechnic displays and the thunder of artillery. A mock castle was constructed and ships floated on a loch in the palace park in a politically-driven re-creation of the 'seige of Lytht' ('siege of Leith').[54] Beyond the chronicle descriptions and reports in state papers, few official records have survived regarding the costs of the occasion or further specific details of the festivities.[55] Thanks to aerial views, maps and sketches, however, scholars have reached tentative conclusions as to which of the three lochs in the park was used, with St Margaret's loch being the closest to the palace, Dunsapie loch favoured by Sarah Carpenter, and Duddingston loch, the largest of the three, favoured by Pesala Bandara.[56] As with the 'palace in the wild' set against Glen Tilt, the waterborne spectacle at Holyrood was performed against the backdrop of Arthur's seat and incorporated the wonders of nature to add to its scale. The use of landscape as a key feature demonstrating power and status has become more prominent in English and European castle studies, and is currently being

---

[53] *Calendar of State Papers Relating to Scotland and Mary, Queen of Scots, 1547–1602*, [hereafter *CSPS*], ed. J. Bain et al., 12 vols (Edinburgh: H.M. General Register House, 1898–1952), vol. 1, no. 1097; *A Diurnal of Remarkable Occurrents That Have Passed Within the Country of Scotland Since the Death of King James the Fourth til the Year MDLXXV [1575]* (Edinburgh: Bannatyne Club, 1833), pp. 72–3; Pitscottie, *Historie*, vol. 2, p. 176. See also Pesala Bandara, 'Mary, Queen of Scots' Aquatic Entertainments for the Wedding of John Fleming, Fifth Lord Fleming to Elizabeth Ross, May 1562', in Margaret Shewring (ed.), *Waterborne Pageants and Festivities in the Renaissance: Essays in Honour of J.R. Mulryne* (Farnham and Burlington, VT: Ashgate, 2013), pp. 199–209.

[54] Sarah Carpenter, 'Performing Diplomacies: The 1560s Court Entertainments of Mary Queen of Scots', *The Scottish Historical Review*, 82.2 (October 2003) 214, pp. 202–3.

[55] *TA*, vol. 11, pp. xxxv–xxxvi, 162; Pitscottie, *Historie and Cronicles*, vol. 2, p. 176; *CSPS*, vol. 1, no. 1111. The surviving accounts for the Master of Works between 1554 and 1594 remain in fragmented Loose Accounts only and there are no entries between 1559, when work was undertaken on a park dyke at Holyrood, and 1576: *Accounts of the Masters of Works for Building and Repairing Royal Palaces and Castles, Vol. I, 1529–1615*, ed. Henry M. Paton (Edinburgh: H.M. Stationery Office, 1957), pp. 299–300.

[56] For example, showing both of these lochs see 'John Dewar Oblique Aerial View of Holyrood Park Looking East, SC431766', *Canmore, Royal Commission for Ancient and Historical Monuments of Scotland website* (2014), http://canmore.rcahms.gov.uk/en/site/52219/details/edinburgh+holyrood+park+ general+and+perimeter+wall/ [Accessed 2 January 2014]; Carpenter, 'Performing Diplomacies', p. 203, suggests the loch used was Dunsapie loch but gives no specific reason for this suggestion; while Bandara, 'Mary, Queen of Scots' Aquatic Entertainments', pp. 203–4, argues that the location was most likely to have been Duddingston loch.

explored by Katherine Buchanan in regard to Scottish noble castles in Angus.[57] Although Edinburgh and the palace of Holyrood have been massively developed during the last 450 years, the park has remained largely intact, and the investigation of how such open spaces were transformed for festival deserves closer attention in the Scottish context.

Perhaps the most famous marriage to take place at Holyrood Palace was that of James IV to Margaret Tudor on 8 August 1503. In the days following the marriage, the Somerset herald, John Young, reported that the tournaments and martial sports were held in front of the palace with the royal couple watching from the windows of their great chambers.[58] John Dunbar's discussions of building projects at the palace have thrown light on the position of the royal chambers of the king and queen in the reign of James IV arguing that they most likely ran along the west arm of the palace quadrangle, with the queen's apartments extending onto the north wing, and an outer court in front of these rooms used for outdoor displays.[59] For the year prior to the wedding the *Treasurer's Accounts* indicate that extensive work was undertaken at the palace and abbey, with significant quantities of timber, iron, roof slates, glass and plaster purchased. The *Accounts* also show payments for craftsmen, while other items hint at the finer touches, such as gold to decorate the king's coat of arms adorning the fore gate.[60]

In Young's contemporary account of the wedding some of the guests watched alongside the king and queen at windows of their great chambers, others from a scaffold that appears to have been built below the windows, and finally there were those – such as officers and trumpeters – who observed the events from alongside the action.[61] None of the timber was specifically listed as being purchased for the scaffolding, but the royal apartments were on the first floor and the scaffold must have been lower than the first floor windows. Dunbar notes references to the 'Queen's gallery' in 1511–1512, and an entry at the time of the wedding also refers to construction works on such a gallery; but unless the gallery and scaffold are one and the same, no reference to the gallery appears in Young's account.[62] While the exact layout of the tilting ground and the surrounding structures is uncertain, the arrangements suggest that structures, both permanent and

---

[57] See n. 13.

[58] John Young, 'Fyancells of Margaret', College of Arms, MS 1st M.13 bis, fols 112v–114v; Ibid., 'The Fyancells of Margaret', in Thomas Hearne (ed.), *Johannis Lelandi antiquarii De rebus Brittannicis Collectanea*, 4 vols (London: Benjamin White, 1774), vol. 4, pp. 298–9.

[59] Dunbar, *Scottish Royal Palaces*, pp. 58–60, sketch of ground plans, illustration 2.9, p. 60.

[60] *TA*, vol. ii, pp. 269–74, 344, 370, 383.

[61] Young, 'Fyancells', CA MS, fols 112v–114v, and in *Lelandi Collectanea*, pp. 298–9.

[62] Dunbar, *Scottish Royal Palaces*, p. 59; *TA*, vol. 2, p. 269. The payment in 1503 is made to William Turnbull, mason, for the gallery and windows – the craftsman's occupation suggests that the gallery was a permanent rather than temporary wooden structure.

temporary, were utilised to provide viewing platforms tiered according to status, or level of access to the monarch and his new bride. Moreover, Katie Stevenson has proposed that access according to status was given greater weight by the choice of a space enclosed within the palace walls, whereas earlier events in James IV's reign – such as Shrove Tuesday tourneys – were held in public spaces outside the walls.[63]

Across the three days of jousts, both indoor and outdoor spaces were used. The decoration of the apartments from which the royal party watched the events – particularly the lavishly-decorated queen's chambers – can be envisaged using the records from the *Treasurer's Accounts* and Young's account. These decorations included rich furnishings in royal colours with huge quantities of blue, red and purple velvet, along with £400-worth of cloth of gold used for the queen's chamber and the bed of state, which stood prominent in the room.[64] Descriptions of the lists are limited, but it is possible to infer that the jousting gear was plentiful and decorative, with banded spears decorated with diamonds amongst those made for the occasion, and the lists themselves appear to have been dressed with damask material on which seven men worked for two days.[65] While the specific colours of this cloth are not stated, the care taken by James IV in the provision of clothing for the attending nobles, courtiers, household officials and servants, including musicians, henchmen and heralds, emphasises a clear understanding of visual display.[66] The costumes and other fabrics often reflected the royal colour scheme as utilised within the apartments, for example, the red taffeta and gold coats of arms purchased for the heralds, thus further amplifying the symbols and colours of royal authority. Costume, gestures and actions in the court of James IV are discussed at length by Sarah Carpenter and Louise Fradenburg, both of whom convincingly argue for a highly-developed ceremonial awareness that enabled the Scottish royal court to produce grander and more sophisticated spectacles under James, an enthusiastic and self-assured monarch.[67] It is therefore reasonable to suggest that interior and exterior spaces were deliberately set in harmony with each other and with the clothing of key royal figures. This interaction between indoor and outdoor spaces takes us back full circle to the first example of the 'palace in the wild' in Glen Tilt,

---

[63] Katie Stevenson, *Chivalry and Knighthood in Scotland, 1424–1513* (Woodbridge: Boydell Press, 2006), p. 93.

[64] Young, 'Fyancells', CA MS, fol. 108v, and in *Lelandi Collectanea*, p. 295; *TA*, vol. 2, pp. 213–14.

[65] Ibid., pp. 388–90. See also Stevenson, *Chivalry and Knighthood*, pp. 92–3.

[66] *TA*, vol. 2, pp. 306–13, 341; Aberdeen City Archives, Council, Baillie and Guild Court Book, vol. 8, CA/1/1/8, fol. 239. The accounts highlight that anyone who had received orders to attend also received instructions to be dressed in their best.

[67] Louise O. Fradenburg, *City, Marriage, Tournament: Arts of Rule in Late Medieval Scotland* (Madison, WI: University of Wisconsin Press, 1991); Sarah Carpenter, '"To Thexaltacyon of Noblesse": A Herald's Account of the Marriage of Margaret Tudor and James IV', *Medieval English Theatre*, 29 (2007), 104–20.

where natural outdoor products were introduced inside the building amongst the manmade luxuries.

In conclusion, the settings for royal ceremony in Scotland – even when focusing on these three core ceremonies only – are many, and use a wide variety of available indoor and outdoor spaces. It is notable that no one ceremonial space is dominant across the four hundred years, as Westminster is in England, or a set combination of spaces such as Reims (coronation) and St Denis (funeral) in France. The outside spaces in Scotland included the outer courts of royal palaces, royal parks and lochs, the exterior landscapes of ecclesiastical monuments, the highland hunting parks of nobles, and the ports, ships and towns of the realm. This use of multiple places in individual royal ceremonies, which often at various stages in the proceedings provided open access for the public, mirrors both the itinerant nature of Scottish kingship and a desire to provide ease of public access to the ruler. Moreover, the interactions between particular spaces can illustrate very real political tensions met with diplomatic skill, while choice of place and level of public access can reflect developments in the manner of kingship practised by different Scottish monarchs.

Bibliography

Manuscript sources

Aberdeen City Archives, Council, Baillie and Guild Court Book, vol. 8, CA/1/1/8
College of Arms, MS 1st M.13 bis [Heraldic collection]

National Records of Scotland [NRS], Exchequer Records, Treasurer's Accounts, E21/40

NRS, Exchequer Records: Exchequer Rolls, E38/9

NRS, Exchequer Records: 'Libri Domicilli' James V, E31/7

Printed primary sources

Accounts of the Lord High Treasurer of Scotland [hereafter *TA*], ed. Thomas Dickson and James Balfour Paul, 12 vols (Edinburgh: H.M. Register House, 1877–1916).

Accounts of the Masters of Works for Building and Repairing Royal Palaces and Castles, Vol. I, 1529–1615, ed. Henry M. Paton (Edinburgh: H.M. Stationery Office, 1957).

Bower, Walter, *Scotichronicon*, trans. and ed. D.E.R. Watt et al., 9 vols (Aberdeen and Edinburgh: Aberdeen University Press and Mercat Press, 1987–1998).

Calendar of Documents Relating to Scotland Preserved in Her Majesty's Public Record Office, London, ed. Joseph Bain et al., 5 vols (Edinburgh: H.M. General Register House, 1881–1986).

Calendar of Entries in the Papal Registers Relating to Great Britain and Ireland: Papal Letters, ed. W.H. Bliss et al., 16 vols (London: H.M. Stationery Office, 1893).

Calendar of State Papers Relating to Scotland and Mary, Queen of Scots, 1547–1602, ed. J. Bain et al., 12 vols (Edinburgh: H.M. General Register House, 1898–1952).

A Diurnal of Remarkable Occurrents That Have Passed Within the Country of Scotland Since the Death of King James the Fourth til the Year MDLXXV [1575] (Edinburgh: Bannatyne Club, 1833).

The Exchequer Rolls of Scotland: Rotuli Scaccarii Regum Scotorum, ed. G. Burnett et al., 23 vols (Edinburgh, 1878–1908).

Hoveden, Roger de, *The Annals of Roger de Hoveden Comprising the History of England and Other Countries of Europe From AD 732 to AD 1201*, trans. and ed. Henry T. Riley, 2 vols (London: H.G. Bohn, 1853).

Legg, Leopold G.W. (ed.), *English Coronation Records* (Westminster: Archibald Constable and Co., 1901).

Leslie, John, *The Historie of Scotland wrytten first in latin by the most reuerrend and worthy Jhone Leslie, Bishop of Ross*, trans. James Dalyrmple (1596), ed. E.G. Cody (Edinburgh and London: William Blackwood and Sons, 1890).

Lindesay of Pitscottie, Robert, *The Historie and Cronicles of Scotland: From the Slauchter of King James the First To the Ane thousande five hundrieth thrie scoir fyftein zeir*, ed. Æ.J.G. Mackay, 2 vols (Edinburgh and London: William Blackwood and Sons, 1899).

Records of the Parliament of Scotland, ed. Gillian H. MacIntosh, Alastair J. Mann and Roland J. Tanner et al. (St Andrews, 2007–2013), www.rps.ac.uk

Wyntoun, Andrew, *The Original Chronicles of Andrew of Wyntoun*, ed. F.J. Amours, 6 vols (Edinburgh and London: William Blackwood and Sons, 1903–1914).

Young, John, 'The Fyancells of Margaret, eldeſt Daughter of King of the King Henry VIIth to James King of Scotland: Together With Her Departure From England, Journey Into Scotland, Her Reception and Marriage There, and the Great Feaſts Held on That Account', in *Johannis Lelandi antiquarii De rebus Brittannicis Collectanea*, ed. Thomas Hearne, 4 vols (London: Benjamin White, 1774), vol. 4, pp. 258–300.

Secondary sources

Bandara, Pesala, 'Mary, Queen of Scots' Aquatic Entertainments for the Wedding of John Fleming, Fifth Lord Fleming to Elizabeth Ross, May 1562', in Margaret Shewring (ed.), *Waterborne Pageants and Festivities in the Renaissance: Essays in Honour of J.R. Mulryne* (Farnham and Burlington, VT: Ashgate, 2013), pp. 199–209.

Boardman, Stephen, 'Robert II', in Keith Brown and Roland Tanner (eds), *Scottish Kingship 1306–1542: Essays in Honour of Norman Macdougall* (Edinburgh: John Donald, 2008), pp. 72–108.

Carpenter, Sarah, 'Performing Diplomacies: The 1560s Court Entertainments of Mary Queen of Scots', *The Scottish Historical Review*, 82.2/214 (October 2003), 194–225.

Carpenter, Sarah, '"To thexaltacyon of noblesse": A Herald's Account of the Marriage of Margaret Tudor and James IV', *Medieval English Theatre*, 29 (2007), 104–20.

Cowan, Samuel, *Three Celtic Earldoms: Atholl, Strathearn and Menteith (Critical and Historical Recital So Far as Know)* (Edinburgh: Norman Macleod, 1909).

Cox, Kevin R., Murray Low and Jennifer Robinson (eds), *The SAGE Handbook of Political Geography* (London: Sage, 2008).

Creighton, Oliver H., *Castles and Landscapes: Power, Community and Fortification in Medieval England* (London: Equinox, 2005).

Dendy, D.R., *The Use of Light in Christian Worship* (London: SPCK, 1959).

Duffy, Eamon, *The Stripping of the Altars: Traditional Religion in England 1400–1580* (New Haven, CT and London: Yale University Press, 1993).

Dunbar, John G., *Scottish Royal Palaces: The Architecture of the Royal Residences During the Late Medieval and Early Renaissance Periods* (East Linton: Tuckwell Press, 1999).

Duncan, Archibald A.M., *Scotland: The Making of the Kingdom* (Edinburgh: Edinburgh University Press, reprint 1996).

Duncan, Archibald A.M., *The Kingship of the Scots, 842–1292: Succession and Independence* (Edinburgh: Edinburgh University Press, 2002).

Fawcett, Richard, *Scottish Abbeys and Priories* (London: Batsford Ltd., 1994).

Fitzpatrick, Elizabeth, *Royal Inauguration in Gaelic Ireland, c. 1100–1600: A Cultural Landscape Study* (Woodbridge: Boydell Press, 2004).

Fradenburg, Louise O., *City, Marriage, Tournament: Arts of Rule in Late Medieval Scotland* (Madison: University of Wisconsin Press, 1991).

Gray, Douglas, 'The Royal Entry in Sixteenth-Century Scotland', in Sally Mapstone and Juliette Hood (eds), *The Rose and the Thistle: Essays on the Culture of Late Medieval and Renaissance Scotland* (East Linton: Tuckwell Press, 1998), pp. 10–37.

Guidicini, Giovanna, 'Municipal Perspective, Royal Expectations, and the Use of Public Space: The Case of the West Port, Edinburgh, 1503–1633', *Architectural Heritage*, 22 (2011), 37–52.

Hansson, Martin, 'Aristocratic Landscape: The Spatial Ideology of the Medieval Aristocracy', *Lund Studies in Historical Archaeology* 2 (2006).

Harrison, John, *Rebirth of a Palace: The Royal Court at Stirling Castle* (Edinburgh: Historic Scotland, 2011).

Houwen, L.A.J.R., Alasdair A. MacDonald and Sally L. Mapstone (eds), *A Palace in the Wild: Essays on Vernacular Culture and Humanism in Late-Medieval and Renaissance Scotland* (Leuven: Peeters, 2000).

Lewis, J.H., G.J. Ewart et al., *Jedburgh Abbey: The Archaeology and Architecture of a Border Abbey* (Edinburgh: Society of Antiquaries of Scotland, 1995).

Liddiard, Robert, *Castles in Context: Power, Symbolism and Landscape, 1066–1500* (Macclesfield: Windgather Press, 2005).

MacDonald, Alasdair A., 'Mary Stewart's Entry to Edinburgh: An Ambiguous Triumph', *The Innes Review*, 42/2 (Autumn 1991), 101–10.

O'Grady, Oliver, 'Scone Abbey and Moot Hill, Perth and Kinross (Scone Parish), Geophysical Survey', *Discovery Excavation Scotland*, 8 (2007), 167–8.

Oram, Richard, *Alexander II, King of Scots: 1214–1249* (Edinburgh: John Donald, 2012).

Sanderson, Margaret H.B., *Cardinal of Scotland: David Beaton, 1494–1546* (Edinburgh: John Donald, 2001).

Stevenson, Katie, *Chivalry and Knighthood in Scotland, 1424–1513* (Woodbridge: Boydell Press, 2006).

Welander, R., D. Breeze, and Tom O. Clancy (eds), *The Stone of Destiny: Artefact and Icon* (Edinburgh: Society of Antiquaries of Scotland, 2003).

Online Sources

Guidicini, Giovanna, 'European Themes and Local Awareness: The Reconstruction of Charles I's Entry Into Edinburgh in 1633', Online Exhibition on *Re-Creating Early Modern Festivals Project Website*, www.recreatingearlymodernfestivals.com/ exhibition_giovanna.htm [Accessed 28 December 2013].

'John Dewar Oblique Aerial View of Holyrood Park looking East, SC431766', *Canmore, Royal Commission for Ancient and Historical Monuments of Scotland website* (2014), http://canmore.rcahms.gov.uk/en/site/52219/details/edinburgh+holyrood+park+ general+and+perimeter+wall/ [Accessed 2 January 2014].

'Stirling Palace Project', see *Historic Scotland website*, www.historic-scotland.gov.uk/index/news/mediaresources/stirling-castle-palace-project.htm [Accessed 28 December 2013].

Unpublished Theses

Buchanan, Katherine, 'The Social, Geographical, and Structural Environments of Minor Noble Castles in Angus, 1449–1542' (unpublished PhD thesis, University of Stirling, 2014).

Dean, Lucinda H.S., 'Crowns, Rings and Processions: Continuity and Change in the Representations of Scottish Royal Authority Through State Ceremony, c.1214–c.1603' (Unpublished PhD thesis, University of Stirling, 2013).

Guidicini, Giovanna, 'Scotland Triumphant: The Relevance of Stewart Triumphal Celebrations in Shaping Scottish Renaissance Architecture' (Unpublished PhD thesis, Edinburgh, October 2009).

O'Grady, Oliver J.T., 'The Setting and Practice of Open-Air Judicial Assemblies in Medieval Scotland: A Multidisciplinary Study' (Unpublished PhD thesis, University of Glasgow, 2008).

Chapter 6

From ephemeral to permanent architecture

The Venetian palazzo in the second half of the seventeenth century

Martina Frank

Around 1700 the range of Venetian palace architecture was enhanced by a small number of unfamiliar structural features. These were intended for the celebration of festivities and were characterised by decorative systems and architectural developments that broke with a well-established tradition. The most spectacular testimony to the thirst for new directions, and an indispensable term of comparison for our present purpose, is the double-height central hall in Palazzo Zenobio (see Plate 9).

In 1695 the Zenobio family, recently assimilated into the patrician class, appointed Antonio Gaspari to renovate a Gothic palace in the ownership of Angelo Raffaele, which the family had bought in 1664 from the Morosini family.[1] Gaspari eliminated, or at least radically modified, a fundamental feature of Venetian houses, namely the *portego*, the rather long and narrow passage hall typical of the *piano nobile* or principal storey of the house. On the ground floor, the architect introduced a colonnaded passageway, narrowing towards the garden, while on the *piano nobile* the *portego* was designed to open up to form a room that breaks not only its lateral confines but also its upper confine as it soars two storeys high. The connection between the ground floor and the *piano nobile* seeks to inspire in the visitor a feeling of wonder and surprise. The grand staircase at the end of the ground-floor colonnaded passageway leads up to a *porteghetto* with a Serlian window looking out on the garden, while a second Serlian arch constitutes a spectacular entrance to a hall, the dimensions, proportions and decorations of which could hardly fail to induce a feeling of awe and wonder. A space such as this was

[1] Massimo Favilla and Ruggero Rugolo, 'Dorigny e Venezia. Da Ca' Tron a Ca' Zenobio e ritorno', in Giorgio Marini and Paola Marini (eds), *Louis Dorigny (1654–1742): Un pittore della corte francese a Verona* (Venice: Marsilio, 2003), pp. 37–59; Massimo Favilla and Ruggero Rugolo, 'Progetti di Antonio Gaspari, architetto della Venezia barocca', *Atti dell'Istituto Veneto di Scienze, Lettere ed Arti, classe di scienze morali, lettere ed arti*, 165 (2006–2007), 139–91.

undoubtedly designed for new functions and new events leading to equally new decoration.

Antonio Gaspari is regarded as the most evidently baroque of Venetian architects, who tried, in his own words, to follow Roman rules and adapt them to Venetian habits, an aim which can clearly be read in the façade of Palazzo Zenobio (see Plate 10).[2] The façade speaks a Venetian language, but interpreted in the light of Roman models, in particular those of Gianlorenzo Bernini's Palazzo Chigi in Piazza SS Apostoli. The pyramid-shaped composition of the façade culminates in a coat of arms enclosed in a curved tympanum, while the balcony indicates the hall's extent, and the Serlian window organises the depth of the space.[3]

The elaborate pictorial scheme in the central hall, which historians call the music room, is situated within an architectural space structured by pilasters and decorated with exquisitely modelled stuccos by Abbondio Stazio.[4] The pyramidal composition of Louis Dorigny's fresco echoes that by Gaspari on the façade, leading towards a skyward-facing opening and depicting a Triumphant Aurora followed by Apollo's chariot.[5] Mezzanine openings are repeated in *trompe l'œil* along the whole perimeter, forming a proscenium for the *orchestra* and for the allegorical figures that belong to the terrestrial realm. The hall thus breaks with the typology of the *portego*, the passage hall that traditionally occupies the centre

---

[2] A drawing of Antonio Gaspari for Villa De Lezze bears the inscription: '*Romanae Architecturae Leges servavi / Ut Venetis Legiis servire*'. The drawing, held in the Biblioteca del Museo Correr, Venice (BMCVe), Raccolta Gaspari, I, 93, is discussed by Martina Frank, 'Appunti su villa da Lezze', in Martina Frank (ed.), *Da Longhena a Selva: Un'idea di Venezia a dieci anni dalla scomparsa di Elena Bassi* (Bologna: Archetipo Libri, 2011), pp. 111–22, 119. For Gaspari's hypothetical stay at the Roman Accademia di San Luca, see Massimo Favilla and Ruggero Rugolo, 'La verità sul caso Gaspari', *Studi Veneziani*, 45 (2003), 243–63, 246–50.

[3] The coat of arms now lies in the garden. For the original state of the façade see Luca Carlevarijs, *Le fabbriche e vedute di Venetia disgnate, poste in prospettiva et intagliate* (Venice: Finazzi, 1703).

[4] Bernard Aikema, 'Il famoso Abbondio: Abbondio Stazio e la decorazione a stucco dei palazzi veneziani, circa 1685–1750', *Saggi e memorie di storia dell'arte*, 21 (1997), 85–122; Massimo De Grassi, 'Filippo Parodi, Pietro Roncaioli e lo stucco tardobarocco a Venezia', *Arte Veneta*, 54 (1999), 55–61.

[5] The decoration can probably be linked to the preparations for the wedding of Carlo Zenobio with Maria Vendramin in 1698. Alessio Pasian, 'Per un catalogo di Louis Dorigny', *Arte in Friuli Arte a Trieste*, 18–19 (1999), 9–38, 17; Massimo Favilla and Ruggero Rugolo, 'Louis Dorigny. Salone e andito al piano nobile (1695–1698 circa). Venezia Ca' Zenobio', in Filippo Pedrocco (ed.), *Gli affreschi nei palazzi e nelle ville venete* (Schio: Sassi, 2008), pp. 162–71, 162–4. A previous collaboration between Gaspari and Dorigny is discussed by Adriano Mariuz and Giuseppe Pavanello, 'La chiesetta di Bernardo Nave a Cittadella', *Arte Veneta*, 50 (1997), 68–85. Dorigny was also active in Villa Da Lezze, see Martina Frank, 'Zu einer kaum bekannten Vita des Ludovico Dorigny', *Wiener Jahrbuch fur Kunstgeschichte*, 40 (1987), 103–7.

of a Venetian palazzo in double or triple superposition, depending on the number of floors. It also completely erases the usual compositional and lighting focus of a nobleman's house on the lagoon, namely the *portego*'s tight sequence of openings on the *piano nobile*. The *portego*'s traditional proportions and orientation prevent the eye from adopting a high focal point, and are usually reinforced by apparently secondary elements such as the shining floor-surfaces, which tend to reflect, in the interior of the building, the quality of the liquid surface outside. In Ca' Zenobio, windows are restricted to serving as sources of light for the decorative scheme overhead, and thereby lose their Venetian essence, namely the quality of connecting the interior with the exterior.

The development of Gaspari's architectural reasoning can be followed in a number of autograph sketches illustrating various stages of the Palazzo Zenobio project. One particularly interesting item documents the concept of the main hall as a transverse oval opening, a solution which would have emphasised even further the break with local tradition (Figure 6.1).[6]

If the plan of Ca' Zenobio's central hall seems to draw inspiration for its T shape from medieval precedents, the fact that it is two storeys high shows that we are in no way dealing with a concession to tradition. And the fact that Gaspari initially considered using an oval for the palazzo's central space suggests his and his patron's wish to introduce a spectacular element of novelty.

I would therefore suggest that, in the case of Ca' Zenobio, the Venetian *portego* abandoned what had always been its characteristic rectangular shape, its real and ideal extension, to conform to a more 'international' taste, in this way nullifying the relationship between inward and outward perspectives. The palazzo's music or ball room is a setting whose claim to permanent significance involves isolating the palazzo from the city, preventing that natural extension of space ensured by the *portego*'s terminal source of light. The room's function as a place designed for music is expressed by the overhanging balcony, its role emphasised by a range of musical instruments carrying iconographical significance, together with other elements extrapolated from theatrical tradition.

The development from *portego* to *salone* (main hall) was not, however, straightforward, and no radical or general reform of the internal distribution of space in the Venetian palazzo was ever actually achieved.[7] It is also true that the period around

---

6 BMCVe, Raccolta Gaspari, III, 34, first published by Elena Bassi, 'Episodi dell'architettura veneta nell'opera di Antonio Gaspari', *Saggi e memorie di storia dell'arte*, 3 (1963), 55–108, 74–6. See also Gianmario Guidarelli, 'L'architettura civile', in Augusto Roca De Amicis (ed.), *Storia dell'architettura nel Veneto: Il Seicento* (Venice: Marsilio, 2008), pp. 224–47, 236.

7 Vincenzo Fontana, 'Dal 'portego' al salone', in Lionello Puppi (ed.), *Giambattista Tiepolo nel terzo centenario della nascita* (Padua: Il Poligrafo, 1998), pp. 115–24; Vincenzo Fontana, 'Scaloni e sale da musica, alcove e ridotti: il rinnovamento dei palazzi veneziani', in Marcello Fagiolo (ed.), *Atlante tematico del barocco in Italia. Residenze nobiliari. Italia settentrionale* (Rome: De Luca, 2009), pp. 251–74.

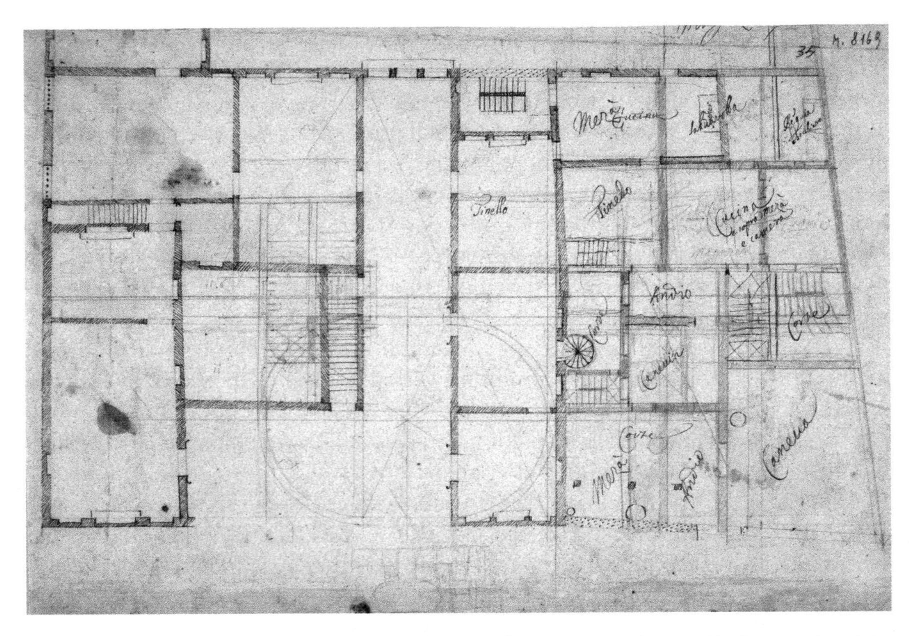

Figure 6.1 Antonio Gaspari, *Project for the ground plan of Palazzo Zenobio*, BMCVe (Biblioteca del Museo Correr, Venice), Raccolta Gaspari, III

1700 is characterised by an extensive range of solutions, which indicates a need for new initiatives. These initiatives are in turn rooted in a process which had started long before, given expression in a series of experiments originating from the second half of the seventeenth century, the aim of which was to redefine the sequence and functions of space in aristocratic houses. Retracing these processes requires a multidisciplinary analysis of a number of factors. Architectural examples are not in themselves sufficient to account for this change, just as the primacy of an unprecedented decorative formula is not sufficient to do justice to the complexity of the phenomenon. Nor is it satisfactory to proceed by historical simplification, for instance, by attributing a spirit of innovation to the new aristocracy.[8]

The construction type adopted by Ca' Pesaro – launched by Giovanni Pesaro, (doge 1658–1659), then taken over after his death by his nephew Leonardo – belongs to the tradition of the *palazzo principalissimo* deriving from the palazzo's position on the Grand Canal as well as its dimensions, materials and architectural vocabulary,

[8] For an analysis of the phenomenon of new membership of the patriciate, see Roberto Sabbadini, *L'acquisto della tradizione: Aristocrazia e nuova nobilità a Venezia* (Udine: Gaspari editore, 1995). The relationship between new and old families in social, cultural and political matters has been studied by Dorit Raines, *L'invention du mythe aristocratique: L'image de soi du patriciat vénitien au temps de la Sérénissime*, 2 vols (Venice: Istituto veneto di scienze, lettere ed arti, 2006).

while also exhibiting a propensity for grand dimensions typical of the second half of the seventeenth century.[9] The long history of its construction stretches from the 1620s to the early-eighteenth century. The palazzo, based on two pre-existing aristocratic structures, which long influenced the project, was a venue for experimentation, especially regarding the relationship between the *portego*, the stairs and the courtyard. Baldassare Longhena's initial conception did not challenge conformity with tradition, and the exceptionally wide and deep *portego* remains the founding element of the design.[10] Leonardo Pesaro and Antonio Gaspari, who, according to Hopkins, came onto the scene in the mid-1670s, brought a new impulse to the project, aiming to find a solution to the problem of an exceedingly deep and dark passage hall while respecting the pre-existing structure of the walls. Furthermore Ca' Rezzonico provides an example where Longhena had already proved his sensitivity to these considerations by reducing the depth of the *portego* through the expedient of an intermediary courtyard. The sketches for Palazzo Pesaro feature the recurring theme of a monumental staircase as a link between the *portego* and the courtyard (Figure 6.2).

Longhena's staircase at San Giorgio Maggiore (1642) had recently shown the architect's capacity for connecting the two levels of the cloister with a strong sense of theatricality, thus creating a dialogue between the various architectural elements. In the case of Palazzo Pesaro, none of the schemes involving a multi-flight staircase on the central axis, opening toward the *portego* and courtyard through a series of light-filled arcades, was ever carried out. After 1700, Antonio Gaspari introduced a one-flight monumental staircase, placed as a semi-autonomous element to the right of the *portego*, near the land entrance. Nevertheless, the objective of breaking the continuity of the *portego* influenced choices relative to the ground-floor entrance hall. The fact that our reading of the façade, even in the completed building, is determined by the same choices as are found in its structure before the definitive resolution of the planimetric aspects, proves that the architectural structure was designed as a whole. On the façade, the two huge twin gates, separated by a recess, were designed to meet the two openings on the courtyard axially, while the 'blind' portion in the middle was supposed to correspond to the central flight of the staircase. This is a complex design which takes into account visual

[9] The expression *palazzo principalissimo* goes back to Francesco Sansovino, *Venetia città nobilissima et singolare* (Venice: Sansovino, 1581), p. 149. He uses it to describe the *palazzi* Loredan (Mauro Codussi), Dolfin, Corner Ca' Granda (both by his father Jacopo Sansovino) and Grimani at San Luca. For the phenomenon in the baroque period see Martina Frank, 'Committenza pubblica e privata', in Augusto Roca De Amicis (ed.), *Storia dell'architettura nel Veneto: Il Seicento* (Venice: Marsilio, 2008), pp. 8–12; Andrew Hopkins, *Baldassare Longhena and Venetian Baroque Architecture* (New Haven, CT and London: Yale University Press, 2012), p. 172.

[10] See the drawings in Archivio di Stato di Venezia (ASVe), *Archivio Gradenigo Rio Marin*, busta 259, published by Alessandro Borgomainerio, 'Due disegni inediti di Baldassare Longhena per Ca' Pesaro', *Arte Veneta*, 66 (2010), 211–15; Hopkins, *Baldassare Longhena*, p. 208, for their dating in the late 1650s.

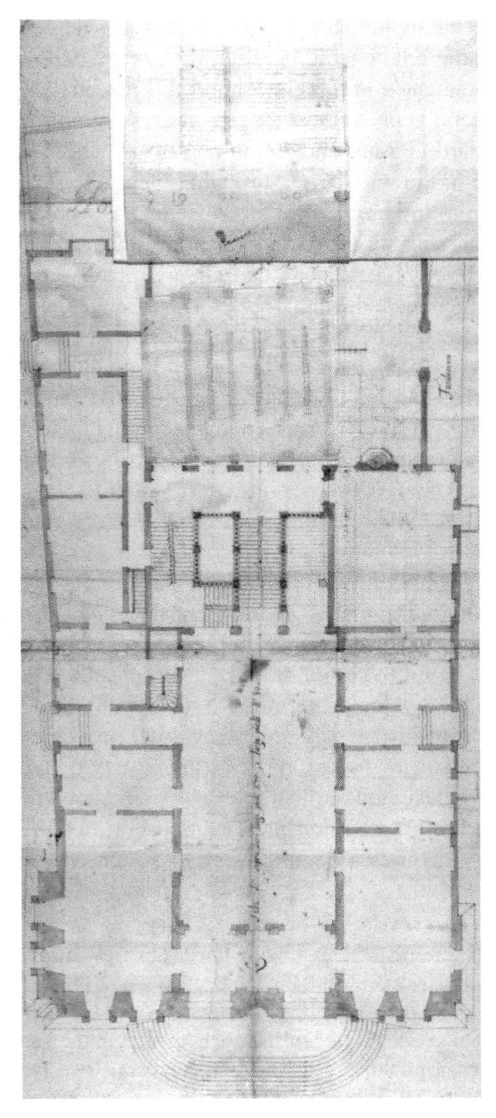

Figure 6.2 Baldassare Longhena and Antonio Gaspari, *Project for the ground plan of Palazzo Pesaro*, BMCVe (Biblioteca del Museo Correr, Venice), Raccolta Gaspari, III

axes, sources of light, and movement within the building.[11] We will not encounter another such instance of theatrical insight applied to the relationship between interior and exterior until Domenico Rossi's project of 1723 for Ca' Corner della Regina, located on the Grand Canal near Ca' Pesaro, which certainly constitutes a response to its seventeenth-century precedent.

Venetian architecture and theatrical and festive space

Giorgio Bellavitis has described the lower part of the façade at Ca' Corner della Regina as a *frons scenae*, capable of being read when the three gates are open (Figure 6.3).[12] The larger, central gate leads to an extremely deep *portego* ending in a courtyard, while the two minor gates offer an axial correspondence that is both visual and functional via the two flights of stairs located on the lateral sides of the entrance hall, which itself therefore takes on a T-shape, with the wider side oriented towards the Grand Canal. The *piano nobile*'s extremely long *portego*, on the other hand, indicates a return to tradition.

In his sketch of the floor plan of Palazzo Mocenigo Casa Vecchia, Antonio Visentini emphasises two staircases, symmetrically located on both sides of the entrance hall. We do not know if his observation corresponds to reality, nor when such a solution might have been conceived.[13] Significantly, however, an etching by Giuseppe Filosi celebrating the visit of Augustus of Saxony to the Mocenigo family in 1716 shows the ideal use of the space, transformed into an elaborate *scena per angolo* to accommodate the reception of the monarch (Figure 6.4).

These 'scenographic' staircases find an important model in Palazzo Priuli Scarpon in San Felice, where in the 1660s Alfonso Moscatelli designed a multi-flight staircase serving not only as a means of connecting one level with another, but also as an autonomous structure of theatrical architecture.[14] Moscatelli, an engineer from Mantua, is known not only for his buildings but also for his work as a set designer; for instance, during the carnival of 1659, he staged *La Costanza di Rosmonda* for the theatre of Santi Giovanni e Paolo.[15]

---

[11] For the use of twin gates in a wider Venetian context see Martina Frank, 'Riflessioni sul Longhena', *Storia dell'arte*, 64 (1988), 241–7.

[12] Giorgio Bellavitis, 'Note sul restauro di Palazzo Corner della Regina e sull'uso temporaneo del pianoterra come spazio espositivo', in *La Biennale di Venezia Annuario 1976* (Venice: La Biennale di Venezia, 1976), pp. 897–908.

[13] Elena Bassi, *Palazzi di Venezia: Admiranda Urbis Venetiae* (Venice: Stamperia di Venezia Editrice, 1976), p. 134.

[14] Bassi, *Palazzi*, pp. 278–81. The staircase was destroyed by fire in 1739 and is documented only by Visentini's drawing published by Bassi.

[15] Jonathan E. Glixon and Beth L. Glixon, *Inventing the Business of Opera: The Impresario and His World in Seventeenth Century Venice* (New York: Oxford University Press, 2006), p. 330.

Figure 6.3 Venice, Palazzo Corner della Regina, scheme of the façade (Giorgio Bellavitis, in *La Biennale di Venezia Annuario*, 1976)

A celebrated exhibition mounted in 1980 was entitled *Venezia e lo spazio scenico* ('Venice and stage space'). In addition to retracing Venice's theatrical life, the exhibition explored the notion of an entire city envisaged as theatrical space, where a change of scene is achieved by the change of location of the viewer-visitor. This is not the place to survey the packed calendar of Venetian festivities, based precisely on processional movement and celebration of the Republic's history. It is necessary to reiterate however that this is not an *a posteriori* interpretation but a well-established and thought-through process which started inside the Serenissima itself. Elements of this process include the *andate ducali* (ducal processions), and historical festivities such as *la Sensa* (the Ascension), together with occasional celebrations such as the

Figure 6.4 Giuseppe Filosi, *The visit of Augustus of Saxony to the Palazzo Mocenigo in 1716* (engraving owned by author)

ingressi (entrances) of the ambassadors and procurators of San Marco, the ceremonies for the arrival of high-ranking visitors, funerals, celebrations of military victories and others. On all these occasions, the itinerary and its point of arrival were marked by ephemeral architecture and decorations resulting from collaborative planning.[16]

To further emphasise the notion of an entire city configured as a stage, it is worth mentioning that even the historiography of Venice (the so-called Myth of Venice and its commentaries) stresses the principles of itinerary and mobility. Although much has been written on the topic, it is worth repeating that Venice as a state without a royal court, or more precisely an oligarchic republic, transferred the concept of central authority onto a carefully-conceived quasi-processional sequence of all those elements capable of ensuring congruence and integrity between the state's various components.

[16] Overviews on religious and civic ceremonies include: Giustina Renier Michiel, *Origine delle feste veneziane*, 2 vols (Milan: Editori degli annuali delle scienze e dell'industria, 1829); Bianca Tamassia Mazzarotto, *Le feste veneziane: i giochi popolari, le cerimonie religiose e di governo* (Florence: Sansoni, 1961); Matteo Casini, *I gesti del Principe. La festa politica a Firenze e Venezia in età rinascimentale* (Venice: Marsilio, 1996); Lina Urban, *Processioni e feste dogali. Venetia est mundus* (Vicenza: Neri Pozza, 1998).

Such a premise, while too briefly described to encompass the phenomenon in all its complexity, may nevertheless draw attention to a distinctive aspect of Venice – the *Città nobilissima et singolare* (most noble and unique city), in the words of Francesco Sansovino – which in 1637 acquired a further distinguishing element: the opera theatre. This initiative was left entirely to individual patricians or groups of patricians, without any state involvement. The culture of musical performance thus presented itself as complementary to the packed calendar of official or semi-official festivities. Between 1637 and the end of the century, twelve theatres were founded, devoted at least periodically to melodrama only. These theatres and their repertoire radically altered the social function of music and its performance, leading to its evolution from a widespread activity into a closed and regulated system. The birth of public theatres involved private individuals, or in any case the owners of residential palazzi, reshaping their role as promoters of festivities and performances staged in domestic spaces. Giovanni Morelli illustrated this process in a masterly essay, underscoring how the state, while not an active participant, exploited the opera season for the purpose of self-celebration.[17] The state thus gained 'at zero cost' a strong attraction in the eyes of foreign visitors, ambassadors and diplomats. The performance characteristics of this theatre-form were distinctive in that it could easily be represented as a synesthetic assemblage of artistic 'wonders', both visual and auditory, simultaneously produced in different strategic venues throughout typical Venetian nights. The fact that Venetian melodrama may also be read as a celebration of the greatness of the Serenissima Repubblica was stressed by Ellen Rosand in her studies of Claudio Monteverdi's last operas, associated with the celebrated achievements of the set designer Giacomo Torelli among others.[18] Indeed, instrumental music and singing gradually lost importance in the face of the sheer spectacle offered by set design and theatrical machinery.

The introduction of paid performance demanded a reaction on the part of those who were accustomed to promote a culture of theatre and music in their own homes. One can indeed observe in seventeenth-century baroque Venice a kind of reversal of trends with respect to the late Renaissance. During the Renaissance and early Baroque periods, a specific event (a wedding or the arrival of an important visitor) occasioned a theatrical performance, addressed to a select audience. In this respect, Venice remained in line with the culture of European courts. In the seventeenth century, however, the calendar of theatrical performances dictated the choice of dates for the celebration of a given event. Foreigners, for example, often planned their travels on the basis of the opera season.

There are numerous witnesses to the changes described above. On the occasion of the wedding between Lorenzo Giustinian and Giustina Mocenigo in 1630, a

[17] Giovanni Morelli, 'La musica', in Gino Benzoni and Gaetano Cozzi (eds), *Storia di Venezia. Dalle origini alla caduta della Serenissima, VII. La Venezia barocca* (Rome: Treccani, 2007), pp. 239–305.

[18] Ellen Rosand, *Monteverdi's Last Operas: A Venetian Trilogy* (Berkeley, CA and Los Angeles: University of California Press, 2007), pp. 12–17.

legendary performance of Monteverdi's *The Rape of Proserpine*, with a libretto by Giulio Strozzi, was staged in the palazzo of the Mocenigo family in calle delle Rasse, an event that proved a culmination and, at the same time, a final expression of a world in decline:

> *Con l'occasione del maridar di D . . . sua figliola in ser Lorenzo Giustinian fu di ser Girolamo fece ser Girolamo Mocenigo fu di ser Andrea un solennissimo & estraordinario banchetto a parenti & amici con apparato veramente regio, dando nel disnare che fece carne & pesce & freddi & caldi tutto ciò che si potea dare . . . doppo il qual desinare, essendosi ballato sino le 24 hore, fece poi la sera con le torcie recitar & rappresentar in musica (cosa non più veduta simile) il rapto di Proserpina con voci & instrumenti perfettissimi, con apparitioni aeree, mutationi di scene & altro, con stupore & meraviglia di tutti gli astanti. Si fece il banchetto nella casa della sua habitazione & ragione in calle delle Rasse solaro di sotto & in quello di sopra di ragione di ca' Gritto fu rappresentata la favola che fu inventione del s[igno]r Giulio Strozzi fiorentino, persona virtuosa habitante di questa città & la musica fu opera del Monteverde Maestro ducale famoso & v'intervennero li duchi di Roan & Candoles francesi con singolar soddisfattione & egual amministratione ancora.*
>
> [Ser Girolamo Mocenigo, son of ser Andrea, on the occasion of the wedding of his daughter D . . . with ser Lorenzo Giustinian, son of the late ser Girolamo, held a most solemn & extraordinary banquet for his family and friends, in a setting worthy of a king, offering for dinner every possible meat & fish & cold & hot dishes . . . After dinner, having danced until midnight, he presented a torch-lit stage and musical performance (such as was never seen before) of *The Rape of Proserpine*, with the most perfect voices and instruments, aerial shows, changes of scenes and other devices, to the awe and amazement of all the guests. The banquet was held in his residence & property on the first floor in calle delle Rasse, while the second floor, the property of ca' Gritto, hosted the performance of a tale written by the celebrated Florentine Giulio Strozzi, who resides in this city, with music composed by the famous ducal maestro Monteverde. The Dukes of Roan and Candoles assisted with singular pleasure.][19]

The celebration of a wedding offered an opportunity to display the prestige of the family, through theatre as well as other means, while the presence of foreign guests ensured the quality and spectacular nature of the event. A performance such as *The Rape of Proserpine* was certainly not the rule during wedding celebrations,

[19] Biblioteca Nazionale Marciana, Venice (BNMVe), ms. it. Cl. VII 2492 (= 10145), *Diari di Girolamo Priuli*. See Luca Zoppelli, 'Il rapto perfettissimo. Un'inedita testimonianza sulla Proserpina di Monteverdi', *Rassegna Veneta di Studi Musicali*, 2–3 (1986–87), 343–5.

but represented rather a particularly significant moment in the history of the birth of melodrama. It is also indicative of how Venetian palazzi were conceived as theatrical spaces.

It remains true that the growth of 'public' theatres gradually eliminated the custom of staging performances in private residences unable to compete with the technical devices available in specialised venues. This does not mean that palazzi lost their theatrical features, but rather that these were conveyed through different modalities and expressive forms. While we know of no performance staged inside a palazzo in the second half of the century, it is possible to point to the rather exceptional case represented by the garden theatre of the Roman prince Altieri, which occupies an intermediate position between public theatre and private staging, and whose very existence seems to be due to the fact that its promoter was a 'foreigner'. Gaspare Altieri became a Venetian nobleman in 1670, but his social behaviour remained that of a Roman outsider. To this day, few studies have appeared of performances staged in the garden of the palazzo on Canal Regio. It seems certain that these were not in fact part of an actual season, but were *impromptu* productions staged for particular occasions such as the wedding of Gaspare's son Emilio and Costanza Chigi in 1697.[20] Meanwhile, most Venetian noblemen had transferred such initiatives to their mainland residences. In Piazzola sul Brenta, Marco Contarini, a virtually unknown figure in the theatrical life of the city, equipped his villa with a series of structures dedicated to theatre and music. In Contarini's case, chronicle accounts describe a famous series of indoor and outdoor spectacles held at the villa on the occasion of the visit of the duke of Brunswick in 1685.[21]

We are indebted to Cristoforo Ivanovich, canon of St Mark's Basilica, for what we might call the first history of musical theatre in Venice. This is not the place to discuss his text, published in 1681 and titled *Minerva al tavolino*, or to verify the accuracy of the information it provides on the world of melodrama. Rather it is pertinent to highlight that the dialectical and complementary relationship between public and private, theatre and palace, performance and festivity, becomes the cornerstone of his thinking. In particular, Ivanovich takes us through the codes of behaviour of the Venetian patrician class, and through the protocols regulating the organisation of events. The main occasions integrating the palazzo into a wider framework of performance and transforming it from a private space into a public venue were, once again, weddings. Referring to this phenomenon, Ivanovich

---

[20] Franco Mancini, Maria Teresa Muraro and Elena Povoledo, *I teatri del Veneto. Venezia*, 2 vols (Venice: Corbo e Fiore, 1995), vol. 1, *Teatri effimeri e nobili imprenditori*, pp. 422–8.

[21] Musical activity in Piazzola started in 1679. Marinella Laini, *Vita musicale a Venezia durante la Repubblica. Istituzioni e mecenatismo* (Venice: Marsilio, 2001), p. 148. The extraordinary event of 1685 is commemorated in a volume by Francesco Maria Piccioli, *Il Vaticinio della Fortuna. Musicali Acclamationi consacrati . . .* (Piazzola: Loco delle Vergini, 1685).

significantly observes that patricians chose to celebrate their nuptials during carnival, in other words during the high point of the theatre season in the Venetian calendar, thus attracting the greatest number of foreign visitors. However, there is another fact which is just as significant: that the author refers to weddings within a text which is intended as a history of theatre.

On these occasions, patricians would throw open the doors of their palazzi in an almost unrestricted fashion. Whereas the public paid to attend theatre, the spectacle of a wedding was free and allowed one to enter a world, that of the family palazzo, which by definition was otherwise closed.[22] Chronicles and the eye-witness accounts of travellers confirm at length how the palazzo was used on these occasions, while archival documents illustrate the lengthy preparations required to provide the palazzo with appropriate decoration, or even at times with adequate architectural adaptation.

The palazzo, which no longer needed to prove its suitability as a theatre venue, could return to being part of the wider mosaic of Venice as a scenic space, as described above. In the eyes of foreign visitors, the palazzo was seen as a place characterised by perfect architectural configuration. The notable arrangement intended to promote free circulation within a venue, a variety of functions and the celebration of the greatness of a family are described, for instance, in a 1680 text by the Frenchman Limojon de Saint Didier who, in the 1670s, had been secretary to the French Embassy in Venice. Limojon links his description of private residences with wedding celebrations, precisely because these are the public occasions *par excellence* of patrician houses:

> *Comme il est necessaire de connoitre en quelque facon la disposition des maisons, je diray que presque toutes les maisons sont baties d'une mesme manière. L'on entre ordinairement dans un long portique, dont les murailles sont bien blanchies, et qui n'est paré que de quelques bancs de bois blanc à dossiers tout unis; mais peints de diverses couleurs, avec des rateliers d'un coté et d'autre où l'on voit des piques et des hallebardes, plutost pour servir d'ornement que de deffence; l'escalier conduit dans un autre portique au dessus du premier, et qui est de toute la longueur de la maison en forme de galerie vitrée par les deux bouts, et qui communique à droite et à gauche dans toutes les chambres, lesquelles ayant leur degagement l'une dans l'autre, donnent le moyen de faire de plain-pied le tour de toute la maison en diverses manieres. Les Gentils hommes qui sont riches, se plaisent à la magnificence des meubles, on y en voit de velours à fond d'or, d'autres en broderie, avec les franges et crépines d'or, quantité de belles tables, et de miroirs de grands prix, mais on ne voit aucun lit dans les chambres de ce premier étage, pour laisser plus d'espace à la foule épouventable qu'il y a dans ces occasions.*

[22] As is indicated, for instance, by the laws setting out the prohibition of access for foreigners.

> [Since it is necessary to have some notion of the arrangement of the houses, I shall mention that most of them are built in the same fashion. People usually enter through a long portico with expertly whitewashed walls, whose sole decorations are several white-wood benches of similar design, painted in a variety of colours and equipped with racks on both sides containing pikes and halberds whose function is more decorative than military. The staircase leads to a second portico above the first one, covering the whole length of the building in the shape of a gallery glazed at both ends and communicating with all the rooms to its left and right. And as all of these rooms also communicate with one another, it is possible to go around the house by different paths. Rich noblemen appreciate luxurious furniture, and their houses boast gilded velvets, embroideries with golden fringes and trimmings, many beautiful tables and precious mirrors, but no beds are to be seen in the rooms on the first floor, so as to allow more space for the overwhelming crowd showing up on these occasions.][23]

Limojon goes on to describe the wedding ceremony and how the dance, led by the bride, turned into a continuous movement through all the rooms of the *piano nobile*. During the two-day celebration, the residents of the palazzo would display all their wealth. Although the *portego* remained the central element of the architectural organism, from a functional viewpoint it was no longer entirely autonomous, but rather complementary to the communicating rooms on both sides of it.

Accounts such as that by Limojon de Saint Didier are important in allowing us to catch a glimpse of life inside patrician residences. There are no systematic studies dealing with the function of spaces in seventeenth-century Venetian palazzi, and the lack of a classic historical account such as that provided by Patricia Fortini Brown with regard to the sixteenth century, is keenly felt.[24]

We can cautiously assume in a specific case that one of the *piani nobili* was devoted to public or semi-public functions, while the second, where access was more limited and selective, was given over to cultural, educational and archival activities. An excellent example of such an arrangement is Palazzo Basadonna in San Trovaso, which can be shown to have had a library and painting gallery on the upper floor in addition to its lower-floor, more public, spaces. Palazzo Grimani in San Marcuola and Palazzo Tassis in San Canciano present a reverse arrangement, with libraries and galleries located, by contrast, on the *piano nobile*.[25]

It may in fact be argued that a development as significant as the emergence of public theatre played an important role in changing the self-celebratory practices of the

---

[23] Alexandre-Toussaint Limojon de Saint Didier, *La Ville et la République de Venise* (Paris: Guillaume de Luyne, 1680), p. 468.

[24] Patricia Fortini Brown, *Private Lives in Renaissance Venice: Art, Architecture and the Family* (New Haven, CT and London: Yale University Press, 2004).

[25] Dorit Raines, 'La biblioteca-museo patrizia e il suo capitale sociale: modelli illuministici veneziani e l'imitazione dei nuovi aggregati', in Caterina Furlan and Giuseppe Pavanello (eds), *Arte, storia, cultura e musica in Friuli nell'età di Tiepolo* (Udine: Forum, 1998), pp. 63–84.

patrician class. This was a long process, interwoven and in parallel with a series of other factors such as the War of Candia and one of its most spectacular consequences, the oft-cited launch of the *Libro d'Oro*, which granted entrance into the patrician class to numerous rich aristocratic families from the mainland and to the city's bourgeoisie.

The family palazzo, having lost – with the emergence of public theatres – the option of functioning as a temporary theatre, eventually modernised and equipped itself with spaces adapted to celebrations which became increasingly family-focused and distinct from the self-advertisement of the state. Such a process was marked by sequential stages featuring multiple aspects such as schools, galleries, libraries and *cameroni*, all of which entered into a new dialogue with the *portego* until, in Palazzo Zenobio, the *portego* emerged as a two-storey-high transverse hall. Within the general configuration of the palazzo, Ca' Zenobio's hall assumes, by its shape and function, a central position which the *portego* never enjoyed. The hall becomes the ultimate goal of an itinerary, rendering obsolete the circular movement described by Limojon de Saint-Didier. On a vertical plan, it abolishes the interplay between floors, as there is no longer space for a second *piano nobile* functioning as complementary to the first.

The goal of preserving the characteristic distribution of a Venetian palazzo while becoming equipped with a modern 'Festivities Hall' could be achieved by moving the Hall into an autonomous building separate from the palazzo, a solution which gradually emerged from the middle of the century, perhaps rooted in the experience of the *casino nobile*. In Palazzo Tron, the venue designated for festivities is confined to an external building in the garden, once again designed by Antonio Gaspari and decorated in 1701 with frescos by Louis Dorigny, or so it may be supposed, and elements of architectural *trompe-l'œil*.[26] Such dislocation of the space designated for celebrations and receptions was relatively widespread at the turn of the century and is inscribed, like the new developments in scenographic staircases, in a period of intense experimentation whose goal was to adapt family residences to their functional or official requirements. It also allows preservation of the integrity of the *portego* and tends to feature new decorative systems and contents. Many of these structures annexed to the property were lost, such as that of Ca' da Lezze in Misercordia, or that of Palazzo Gradenigo in rio Manin. However, on the eve of the construction of Palazzo Zenobio, the now renovated *casino* of Ca' Zane in S. Stin plainly represents the significant endpoint of this evolution. On the rear part of the garden, and overlooking rio Manin, Antonio Gaspari designed a building consisting of a double-height room surrounded by a balcony, a well-established typology for the central halls of villas.[27]

---

[26] The building was demolished in the nineteenth century. For documentary evidence, see Favilla and Rugolo, 'Dorigny e Venezia', pp. 50–3.

[27] Massimo Favilla and Ruggero Rugolo, 'Palazzetto Zane', in Filippo Pedrocco (ed.), *Gli affreschi nei palazzi e nelle ville venete* (Schio: Sassi, 2008), pp. 178–83; also for the ceiling painted by Sebastiano Ricci. For the Venetian casinos see: Martina Frank, 'The Venetian Casino: Form and Function', in Sylva Dobalova & Ivan P. Muchka (eds.), Looking for Leisure. Court Residences and their Satellites 1400–1700 (Prague: Artefactum, 2017), 231–251.

The 'originality' of Ca' Zenobio

Finally, it may be pertinent to emphasise once more an element that might already be obvious from the last examples discussed, that is Ca' Zenobio's eccentric position in this phase. Finding a similar development, albeit in a completely different form, would entail waiting until the *Magnifica sala* of Palazzo Dolfin in S. Pantalon, set up in an architectural context defined by Domenico Rossi, with frescos painted between 1711 and 1715 by Nicolò Bambini and the quadraturists Antonio Felice Ferrari and Gerolamo Mengozzi Colonna (see Plates 11 and 12).[28] The solution adopted in this case appears as a synthesis between the music room of Palazzo Zenobio and independent, displaced salons. The room, which stretches across the whole width of the palazzo, does not replace the *portego*, and any ambiguity as to its connection with other spaces in the palazzo has been avoided. All elements that would lead to its being perceived as the centre of the palazzo are missing and only its location on the top floor suggests at least an unavoidable path through a hall and up a staircase. Structural changes have deeply altered the internal distribution and no historical documentation can be constructed, no hypothesis about the connection between the room and other spaces of the residence. In its present configuration, the prominence of its massive space suggests that in this case the room itself *is* the palazzo. Palazzo Dolfin had been one of the venues chosen for the staging of festivities to honour the Danish king, Frederic IV, who paid a private visit to Venice between the end of 1708 and February 1709. Chronicles tell how – as the palazzo had no adequate space for dancing – it was decided that a temporary hall should be built in the garden, between the two wings of the building.[29] Re-ordering of the palazzo shortly thereafter seems aimed at commemorating this event by making a temporary installation permanent, and at redesigning a palazzo without an adequate space for theatrical display.

Once more, the palazzo had been called on to respond to the competition of the theatre. In Frederic's honour, the Grimani theatre in San Giovanni Crisostomo had promoted the staging of an opera and at the end of the performance the king had been offered a sumptuous dinner in a nearby location. After dinner the guests went back to the theatre, which had meanwhile been turned into a ball-room.[30] At that

---

[28] Elena Bassi, *Architettura dei sei e settecento a Venezia* (Naples: Edizioni scientifiche italiane, 1962), p. 213. Adriano Mariuz, 'La Magnifica Sala di Palazzo Dolfin a Venezia: Gli affreschi di Nicolò Bambini e Antonio Felice Ferrari', *Arte Veneta*, 35 (1981), 182–6. The correct dating of the ceiling fresco appears first in Valentina Conticelli, 'Ca' Dolfin a San Pantalon: Precisazioni sulla committenza e sul programma iconografico della Magnifica Sala', in Lionello Puppi (ed.), *Giambattista Tiepolo nel terzo centenario della nascita* (Padua: Il Poligrafo, 1998), pp. 231–8.

[29] There are several manuscripts which describe the visit of the king. I used a copy in BMCVe, Codice Cicogna 3283. See also Renier Michiel, *Origine delle feste*, pp. 106–7; Conticelli, 'Ca' Dolfin a San Pantalon', pp. 231–2.

[30] Michiel, *Origine delle feste*, p. 108.

point, what previously might have seemed one of Venice's many public theatres returned to functioning as the 'Festivities Hall' of the Grimani family, a role given emphasis by the huge coat of family arms on the stage.

Abbreviations

ASVe – Archivio di Stato di Venezia
BMCVe – Biblioteca del Museo Correr, Venice
BNMVe – Biblioteca Nazionale Marciana, Venice

Bibliography

Printed primary sources

Carlevarijs, Luca, *Le fabbriche e vedute di Venetia disegnate, poste in prospettiva et intagliate* (Venice: Finazzi, 1703).
Ivanovich, Cristoforo, *Minerva al tavolino* (Venice: Nicolò Pezzana, 1681).
Limojon de Saint Didier, Alexandre-Toussaint, *La Ville et la République de Venise* (Paris: Guillaume de Luyne, 1680).
Piccioli, Francesco Maria, *Il Vaticinio della Fortuna. Musicali Acclamationi consacrati* . . . (Piazzola: Loco delle Vergini, 1685).
Sansovino, Francesco, *Venetia città nobilissima et singolare* (Venice: Sansovino, 1581).

Secondary sources

Aikema, Bernard, 'Il famoso Abbondio: Abbondio Stazio e la decorazione a stucco dei palazzi veneziani, circa 1685–1750', *Saggi e memorie di storia dell'arte*, 21 (1997), 85–122.
Bassi, Elena, *Architettura dei sei e settecento a Venezia* (Naples: Edizioni scientifiche italiane, 1962).
Bassi, Elena, 'Episodi dell'architettura veneta nell'opera di Antonio Gaspari', *Saggi e memorie di storia dell'arte*, 3 (1963), 55–108.
Bassi, Elena, *Palazzi di Venezia: Admiranda Urbis Venetiae* (Venice: Stamperia di Venezia Editrice, 1976).
Borgomainerio, Alessandro, 'Due disegni inediti di Baldassare Longhena per Ca' Pesaro', *Arte Veneta*, 66 (2010), 211–15.
Bellavitis, Giorgio, 'Note sul restauro di Palazzo Corner della Regina e sull'uso temporaneo del pianoterra come spazio espositivo', in *La Biennale di Venezia Annuario 1976* (Venice: La Biennale di Venezia, 1976), pp. 897–908.
Casini, Matteo, *I gesti del Principe. La festa politica a Firenze e Venezia in età rinascimentale* (Venice: Marsilio, 1996).

Conticelli, Valentina, 'Ca' Dolfin a San Pantalon: Precisazioni sulla committenza e sul programma iconografico della Magnifica Sala', in Lionello Puppi (ed.), *Giambattista Tiepolo nel terzo centenario della nascita* (Padua: Il Poligrafo, 1998), pp. 231–8.

De Grassi, Massimo, 'Filippo Parodi, Pietro Roncaioli e lo stucco tardobarocco a Venezia', *Arte Veneta*, 54 (1999), 55–61.

Favilla, Massimo and Ruggero Rugolo, 'Dorigny e Venezia: Da Ca' Tron a Ca' Zenobio e ritorno', in Giorgio Marini and Paola Marini (eds), *Louis Dorigny (1654–1742): Un pittore della corte francese a Verona* (Venice: Marsilio, 2003), pp. 37–59.

Favilla, Massimo and Ruggero Rugolo, 'La verità sul caso Gaspari', *Studi Veneziani*, 45 (2003), 243–63.

Favilla, Massimo and Ruggero Rugolo, 'Progetti di Antonio Gaspari, architetto della Venezia barocca', *Atti dell'Istituto Veneto di Scienze, Lettere ed Arti, classe di scienze morali, lettere ed arti*, 165 (2006–2007), 139–91.

Favilla, Massimo and Ruggero Rugolo, 'Louis Dorigny. Salone e andito al piano nobile (1695–1698 circa). Venezia Ca' Zenobio', in Filippo Pedrocco (ed.), *Gli affreschi nei palazzi e nelle ville venete* (Schio: Sassi, 2008), pp. 162–71.

Favilla, Massimo and Ruggero Rugolo, 'Palazzetto Zane', in Filippo Pedrocco (ed.), *Gli affreschi nei palazzi e nelle ville venete* (Schio: Sassi, 2008), pp. 178–83.

Fontana, Vincenzo, 'Dal 'portego' al salone', in Lionello Puppi (ed.), *Giambattista Tiepolo nel terzo centenario della nascita* (Padua: Il Poligrafo, 1998), pp. 115–24.

Fontana, Vincenzo, 'Scaloni e sale da musica, alcove e ridotti: il rinnovamento dei palazzi veneziani', in Marcello Fagiolo (ed.), *Atlante tematico del barocco in Italia. Residenze nobiliari. Italia settentrionale* (Rome: De Luca, 2009), pp. 251–74.

Fortini Brown, Patricia, *Private Lives in Renaissance Venice: Art, Architecture and the Family* (New Haven, CT and London: Yale University Press, 2004).

Frank, Martina, 'Zu einer kaum bekannten Vita des Ludovico Dorigny', *Wiener Jahrbuch fur Kunstgeschichte*, 40 (1987), 103–7.

Frank, Martina, 'Riflessioni sul Longhena', *Storia dell'arte*, 64 (1988), 241–7.

Frank, Martina, 'Committenza pubblica e privata', in Augusto Roca De Amicis (ed.), *Storia dell'architettura nel Veneto. Il Seicento* (Venice: Marsilio, 2008), pp. 8–12.

Frank, Martina, 'Appunti su villa da Lezze', in Martina Frank (ed.), *Da Longhena a Selva. Un'idea di Venezia a dieci anni dalla scomparsa di Elena Bassi* (Bologna: Archetipo Libri, 2011), pp. 111–22.

Martina Frank, 'The Venetian Casino: Form and Function', in Sylva Dobalova & Ivan P. Muchka (eds.), Looking for Leisure. Court Residences and their Satellites 1400–1700 (Prague: Artefactum, 2017), 231–251.

Glixon, Jonathan E. and Beth L. Glixon, *Inventing the Bussiness of Opera: The Impresario and His World in Seventeenth Century Venice* (New York: Oxford University Press, 2006).

Guidarelli, Gianmario, 'L'architettura civile', in Augusto Roca De Amicis (ed.), *Storia dell'architettura nel Veneto. Il Seicento* (Venice: Marsilio, 2008), pp. 224–47.

Hopkins, Andrew, *Baldassare Longhena and Venetian Baroque Architecture* (New Haven, CT and London: Yale University Press, 2012).

Laini, Marinella, *Vita musicale a Venezia durante la Repubblica: Istituzioni e mecenatismo* (Venice: Marsilio, 2001).

Mancini, Franco, Maria Teresa Muraro and Elena Povoledo, *I teatri del Veneto: Venezia*, 2 vols (Venice: Corbo e Fiore, 1995).

Mariuz, Adriano, 'La Magnifica Sala di Palazzo Dolfin a Venezia: Gli affreschi di Nicolò Bambini e Antonio Felice Ferrari', *Arte Veneta*, 35 (1981), 182–6.

Mariuz, Adriano and Giuseppe Pavanello, 'La chiesetta di Bernardo Nave a Cittadella', *Arte Veneta*, 50 (1997), 68–85.

Morelli, Giovanni, 'La musica', in Gino Benzoni and Gaetano Cozzi (eds), *Storia di Venezia. Dalle origini alla caduta della Serenissima, VII. La Venezia barocca* (Rome: Treccani, 2007), pp. 239–305.

Pasian, Alessio, 'Per un catalogo di Louis Dorigny', *Arte in Friuli Arte a Trieste*, 18–19 (1999), 9–38.

Raines, Dorit, 'La biblioteca-museo patrizia e il suo capitale sociale: modelli illuministici veneziani e l'imitazione dei nuovi aggregati', in Caterina Furlan and Giuseppe Pavanello (eds), *Arte, storia, cultura e musica in Friuli nell'età di Tiepolo* (Udine: Forum, 1998), pp. 63–84.

Raines, Dorit, *L'invention du mythe aristocratique. L'image de soi du patriciat vénitien au temps de la Sérénissime*, 2 vols (Venice: Istituto veneto di scienze, lettere ed arti, 2006).

Renier Michiel, Giustina, *Origine delle feste veneziane*, 2 vols (Milan: Editori degli annuali delle scienze e dell'industria, 1829).

Rosand, Ellen, *Monteverdi's Last Operas: A Venetian Trilogy* (Berkeley, CA and Los Angeles, CA: University of California Press, 2007).

Sabbadini, Roberto, *L'acquisto della tradizione: Aristocrazia e nuova nobilità a Venezia* (Udine: Gaspari editore, 1995).

Tamassia Mazzarotto, Bianca, *Le feste veneziane: i giochi popolari, le cerimonie religiose e di governo* (Florence: Sansoni, 1961).

Urban, Lina, *Processioni e feste dogali. Venetia est mundus* (Vicenza: Neri Pozza, 1998).

Zoppelli, Luca, 'I rapto perfettissimo. Un'inedita testimonianza sulla Proserpina di Monteverdi', *Rassegna Veneta di Studi Musicali*, 2–3 (1986–87), 343–5.

Chapter 7

Contested ideals

Designing and making temporary structures for the *Entrée* of Louis XIV into Paris, August 1660

Elaine Tierney[1]

Early modern festival was a form of rhetorical design. Studies have explored how narrative, symbolism and allegory, location and material splendour were all harnessed to produce performances that met the needs of the political moment. Rituals, ceremonies and performances were also translated into enduring objects, which gave permanent form to the rhetorical ideals invested in specific occasions. Most notably, scholars have made extensive use of the presentational texts and visual images employed to commemorate and disseminate events. These studies have considered the complex relationships between performance and record, as well as the crucial functions performed by texts, both in explaining the recondite symbolism of occasions and conveying their political agendas to elite audiences at home and further afield.[2] What follows is intended as a suggestive case study of one event, Louis XIV's *entrée* into Paris in August 1660. While iconographical readings of festival are vital, a methodological focus on iconography has resulted in omissions from the subject's treatment, which can be remedied through the application of an object and process-focussed approach.[3] It is not my intention,

---

[1] Many thanks to Jasmine Kilburn-Toppin, Jack Rollo, Christina Petrie and Angela McShane and the editors for commenting on versions of this text; all subsequent errors are entirely my own.

[2] These studies are too numerous to mention here, but I have found the work of Helen Watanabe-O'Kelly especially useful: 'Early Modern Court Festivals: Politics and Performance, Event and Record', in J.R. Mulryne and Elizabeth Goldring (eds), *Court Festivals of the European Renaissance: Art, Politics and Performance* (Aldershot and Burlington, VT: Ashgate, 2002), pp. 15–25; Helen Watanabe O'Kelly, 'The Early Modern Festival Book: Function and Form', in J.R. Mulryne, Helen Watanabe-O'Kelly and Margaret Shewring (eds), *Europa Triumphans: Court and Civic Festival in Early Modern Europe*, 2 vols (Aldershot and Burlington, VT: Ashgate, 2004), vol. 1, pp. 3–17.

[3] Although not within its chronology or geographical scope, the present work is sympathetic to the aims of the following: Eric Monin, 'The Construction of Fantasy: Ephemeral Structures and Urban Celebrations in France During the Eighteenth Century', in Santiago Huerta (ed.), *Proceedings of the First International Congress on Construction History*, Madrid, 20–24 January 2003, (Madrid: Instituto Juan de Herrera, 2003), pp. 1475–87; 'The

therefore, to tease out nuance or to reframe the *entrée*'s complex symbolism and allegory. Instead, using the design and construction of two types of temporary structures made for the event, I will explore how urban festival marked both the conjuncture and disjuncture between a rhetorical ideal and the challenges inherent in its practical realisation.

The first type of structure, triumphal or occasional architecture, has received a substantial amount of scholarly attention elsewhere, reflecting the monumentality and scale of the structures, as well as the ideological and iconographical information inscribed on them.[4] By contrast, the second has remained much more elusive. This relates to the viewing platforms, 'scaffolds' in English and '*échafauds*' in French, which permitted some spectators an elevated view of proceedings.[5] Gabriel Ladame's single-sheet engraving (see Figure 7.1) provides a rare view of *échafauds* in situ, but more typically this type of temporary addition to the urban landscape was removed from the visual images and textual descriptions intended to advertise, explicate or commemorate events.

Together, triumphal architecture and viewing platforms transformed Paris, both physically and materially, to make it a more suitable site for celebration. The following discussion focuses on the preparations before the *entrée* in order to demonstrate the wider spatial and temporal impact of events on this scale. Issues of design, construction and project management will be used to highlight the range of social, cultural and political ideals invested in the occasion. More importantly, Paris is conceptualised, not as the ideal celebratory city found in festival literature and presentational images – the sources most often consulted in analyses of festival – but as an early modern metropolis, with other distinct, sometimes contested, uses and identities. In combination, these concerns demonstrate the extent to which planning and realising events required collaboration and negotiation and, on occasion, resulted in disorder and chaos.

Speculative Challenges of Festival Architecture in Eighteenth-Century France', in Sarah Bonnemaison and Christine Macy (eds), *Festival Architecture* (London and New York: Routledge, 2008), pp. 155–80; Margit Thøfner, *A Common Art: Ceremonial in Antwerp and Brussels During and After the Dutch Revolt* (Zwolle: Waanders, 2007), pp. 59–77.

[4] Although not an exhaustive list, the following have informed this discussion: J. D. Loach, 'Pageant and Festival Arts', *Grove Art Online. Oxford Art Online*, www.oxfordartonline.com/subscriber/article/grove/art/T064588 [Accessed 23 September 2013]; Margaret M. McGowan, 'The Renaissance Triumph and Its Classical Heritage', in Mulryne and Goldring, *Court Festivals of the European Renaissance*, pp. 26–47; Christine Stevenson, 'Occasional Architecture in Seventeenth-Century London', *Architectural History*, 49 (2006), 35–74; Christine Stevenson, *The City and the King. Architecture and Politics in Restoration London* (New Haven, CT and London: Yale University Press, 2013), pp. 63–118.

[5] The scaffolding built for festival is not exceptional: all forms of early modern scaffolding have received little attention from scholars, with treatments of the subject lurking on the peripheries of other histories, including those of building and construction, judicial punishment, horseracing and hunting.

Figure 7.1 Gabriel Ladame, *La Magnifique Entrée du Roy et de la Royne dans leur bonne Ville de Paris, le 26 aoust 1660* (1660), engraving and etching on paper (© Bibliothèque nationale de France, Paris, département des Estampes et de la photographie, Hennin: 3977)

'No preparations necessary': where were design and making in presentational accounts of Louis's *entrée*?

Politically and historically, Louis's *entrée* in August 1660 was a headline event. It was one of a suite of occasions that marked peace with Spain after 24 years of devastating war. Ratification of the Treaty of Pyrenees (1659) was followed by Louis's marriage to Maria-Teresa, daughter of the Spanish king, Felipe IV.[6] This, in turn, was followed by two months of progresses across south and central France.[7] Traditionally, the royal entry into Paris had come immediately after the new king's coronation; although Louis XIV had been crowned in Reims in June 1654, his *entrée* had been delayed because of the upheaval that characterised the early part of his reign and, more pertinently, Paris's perceived role in it.[8] The elaborate *entrée* in 1660 has, in fact, been described as Louis's public act of forgiveness, with the city spending an estimated 100,000 lire in what Guy Patin labelled an 'expiation' for its role in the Fronde.[9]

The relationship between the *entrée*'s political moment, its iconographical design and lavish production values has, to some extent, been taken for granted. Previous studies have explained the event's conceptual execution as a presentation of the young king, then on the cusp of his majority, as Louis '*le Donneur de Paix*': a theme that made absolute sense in the context of recent history.[10]

---

[6] Marriage by proxy in 1659 was formalised by a religious service on 9 June 1660 (NS), when Louis wed Maria-Teresa in the French port of Saint-Jean-de-Luz, close to the Spanish border. Abby E. Zanger, *Scenes From the Marriage of Louis XIV. Nuptial Fictions and the Making of Absolute Power* (Stanford, CA: Stanford University Press, 1997), pp. 1–2.

[7] Hubert Delpont, *Parade pour une Infante: Le périple nuptial de Louis XIV à travers le Midi de la France, 1659–1660* (Bouloc: Editions d'Albret, 2007), *passim*, but especially pp. 9–11; Christoph Daniel Frank, *The Mechanics of Triumph: Public Ceremony and Civic Pageantry Under Louis XIV* (PhD dissertation, Warburg Institute, University of London, 1993), pp. 90–9.

[8] Lawrence M. Bryant, *The King and the City in the Parisian Royal Entry* (Geneva: Droz, 1986), pp. 18–19.

[9] All amounts of money cited in this discussion are in *livres tournois* unless otherwise specified. Frank, *The Mechanics of Triumph*, pp. 100–1; Chantal Grell, 'The Financing and Material Organisation of Court Festivals Under Louis XIV', in *Court Festivals of the European Renaissance*, pp. 118–33, 120–1; Peter Burke, *The Fabrication of Louis XIV* (New Haven, CT and London: Yale University Press, 1992), p. 13. Further details of the *entrée's* budget can be found in minutes from a preliminary meeting held by the event's organising committee on 21 May 1660; Frank describes a second meeting that saw more funds allocated to the event at the beginning of July. Archive nationales, Paris, H2.1815, fols. 229v–232r; Frank, *The Mechanics of Triumph*, p. 101.

[10] See, for example: Lawrence M. Bryant, 'The Decline of the Entry Ceremony', in *The King and the City*, pp. 207–24, 208–13; Lawrence M. Bryant, 'From Communal Ritual to Royal Spectacle: Some Observations on the Staging of Royal Entries (1450–1600)', in *Ritual, Ceremony and the Changing Monarchy in France*, pp. 243–81, 263; Frank, *The Mechanics of Triumph*, pp. 112–18, 121–4, 125–9, 130–1; Möseneder, *Zeremoniell und monumentale Poesie*, *passim*, but especially pp. 17–21, 81–145.

Historiographical emphasis on the politicised, as opposed to practical, dimensions of the design reflected the concerns of contemporary printed descriptions and visual representations of the occasion, which devoted almost all their attention to the performance of the ceremony, or to detailed accounts of its completed decorative features. *L'Entrée Triomphante de Levrs Maiestez. . .*, usually attributed to Jean Tronçon, was the event's official chronicle and almost two years in the making.[11] And yet, for a volume so preoccupied with things, with a substantial section titled '*Preparatifs dans la Ville de Paris, pour la reception de leurs Maiestez*', ('Preparations in the city of Paris for the reception of their Majesties') very little of its copious text provided any insight into how the *entrée* was actually made.[12]

The qualities associated with processes of designing and making, such as diligence in preparation and virtuoso craftsmanship, were instead used rhetorically to demonstrate Paris's veneration of Louis and his new bride. The royal couple's short stay before the *entrée* in Vincennes, to the east of city, was framed as a reciprocal necessity as, '*La ville n'auoit pas encore peu disposer les choses qu'elle preparoit pour vn Triomphe de cette importance*' ('The city did not have things ready for a Triumph of this importance').[13] Similarly, the poet François Colletet harnessed the time taken to prepare for the *entrée*, ('*le loisir qu'il leur donne de preparer de si belles choses pour son Entrée*'), ('it gives them the leisure to prepare such beautiful things for his *Entrée*') as evidence of Louis's indulgent love of his capital city and its inhabitants, as '. . . *iamais Roy n'aima mieux ses sujets; & particulierement ceux qui composent la Ville de Paris*' ('. . . never did a king love his subjects better and, in particular, those who made up the City of Paris').[14]

---

[11] The title in full: *L'Entrée Triomphante de Levrs Maiestez Lovis XIV. Roy de France et de Navarre et Marie Theresa d'Avstriche son Epovse, dans la Ville de Paris Capitale de Levrs Royavmes, av Retour de la Signatvre de la Paix Generalle et de Levr Herevx Mariage. Enrichie de plusher Figvres, des Harangves & de Diuerse Pieces Considerables Pour l'Histoire. Le tout exactement recuielly par l'ordre de Messievrs de Ville* (Paris: Le Petit, Joly and Bilaine, 1662). Although authorship of the *entrée*'s official relation is usually solely credited to Tronçon, an attribution that can be traced to Jacques Lelong, Frank makes a partially convincing case that André Félibien, best known for his chronicles of later 'fêtes' held at Versailles, was responsible for the descriptions of the triumphal architecture. Jacques Lelong, *Bibliothèque historique de la France, contenant le catalogue des ouvrages, tant imprimés que manuscrits qui traitent de l'Histoire de ce Roïaume, ou qui y ont Rapport* (Paris: Gabriel Martin, 1719), p. 561, no. 10780; Frank, *The Mechanics of Triumph*, pp. 104–6.

[12] The exception was a short passage commenting on '*le corps solide & interieur estoit d'vne forte Charpenterie*' ('the sturdy Carpentry of the solid frame and interior', which was '*taillée & dressée par l'ordre de Sieur Cochy, Maistre de oeuvres de Charpenterie de la Ville*' ('cut and drawn on the orders of Sire Cochy, Master of Carpentry for the City'); 'Preparatifs', *L'Entrée Triomphante de Levrs Maiestez . . .*, p. 31.

[13] 'Retovr dv Roy et son seiovr a Vincennes', *L'Entrée Triomphante de leurs Maiestez . . .*, p. 9.

[14] François Colletet, *Ordre Generale et Particuliere de la Marche qvi doit estre Observee dans les trois iours consecutifs pour l'Entrée de leurs Majestez dans leur bonne Ville*

The delay was, in all probability, more than literary hyperbole. In a letter to his friend André Falconet, dated 10 August, Patin wrote of Paris's heightened state of expectation as it waited for the increasingly overdue *entrée*, speculating that the decision to stall until 26 August was political, as this was the '*pareil jour que l'on fit les barricades*' ('the same day as the barricades were made') in 1648.[15]

Material magnificence and luxury was part of the rhetoric of festival books. Descriptions of Louis's *entrée* were no exception, and the extravagant materiality of the occasion could, of course, be seen as part of Paris's attempt to repay its 'debt' for the city's role in the *Fronde*: in Colletet's telling phrase, Paris '*épuise tous le Tresors*' ('exhausts all its treasures').[16] Similarly, *L'Entrée Triomphante de Levrs Maiestez* . . . revelled in the rich material culture generated by a royal occasion on this scale, describing in sumptuous detail the event's elaborate occasional architecture; bonfires, torches and lanterns; the gorgeous clothes and jewels worn by participants and costly hangings used to decorate the façades of houses. Notably, in these descriptions the focus was explicitly on itemising and explaining the finished product rather than revealing processes of organising, designing and making.

The preoccupation with finished products was characteristic, too, of visual representations. Take, for example, Jean Marot's etching of the triumphal arch erected in the Faubourg Saint-Antoine (see Figure 7.2), an illustration from *L'Entrée Triomphante de leurs Maiestez* . . . Marot depicted the arch in glorious isolation, looking more like a permanent stone edifice than a temporary construction crafted out of canvas, plaster and wood.

---

de Paris, par Messieurs du Clergé, par Messieurs les Preuost des Marchands, Eschevins & Bourgeois de ladite Ville, Preuost de l'Isle, Chevalier & Lieutenant du Guet, & co. / Avec la description des Superbes Appareils de la Cour, & des Magnificence de la Milice Bourgeoise (Paris: Loyson, 1660), p. 3.

[15] Letter to André Falconet, 10 August 1660, *Correspondance française de Guy Patin*, ed. Loïc Capron (Paris: Bibliothèque interuniversitaire de santé, 2015), www.biusante.parisdescartes.fr/patin/?do=pg&let=0632; Letter to André Falconet, 26 August 1660, *Correspondance française de Guy Patin*, ed. Loïc Capron (Paris: Bibliothèque interuniversitaire de santé, 2015), www.biusante.parisdescartes.fr/patin/?do=pg&let=0632. Patin's vision of Paris on tenterhooks was echoed, too, in two poems by Colletet. '*Reqveste Presentée a Monsieur le Prevost des Marchands par Cent-Mil Provinciaux Ruinez, Attendez L'Entrée*' ('Request Presented to Monsieur the Prévôt des Marchands by Ten Thousand Ruined Provincials, Attending the Entrée') was framed as a humorous address from all those from across France whom had descended on Paris before the *entrée* and were rapidly running out of funds the longer it was delayed. The second, 'Sovhait des Prouinciaux pour l'entrée du Roy et de la Reyne', made a similar case but this time directed at Louis XIV and his Queen. The poems were printed together as: *Reqveste Presentée a Monsieur le Prevost des Marchands par Cent-Mil Provinciaux Ruinez, Attendez L'Entrée* (Paris: Loyson, 1660).

[16] François Colletet, *Le Triomphe de la France svr l'Entrée Royale de Levrs Maiestez dans leur Bonne Ville de Paris, Avec les Discours Heroïques sur les Vies des Roys de Frances, depuis Pharamond iusqu'à nostre Grand Monarque Lovis XIV. Ensemble les Eloges de la Reyne, de la Reyne Mere, & de son Eminence. Dedié à Messieurs les Prevost des Marchands & Eschevins de la Ville* (Paris: Loyson, 1660), p. 5.

Figure 7.2 Jean Marot, *Triumphal arch erected in the Faubourg Saint-Antoine* (1662), etching on paper (© Houghton Library, Harvard University, Typ 615.62.363)

In fact, the format of the image represents a variation on the orthographic set of plan and elevation that has informed working representations of architecture from the sixteenth century onwards.[17] Noticeably, the accompanying text provided few additional clues as to the materiality of the arch, beyond the cursory observation that its fabrication '*a esté conduit par le Sieur Melin*' ('has been managed by Sire Melin').[18] Instead, the accompanying text echoed and reinforced Marot's visual format, treating the structure in the context of the Classical architectural orders, before moving on to a detailed account of the symbolic resonances embedded in its decorative scheme.[19]

In effect, these examples embodied the notion that festival in print was 'pre-packaged', showing and telling its reader how to interpret the event being documented, as well as presenting the occasion in its best light.[20] Magnificence, material extravagance and symbolic content were rallied, here, to make Paris a more suitable site for celebration and demonstrate the city's loyalty and affection towards Louis XIV and his new bride. As part of this process, artists and writers created a permanent version of an ideal celebratory city by excising those parts of the wider urban environment that might compromise the vision. Similarly, while the superlative, highly finished objects made for the *entrée* were documented in fine-grain detail, design and making were almost entirely absent from accounts of the event. To return to a question raised earlier, what can be gained if we shift our focus from these carefully-framed accounts of the *entrée* and concentrate, instead, on sources that reveal more about the design, construction and project management involved in the practical realisation of the triumphal arches and *échafauds*?

---

[17] Eve Blau and Edward Kaufman, 'Introduction', in Eve Blau and Edward Kaufman (eds), *Architecture and Its Image: Four Centuries of Architectural Representation. Works From the Collection of the Canadian Center for Architecture* (Montreal: Canadian Center for Architecture, 1989), pp. 13–15, p. 13; Caroline van Eck, 'Verbal and Visual Abstraction: The Role of Pictorial Techniques of Representation in Renaissance Architectural Theory', in Christy Anderson (ed.), *The Built Surface. Volume 1: Architecture and the Pictoral Arts From Antiquity to the Enlightenment* (Aldershot and Burlington, VT: Ashgate, 2002), pp. 162–80. Marot was well-regarded as an architect and engraver. His two best-known volumes, often termed the *Petit Marot* (1654–1660) and *Grand Marot* (pub. 1670), were collections of engravings that celebrated the most accomplished examples of contemporary French architecture, with the emphasis on buildings in Paris. Marot also included some of his own designs for speculative projects encompassing church facades, tombs, city gates and, in the *Grand Marot*, ten plates of triumphal arches; it is unclear whether the latter were ever realised.

[18] 'Preparatifs dans la Ville de Paris pour l'Entrée de leurs Majestez', *L'Entrée Triomphante de Levrs Maiestez. . .*, p. 1.

[19] Ibid., pp. 1–4.

[20] Watanabe-O'Kelly, 'Politics and Performance, Event and Record', pp. 19–20, 22–3.

Designing and making triumphal arches for Louis XIV's *entrée*

The appearance of elaborate occasional architecture across Paris in the summer of 1660 was the most eye-catching indication that something special was about to happen. In all, seven huge temporary structures were erected along the processional route in the months before 26 August 1660. These included the five huge triumphal arches, as well as the '*trône-dias*' erected in the Place du Trône (present-day Place de la Nation) and the semi-circular amphitheatre built in Place Dauphine, which will be treated below. Although not the explicit focus of this discussion, other permanent improvements were also made to the city, illustrating the *entrée* longer-term impact: Pont Notre-Dame's decorative elements were refreshed under the supervision of Pierre Vion, while the sculptor Thomas Regnaudin received 1,000 lire to produce stone statues of Hercules and Minerva to adorn two niches in the permanent Porte Saint-Antoine.[21]

As noted, Marot's etching of the triumphal arch erected in Faubourg Saint-Antoine (see Figure 7.2) showed the structure in glorious isolation, occupying a space devoid of topographical specificity and quite unlike the busy, built-up locale suggested by other forms of evidence.[22] Quite simply, the etching avoided engagement with just how much the addition of major temporary architecture constituted imposing, sometimes inconvenient, incursions into the urban landscape. If we consider the main material properties associated with triumphal architecture, we may draw the following conclusions. Firstly, the most impressive temporary structures were built on a colossal scale and intended to inspire awe in those who saw, sat on, stood by and passed under them. For the 1660 *entrée*, the tallest structure was the arch erected in Place Dauphine (see Figure 7.3), measuring around 100 ft in height.[23]

In Colletet's hyperbolic description, this arch was so tall that '*le sommet se perd dans les nuës*' ('the peak is lost in the clouds').[24] But even the 'smaller' arches – the arch in what is today Montparnasse (see Figure 7.4) and the arch built at Pont Notre-Dame (see Figure 7.5) – reached the extraordinary height of

---

21 Archives nationales, Paris, Minutier central, LXXXVII, 579, fol. 1r (3 May 1660); H2.2012, fol. 1r (11 May 1660). See also: 'Preparatifs', *L'Entrée Triomphante de Levrs Maiestez. . .*, pp. 5–8, 11; Frank, *The Mechanics of Triumph*, pp. 114, 119–20; M. Christoph Frank, 'Les artistes de l'entrée de Louis XIV en 1660', *Bulletin de la Société de l'Histoire de l'Art français* (1989/1990), 53–74, 55–7, 58–9, 64–5, 66–7.

22 See, for example, Gabriel Pérelle's 1671 pen and ink drawing of the Bastille and Porte Saint-Antoine, which showed one of the main points of entry into the city as a bustling neighbourhood. No. FRBNF40311583, département Estampes et photographie, Bibliothèque nationale de France, Paris.

23 Archives nationales, Paris, Minutier central, LXXXVII, 579, fol.1 [r]: 16 June 1660. Frank, *The Mechanics of Triumph*, pp. 124–5.

24 Colletet, *Descriptions des Arcs de Triomphes*, p. 23.

Figure 7.3 Jean Lepautre, *Triumphal arch and amphiteatre in Place Dauphine* (1662), etching on paper (© Houghton Library, Harvard University, Typ 615.62.363)

45 ft.[25] Secondly, occasional architecture was built in canvas, wood and plaster, but painted to imitate more durable materials, such as precious metals, marble, jasper and porphyry.[26] And finally, by comparison with permanent, monumental additions to the urban landscape, temporary structures could be erected, and dismantled, relatively quickly.[27] In combination, such factors meant occasional architecture was transformative, with the ability to alter the appearance and experience of urban space in a short space of time, enhancing what architectural historian Judi Loach has described as the 'trance-like' effect of festival.[28]

In 1660, the *marchés* (contracts) drawn up between representatives of Paris's municipal elite and the personnel charged with designing the occasional architecture, offered clear evidence as to how this transformation was achieved. Where images of the triumphal arches were usually monochrome and provided only a

[25] The Faubourg Saint-Antoine arch measured approximately 50 by 60 feet, while Tortebat and Dorigny's Marché-Neuf arch was roughly 60 by 45 feet; Archives nationales, Paris, Minutier central, LXXXVII, 579, fol.1 [r]: 5 May 1660; 11 May 1660.

[26] Alice Jarrard, *Architecture as Performance in Seventeenth-Century Europe: Court Ritual in Modena, Rome and Paris* (Cambridge: Cambridge University Press, 2003), pp. 12, 24, 27; Monin, 'The Construction of Fantasy', p. 1479.

[27] Anthony Gerbino, *François Blondel: Architecture, Erudition and the Scientific Revolution* (London and New York: Routledge, 2010), pp. 71–117; Loach, 'Pageant and Festival Arts', www.oxfordartonline.com/subscriber/article/grove/art/T064588; Monin, 'Construction of Fantasy', pp. 1482–84; Antoine Picon, *Claude Perault ou la curiosité d'un classique* (Paris: Picard, 1988), pp. 223–30.

[28] Judi Loach, 'Reflections on Triumphal Arches, Wine Fountains and Firework Displays in Baroque Festivals' (presentation, Society of Architectural Historian of Great Britain Annual Symposium, London, 18 May 2013).

Figure 7.4 Jean Lepautre, *Montparnasse erected at the Saint-Gervais Fountain* (1662), etching on paper (© Houghton Library, Harvard University, Typ 615.62.363)

Figure 7.5 Jean Lepautre, *Triumphal arch erected at Pont Notre-Dame* (1662), etching on paper (© Houghton Library, Harvard University, Typ 615.62.363)

single, typically frontal, view, the *marchés* put flesh on these bare bones, suggesting how the structures worked as polychromatic, three-dimensional entities by detailing scale, materials used, construction techniques, colour and finish; where necessary they also provided precise instructions for the composition of large-format canvases, heraldic devices and deployment of architectural orders.

Each structure was in practice effectively treated as a separate project under the supervision of a single artist or, more typically, pair of artists, with painters taking the lead in designing the triumphal architecture.[29] Pierre Mélin designed the first freestanding triumphal arch at Porte Saint-Antoine (see Figure 7.2) with the master carpenter Fleurent Lenoir drafted in to supervise its construction.[30] Mélin was also put in charge of a second structure, the 'Montparnasse' (see Figure 7.4) at Carrefour de la Fontaine Saint-Gervais, not far from the Hotel de Ville.[31] The cousins Henri and Charles Beaubrun received the commission to devise the third arch for Pont Notre-Dame (see Figure 7.5), at the *Cité*-end of the bridge.[32] Michel Dorigny and François Tortebat were responsible for the arch at Marché-Neuf (see Figure 7.6), on the Île de la Cité, which was more akin to an elaborate frame for Dorigny and Tortebat's canvas, which measured 15 ft by 12 ft on its own, and was set at a height of 6 ft '*affin de résister à ce que le thoilles ne puissant ester crevée par la foulle*' ('to prevent crowds bursting through the canvas').[33] Finally, Daniel Hallé and Charles Poërson supervised the construction of the huge Place Dauphine arch (see Figure 7.3). The latter's design was actually supplied by Charles Le Brun, '*premier peintre du roy*', with Hallé and Poërson employed to oversee and execute the arch's figurative devices and large-format canvas.[34] Three additional painters, Jacques L'Homme, François Francart and Charles Bacot, were contracted to paint its architectural details and make it look like gold and marble, with Hallé and Poerson acting as senior partners in the enterprise.[35]

The process for commissioning, designing and making the triumphal arches for Louis's *entrée* is revealing. Arguably, it can be framed in terms of the 'centre' and 'periphery': in this instance, those with bureaucratic control over the event's ideologically-loaded appearance had to entrust a team of 'creatives' with the business of giving material form to the occasion's political ideals. Although one can only imagine the kinds of discussion which took place and the different

---

[29] Unfortunately available sources do not tell us the size or professional composition of the wider personnel involved, but it seems reasonable to believe that each 'project' involved a much larger team of anonymous workers.

[30] Archives nationales, Paris, Minutier central, LXXXVII, 579, fol.1 [r]: 5 May 1660; Minutier central, LXXXVII, 579, fol.1 [r]: 6 May 1660.

[31] Archives nationales, Paris, Minutier central, LXXXVII, 579, fol.1 [r]: 17 June 1660.

[32] Archives nationales, Paris, Minutier central, LXXXVII, 579, fol.1 [r]: 11 May 1660.

[33] Archives nationales, Paris, Minutier central, LXXXVII, 579, fol.1 [r]: 11 May 1660.

[34] Archives nationales, Paris, Minutier central, LXXXVII, 579, fol.1 [r]: 16 June 1660.

[35] Archives nationales, Paris, Minutier central, LXXXVII, 579, fol.1 [r]: 16 June 1660.

Figure 7.6 Jean Marot, *Triumphal arch erected in Marché-Neuf* (1662), etching on paper (© Houghton Library, Harvard University, Typ 615.62.363)

personalities which shaped them, the *marchés* function as partial records of key planning meetings during the design process, as well as indicating who was present.[36] More importantly, this part of the process highlights the professional anxieties that informed the *entrée*, as a headline political event, by showing how the event's organising committee used a range of supervisory practices and incentive mechanisms to ensure the job was done properly.

In common with other major building projects in late-seventeenth-century Paris, the artists involved had to submit designs for approval.[37] The *maître-menuisier* Lenoir's *marché* noted that although Mélin oversaw work on the Saint-Antoine arch, he was, in turn, answerable to *Messieurs les prévost des marchandz et eschevins*: '*Le tout sera faict suivant le dessein dudict Melin peintre qui en a esté montré ausdicts sieurs*'.[38] ('Everything is to be made according to the design provided by the aforementioned Mélin, painter, as shown to the aforementioned sires'). Other *marchés* revealed the crucial role played by Michel Noblet, Paris's *Maître des oeuvres*, in the preparations. Tortebat and Dorigny's contract for the Marché-Neuf arch indicates that, although they were responsible for the 'look' of the structure, '*le tout fait suivant la visite et controlle du sieur Noblet maître de œuvres de la ville et gens à ce cognoissans*' ('all was done under the surveillance and control of Sieur Noblet, master of town works, and the people known to him').[39] For ease of supervision, Tortebat and Dorigny were even provided '*d'un lieu convenable par mesdits sieurs pour pouvoir travailler, faire et construire ledit ouvrage*' ('a suitable place by the aforementioned sires to work in, make and build the said works'), suggesting the arch was partially constructed off-site before being installed in situ.[40] Noblet also provided labour to build the framework for Mélin's 'Montparnasse' and directed construction of the arches for Pont Notre-Dame and the Marché-Neuf.[41]

With so many projects running simultaneously, it mattered that work on the triumphal arches was initiated well in advance of the *entrée* on 26 August. All the named artists involved in the project were contracted between 5 May and 16

[36] The same group of high-ranking civic dignitaries signed all but two of the *marché*: Alexandre de Sève, the *prévôt des marchands*; Nicolas Baudequin, *conseiller de ville*; Claude Provost and Charles du Jours, *conseillers du roy au siege présidial du Châtelet*; Nicolas Boucot, Paris's *receveur* and Gaultier, an *échevin*. Each agreement was countersigned by the notary, Leroy, as well as the painter, sculptor or master carpenter concerned. The only exceptions were those contracts made with the sculptor, Regnaudin, who made the two permanent statues for Porte Saint-Antoine, which was only signed by the sculptor and Gautier, and that made with the painter Jacques de Haynault.

[37] Gerbino, *François Blondel*, pp. 71–117; Picon, *Claude Perrault*, pp. 223–30.

[38] Archives nationales, Paris, Minutier central, LXXXVII, 579, fol.1 [r]: 11 May 1660.

[39] Archives nationales, Paris, Minutier central, LXXXVII, 579, fol.1 [r]: 11 May 1660.

[40] Ibid.

[41] Archives nationales, Paris, Minutier central, LXXXVII, 579, fol.1 [r]: 17 June 1660; 11 May 1660.

June. More tellingly, deadlines for completion of work were set months ahead. Mélin was contracted to finish by 15 June, and Lenoir, the Beaubruns, Tortebat and Dorigny by 20 June.[42] The final major deadline, for completion of all work on the Place Dauphine arch, was 15 July, still over a month before the date appointed for the *entrée*.[43] Mélin appears to have been a particularly adept project manager, as he signed an additional *marché* on 17 June, agreeing to produce the 'Montparnasse'; this would suggest that by this date work on the Saint-Antoine arch was already completed, or at an advanced stage.[44] This was, for want of a better phrase, the concept of the 'false' deadline. By setting deadlines so far in advance, the *entrée*'s organisers gave themselves breathing space, setting aside time to resolve any problems that arose and, where necessary, allowing the construction of individual arches to overrun. It was common sense that did not go to waste: work on the Marché-Neuf arch seems to have fallen behind the deadline, as another artist, Jacques de Heynault, was subcontracted to paint architectural details and finish, while Tortebat and Dorigny's deadline was extended from 20 to 25 June.[45]

'False' deadlines weren't the only strategy available to the *Bureau de la Ville*, which had other, more hard-nosed tactics at its disposal. Payment for work on the triumphal arches was made in stages: typically a sum was paid up front, with another instalment half way through the job and the rest on completion. The arrangement made with Poerson and Hallé was typical: they received a total of 4,000 lire to realise Le Brun's design for the mammoth Place Dauphine arch, with 1,500 lire paid at the beginning of the job, to cover the cost of materials and labour, and the remaining 2,500 lire paid once work had reached a visibly advanced stage.[46] As in the other contracts, Poerson and Hallé were threatened with a financial penalty should they fail to complete the arch on time and to specification. Other payments were partly made in cash, with the balance 'paid' in materials. In addition to their monetary fee, Jacques L'Homme, François Francart and Charles Bacot, the painters, under contract to apply decorative paint finishes to the Place Dauphine arch, were permitted after the event to take possession of '*les thoilles et chassis*' ('the canvas and framework'), but only those materials used to make the back of the structure.[47]

---

[42] Archives nationales, Paris, Minutier central, LXXXVII, 579, fol.1 [r]: 5 May 1660; 11 May 1660.

[43] Archives nationales, Paris, Minutier central, LXXXVII, 579, fol.1 [r]: 16 June 1660.

[44] Archives nationales, Paris, Minutier central, LXXXVII, 579, fol.1 [r]: 17 June 1660.

[45] Archives nationales, Paris, Minutier central, LXXXVII, 579, fol.1 [r]: 15 May 1660.

[46] Archives nationales, Paris, Minutier central, LXXXVII, 579, fol.1 [r]: 16 June 1660. For a full account of the amounts paid for each component of the occasion's architecture, both ephemeral and permanent, see: Frank, 'Les artistes de l'entrée de Louis XIV', pp. 54–62.

[47] Archives nationales, Paris, Minutier central, LXXXVII, 579, fol.1 [r]: 16 June 1660.

In combination, supervision, financial incentives and false deadlines were all suggestive of the tight hold the *Bureau de la Ville* kept over the design and execution of triumphal architecture in 1660. And yet, close attention to the wording of the *marchés* indicates that the process could be much less prescriptive. While some aspects of the arches' decoration were described in minute detail, others seemed to be left to the imagination of those involved. Where another discussion might concentrate on unravelling the symbolic meanings embedded in the decoration, the following brief remarks are directed towards revealing levels of information: that is, the extent to which the specificity – or otherwise – of the language employed in relation to different aspects of the *entrée*'s design may be used to uncover the full spectrum of professional responsibilities and anxieties that informed an event on this scale.

Most care was taken with the description of large figurative canvases and heraldic devices, namely those aspects of the *entrée*'s design that were most closely allied with its political and cultural identity, and helped convey the peace, plenty and prosperity that were actively stressed as part of the occasion's principal message. The Beaubruns' contract described at length the large canvas that was the centrepiece of the Pont Notre-Dame arch (see Figure 7.5), depicting '*une Junon soubz le visage de la resemblance de la royne mère*' ('a Juno, whose face resembled the Queen Mother's'), sending Iris and Mercury, messengers of the Roman gods, to Hymen, Greek god of wedding ceremonies.[48] Likewise, Poerson and Hallé's *marché* included an equally rigorous account of the canvas that adorned the arch at Place Dauphine (see Figure 7.3), which showed Louis and his bride in Hymen's chariot being pulled by a cockerel and a lion, the heraldic beasts of France and Spain respectively.[49] Smaller symbolic devices were also described in some detail. In this instance, the painting was intended to mimic the finish of more expensive tapestry ('*sera fein comme une tappisserye*').[50] A thick border surrounded the main composition to make room for more symbolic content: the two verticals were '*chargé de fleur de lis d'or*' ('filled with gold *fleur-de-lis*'), with the horizontals decorated with the motif of *l'Ordre du Sainct Esprit*, the senior chivalric order in France.[51]

And yet, elsewhere, the *marchés* were noticeably less prescriptive, suggesting comparative free rein with aspects of the decoration that didn't explicitly relate to the *entrée*'s iconographical programme. Mélin was asked to devise '*des trophées de symphonies ou telles autres qu'ilz désireront mesdits sieurs*' ('trophies of musical instruments, or such others that the Sires desired') for the arch in Faubourg Saint-Antoine, while the Beaubruns received vague instructions to embellish the arch at Pont Notre-Dame with four figures '*plus grande que nature représentant*

[48] Archives nationales, Paris, Minutier central, LXXXVII, 579, fol.1 [r]: 11 May 1660.

[49] Archives nationales, Paris, Minutier central, LXXXVII, 579, fol.1 [r]: 16 June 1660.

[50] Ibid.

[51] Ibid.

telle personne ou figure qui sera donné par lesdits sieurs' ('larger than life, representing such person[s] or figure[s] that will be specified by the Sires').[52] The reference in both instances to 'Sieurs' suggests the opportunity for additional involvement for the event's organising committee. This may indicate that not all aspects of the design had been finalised when the contracts were drawn up, or that the artists employed were trusted to interpret less symbolically significant decorative features as they saw fit. The construction of the arches was informed by a similar pragmatism. This was particularly evident in those *marchés* that mention the back of structures, which confirms the efforts made to save time, money and materials, or to ensure more efficient working practices. At Pont Notre-Dame, the back of the Beaubruns' triumphal arch (see Figure 7.5) was swathed in '*tapissé au soings*' ('silken tapestries'), while the arch erected at Marché-Neuf (see Figure 7.6) was only painted on the side that faced onto Place Notre-Dame.[53] Such tantalising glimpses revealed the theatricality inherent in occasional architecture, with some structures only decorated on those sides that faced the audience.

Seeing and being seen: planning, using and leasing *échafauds* during Louis XIV's entrée in 1660

Gabriel Ladame's 1660 engraving (see Figure 7.1) provides a very different perspective on Louis's *entrée*. Rather than present individual structures in glorious isolation, Ladame compresses much of the occasion's triumphal architecture into one scene, creating a single-sheet distillation of the event's key sights. Four of the temporary triumphal arches are scattered across the integrated scene – Faubourg Saint-Antoine, Mélin's 'Montparnasse', Marché-Neuf and Place Dauphine – with the '*trône-dias*' visible to the left and the permanent stone Porte Saint-Antoine on the right. Notably, the image is full of people, showing part of the procession as it snaked from Place du Trône through the first of the triumphal arches, as well as the militia and 'civilian' spectators. In fact, the middle of the composition is dominated by a highly unusual addition: a series of covered viewing platforms that were intended to support the weight of the wealthier people present.

By comparison with other types of occasional architecture, *échafauds*, or 'scaffolds', have received little attention from scholars. As is so often the case, it is a question of sources: where triumphal arches were commemorated in visual images, such as those which illustrate this discussion, and close textual descriptions, *échafauds* were routinely excised from contemporary descriptions and visual representations. Quite simply, unlike carefully designed and decorated triumphal architecture, functional viewing platforms do not explicitly communicate

[52] Archives nationales, Paris, Minutier central, LXXXVII, 579, fol.1 [r]: 5 May 1660; 11 May 1660.

[53] Archives nationales, Paris, Minutier central, LXXXVII, 579, fol.1 [r]: 11 May 1660.

Figure 7.7 Jean Marot, *Trône-dais erected in Place du Trône* (1662), engraving on paper (© Houghton Library, Harvard University, Typ 615.62.363)

an event's iconographical or ideological programme. And yet, as the following discussion shows, the design, construction and use of *échafauds* in 1660 offers a different perspective on the social, commercial and political world of Louis's *entrée*.

Revealingly, when scaffolds did make an appearance in depictions or descriptions of early modern festival, it was in a supporting role: to put the most important people present on show. This calls to mind Helen Watanabe-O'Kelly's remarks on the legitimating visibility that was at the heart of early modern festival, where 'the audience is there as a witness and without it the event would not be legal or binding'.[54] This impulse was present in Marot's etching of the *trône-dais* (see Figure 7.7).

Its inclusion as an illustrative plate in *L'Entrée Triomphante de leurs Maiestez . . .* speaks not of the significance of the structure or the beauty of its design, but of the people on it.[55] The dais was designed to accommodate Louis XIV and

[54] Helen Watanabe-O'Kelly, 'Politics and Performance, Event and Record', p. 16.

[55] The textual description of the *trône-dais* was certainly impressive, reflecting its status as the *échafaux par excellence* built for the occasion: '*vne Estrade de trente-six pieds de long, sur vingt & vn de large, à laquelle on montoit de trois costez par dix-huict marches, & plus en quelques endroits à cause de l'inegalité du rez de chaussée, chacune d'vn pied de giron; sa couuerture en forme de pauillion, estoit portée sur quatre pilaster de*

his new bride, Maria-Teresa, while they received homage from representatives of the *Cité*, *Université* and the Church.[56] Similarly, Marot's etching of the '*amphiteatre*' in Place Dauphine (see Figure 7.3) from the same volume shows a sturdy construction, made with masonry as well as wood, and composed of two semi-circular banks of tiered seats arranged in an oval formation. Again, its careful representation in print attests to the importance of the audience it contained, with the amphitheatre intended to seat members of the local high nobility and judiciary, as well as the king's twenty-four violinists.[57]

Not all *échafauds* built for the *entrée* in 1660 were such elaborate affairs, nor was all space on viewing platforms reserved exclusively for royalty or local dignitaries. Most of the structures appear to have been semi-private, with groups or individuals applying for planning permission to build stands on the processional route. '*Messieurs les Payeurs de Rentes*' were given permission to build 'un arcade un Echauffeur un Amphiteatre' ('an arcade, a scaffold and an amphitheatre') at the top of rue Saint-Marguerite; Thomas Endebert and associates were allowed to build '*galeries, Loges Et Eschaffaux*' ('galleries, loggias and scaffolds') in an unspecified location in the city, while permission was given for an additional anonymous applicant to build an *échafaud* on rue Saint-Antoine, close to the city walls.[58] Some *échafauds* were explicitly commercial ventures, with those that could afford to do so paying for a better quality of experience. When René Deschamps and Joannes Dancerains sought permission to build three *échafauds* at various points along the rue Faubourg Saint-Antoine, it was so they might '*loüer par eux les places de dessus lesdits Eschaffaux à telles personnes ques bon leur semblera*' ('hire out space on the said scaffolds to such persons as seemed respectable to them').[59]

Demand for space on *échafauds* can be explained by the size, density and unpredictable behaviour of festival crowds. Although not within the scope of the present discussion, the challenges inherent in being a spectator at major urban festivals were considerable.[60] Structures such as those depicted in Ladame's engraving (see Figure 7.1) offer a design solution to these problems by providing

---

hauteur, & de force proportionée à la grandeur de l'Edifice, qui soustenoient vne corniche taillée en saillie, selon l'ordre Corinthien' ('a platform thirty-six feet long and twenty-one feet wide, which could be ascended by eighteen steps on three of its sides – more in some places because of its unequal height at ground level – the tread of each step being one-step wide; its roof, in the style of a pavilion, was supported by four tall pillars, as strong as the edifice was grand, which held a projecting cornice, which was carved, following the Corinthian order'.) 'Preparatifs. . .', *L'Entrée Triomphante de Levrs Maiestez. . .*, p. 33.

56 Ibid.

57 Archives nationales, Paris, H2.1815, fol. 556r.

58 Archives nationales, Paris, K1000, no. 253.278 [4r]; no.253.390 [13r]; no.253.283 [5r–5v].

59 Archives nationales, Paris, K1000, no. 299.

60 The role of the crowd in festival design is a matter that deserves significant further attention. The following is a provocative interrogation of events in late eighteenth-century

an elevated, stable, secure view of proceedings. In this example, the *échafauds* comprise a series of raised platforms adjacent to the processional route, equipped with rails at the front and a partial roof, which would have offered protection from the August sun; crucially the stands were robust enough to hold a sizeable crowd without collapsing.

In combination, differences in terminology and visual evidence can be used to establish key differences in construction and design. The 1694 edition of the *Dictionnaire de l'Académie française* defined the '*eschafauts*' built for festival as:

> *ouvrage de Charpenterie eslevez ordinairement par degrez en forme d'amphitheatre, pour voir plus commodément des ceremonies publiques ou autres spectacles. On avoit dressé des eschafauts pour les Ambassadeurs, pour la Cour, pour la musique'*.[61]
>
> [wooden structures typically erected in tiers in the form of an amphitheatre to facilitate a better view of public rituals or other spectacles. Scaffolds were built for ambassadors, the court [and] musical performers.]

That a variety of terms were used in 1660 also suggests the existence of a range of structures. Baldly put, differences in design and construction come down to roofs, walls, seating and steps. Some viewing platforms were covered – the 'arcade' and 'gallery'. Others were almost completely enclosed, granting those inside protection from the weather and seclusion from less savoury elements in the crowd – those people who would not have seemed respectable to Deschamps and Dancerains. In particular, the 'loge', meaning a '*petite hutte faite à la haste*' ('small, speedily constructed hut') or '*un petit reduit fait de cloisonnage, & capable de contenir cinq ou six personnes*' ('little room, partitioned off, to hold 5 or 6 people'), feels reminiscent of the temporary 'grandstands' built to accommodate spectators at horseracing, which appeared in contemporary visual representations and textual descriptions as elevated huts or sheds with roofs and walls; the most elegantly presented examples, such as those devised for royalty, were draped with expensive textiles.[62]

France from the perspective of a scholar with prior architectural training: Eric Monin, 'The Speculative Challenges of Festival Design', *passim*, but especially pp. 153–62.

[61] *Dictionnaire de l'Académie française*, 1st edition, *Dictionnaires d'autrefois* (Chicago: University of Chicago, 1694), http://artflx.uchicago.edu/cgi-bin/dicos//pubdico1look.pl?strippedhw=eschafaut [Accessed 23 September 2013]. Notably, this definition of 'festival scaffolding' does not change in later editions of the *Dictionnaire de l'Académie française*; it was only in the 8th edition (1932–35) that the following proviso was added, '*On dit plutôt aujourd'hui TRIBUNE ou ESTRADE*' [Today it is more often 'Rostrum' or 'Platform'].

[62] *Dictionnaire de l'Académie française*, 1st edition, *Dictionnaires d'autrefois* (Chicago: University of Chicago, 1694), http://artflx.uchicago.edu/cgi-bin/dicos/

As these examples suggest, the design and structural properties of *échafauds* can be mined for social and cultural values. Elaborate scaffolds, like the *trône-dais* or *amphiteatre*, were designed to put key individuals, such as the king and queen, on show. Other structures allowed spectators to 'publicise' differences in social status, with wealthier members of the festival crowd paying for a better quality of view on commercial stands: a transaction that was necessarily made and performed in public. The *échafauds*, commercial or otherwise, were supporting structures that showcased the magnificently dressed spectators, who enhanced the urban environment and, by extension, the ideals of the occasion. Colletet's description of the *entrée* in 1660 employed this notion to rhetorical effect: the scaffolds, in addition to roofs, windows and balconies, made it easier to place the large number of people, who:

> *rendra le triomphe encore plus magnifique, puis que l'on verra les maisons ornées de beau monde, & particulierement de belles Dames, qui sans doute seront superbement parées, & qui n'oubliront rein de ce qui doit releuer leur beauté éclattante.*[63]

> [will make the triumph even more magnificent, then we shall see the houses adorned with the *beau monde* and, in particular, the beautiful women, who will be, without doubt, stunningly arrayed, and who will forget nothing that enhances their dazzling beauty.]

---

pubdico1look.pl?strippedhw=loge&headword=&docyear=ALL&dicoid=ALL [Accessed 23 September 2013].

For an example of a depiction of a 'grandstand', see Francis Barlow's 1687 engraving of Charles II at the horseracing at Windsor (Museum no. 1972, U.941, Department of Prints and Drawings, British Museum, London). Maurice Howard's account of sixteenth- and seventeenth-century hunting lodges accounts for remarkably similar-sounding structures; see: Maurice Howard, 'The Hunting Lodge in England 1500–1650', in Monique Chatenet (ed.), *Maisons des champs dans l'Europe de la Renaissance* (Paris: Picard, 2006), pp. 291–8, 293–4.

[63] François Colletet, *La Liste Generale et Particuliere De Messieurs les Colonels, Capitaines, Lieutenants, Enseigns, & autres Officiers, & Bourgeois de la Ville & Fauxbourgs de Paris; Auec l'ordre qu'ils doiuent tenir dans leur marche, & dans les autres Ceremonies qui s'obserueront à l'Entrée Royale de leurs Majestés* (Paris: Loyson, 1660), p. 10. Both Abby Zanger and Marie-Claude Canova-Green discuss the less public-face of the scaffolds for Louis's entrée, using the prologue to Madeleine de Scudéry's *Célinte* (Paris: Courbé, 1661) to tease out very different ideas about the literary function of the structures as loci of 'curiousity'. See: Zanger, *Scenes From the Marriage of Louis XIV*, pp. 133–46; Marie-Claude Canova-Green, 'From Object of Curiosity to Subject of Conversation: Mlle de Scudéry and the Paris Entry of Louis XIV and Maria Teresa (1660)', in M.-C. Canova-Green, J. Andrews and M.-F. Wagner (eds), *Writing Royal Entries in Early Modern Europe* (Turnhout: Brepols, 2013), pp. 323–38, 332–8.

The viewing platforms built in 1660 also attest to the small-scale conflicts that impacted on major public celebrations. Although the design and construction of the *échafauds* for Louis's *entrée* were subject to comparatively looser controls than those applied to triumphal architecture, it is important to note that designs still had to be submitted to Noblet, Paris's *maître d'oeuvres*.[64] However, the chains of command for the construction of *échafauds* were much less clearly delineated; instead of being tightly controlled from the 'centre', networks of patronage and the operation of planning permission influenced this aspect of the event's design. The key players in the deployment of viewing platforms were the *entrée*'s municipal organising committee and the *Trésoriers de France*, one of the main institutions responsible for handling royal finances during the *ancien régime*.[65] As we shall see, the right to grant planning permission for *échafauds* in 1660 could be framed as a tussle between representatives of royal and municipal interests.

The first reference to scaffolds on 19 July 1660 was uncontroversial: the *Bureau de la Ville* granted permission to the '*Payeurs de Rentes*' and for the construction of the anonymous scaffold on rue Saint-Antoine.[66] At most, like the contracts for the triumphal arches, this demonstrated that large-format apparatus were made well in advance of the *entrée*. However, a few days later, on 24 July, the situation began to get out of hand, when the King's Privy Council issued an *arrêt*, or ruling, about several scaffolds that had been demolished on the previous day, supposedly on the orders of the *Trésoriers*.[67] This document lays bare the tensions between parties involved in organising the *entrée*, as the demolished scaffolds were under the jurisdiction of the *entrée's* municipal organising committee. As a consequence of the damage that had been done, the *Trésoriers* were compelled to see that the scaffolds were entirely rebuilt, with the Privy Council seeking additional information as to the identities of '*les officiers [et] ouvriers et au[tres] qui ont fait les Démolir*' ('the officers and workers and others who had them [the scaffolds] demolished').[68] Additional minutes from this meeting evoke a rather dramatic scene, with the *Trésoriers* accused of going to several places in the city on 23 July and:

> *firent abattre les Eschaffaux posez pour l'ordre des Supplians [the Prevôt des marchands et échevins] en quelques endroits de rües non incommodes, mais necessaries à placer les personnes qui seruent à releuer la ceremonie: & pour paruenir à leurs desseins exciterent le people à demolir lesdits Eschauffaux, ce qui est [un] mauvais exemple, tend à sedition.*[69]

---

[64] Archives nationales, Paris, K1000, no. 253.278 [4r]; no. 253.317 [8r–8v].

[65] Roland E. Mousnier, *The Institutions of France Under the Absolute Monarchy*, trans. Arthur Goldhammer, 2 vols (Chicago and London: University of Chicago Press, 1979–80), vol. 1, pp. 435–7, 763.

[66] Archives nationales, Paris, K1000, no. 253.278 [4r]; no. 253.283 [5r–5v].

[67] Archives nationales, Paris, K1000, no. 253.292 [7v–8r].

[68] Ibid.

[69] Archives nationales, Paris, K1000, no. 294.

> [having pulled down scaffolds erected on the order of the suppliants in parts of the street that were not inconvenient, but [in fact] necessary to place the spectators to see the ceremony; and to accomplish their designs incited the people to demolish the said scaffolds, setting a bad example, that tended towards sedition.]

The episode was significant. Not only were the *Trésoriers* accused of impeding practical preparations for the *entrée*, they were also held account for setting a bad example to the wider populace by encouraging disorderly behaviour. The chaotic nature of the scene also highlights the potential nuisances caused by festival preparations. Less dramatic, although no less suggestive, was a directive issued in relation to a scaffold built by Deschamps and Dancerains, which ordered that residents on rue de Neuilly be permitted free access to their houses; the implication being that locals, finding it difficult to go about their business in the midst of a building site, had complained to the *Bureau de la Ville*.[70]

On 28 July, the situation was further confused, when Louis used his *Brevet du Roy* to grant Deschamps and Dancerains permission to build their three *échafauds*, a decision confirmed two days later on 30 July by printed proclamation.[71] The case highlights the networks of royal patronage that informed planning permission for *échafauds* and the desirability of building – and leasing space on – scaffolds. Notably, the two men were part of the royal household; as two of Louis's *grand valets de pied* they were part of the *grand écuyer*, or Royal Stables, under the jurisdiction of the *Grand écuyer de France*.[72] In this instance, the *Trésoriers* acted as middlemen, with Deschamps and Dancerains approaching them first; it was on the basis of their counsel that Louis granted his permission in recognition of the *valets' 'bons & agreables Seruices*' ('good and pleasing service').[73]

Barely two days later, on 2 August, an *Ordonnance du Roy* gave categorical support to the *Bureau de la Ville*. The *Trésoriers* were taken out of the equation, with the *Prévôt des marchands et échevins* granted sole jurisdiction over '*les Eschaffaut et autres choses pour lentrée de leurs Majestes*' ('the scaffolds and other things for the entry of their majesties') in recognition of the role they played in organising and paying for the rest of the event.[74] The comprehensiveness of the new *Ordonnance* was underlined by a reference to Dancerains and Deschamps: it was specified that even they would not receive special treatment, in spite of their loyal service to the Crown.

---

[70] Archives nationales, Paris, K1000, no. 253.393 [13r–13v].

[71] Archives nationales, Paris, K1000, no. 253.316 [8r]; K1000, no. 299.

[72] Joseph-Nicolas Guyot, *Traité des Droits, Fonctions, Franchises, Exemptions, Prérogatives et Privilèges Annexés en France à chaque Dignité, à chaque Office & à chaque État, soit Civil, soit Militaire, soit Ecclésiastique*, 4 vols (Paris: Visse, 1786), vol. 1, pp. 618, 624; Mousnier, *Institutions of France*, vol. 2, pp. 116–17.

[73] A.N., Paris, K1000, no. 399.

[74] A.N., Paris, K1000, no. 253.339 [10r–10v].

The conflict over *échafauds* in 1660 put the issue of planning permission at the centre of social and economic networks. Here, as elsewhere, the scaffolding built as viewing platforms was potentially hugely profitable, which explained the high level of contestation that attended its construction before the *entrée*. From the perspective of Paris as a heterogeneous, contested space, the commotion caused in building *échafauds* also evidenced the extent to which preparations for major celebrations actively, and sometimes disruptively, 'colonised' urban spaces with other competing uses. Significantly, while the *échafauds* erected in 1660 were documented in remarkable detail, relevant sources include fewer references to scaffolds being built for similar events in the following period.[75] One wonders if, perhaps, the chaotic nature of this part of the preparations led to greater restrictions on their construction.

Conclusion

This discussion has shown how evidence of designing and making temporary structures can expose tensions between the representations of Louis XIV's *entrée* into Paris and the processes of project management, collaboration, delegation and negotiation that underpinned its realisation as a temporally and spatially located event. Where previous studies have stressed the iconographical design of the occasion and its political contexts, this treatment has taken an object and process-focussed approach, using the commission and manufacture of temporary structures to explore the extent to which festival was a product of negotiated and, in some instances, conflicting interests and ideals. The structures, whether decorative or functional, contributed to the overall experience of the event, and the ideas and ideals invested in it. However, their design and construction had to be devolved to decentralised personnel, with individual structures being the end product of periods of discussion between those responsible for the overall design of an occasion and the personnel charged with devising its individual components.

Attending to issues of design and making has, in addition, highlighted the tensions between representatives of state and civic interests in preparing for the event. The elaborate triumphal architecture built for Louis's *entrée* was closely monitored by the event's organising committee, composed of men with vested political

[75] This study is based on a survey of the Délibérations de la bureau de la Ville de Paris from 1650 until 1720. 'Semi-private' scaffold building does not seem to revive until the first decade of the eighteenth century, when the Bureau de la Ville attempted to crack down on entrepreneurial Parisians building *échafauds* in Place Greve for the annual Fête Saint-Jean celebrations and for those devised to mark early victories in the War of the Spanish Succession. See, for example: Archives nationales, Paris, H2. 1840 (141r); H2. 1840 (206v); H2. 1840 (212r). At present, it is impossible to say whether these instances are merely indicative of a constant strain of rogue scaffold building on days of occasion, or, indeed, whether the practice intensified from 1700.

interests in the quality and execution of the finished product. This had particular importance in relation to decorative motifs with special ideological significance. Although less emphasis was placed on the decoration of the *échafauds* built for Louis's *entrée*, surviving documentation reveals the bureaucratic and commercial interests underpinning their construction, as well as the social and cultural values invested in their use. Most notably, these scaffolds highlight the conflict between municipal and royal interests in relation to the occasion, with both the *Bureau de la Ville* and the *Trésoriers de France* attempting to take control of this aspect of the event's design.

Bibliography

Primary sources

MANUSCRIPT

Archive nationales, Paris:
H2.2012, fol. 1r
H2.1815, fols 229v–232r
H2.1815, fol. 556r
H2. 1840, fol. 142r
H2. 1840, fol. 206r
H2. 1840, fol. 212r
K1000, no. 253.278, fol. 4r
K1000, no.253.283, fols 5r–5v
K1000, no. 253.292, fols 7v–8r
K1000, no. 253.316, fol. 8r
K1000, no. 253.317, fols 8r–8v
K1000, no. 253.339, fols 10r–10v
K1000, no. 253.390, fol. 13r
K1000, no. 253.393, fols 13r–13v
K1000, no. 294
K1000, no. 299
K1000, no. 399
Minutier central, LXXXVII, 579

Primary sources

ONLINE

Correspondance française de Guy Patin, ed. by Loïc Capron (Paris: Bibliothèque interuniversitaire de santé, 2015), www.biusante.parisdescartes.fr/patin/?do=pg&let=0632

PRINTED

Colletet, François, *Descriptions des Arcs de Triomphes Eslevés dans les places Publiques pour l'Entrée de la Reyne* (Paris: Loyson, 1660).

Colletet, François, *La Liste Generale et Particuliere De Messieurs les Colonels, Capitaines, Lieutenants, Enseigns, & autres Officiers, & Bourgeois de la Ville & Fauxbourgs de Paris; Auec l'ordre qu'ils doiuent tenir dans leur marche, & dans les autres Ceremonies qui s'obserueront à l'Entrée Royale de leurs Majestés* (Paris: Loyson, 1660).

Colletet, François, *Le Triomphe de la France svr l'Entrée Royale de Levrs Maiestez dans leur Bonne Ville de Paris, Avec les Discours Heroïques sur les Vies des Roys de Frances, depuis Pharamond iusqu'à nostre Grand Monarque Lovis XIV. Ensemble les Eloges de la Reyne, de la Reyne Mere, & de son Eminence. Dedié à Messieurs les Prevost des Marchands & Eschevins de la Ville* (Paris: Loyson, 1660).

Colletet, François, *Ordre Generale et Particuliere de la Marche qvi doit estre Observee dans les trois iours consecutifs pour l'Entrée de leurs Majestez dans leur bonne Ville de Paris, par Messieurs du Clergé, par Messieurs les Preuost des Marchands, Eschevins & Bourgeois de ladite Ville, Preuost de l'Isle, Chevalier & Lieutenant du Guet, & co./Avec la description des Superbes Appareils de la Cour, & des Magnificence de la Milice Bourgeoise* (Paris: Loyson, 1660).

Colletet, François, *Reqveste Presentée a Monsieur le Prevost des Marchands par Cent-Mil Provinciaux Ruinez, Attendez L'Entrée* (Paris: Loyson, 1660).

Guyot, Joseph-Nicolas, *Traité des Droits, Fonctions, Franchises, Exemptions, Prérogatives et Privilèges Annexés en France à chaque Dignité, à chaque Office & à chaque État, soit Civil, soit Militaire, soit Ecclésiastique*, 4 vols (Paris: Visse, 1786).

Lelong, Jacques, *Bibliothèque historique de la France, contenant le catalogue des ouvrages, tant imprimés que manuscrits qui traitent de l'Histoire de ce Roïaume, ou qui y ont Rapport* (Paris: Gabriel Martin, 1719).

L'Entrée Triomphante de Levrs Maiestez Lovis XIV. Roy de France et de Navarre et Marie Theresa d'Avstriche son Epovse, dans la Ville de Paris Capitale de Levrs Royavmes, av Retour de la Signatvre de la Paix Generalle et de Levr Herevx Mariage. Enrichie de plusher Figvres, des Harangves & de Diuerse Pieces Considerables Pour l'Histoire. Le tout exactement recuielly par l'ordre de Messievrs de Ville (Paris: Le Petit, Joly and Bilaine, 1662).

Secondary sources

PRINTED

Blau, Eve and Edward Kaufman, 'Introduction', in E. Blau and E. Kaufman (eds), *Architecture and Its Image: Four Centuries of Architectural Representation. Works From the Collection of the Canadian Center for Architecture* (Montreal: Canadian Center for Architecture, 1989), pp. 13–15.

Bryant, Lawrence M., *The King and the City in the Parisian Royal Entry* (Geneva: Droz, 1986).

Bryant, Lawrence M., 'From Communal Ritual to Royal Spectacle: Some Observations on the Staging of Royal Entries (1450–1600)', in *Ritual, Ceremony and the Changing Monarchy in France* (Farnham and Burlington, VT: Ashgate Valorium, 2010), pp. 243–81.

Bryant, Lawrence M., 'Royal Ceremony and the Revolutionary Strategies of the Third Estate', in *Ritual, Ceremony and the Changing Monarchy in France 1350–1789* (Farnham: Ashgate Valorium, 2010), pp. 283–320.

Burke, Peter, *The Fabrication of Louis XIV* (New Haven, CT and London: Yale University Press, 1992).

Canova-Green, Marie-Claude, 'From Object of Curiosity to Subject of Conversation: Mlle de Scudéry and the Paris Entry of Louis XIV and Maria Teresa (1660)', in M.-C. Canova-Green, J. Andrews and M.-F. Wagner (eds), *Writing Royal Entries in Early Modern Europe* (Turnhout: Brepols, 2013), pp. 323–38.

Delpont, Hubert, *Parade pour une Infante: Le périple nuptial de Louis XIV à travers le Midi de la France, 1659–1660* (Bouloc: Éditions d'Albret, 2007).

Frank, Christoph Daniel, *The Mechanics of Triumph: Public Ceremony and Civic Pageantry under Louis XIV* (PhD dissertation, Warburg Institute, University of London, 1993).

Frank, M. Christoph, 'Les artistes de l'entrée de Louis XIV en 1660', *Bulletin de la Société de l'Histoire de l'Art français* (1989/90), 53–74.

Gerbino, Anthony, *François Blondel. Architecture, Erudition and the Scientific Revolution* (London and New York: Routledge, 2010).

Grell, Chantal, 'The Financing and Material Organisation of Court Festivals Under Louis XIV', in J.R. Mulryne and Elizabeth Goldring (eds), *Court Festivals of the European Renaissance: Art Politics and Performance* (Aldershot and Burlington, VT: Ashgate, 2002).

Howard, Maurice, 'The Hunting Lodge in England 1500–1650', in Monique Chatenet (ed.), *Maisons des champs dans l'Europe de la Renaissance* (Paris: Picard, 2006), pp. 291–8.

Jarrard, Alice, *Architecture as Performance in Seventeenth-Century Europe: Court Ritual in Modena, Rome and Paris* (Cambridge: Cambridge University Press, 2003).

Loach, J. D., 'Pageant and Festival Arts', *Grove Art Online*, *Oxford Art Online*, www.oxfordartonline.com/subscriber/article/grove/art/T064588

McGowan, Margaret M., 'The Renaissance Triumph and Its Classical Heritage', in J.R. Mulryne and Elizabeth Goldring (eds), *Court Festivals of the European Renaissance: Art Politics and Performance* (Aldershot and Burlington, VT: Ashgate, 2002), pp. 26–47.

Monin, Eric, 'The Construction of Fantasy: Ephemeral Structures and Urban Celebrations in France During the Eighteenth Century', in Santiago Huerta (ed.), *Proceedings of the First International Congress on Construction History, Madrid, 20–24 January 2003* (Madrid: Instituto Juan de Herrera, 2003), pp. 1475–87.

Monin, Eric, 'The Speculative Challenges of Festival Architecture in Eighteenth-Century France', in Sarah Bonnemaison and Christine Macy (eds), *Festival Architecture* (London and New York: Routledge, 2008), pp. 155–80.

Möseneder, Karl, *Zeremoniell und monumentale Poesie: die 'Entrée Solennelle' Ludwigs XIV 1660 in Paris* (Berlin: Gebr. Mann Verlag, 1983).

Mousnier, Roland E., *The Institutions of France under the Absolute Monarchy*, trans. Arthur Goldhammer, 2 vols (Chicago and London: University of Chicago Press, 1979–80).

Picon, Antoine, *Claude Perault ou la curiosité d'un classique* (Paris: Picard, 1988).

Stevenson, Christine, 'Occasional Architecture in Seventeenth-Century London', *Architectural History*, 49 (2006), 35–74.

Stevenson, Christine, *The City and the King: Architecture and Politics in Restoration London* (New Haven, CT and Londen: Yale University Press, 2013).

Tierney, Elaine, *Strategies for Celebration: Realising the Ideal Celebratory City in London and Paris 1660–1715* (DPhil dissertation, University of Sussex/ Victoria and Albert Museum, 2012).

Thøfner, Margit, *A Common Art: Ceremonial in Antwerp and Brussels During and After the Dutch Revolt* (Zwolle: Waanders, 2007).

Van Eck, Caroline, 'Verbal and Visual Abstraction: The Role of Pictorial Techniques of Representation in Renaissance Architectural Theory', in Christy Anderson (ed.), *The Built Surface. Volume 1: Architecture and the Pictoral Arts From Antiquity to the Enlightenment* (Aldershot and Burlington, VT: Ashgate, 2002), pp. 162–80.

Watanabe-O'Kelly, Helen, 'Early Modern Court Festivals: Politics and Performance, Event and Record', in J.R. Mulryne and Elizabeth Goldring (eds), *Court Festivals of the European Renaissance: Art, Politics and Performance* (Aldershot and Burlington, VT: Ashgate, 2002), pp. 15–25.

Watanabe-O'Kelly, Helen, 'The Early Modern Festival Book: Function and Form', in J.R. Mulryne, Margaret Shewring and Helen Watanabe-O'Kelly (eds), *Europa Triumphans: Court and Civic Festival in Early Modern Europe*, 2 vols (Aldershot and Burlington, VT: Ashgate, 2004), vol. 1, pp. 3–17.

Zanger, Abby E., *Scenes From the Marriage of Louis XIV. Nuptial Fictions and the Making of Absolute Power* (Stanford, CA: Stanford University Press, 1997).

Chapter 8
Overcrowding at court
A Renaissance problem and its solution: temporary theatres and banquet halls

Sydney Anglo

Most students of court festivals will be familiar with the disaster at Isabelle of Bavaria's Paris reception in 1389. A brilliant banquet and mock-siege entertainment had been arranged but, as Froissart tells us, the show was doomed to be short-lived because of the crush of people: '*il y eut là des gens échauffés par la chaleur et mal à leure aise dans la foule*' ('there were people there, overcome by the heat and ill at ease in the crowd'). A table was knocked over and everything was in disorder. The queen was nearly sick; a window had to be smashed to let in some air, and many of the more-than-500 women present were exhausted by the sweltering atmosphere.[1] Was a good time had by all? Definitely not. And there is the problem in a nutshell: too many people, and not enough room.

Was there a solution? One answer might have been simply to find a larger space or invite fewer guests; and certainly, for feasts and indoor spectacles, it was sometimes possible to locate an existing area sufficiently capacious to provide what was required. For large-scale outdoor festivals, such as tournaments and horse ballets, the problem was easier to resolve and, all over Europe, squares and the courtyards of palaces were transformed into something recognisably like theatres, with richly-decorated galleries and boxes, erected in the most advantageous positions, for royalty, nobility, important visitors, and civic dignitaries, and with tiers of wooden stands raised on scaffolding for the commonalty.[2]

Quite often, however, more ingenious solutions were found to meet the logistical problems posed by the confluence of a large number of diners, revellers, performers and onlookers, and, from time to time, there was a kind of half-way house between an outdoor and indoor setting. At Rome in 1474, for example, the Piazza de' Santi Apostoli was roofed over to form a banqueting hall for Leonora

---

[1] Jean Froissart, *Les Chroniques*, ed. Madame De Witt, née Guizot (Paris: Hachette, 1881), p. 742.

[2] For a typical example, see Sydney Anglo, 'Anglo-Burgundian Feats of Arms: Smithfield, June 1467', *The Guildhall Miscellany*, II (1965), 276–7. For a valuable discussion of the provision of tournament space in England, see Alan Young, *Tudor and Jacobean Tournaments* (London: George Philip, 1987), pp. 74–122.

daughter of Ferdinand of Naples; and in 1492, as part of the festivities to mark the fall of Granada, the courtyard of the Palazzo della Cancelleria Apostolica was *umbraculis tecto* (covered over with cloth), to protect the audience from the sun.[3] A similar scheme was adopted in April and May 1518 at the Château d'Amboise for celebrations to mark the baptism of the Dauphin together with the marriage of Madeleine de La Tour d'Auvergne and Lorenzo de' Medici, when '*la grand court toute tendue et couverte en forme de pavillons de toilles semées de fleurs de lys soubstenues de corde attachées à troys grans mastz de basteaulx*' ('when the great court was all covered over with drapery, like pavilions strewn with *fleurs de lys*, supported by ropes attached to three great ship's masts').

And then, barely a month later, Francis I arranged a banquet and ball at Clos-Lucé where a special hall was created by covering the courtyard of the castle with sky-blue cloths '*avec les étoiles d'or à l'imitation du ciel, ensuite il y avait les principales planètes, le soleil d'un coté et la lune en face, ce qui faisait un spectacle admirable; Mars, Jupiter et Saturne étaient mis à leur rang, avec les douze signes célestes*' ('with golden stars in imitation of the heavens, together with the principal planets, the sun on one side and the moon opposite, which was an admirable spectacle; Mars, Jupiter and Saturn were in their place. with the twelve celestial signs').[4] At Florence, too, the technique of covering an open courtyard was sometimes adopted as a way to provide the space needed for a large-scale festival. Thus, for the marriage of Cosimo I in 1539, the second cortile of the Palazzo de' Medici was roofed over with an artificial sky of bright blue baize for a performance of Antonio Landi's *Il Commodo*. In 1579 the Cortile of the Palazzo Pitti was protected overhead by a great cloth, for the *Sbarra* to entertain Bianca Cappello; and 10 years later the same cortile was roofed over again for the tournament and *naumachia* which formed part of the entertainments for the marriage of the Grand Duke Ferdinand.[5]

Nevertheless, such *ad hoc* expedients could never have been entirely satisfactory either for their immediate purpose or for demonstrating wealth and artistic resource. Something more ingenious, impressive and, at the same time, more practical was required; and so, from at least the early fifteenth century, kings and princes used their wealth to deploy armies of designers, artists, craftsmen and

---

[3] Filippo Clementi, *Il Carnevale Romano nelle cronache contemporanee* (Rome: Tipografia Tiberina, 1899), pp. 79, 92–3.

[4] Anne-Marie Lecoq, 'Une fête italienne à la Bastille en 1518', in *'Il se rendit en Italie': Etudes offertes à André Chastel, CNRS* (Paris: Flammarion, 1987), pp. 149–68.

[5] A.M. Nagler, *Theatre Festivals of the Medici 1539–1637* (New Haven, CT and London: Yale University Press, 1964), pp. 6, 50, 91–2. Similar expedients were still being employed nearly a century later. See, for examples, *Mercurio e Marte discordi* (Munich, 1654), p. 210, and *Atiopa giustificata* (Munich, 1662), p. 5. See also J.R. Mulryne, 'Arbitrary Reality: Fact and Fantasy in the Florentine *Naumachia*, 1589', in Margaret Shewring (ed.), *Waterborne Pageants and Festivities in the Renaissance* (Farnham and Burlington, VT: Ashgate, 2013), pp. 143–75.

artisans to create ephemeral buildings within which they could feed, entertain and impress their chosen guests. Such was the banquet house built at Bruges in 1429 for the feasts celebrating the marriage of Isabelle of Portugal. This was a substantial structure, 146 feet long and 73 feet wide, newly made but destined for demolition when the festival was over.[6] Also at Bruges, for the marriage of Margaret of York and Charles Duke of Burgundy in 1468, the Ducal *jeu de paume* space was turned into a '*chambre faicte hastivement de charpenterie, moult grande, moult haulte et moult spacieuse*' ('quickly fashioned of timber, very large, very high, and very spacious'); covered with a roof of blue and white cloth; hung with rich tapestries; and illuminated by highly-wrought candelabras.[7] In 1507, to entertain Louis XII during his visit to Milan, Giovan Jacopo Trivulzio built a banquet hall and ballroom, some 120 paces long: '*a deux rangz de pilliers de verdure, couverte de draps de bleu, tous semez de fleurs de lys d'or et d'estoilles d'or*' ('with two rows of pillars made of greenery, covered with blue cloths, the whole structure strewn with golden *fleurs de lys* and golden stars').[8] Even more elaborate, and better documented, was the masking theatre and banquet hall, with a celestial ceiling and zodiacal decorations, built within a courtyard of the Bastille for the entertainment of an English embassy to Paris in 1518.[9] The chronicler Edward Hall, describing the building, pays particular attention to the construction of its roof and ceiling: 'this house was covered with coardes strayned by craft and every coarde was wound great knop gilt with gold foyle. Over theyr coardes was streyned wollen clothes of light blew: this roofe was lxxx. fote high . . . set full of starres gilt furnished with glasses betweene the fretes'.[10]

This ambassadorial festival in Paris was a success and the temporary building served its purpose well. But sometimes these structures proved to be so ephemeral that they did not even remain standing long enough to be used at all. Such was the fate of François Ier's great pavilion at the Field of Cloth of Gold in 1520. This was an ambitious round building some 60 paces in circumference, with a central column formed by several ship's masts supporting a canvas roof decorated on the interior with stars of gold foil and a representation of 'the Orbes of the heavens . . . in manner like the sky or firmament'.[11] Fleurange observed that this building was built '*de la façon comme du temps passé les Romains faisoient leur théâtre, tout en rond, à ouvrage de bois, chambres, salles, galleries, trois estages l'un sur lautre*'

6 Saint-Remy, *Chronique de Jean le Févre Seigneur de Saint-Remy*, ed. François Morand, 2 vols (Paris: Société de l'Histoire de France, 1871), vol. 2, p. 160.

7 Olivier de la Marche, *Mémoires*, ed. H. Beaune and J.D'Arbaumont, 4 vols (Paris: Société de l'Histoire de France, 1885), vol. 3, pp. 117–19.

8 Jean d'Auton, *Chroniques de Louis XII*, ed. R. de maulde la Clavière, 4 vols (Paris: Société de l'Histoire de France: 1889–95), vol. 4, pp. 307–313.

9 See note 4 in this chapter.

10 Edward Hall, *The Union of the Two Noble and Illustre Famelies of Lancastre and York*, ed. Henry Ellis (London: J. Johnson, 1809), p. 596.

11 Ibid., p. 607.

('in the same way as in times past the Romans used to fashion their theatres, in the round, made of wood, with chambers, rooms, and galleries, three storeys one above the other').[12] Unfortunately, a gale demolished the masterpiece, and Francis and his court were obliged to do their entertaining in Ardres itself.

On the other hand, the temporary architecture sometimes proved so permanent that appropriate refurbishment might keep these buildings going for decades. This was the case with Elizabeth I's banquet house and theatre built at Whitehall in 1581, where the cosmic decoration, 'most cunninglie painted [with] the cloudes, with the starres the sunne and sunne beames', proved more enduring than temporary, so that the building was still in use (patched, restored and enlarged) for Jonson's *Masque of Blackness* in 1605.[13]

Several of these ephemeral sructures have achieved a measure of lasting fame through a kind of verbal conservation process in chronicles, letters, archival records and research papers of academe. One early example was a wooden structure built for René d'Anjou at Saumur for a tournament in 1448. It was named after Lancelot's castle, the Chasteau de la Joyeuse Garde, *'a l'imitation des anciens romans'* ('in imitation of the old romances'), and must have been of considerable size, since René was able to entertain his court there amidst luxury and revelry for 40 days.[14] It was not, however, comparable to the largest, most elaborate, and most famous of all the temporary palaces of Renaissance Europe – that built for Henry VIII at the Field of Cloth of Gold, which, said one Italian admirer, could not have been bettered by Leonardo himself.[15] (See Plate 13.)

The ground floor, consisting of wine cellars and offices, was set within a quadrant, each side of which was about 300 feet in length, and formed by brick walls 8 feet in height. Above these walls was the main storey arranged in four blocks comprising huge suites of apartments for the royal entourage together with a 60 foot gallery, a 100 foot chapel, and a 220 foot banquet hall. Externally, the walls above the brickwork were about 30 feet high and made of canvas mounted on timber frames, all painted to resemble stone or brickwork so that they 'seemed to be that which they were not, and were that which they did not appear to be'. Especially remarkable were the large windows of fine white glass which, according to Soardino, the Mantuan ambassador to the French court, made the building so bright that it might almost have been open to the daylight; while Fleurange

---

[12] Robert de la Marck, Maréchal de Fleurange, *Les Mémoires*, eds J.J.P. Poujoulat and J.J. Michaud (Paris: L'Editeur du commentaire analytique du Code Civil, 1838), p. 69. This text is ambiguous, and it is not clear whether Fleurange is describing Francis's great pavilion or another of similar structure.

[13] See John Orrell, *The Human Stage: English Theatre Design, 1567–1640* (Cambridge: Cambridge University Press, 1988), pp. 38–41.

[14] Marc de Vulson sieur de La Colombière, *Le Vray Théâtre d'honneur*, 2 vols (Paris, 1648), vol. 1, pp. 82–3.

[15] See Sydney Anglo, 'The Hampton Court Painting of the Field of Cloth of Gold Considered as an Historical Document', *The Antiquaries Journal*, XLVI (1966), 287–307.

declared that it was the most beautiful glass that he had ever seen and that *'la moitié de la maison estoit toute de verrine; et vous asseure qu'il y faisoit bien clair'* ('half of the building was made entirely of glass, and you may be sure that it made it all very light'). This English palace was a triumph and was acknowledged as such by the competitive French; but no less interesting was the 16-sided masking theatre and banquet hall built at Calais, by the same team of English craftsmen, for the meeting of Henry VIII and the Emperor Charles V immediately after the Field of Cloth of Gold. This remarkable building was closed in by a double roof: an outer weather covering and an inner canvas of blue which formed the ceiling and was decorated with a vast *mappa mundi* displaying the four elements painted in four bands around the entire circumference and culminating in a meticulous representation of the heavens and a sphere of flames. Unfortunately, like the French King's great pavilion, it was unable to resist the stormy weather and was reduced to ruins before it could be used.[16]

Despite that setback, the English team of craftsmen had become so skilled that when, in the Spring and Autumn of 1527, two French embassies were entertained at Greenwich, another double building was created: a huge banquet house and a theatre with a ceiling depicting the 'whole earth environed with the sea, like a very mappe or carte, and by a cunning making of another cloth, the zodiacke with the xii. signes', and the Sun, Moon and the planets 'everyone in their proper houses made according to their properties'. This cosmic vision had been designed by Nicholas Kratzer, the King's astronomer, and painted by none other than Hans Holbein; so it is no wonder that the chronicler Edward Hall thought it 'a pleasant sight to beholde'.[17]

The English court, it seems, especially favoured the temporary theatre and banquet hall as a method of accommodating large numbers of visitors, and there were at least 14 such buildings erected in and around London between 1546 and 1626.[18] There were relatively fewer such structures on the Continent due possibly to the existence of many more permanent palaces with more capacious halls, rather than to a difference in taste. Several examples of the genre can, however, be cited such as the Milan banquet house of 1507;[19] the enormous wooden theatre built on the

---

[16] See Sydney Anglo, *Spectacle, Pageantry and Early Tudor Policy* (Oxford: Clarendon Press, 1969), pp. 159–68; and Richard Hosley, 'The Theatre and the Tradition of English Playhouse Design', in Herbert Berry (ed.), *The First Public Playhouse: The Theatre in Shoreditch 1576–1598* (Montreal: McGill-Queen's University Press, 1979), pp. 47–79.

[17] See Sydney Anglo, 'La salle de banquet et le théatre construits à Greenwich pour les fêtes Franco-Anglaises de 1527', in Jean Jacquot (ed.), *Le lieu théatral à la Renaissance* (Paris: Centre Nationale de la Recherche Scientifique, 1963), pp. 273–88.

[18] For references, see H.M. Colvin (ed.), *The History of the King's Works*, 4 vols (London: Her Majesty's Stationery Office, 1982), vol. 4, Pt II, pp. 30–1, 107, 109, 157, 203, 261, 319, 322–5, 341.

[19] See note 8 in this chapter.

Campidoglio at Rome in 1513;[20] a theatre with a golden celestial ceiling, sun and moon, at Constantinople in 1524;[21] and yet another at Rome in 1550.[22]

Cosmic decor

A recurrent feature of festival buildings, both permanent and temporary, was the way in which ceiling decorations tended towards the astronomical, astrological or celestial. Images of the sky in general, and of the Sun, Moon, Stars and Zodiacal signs in particular, abound. These do not occur invariably, but are common enough to merit comment. Anne-Marie Lecoq, in her study of the 1518 temporary palace at the Bastille, has suggested that these themes may be related to several specifically-horoscopic astrological decorations found in some fifteenth-century Italian palaces and chapels.[23] But these are, at best, merely analogous and were unlikely to have been widely known.[24] I believe that the cosmic decorations may be related to other traditions which, although abstruse, are far more cogent.

It may be helpful to imagine some vast conceptual cauldron into which many ingredients may be thrown to add richness to the mixture. First, there is Pliny's brief reference to 'linen cloths [that] were used in the theatres as awnings'. Some of these were 'of sky blue and spangled with stars' and were stretched over the amphitheatres with ropes.[25] This text must have been well-known to Renaissance readers as would have been Alberti's augmented description of an ancient theatre where 'to keep off the Weather, and to retain the Voice' the auditorium was shielded by a sail, 'strewed over with Stars' and suspended by ropes from poles 'like the masts of ships'.[26] There is an obvious parallel here with both the theatre and banquet hall built at the Bastille in 1518; with Francis I's great pavilion built like the ancient Roman theatres; and with English temporary theatres and the London public playhouses as they developed in the latter part of the sixteenth century.[27] These buildings, sometimes described as 'round', were really polygonal

---

[20] Clementi, *Carnevale Romano*, pp. 145–8; Bonner Mitchell, *Italian Civic Pageantry*, pp. 120–4.

[21] Marino Sanuto, *I Diarii di Marino Sanuto*, ed. F. Stefani (Venice: F. Visentini, 1879–1902), XXXV, col.118.

[22] Clementi, *Carnevale Romano*, pp. 206–8; Mitchell, *Italian Civic Pageantry*, pp. 131–2.

[23] Lecoq, 'Un fête italienne', pp. 159–60.

[24] Especially since their secret meanings have only been revealed by the erudite analyses of scholars such as Warburg, Saxl and Seznec.

[25] Pliny the Elder, *Natural History*, Book XIX, (Paris: A-U Coustelier, 1723), cap. vi.

[26] Leon Battista Alberti, *The Architecture*, trans. James Leoni (London: Robert Alfray, 1755), VIII.vii, pp. 178–9.

[27] The similarities between Alberti's description, the Calais 'round house', and the later English public theatres did not escape the notice of Orrell, *Human Stage*, pp. 61–2.

and had terraced auditoria, with seats placed in horseshoe fashion around the stage or performing area. Similarly, the so-called 'round-house' at Calais in 1520 had three tiers of galleries, one above the other – each tier raked so that people could see over the heads of those standing in front of them. And, most suggestive of all, the later theatres were similarly decorated with representations of the 'heavens', sometimes vestigial, but still recognisably celestial.

There are other cosmic ingredients, too. Both religious and court festivals often included working mechanical models of the heavens. Vasari provides considerable technical information concerning the apparatus devised by Brunelleschi for Florentine churches where stars, angels, God the Father, numerous lights and sweet music, all combined to represent Paradise 'most realistically'.[28] For the marriage entertainment of Costanzo Sforza and Camilla d'Aragona at Pesaro in May 1475, the great hall of the ducal palace was laid out for the banquet 'like a theatre' with a cosmic *mise-en-scène*. The ceiling of the hall had been completely covered with a blue cloth stretched and decorated to represent the sky, and in the centre across nearly the whole width of the room were all the signs of the Zodiac, each the size of a man. The degrees and divisions were marked in silver, while the stars related to the signs were made of mirrors and arranged 'according to what had been written by astrologers'. There were also five large planets with, at the very centre, the Sun and Moon. Suddenly a circular door opened in the heavens revealing *uno Paradiso splendentissimo* whence, to the sound of music, there descended the golden Sun and silver Moon supervising, as it were, the service of the various courses of the banquet.[29] In 1490, for the marriage of Gian Galeazzzo Sforza in Milan, Leonardo da Vinci designed a Paradiso, although it is not clear that this was a heavenly vault above the revellers.[30] On the other hand, the theatre built in the Castello at Mantua in 1501 had a roof blazing with stars and an artificial circle 'showing the signs of the zodiac' with 'the sun and moon moving in their accustomed orbits'.[31] At Binche in 1549 there was an astrological ceiling and mechanism for the 'Chambre enchantée',[32] and in 1572, for the marriage of Henry of Navarre and Marguerite

[28] Giorgio Vasari, *Vite de' piu' eccellenti pittori scultori e architetti* (Milan: Società Tipografica de' Classici Italiani: 1807–11), IV, pp. 253–8.

[29] A detailed, yet imprecise, contemporary account was published by Marco Tabarrini, *Descrizione del convito e delle feste fatte in Pesaro. . . . . nel Maggio mcccclxxv* (Florence, 1870), and there is an annotated and handsomely illustrated translation by Jane Bridgeman and Alan Griffiths, *A Renaissance Wedding* (London: Harvey Miller, 2013), especially at pp. 57–95.

[30] E. Solmi, 'La festa del Paradiso di Leonardo da Vinci', *Archivio Storico Lombardo, anno* XXXI, fasc. 1 (1904).

[31] See Cantelmo's description of the theatre which is quoted at length in Julia Cartwright, *Isabella d'Este Marchioness of Mantua, 1474–1539: A Study of the Renaissance*, 2 vols (London: John Murray, 1903), vol. 1, pp. 183–5.

[32] For an illustration of the Binche ceiling, see Hugo Soly and Johan Van de Wiele, *Carolus. Charles Quint 1500–1558* (Ghent: Snoek-Ducau & Zoon, 2000), pp. 222–3.

de Valois, a *Paradis d'Amour* included a mechanical wheel which replicated the movement of the heavens, planets and signs of the Zodiac.[33] Nor should we overlook Jean Dorat's description of the great amphitheatre in the théâtre pompeux, for the *Joyeuse Magnificences* in 1581, with its seven fiery globes performing their regular courses in an artificial heaven. This, although wholly imaginary, is also relevant to the idea of a working celestial model.[34]

Cosmological mechanisms were also popular in civic pageants for royal entries as, for example, at Paris in 1389, at Lyon in 1515, and again at Lyon in 1533.[35] London pageant-masters similarly used celestial mechanisms to enhance their shows (as for example in 1501, 1522 and 1547) where onlookers could see 'conclusions of astronomy', a princely horoscope, and the 'Elements, the Planets and stars in their places'.[36]

The cosmic mixture becomes even more interesting when ingredients from other, less obvious, sources are added. There was, for example, the *dormitorium* of Adele of Blois, fashioned like a cosmos, its floor decorated with a *mappa mundi* and its ceiling painted with a starry sky. There was the Graal Temple in *Der Jüngere Titurel*, with its sapphire roof and a starry heaven moving in its true order. And there was a description of the palace of the legendary Eastern Emperor, Prester John, with its council room turning like a wheel and bearing 'a roof vaulted like the heavens, shining at night with the brightness of day', a chapel with an immensely high dome and a star-spangled sky revolving as the firmament does, and a *dormitorium* with another starry ceiling and a Sun, Moon and planetary spheres 'each pursuing its course as in heaven'. The most likely historic sources for these imaginary cosmic chambers are even more striking. In the domed roof of the throne room of Khusrau the Ancient Eastern King, the ruler was portrayed as though in heaven, and the room literally revolved 'on its axis with the help of horses pulling in a circular motion in a subterranean room'. Yet further back in time was Nero's *Domus Aurea* with its cosmic hall described as a rotunda, revolving about its own axis day and night 'just like the world'.[37]

---

[33] See Margaret M. McGowan, *Dance in the Renaissance: European Fashion, French Obsession* (New Haven, CT and London: Yale University Press, 2008), pp. 88–9.

[34] See Monique Chatenet and Luisa Capodieci, 'Les triomphes des noces de Joyeuse (17 septembre–19 octobre 1581) à travers la correspondance diplomatique italienne et l'Epithalame de Jean Dorat', *Bulletin de la Société de l'Histoire de l'Art français* (Paris: Société de l'Histoire de l'Art français, 2007), pp. 9–54 (especially pp. 28–30).

[35] Froissart, *Chroniques*, p. 737; Georges Gigue, *L'Entrée de François Premier Roy de France en la cité de Lyon le 12 Juillet 1515* (Lyon: Société des Bibliophiles Lyonnais, 1899), Plate on pp. 26–7; Théodore Godefroy, *Le Céremonial françois* (Paris, 1649), I, pp. 808–9.

[36] Anglo, *Spectacle*, pp. 69–70, 76, 196–7, 289.

[37] A comprehensive treatment of this materal is in H.P. L'Orange, *The Iconography of Cosmic Kingship in the Ancient World* (Oslo: H. Aschehoug & Co., 1953), pp. 9–34.

I am not suggesting that – every time it was decided to build a pavilion, theatre, or banquet house – the organisers consciously decided to imitate Alberti, Nero, Khusrau or Prester John. Rather, it seems to me, we have something analogous to the chivalric challenge and response at a tournament, when knight challengers would hang shields on a tree or column to indicate the different modes of combat on offer; and the answerers would strike the relevant shield with their lance. These knights were, in fact, re-enacting the rain-making challenges of the priest king at the ancient oracle of Dodona.[38] Yet it is unlikely that the participants had any idea that this is what they were doing, and this, I think, was the case with the cosmic decor of so many festival buildings.

Occasionally, someone like Dorat or the English artisan Clement Urmeston (who worked on the Calais 'round-house' and the Greenwich theatre) propounded theories concerning the possibility of bringing celestial forces to bear upon an important occasion, linking, as it were, courtly and theatrical space with cosmic space.[39] But mostly it must have been an unthinking tradition. Like knights banging shields suspended on trees or columns, the decoration of ceilings with astrological and astronomical images was simply what people thought appropriate to the occasion.

Bibliography

Primary sources

Alberti, Leon Battista, *The Architecture*, tr. James Leoni (London: Robert Afray, 1755).

Antiopa giustificata. Drama Guerriero (Munich: Johann Jäcklin, 1662).

Auton, Jean d', *Chroniques de Louis XII*, ed. R. de Maulde la Clavière, 4 vols (Paris: Société de l'histoire de France, 1889–1895), vol. 4, pp. 307–313.

Bridgeman, Jane and Alan Griffiths (trans. and ed.), *A Renaissance Wedding: The Celebrations at Pesaro for the marriage of Costanzo Sforza & Camilla Marzano d'Aragona 26–30 May 1475* (London: Harvey Miller, 2013).

Descrizione del convito e delle feste fatte in Pesaro . . . nel Maggio mcccclxxv, ed. Marco Tabarrini (Florence, 1870).

Fleurange, Robert de la Marck, Maréchal de, *Les Mémoires*, ed. J.J. Michaud and J.J.P. Poujoulat (Paris, 1838).

38 On the origins of the tree-borne challenge, see Sydney Anglo, 'L'arbre de chevalerie et le perron dans les tournois', in Jean Jacquot (ed.), *Les Fêtes de la Renaissance* (Paris: Editions du Centre National de la Recherche Scientifique, 1975), pp. 283–98.

39 For Dorat's theories and court festivals, see Chatenet and Capodieci, *Les triomphes*; for Urmeston, see Sydney Anglo, *Images of Tudor Kingship* (London: Seaby, 1992), pp. 24–8.

Froissart, Jean, *Les Chroniques*, ed. Madame De Witt, née Guizot (Paris: Hachette, 1881).
Gigue, Georges, *L'Entrée de François Premier Roy de France en la cité de Lyon le 12 Juillet 1515* (Lyon: Société des Bibliophiles Lyonnais, 1899).
Godefroy, Théodore, *Le Céremonial françois* (Paris, 1649).
Hall, Edward, *The Union of the Two Noble and Illustre Famelies of Lancastre and York*, ed. Henry Ellis (London: J. Johnson, 1809).
Marche, Olivier de la, *Mémoires*, ed. H. Beaune and J. D'Arbaumont, 4 vols (Paris: Société de l'Histoire de France, 1885).
Mercurio e Marte discordi. Torneo a piedi (Munich, 1654).
Pliny the Elder, *Natural History*, Book XIX (Paris: A-U Coustelier, 1723).
Sanuto, Marino, *I Diarii di Marino Sanuto*, ed. F. Stefani (Venice: F. Visentini, 1879–1902).
Saint-Remy, *Chronique de Jean le Févre Seigneur de Saint-Remy*, ed. François Morand, 2 vols (Paris: Société de l'Histoire de France, 1871).
Vasari, Giorgio, *Vite de' piu eccellenti pittori scultori e architetti* (Milan: Società Tipografica de' Classici Italiani, 1807–11).
Vulson, Marc de, sieur de La Colombière, *Le Vray Théâtre d'honneur*, 2 vols (Paris: Chez Augustin Courbé, 1648).

Secondary sources

Anglo, Sydney, 'La salle de banquet et le théatre construits à Greenwich pour les fêtes Franco-Anglaises de 1527', in Jean Jacquot (ed.), *Le lieu théatral à la Renaissance* (Paris: Centre Nationale de la Recherche Scientifique, 1963), 273–88.
Anglo, Sydney, 'Anglo-Burgundian Feats of Arms: Smithfield, June 1467', *The Guildhall Miscellany*, II (1965), 271–83.
Anglo, Sydney, 'The Hampton Court Painting of the Field of Cloth of Gold Considered as an Historical Document', *The Antiquaries Journal*, XLVI (1966), 287–307.
Anglo, Sydney, *Spectacle, Pageantry and Early Tudor Policy* (Oxford: Clarendon Press, 1969).
Anglo, Sydney, 'L'arbre de chevalerie et le perron dans les tournois', in Jean Jacquot (ed.), *Les Fêtes de la Renaissance* (Paris: Centre National de la Recherche Scientifique, 1975), pp. 283–98.
Anglo, Sydney, *Images of Tudor Kingship* (London: Seaby, 1992).
Cartwright, Julia, *Isabella d'Este Marchioness of Mantua, 1474–1539: A Study of the Renaissance*, 2 vols (London: John Murray, 1903).
Chatenet, Monique and Luisa Capodieci, 'Les triomphes des noces de Joyeuse (17 septembre–19 octobre 1581) à travers la correspondance diplomatique italienne et *l'Epithalame* de Jean Dorat', *Bulletin de la Société de l'Histoire de l'Art français* (Paris: Société de l'Histoire de l'Art français, 2007), 9–54.

Clementi, Filippo, *Il Carnevale Romano nelle cronache contemporanee* (Rome: Tipografia Tiberina, 1899).

Colvin, H.M. (ed.), *The History of the King's Works*, 4 vols (London: Her Majesty's Stationery Office, 1982).

Hosley, Richard, 'The Theatre and the Tradition of English Playhouse Design', in H. Berry (ed.), *The First Public Playhouse: The Theatre in Shoreditch 1576–1598* (Montreal: McGill-Queen's University Press, 1979), pp. 47–79.

L'Orange, H.P., *The Iconography of Cosmic Kingship in the Ancient World* (Oslo: H. Aschehoug, 1953).

Lecoq, Anne-Marie, 'Une fête italienne à la Bastille en 1518', in *'Il se rendit en Italie': Etudes offertes à André Chastel, CNRS* (Paris: Flammarion, 1987).

McGowan, Margaret M., *Dance in the Renaissance: European Fashion, French Obsession* (New Haven, CT and London: Yale University Press, 2008).

Mitchell, Bonner, *Italian Civic Pageantry in the High Renaissance* (Florence: Leo S. Olschki, 1979).

Nagler, A.M., *Theatre Festivals of the Medici 1539–1637* (New Haven, CT and London: Yale University Press, 1964).

Orrell, John, *The Human Stage. English Theatre Design, 1567–1640* (Cambridge: Cambridge University Press, 1988).

Solmi, E., 'La festa del Paradiso di Leonardo da Vinci', *Archivio Storico Lombardo*, XXXI, fasc. 1 (1904).

Soly, Hugo and Johan Van de Wiele, *Carolus. Charles Quint 1500–1558* (Ghent: Snoek-Ducau & Zoon, 2000).

Young, Alan, *Tudor and Jacobean Tournaments* (London: George Philip, 1987).

Chapter 9

Transformed gardens

The *trompe-l'œil* scenery of the Versailles festivals (1664–1674)

Marie-Claude Canova-Green[1]

Tout le monde a ouï parler des merveilles de cette fête, des palais devenus jardins, et des jardins devenus palais

[Everybody has heard of the marvels of this festival, of palaces transformed into gardens, and gardens into palaces].[2]

The lavish festivals given at Versailles by Louis XIV in the spring and summer of 1664, 1668 and 1674 were an ideal opportunity not only to demonstrate his magnificence, but also to display the beauty of the gardens designed by André Le Nôtre. Carriage rides in the *petit parc* were arranged so that the guests could admire the *parterres* and the ingenious forms the water took as it gushed out of the many fountains. At night, both the palace and the gardens were illuminated and splendid fireworks were set off over the grand canal and other reflecting pools. *Bosquets* were converted into ballrooms, concert halls or open-air theatres that attempted to blend in with the shrubbery, or whose *trompe-l'œil* sets led to the confusion between artifice and reality.[3] Some of the decors opened onto the outside

[1] This chapter draws on research done for my book on Molière's *comédies-ballets*, *'Ces gens-là se trémoussent bien . . . ' Ébats et débats dans les comédies-ballets de Molière* (Tübingen: Gunter Narr, 2007).

[2] Jean de La Fontaine, 'Les Amours de Psyché et de Cupidon', in Pierre Clarac (ed.), *Œuvres diverses* (Paris: Gallimard, 1978), p. 187.

[3] Robert Ballard and the Imprimerie Royale published folio descriptions of the three festivals, which included magnificent engravings of the garden arrangements by Israel Silvestre, Jean Le Pautre and François Chauveau, *Les Plaisirs de l'Isle Enchantée. Course de Bague, Collation ornée de Machines, Comedie meslée de Danse & de Musique, Ballet du Palais d'Alcine, Feu d'Artifice: Et autres Festes galantes & magnifiques; faites par le Roy à Versailles, le 7. May 1664. Et continuées plusieurs autres Jours* (Paris: Robert Ballard, 1664), incl. 9 plates by Israel Silvestre; this was reprinted as *Les Plaisirs de l'Isle Enchantée. Course de Bague; Collation ornée de Machines; Comedie meslée de Danse et de Musique; Ballet du Palais d'Alcine; Feu d'Artifice: Et autres Festes galantes et magnifiques, faites par le Roy à Versailles, le VII. May M.DC.LXIV. Et continuées plusieurs*

space, allowing a glimpse of the royal palace in the distance, or revealing the surrounding gardens in such a way that they seemed to be a continuation of the stage set. Elsewhere, the scene was an exact copy of the latest garden embellishments, which also left the audience in doubt as to what was painted decor or real landscape.

The actual or symbolic opening of the sets onto the landscape of elaborate gardens surrounding the open-air theatre not only disclosed a world of natural beauty that was identical to the one represented on stage and with which the spectators were familiar, it also revealed that the space around the theatre was a space controlled and shaped by the royal will and imagination in the same way as the illusionistic scenery on stage showed the designer's ability to shape matter.[4] In other words, the image of the royal palace and gardens that was offered to the spectators whether on stage or off stage was the image of an enchanted world in which nature and culture combined for the greater glory of a monarch whose every action was said to be a miracle or an illusion. It was also the image of a mythical world, be it Arcadia or the Vale of Tempe in ancient Greece,[5] revisited within the space of a festival and superimposed on the world of everyday courtly intrigue and manoeuvring.

First attempts: Fontainebleau and *Le Ballet des saisons* (1661)

As early as 23 July 1661, the poet Isaac de Benserade and Carlo Vigarani, the Italian architect and stage designer in charge of Louis XIV's court entertainments, devised an '*apareil si nouveau*' ('a very novel machine') for the performance of the *Ballet des saisons* at Fontainebleau. Madame de La Fayette expressed her admiration in her *Memoirs*:

> *L'on répétoit alors à Fontainebleau un Ballet, que le Roi et Madame dancerent, et qui fut le plus agreable qui ait jamais été, soit par le lieu où il se dançoit, qui étoit le bord de l'étang, ou par l'invention qu'on avoit trouvée, de faire venir du*

autres Jours (Paris: Imprimerie Royale, par Sébastien Marbre-Cramoisy, 1673), incl. 9 plates by Israel Silvestre; André Félibien, *Relation de la Feste de Versailles. Du 18. Juillet mil six cens soixante-huit* (Paris: Imprimerie Royale, 1679), incl. 5 plates by Jean Le Pautre; André Félibien, *Les Divertissemens de Versailles, donnez par le Roy [. . .] au retour de la conqueste de la Franche-Comté, en l'année MDCLXXIV* (Paris: Imprimerie Royale, par Sébastien Marbre-Cramoisy, 1676), incl. 6 plates by Jean Le Pautre and François Chauveau.

[4] See Stephen Orgel, *The Illusion of Power: Political Theater in the Renaissance* (Berkeley: University of California Press, 1975).

[5] Both locations were used as settings for the action in Molière's *La Princesse d'Elide* and *Les Amants magnifiques*, performed at Versailles in 1664 and at Saint-Germain-en-Laye in 1670.

> *bout d'une Allée le Theâtre tout entier, chargé d'une infinité de personnes, et qui faisoient une Entrée, en dansant devant le theâtre.*
>
> [At the time, they were rehearsing a ballet at Fontainebleau, in which the King and Madame [Henriette d'Angleterre, Duchesse d'Orléans] took part and which was the most pleasant ever danced, both because of its location by the lake, and because they had found the means to bring the whole theatre from the far end of an *allée*, carrying a large number of performers, who alighted and danced their entry in front of it].[6]

The natural setting for this *al fresco* production had provided not only the idea for the decoration of the stage, but also the general theme of the evening entertainment. As the *Argument* explains, '*[l]e sujet de ce Ballet est tiré du lieu où il se danse*' ('the subject of the ballet is drawn from the location where it is danced').[7] As the seasons came and went during the course of the ballet, each with its own specific pleasures and occupations, the set changed, successively representing a wooded landscape with cascading waters, a garden adorned with *parterres* of flowers, wheat fields with harvesters, vineyards and grape-pickers, a winter scene, and finally another delightful garden to mark the definitive return of spring.

In a way, the *Ballet des saisons* inaugurated the royal open-air festival with its blurring of distinctions between illusion and reality and, above all, the mutation of the festive royal space into a mythical land where courtiers were offered the innocent pleasures of *galant* love and lavish entertainments under the aegis of the all-powerful monarch. As Volker Kapp remarks, 'in staging the pleasure-civilization in which they participated because they belonged to the king's sphere', the ballet was the tangible manifestation of the new political order being established; it also represented 'the fulfilment of that promised happiness'.[8] Once they had been excluded from political decision-making by Louis XIV, who built on his father's policy of extending absolute rule and preferred to rely on trusted *hommes de robe*, a life of leisure and pleasure was all that noble courtiers could hope for.

Les Plaisirs de l'île enchantée (1664)

Together with the dramatist Molière, Vigarani was responsible for the *al fresco* dramatic productions given in *théâtres de verdure* at the 1664 and 1668 Versailles

---

[6] Marie-Madeleine Pioche de la Vergne, comtesse de La Fayette, *Histoire de Madame Henriette d'Angleterre* (Amsterdam: M.-C. Le Cène, 1720), p. 61.

[7] Isaac de Benserade, 'Ballet des saisons', in Marie-Claude Canova-Green (ed.), *Benserade. Ballets pour Louis XIV*, 2 vols (Toulouse: SLC/Klincksieck, 1999), vol. 2, p. 537.

[8] Volker Kapp, 'Félibien interprète des *Quatre Saisons* de Le Brun. Analyse d'un thème des thuriféraires de Louis XIV et réflexions méthodologiques sur l'étude de la littérature panégyrique', *Cahiers de littérature du XVIIe* siècle, 8 (1986), 179–96, 186–7. Author's translation.

festivals. These plays included a number of pastoral interludes that mirrored the surrounding location. Indeed, the Italian designer seems to have gone to great lengths to confuse illusion and reality in their settings, notably by using one of the garden *allées* leading to the palace instead of a painted backcloth on at least one occasion to close the perspective. It goes without saying that he might have made use of the natural setting for purely practical reasons. But doing so also enabled him to remind the monarch (and the court audience) of the extensive and costly redevelopment of the royal park and gardens and thus pay homage to Louis XIV's transforming power over nature.

For the production of *La Princesse d'Elide* on 8 May 1664, on the second day of the festival known as *Les Plaisirs de l'île enchantée*, a temporary structure was erected in the middle of the narrow *Allée Royale* leading from the palace to the *Rondeau des Cygnes* (soon to become the *Bassin d'Apollon*).[9] This structure was hung around with tapestries to prevent the wind from blowing out the hundreds of candles that lit the stage. To give the impression of a close connection between the stage and the auditorium, leafy trees were painted on the inside of the side panels delimiting the hall to resemble the ones painted on the four pairs of parallel flats that composed the set.[10] Spectators were also painted sitting in the trees with their heads turned towards the stage and the actors. Even the proscenium arch was covered in foliage. Judging from the engraving by Israel Silvestre for *La Princesse d'Élide* (see Figure 9.1), Vigarani had also endeavoured to blur the distinction between the decor and the surrounding location by using a painted backcloth with a perspective view of a palace and an *allée* lined with perfectly clipped hedges to give the impression that the rear of the stage, beyond the disproportionately tall trees painted on the flats, was open. To add to the illusion, the zone beyond the lit proscenium where the comedy took place had also been shaded on the engraving so as to suggest a difference between the sloping boards of the stage and the sand or gravel of the *Allée* and to make it look as though a raised platform had been erected right across the *Allée* to serve as a stage for the comedy.

This engraving has led a number of scholars to assume wrongly that the rear of the stage was indeed open,[11] thus allowing the spectators to see the perspective of the *Allée Royale* with a palace in the distance. Some have argued that the palace was the royal palace itself, which, in 1664, was still the modest *pavillon de chasse* built in 1623 for Louis XIII.[12] The references in the play to the *palais* of the

---

[9] This was where the *Bosquet des Dômes* now stands. For the exact location of the various events, see Marie-Christine Moine, *Les Fêtes à la cour du roi Soleil (1653–1715)* (Paris: Éditions Lanore, 1984), as well as Sabine Du Crest, *Des fêtes à Versailles. Les Divertissements de Louis XIV* (s.l.: Aux Amateurs de livres, 1990).

[10] See Helen M.C. Purkis, 'L'Illusion théâtrale', *Studi francesi*, 63 (1977), 407–24.

[11] The acoustic implications of having a stage open to the rear would have been considerable. I am grateful to Jan Clarke for pointing this out to me.

[12] Helen M.C. Purkis, 'Le Chant pastoral chez Molière', *Cahiers de l'Association Internationale des Études Françaises*, 28 (May 1976), 133–44, 136.

Figure 9.1 Israel Silvestre, 'Theatre fait dans la mesme allée, sur lequel la Comédie, et le Ballet de la Princesse d'Elide furent representez', *Les Plaisirs de l'Isle enchantée, Seconde Journée* (Paris: Imprimerie Royale, 1673) (© The British Library Board, 562*g.25(1)). Reproduced by kind permission of the British Library Board). (f.s.)

Prince d'Ithaque, the eponymous heroine's father, and the mirror effects between comedy and reality would seem to support such an interpretation. However, even if the rear of the stage had been open, it would have been unlikely that Vigarani would have arranged the perspective so that the spectators would be looking up towards the royal palace. Moreover, contemporary accounts appear to suggest that the spectators were facing away from the palace and towards the *Rondeau des Cygnes*, where the next day's entertainment, known as *Le Palais d'Alcine*, took place at the bottom of the *Allée Royale*.[13] As a result, other scholars have argued that the palace closing the perspective on the engraving was in fact the temporary structure erected in the middle of the *Rondeau* for this entertainment, which

---

[13] *'Le lendemain, toute la Décoration ayant esté changée, on apperçeut au delà du Portique qui estoit en face, une tres-grande Sale, remplie de siéges & d'Eschafaux, vis à vis un autre Portique fermé par un Rideau'* ('The next day, the decoration was changed and now showed, beyond the arch opposite, a very large room with tiered seating, opposite another arch concealed by a curtain'), 'Les Particularitez des Divertissemens pris à Versailles, par leurs Majestez', *La Gazette*, no. 60, 21 May 1664, pp. 491–2.

Figure 9.2 Israel Silvestre, 'Theatre dressé au milieu du grand Estang representant l'Isle d'Alcine', *Les Plaisirs de l'Isle enchantée, Troisiesme Journée* (Paris: Imprimerie Royale, 1673) (© The British Library Board, 562*g.25(1). Reproduced by kind permission of the British Library Board)

included a ballet as well as a firework display.[14] The two palaces are quite similar, although Silvestre has not represented the two smaller islands that frame the island on which Alcine's palace was built for the following entertainment (as shown on another of his engravings; see Figure 9.2).[15]

The text of the official festival book lends credence to this hypothesis:

> *Lorsque la nuit du second jour fut venue, Leurs Majestés se rendirent dans un autre rond environné de palissades comme le premier, et sur la même ligne, s'avançant toujours vers le Lac, où l'on feignait que le Palais d'Alcine était bâti*

---

[14] This is the interpretation given by Jérôme de La Gorce, *Carlo Vigarani, intendant des plaisirs de Louis XIV* (Paris: Éditions Perrin/Établissement public du musée et du domaine national de Versailles, 2005), pp. 60–1. This is also the interpretation favoured by Helen M.C. Purkis in 'L'Illusion théâtrale', although she had earlier suggested that the palace closing the perspective was the royal palace.

[15] Remark made by Thomas Edward Lawrenson, *The French Stage in the Seventeenth Century* (Manchester: Manchester University Press, 1957), p. 133.

[On the second day, when night came, Their Majesties went to another *rond*, which, like the first one, was surrounded with a fence. It was situated on the same axis but closer to the lake where Alcine's palace was supposed to have been built].[16]

However this confronts us with a problem. We know from the account given in the *Gazette* that Alcine's palace was hidden from view until the evening of 9 May and that only once the spectators were seated,

[à] l'instant, par un admirable artifice, le Rocher se séparant aux deux bords de l'Isle, laissa voir ce Palais qui surprit également les Spectateurs par sa magnifique structure, & par l'élévation qui s'en fit, à mesure que le Rocher s'ouvroit, jusques à la hauteur de 25 pieds, s'élargissant, aussi, à proportion, jusques à 30

[All of a sudden, by an ingenious device, the rock split in two and revealed a palace which surprised the spectators by its magnificent structure and by the way it grew taller and wider as the rock opened, eventually reaching a height of 25 feet and a width of 30 feet].[17]

If the palace had been visible (and also lit) the day before, that is during the performance of *La Princesse d'Élide*, there would have been no surprise the next day, no sudden revelation of what was obviously meant to be one of the highlights of the evening. The spectators would have experienced no wonder, no astonishment, in spite of the fact that the search for *maraviglia* was at the heart of Louis XIV's festive aesthetics.[18] In other words, the palace seen on the first engraving *cannot* be Alcine's palace.[19]

All the evidence seems to point to the fact that the stage was not open at the rear between the side flats. Instead, the gap was filled by a perspective backcloth. So why is Silvestre at pains to suggest the opposite? Was it to place the evening's entertainment under the aegis of the monarch (shown seated in the foreground) and to locate the dramatic action in a space expressing, and visibly circumscribed by, the royal domain? The palace and trees were painted on canvas, but it was essential that the engraved record of the performance showcased the commanding

---

[16] 'Les Plaisirs de l'île enchantée', in Molière, *Œuvres complètes*, ed. Georges Forestier et al., 2 vols (Paris: Éditions Gallimard, 2010), vol. 1, p. 535.

[17] *La Gazette*, p. 494.

[18] See Louis Marin, 'Le Roi magicien ou la fête du prince', in Louis Marin (ed.), *Le Portrait du roi* (Paris: Éditions de Minuit, 1974), pp. 236–50.

[19] Nevertheless, as Helen M.C. Purkis suggests, it is quite possible that the royal palace was visible through the proscenium arch framing the entrance to the theatre directly opposite the stage, as it had been on the first day of the *Plaisirs de l'île enchantée* through the entrance to the lists. See Purkis, 'L'Illusion théâtrale', p. 411.

presence of the monarch.[20] In the same way, the third-day entertainment of *Les Plaisirs de l'île enchantée* strongly emphasised the impression of circularity and concentricity created by the spatial arrangements, in order to turn the festive royal space into a closed, protected, utopian world of happiness or, at the very least, pleasure. The engraving by Israel Silvestre (see Figure 9.2) not only revealed the rationale behind the Versailles festivals, it turned the royal domain into an island literally and metaphorically separated from the rest of the country.[21]

Le Grand Divertissement Royal (1668)

Vigarani used an even more ingenious set for his and Molière's production of *Les Fêtes de l'Amour et de Bacchus* for the *Grand Divertissement Royal* on 18 July 1668. According to André Félibien, an open-air theatre had been erected on one of the side *allées* parallel to the *Allée Royale*, at an intersection with one of the cross-walks, where the *Bassin de Saturne* now stands:

> *C'est dans cet endroit de l'allée du Roi que le sieur Vigarani avait disposé le lieu de la comédie. Le théâtre qui avançait un peu dans le carré de la place s'enfonçait de dix toises dans l'allée qui monte vers le château*
>
> [This is where, in the *allée du Roi*, Vigarani had set up the stage for the comedy. The theatre, which projected a little into the square at the intersection, was sixty feet deep in the alley going up towards the palace].[22]

Félibien reported that the king himself had chosen the location as particularly appropriate: '*Il leur marqua lui-même les endroits où la disposition naturelle du lieu pouvait par sa beauté naturelle contribuer davantage à leur décoration*' ('He showed them himself those places whose natural beauty would contribute best to their décor').[23]

---

[20] In an earlier article I argued that there was an opening in the backcloth, showing the surrounding gardens, see Marie-Claude Canova-Green, 'Le Jeu du fermé et de l'ouvert dans les comédies-ballets de Molière', in Georges Forestier and Lise Michel (eds), *La Scène et la coulisse dans le théâtre du XVIIe siècle en France* (Paris: PUPS, 2011), pp. 261–77. I have since come to think that this was not the case.

[21] For a full discussion of these ideas see Marie-Claude Canova-Green, 'L'Île comme métaphore politique dans le spectacle de cour au XVIIe siècle', in Christian Zonza (ed.), *L'Île au XVIIe siècle. Jeux et enjeux* (Tübingen: Gunter Narr, 2010), pp. 259–72.

[22] André Félibien, 'Relation de la fête de Versailles', in Martin Meade (ed.), *Les Fêtes de Versailles. Chroniques de 1668 & 1674* (Paris: Éditions Dédale, Maisonneuve et Larose, 1994), p. 41.

[23] Ibid., p. 32.

To blend in with the surrounding shrubbery, the theatre had been made to look like an

> *Edifice d'apparence rustique, qui s'eslevant presque a la hauteur des arbres, & n'ayant pour descoration exterieure que la dépoüille des Forests & des Jardins, effaçoit la Pompe des Palais, & donnoit de l'éclat a des choses simples & champestres*
>
> [edifice of rustic appearance that, rising almost to the level of the tops of the trees and having no other exterior decoration than what had been stripped from forests and gardens, effaced the pomp of palaces and gave sophisticated style to rural simplicity].[24]

Its walls inside and out had been covered with leaves as if it too were a *bosquet* built by Le Nôtre. As for the set itself, which provided the background to both the pastoral and the comedy written by Molière, it was a *trompe-l'œil* garden, whose terraces, fountains and canal not only imitated the layout of the park and gardens, but opened out onto them, to the extent that '[the spectators'] eyes were totally fooled, and they thought they were in fact seeing a garden of extraordinary beauty':[25]

> *A l'entrée de ce jardin, on découvrait deux palissades si ingénieusement moulées qu'elles formaient un ordre d'architecture dont la corniche était soutenue par quatre termes qui représentaient des satyres. . . . [E]t sur les piédestaux de marbre qui soutenaient ces mêmes termes, il y avait de grands vases dorés, aussi remplis de fleurs. Un peu plus loin paraissaient deux terrasses revêtues de marbre blanc qui environnaient un long canal. . . . On montait sur ces terrasses par trois degrés et, sur la même ligne où étaient rangés les termes, il y avait, d'un côté et d'autre, une longue allée de grands arbres entre lesquels paraissaient des cabinets d'une architecture rustique. . . . Le bout du canal le plus proche était bordé de douze jets d'eau qui formaient autant de chandeliers; et à l'autre extrémité on voyait un superbe édifice en forme de dôme. Il était percé de trois portiques au travers desquels on découvrait une grande étendue de pays.*
>
> [At the entrance to the garden, two fences were ingeniously shaped to look like an order of architecture, whose cornice was supported by four terms representing satyrs. . . . And on the marble pedestals supporting these terms there were large golden vases, which were also filled with flowers. A little further away

---

[24] Abbé de Montigny, 'La Feste de Versailles. Du 18 juillet 1668. À Monsieur le Marquis de la Füente', in *Recueil de diverses pièces faites par plusieurs personnages* (The Hague: J. & D. Steucker, 1669), p. 9.

[25] '*Et alors, les yeux se trouvant tout à fait trompés, l'on crut voir effectivement un jardin d'une beauté extraordinaire*'. Félibien, 'Relation de la fête de Versailles', p. 43.

> two terraces covered with white marble could be seen on either side of a long canal. . . . These terraces could be reached by three steps and on each side, on a level with the row of terms, there was a long walk planted with trees, between which rustic looking arbours could be seen. . . . At the end of the canal closest to the spectators, there were twelve water jets forming the shape of candelabra as the water gushed out; at the other end was a superb building in the shape of a dome. It had three porticoes through which could be seen vast expanses of landscape.][26]

In other words, *George Dandin*, the *al fresco* marital farce inserted in the pastoral *Les Fêtes de l'Amour et de Bacchus*, was performed in a setting which bore no relation to the spatial or social indications given in the comedy's text. It took place in an ideal space that may have weakened the effect of reality suggested by its plot, but that established a link with the actual location of the theatre and ensured the continuity between the comedy and the wider festival. For, in its smaller space, the decor replicated the larger spaces inhabited by the court. It used the same materials (marble, bronze), the same decorative elements (flowers, trees, fountains), the same architectural features (terraces, *allées*, canal). It set an illusionistic garden within the true garden that it resembled.[27] In other words, it turned the scenic space into 'a kind of hall of mirrors, where there was little difference between the actual and the virtual'.[28]

I would also argue that the emphasis on water features, fountains, pools, basins and the like, together with the view of terraces sloping down towards a canal, were a way to pay homage to the recent developments ordered by the King to improve the water supply to the palace gardens. The many fountains with their spectacular *grandes eaux* had been made possible by the completion of the pumping machine and the *Tour d'eau* in 1665. The canal (the first one to be dug in Versailles) was an even more recent addition to the marvels of the gardens since its construction had only just begun.[29] In fact the King's instructions to the stage designer had been quite specific. Vigarani had been instructed,

---

[26] Ibid., p. 44–5. Madeleine de Scudéry concurs: '*La premiere face du theatre fut un superbe jardin orné de canaux, de cascades, de la veuë d'un palais, et d'un lointain au delà*' ('the first set was a superb garden ornamented with canals, waterfalls, the view of a palace, and the prospect beyond'), Madeleine de Scudéry, 'La Feste de Versailles, à M.***', in *La Promenade de Versailles* (Paris: Claude Barbin, 1669), p. 585.

[27] Roger Chartier, 'De la fête de cour au public citadin', in Roger Chartier (ed.), *Culture écrite et société. L'ordre des livres (XIVe–*XVIIIe siècle) (Paris: Albin Michel, 1996), pp. 155–204, p. 176.

[28] Gretchen Elizabeth Smith, *The Performance of Male Nobility in Molière's comédies-ballets* (Aldershot: Ashgate, 2005), p. 126.

[29] See Pierre de Nolhac, *La Création de Versailles* (Versailles: Librairie L. Bernard, 1901) and Alfred Marie, *Naissance de Versailles* (Paris: Éditions Vincent, 1968).

parce que l'un des plus beaux ornements de cette maison est la quantité des eaux que l'art y a conduites malgré la nature qui les lui avait refusées, . . . de s'en servir le plus qu'il pourrait à l'embellissement de ces lieux

[because one of the best ornaments of this house is the abundance of the waters that art has brought here in spite of nature which had denied them, . . . to use them as much as possible for the embellishment of the location].[30]

Similarly the engraver's insistence on trees and *bosquets*, often represented larger than life (as in Silvestre's engraving for *La Princesse d'Elide*), were a way to showcase Le Nôtre's achievements as well as to emphasise their importance as a resource for the country, since trees provided the timber necessary for shipbuilding and military fortifications.[31] The exaggerated size of the trees was a way to project into the future and to show them as they would look once they had reached their maturity, although in some cases fully-grown trees had even been transplanted to give an immediate effect.[32] In other words, official engravings, whether of the Versailles festivals or of the palace gardens, always represented the gardens in an imagined state of completion and perfection, thus showing the elements yielding to the will of the monarch; nature was disciplined as if by miracle.

The production of *Les Fêtes de l'Amour et de Bacchus* also gave Vigarani the chance to replicate the kind of temporary structure and sets that had elicited the admiration of the court in previous years. A *théâtre de verdure* decorated with '*un nombre infiny de Fontaines, de Jets d'eau, & de Cascades*' ('an infinite number of fountains, jets of water and cascades')[33] was erected for the *al fresco* production of the *Ballet des saisons* at Fontainebleau on 23 July 1661. Another *théâtre de verdure* was built for the performance of Mme de Villedieu's *Le Favori* at Versailles on 13 June 1665, in exactly the same spot where *La Princesse d'Elide* had been given the year before:

Dans un aimable bois dont les sombres allées,
Pour les rayons du jour semblent être voilées,
Dans un endroit bordé, de rameaux toûjours vers,
Où viennent aboutir quatre sentiers divers.
Au sortir d'un parterre, Ouvert & magnifique,
Fut trassé le dessein d'un Theâtre rustique,
Où se montroit aux yeux, comme en éloignement,
De mille chûtes d'eau, le liquide ornement

---

30 Félibien, 'Relation de la fête de Versailles', p. 32.

31 See Chandra Mukerji, *Territorial Ambitions and the Gardens of Versailles* (Cambridge: Cambridge University Press, 1997), pp. 73–6.

32 Madame de Sévigné wrote in a letter that while out riding she had seen 'entire leafy forests being carried to Versailles', quoted in Helen M. Fox, *André Le Nôtre, Garden Architect to Kings* (London: B.T. Batsford, 1962), p. 106.

33 Benserade, 'Ballet des saisons', vol. 2, p. 538.

> [In a pleasant wood whose dark *allées*
> Seem shielded from the rays of the sun,
> In a place lined with evergreen boughs,
> Where four different paths converge,
> At the end of an open and magnificent *parterre*,
> A rustic looking theatre was designed,
> Which revealed, as if in the distance,
> The liquid ornament of a thousand cascades].[34]

The decor used for *Les Fêtes de l'Amour et de Bacchus* not only offered a glimpse of the real palace gardens, it cited and even overemphasised the features in them which helped to construct a particular image of the King and the King's space. It was shown to belong to a world of *otium* and pleasure, whose existence was guaranteed by the restoration of the peace in Europe.[35] In the same way, *La Princesse d'Elide* in May 1664 had encouraged a correspondence, if not a complete identification, between the fictional site and the actual site of Versailles, between the mythical Arcadia where the dramatic action was supposed to take place, and the new Arcadia represented by the royal gardens with their groves, turf, and murmuring waters, a modern-day *locus amoenus* given over to the pleasures of love and *galanterie*.

An outcome was the surprise the spectators must have felt at the last scene change of *Les Fêtes de l'Amour et de Bacchus* in July 1668. The new set revealed a landscape gone wild, with trees and large rocks, as if Versailles had reverted to its original state, to what it used to look like before Le Nôtre's transformation of the gardens (see Figure 9.3):[36]

> *Ici, la décoration du théâtre se trouve changée en un instant et l'on ne peut comprendre comment tant de véritables jets d'eau ne paraissent plus ni par quel artifice, au lieu de ces cabinets et de ces allées, on ne découvre sur le théâtre*

---

[34] Marie-Catherine de Villedieu, 'Description d'une des fêtes que le Roi a faite à Versailles', in *Œuvres de Mme de Villedieu* (Paris: Vve Barbin, 1702), pp. 403–4.

[35] The *Grand Divertissement Royal* was given to celebrate the signature of the peace treaty of Aix-La-Chapelle on 2 May 1668, which ended the War of Devolution and Louis XIV's successful military campaign in Flanders: '*Le roi, ayant accordé la paix aux instances de ses alliés et aux vœux de toute l'Europe, . . . ne pensait plus qu'à s'appliquer aux affaires de son royaume lorsque, pour réparer en quelque sorte ce que la cour avait perdu dans le carnaval pendant son absence, il résolut de faire une fête dans les jardins de Versailles*' ('Having granted peace at the request of his allies and the wishes of the whole of Europe, the King was thinking of nothing more than devoting himself to the affairs of his kingdom when he decided to give a festival in the gardens of Versailles to compensate the court for what they had lost in his absence during the Carnival'), Félibien, 'Relation de la fête de Versailles', p. 31.

[36] Only the structure with the three arches closing the perspective seems to have been retained for this last scene (see Figure 9.3).

Figure 9.3 Jean Le Pautre, 'Les Festes de l'Amour et de Bacchus, Comedie en Musique representée dans le petit Parc de Versailles', *Relation de la Feste de Versailles* (Paris: Imprimerie Royale, 1679) (© The British Library Board, 562*g.25(2)). Reproduced by kind permission of the British Library Board

que de grandes roches entremêlées d'arbres, où l'on voit plusieurs bergers qui chantent et qui jouent de toutes sortes d'instruments

[Now the scene changed in an instant and one could not understand how so many real fountains could no longer be seen, nor by what ingenious device arbours and walks were replaced by great rocks interspersed with trees, amidst which many shepherds could be seen singing and playing all sorts of instruments].[37]

It was as if the landscape had changed to mimic the mood and behaviour of Bacchus and his unruly followers, who came onto the stage to oppose the shepherds and the shepherdesses, devotees of the god of Love, and end the evening's entertainment on a more raucous note. It therefore contrasted vividly with the harmoniously laid-out auditorium and its audience, hierarchically seated around

[37] Félibien, 'Relation de la fête de Versailles', p. 52.

the King, whose plumed hat seems to centre the decor in Le Pautre's engraving of the production (see Figure 9.3).

Les Grands Divertissements de Versailles (1674)

Vigarani was to design another set for the performance of an operatic version of *Les Fêtes de l'Amour et de Bacchus*[38] staged on the fourth day (28 July 1674) of the third and last of the Versailles festivals, known as *Les Grands Divertissements de Versailles*. This time the performance took place in a temporary theatre at the top of the *Allée du Dragon*, close to the *Tour d'Eau*. According to the description published by Félibien, there were no longer distant prospects, with the view stretching as far back as the horizon; instead the set revealed a garden symmetrically designed:

> *Au-delà de cette face paraissait un jardin fort délicieux; il était disposé par grandes allées bordées de part et d'autre de palissades d'arbres verts, industrieusement taillés en diverses manières. Plusieurs figures représentant des termes portaient des consoles et des corniches taillées dans les palissades mêmes. Et entre ces termes, il y avait des bassins de fontaines d'où sortait de l'eau*
>
> [A delightful garden could be seen beyond the proscenium arch; it was divided by wide *allées* which were lined with *palissade* hedges of green trees, painstakingly clipped in different ways. Several figures representing terms supported consoles and cornices cut out of the hedges. Between these terms were pools with fountains of gushing water].[39]

The set used for the last *intermède* also showed some differences. The scene was now markedly pastoral and revealed a succession of '*portiques de verdure*' ('arches of foliage')[40] ornamented with grapes and vine leaves, which could be seen receding into the distance. Seated shepherds played music. However it seems that on this occasion Vigarani had to make do with flats and backcloths rather than try to integrate elements of the natural setting as he had done in July 1668.

---

38 This operatic version of the 1668 *Fêtes* had first been performed at the Académie Royale de Musique in Paris on 11 November 1672. It was in fact a hotchpotch of extracts not only from the original work performed at Versailles on 18 July 1668 but also from other court entertainments by Molière and Lulli, notably *Le Bourgeois Gentilhomme* (Chambord, 14 October 1670), *Les Amants magnifiques* (Saint-Germain-en-Laye, 4 February 1670) and *La Pastorale Comique* (Saint-Germain-en-Laye, 5 January 1667).

39 Félibien, *Les Divertissements de Versailles*, p. 133.

40 Ibid.

Figure 9.4 Jean Le Pautre, 'Le Malade imaginaire, Comedie representée dans le Jardin de Versailles devant la Grotte', *Les Divertissemens de Versailles* (Paris: Imprimerie Royale, 1676) (© The British Library Board, 562*g.25(3). Reproduced by kind permission of the British Library Board)

The set used for the posthumous production of Molière's *Le Malade imaginaire* on 19 July 1774,[41] on the third day of *Les Grands Divertissements*, raises some interesting issues. A temporary stage had been constructed outside the *Grotte de Thétis*, whose façade showed a blazing sun and whose normally closed *grilles* were open to reveal the interior and the three Apollo groups (Figure 9.4):

> *L'aspect de la Grotte servait de fond à ce théâtre élevé de deux pieds et demi de terre. Le frontispice était une grande corniche architravée, soutenue aux deux extrémités par deux massifs avec des ornements rustiques et semblables à ceux qui paraissaient au-dehors de la Grotte. Dans chaque massif, il y avait deux niches où, sur des piédestaux, on voyait deux figures représentant, d'un côté Hercule tenant sa massue et terrassant l'Hydre et, de l'autre côté, Apollon appuyé sur son arc et foulant aux pieds le serpent Python. Au-dessus de la corniche s'élevait un fronton dont le tympan était rempli des armes du roi. Sept*

[41] This is the date given by Félibien in *Les Divertissements de Versailles*, the official account of the festival published two years later. However, in the issue dated 21 July 1674, the *Gazette* describes the entertainment as having taken place on 18 July (no. 87, p. 714).

> *grands lustres pendaient sur le devant du théâtre qui était avancé au-devant des trois portes de la Grotte. Les côtés étaient ornés d'une agréable feuillée. Mais au travers des portes où le théâtre continuait de s'étendre, l'on voyait que la Grotte même lui servait de principale décoration*
>
> [The view of the Grotto served as a backdrop for the stage, which was raised by two and a half feet above the ground. The proscenium arch was a large corniced architrave that was supported on each side by a pillar with rustic decoration, similar to pillars seen on the outside of the Grotto. In each pillar there was a niche for a statue on a pedestal: one represented Hercules with his club felling the Hydra, the other Apollo leaning on his bow and trampling Python underfoot.
>
> The cornice was topped by a pediment whose tympanum bore the arms of the king. Seven great chandeliers hung above the apron of the stage which jutted out in front of the three entrances to the Grotto. The sides were pleasantly decorated with foliage. But through the entrances one could see that the stage extended well into the Grotto and that the Grotto itself was used as the main decor].[42]

According to the stage directions, the scene was '*un Lieu Champêtre . . . fort agréable*' ('a very pleasant rural setting')[43] and as such was reminiscent of previous decors also symbolic of an idealised representation of the French court. With its arrangements of rocks and sea-shells, its cascading waters and the artificial birdsong which could be heard by an audience once inside the theatre, the decoration of the grotto added a pastoral note to the overt solar symbolism of the statuary. This was in keeping with the implications of the prologue,[44] which featured a musical contest between two groups of shepherds, presided over by a number of pastoral deities, while also celebrating the latest victories of Louis XIV, hailed not only as an invincible conqueror but also as a peace-maker, the protector of the arts and the sciences.

The original proscenium arch devised by Vigarani for the production of *Le Malade imaginaire*[45] used decorative motifs inspired by the grotto as if, yet again, the stage designer had tried to blur the distinctions between natural setting and artificial decor. Trees had been planted on either side (later replaced by painted

---

[42] Félibien, *Les Divertissements de Versailles*, pp. 124–6.

[43] See the *Prologue* of 'Le Malade imaginaire', in Molière, *Œuvres complètes*, vol. 2, p. 631.

[44] As John S. Powell, *Music and Theater in France 1600–1680* (Oxford: Oxford University Press, 2000), p. 272, surmises, presumably the original pastoral prologue, written in 1673, was performed on that day. As France had just annexed Franche-Comté, the singing shepherds had a legitimate victory to celebrate.

[45] See Jérôme de La Gorce, *Carlo Vigarani*, p. 154, and 'Un lieu de spectacle à Versailles au temps de Louis XIV: la grotte de Thétis', in Charles Mazouer (ed.), *Les Lieux du spectacle dans l'Europe du XVIIe siècle* (Tübingen: Gunter Narr, 2006), pp. 307–18.

flats), in front of which potted orange trees stood on pedestal tables, lined up like side wings so as to form a perspective. Orange trees had become something of a status symbol at the time and their presence on stage served to reveal the wealth and taste of their royal owner. But they also gestured towards the orange trees that had been used on 17 August 1661 for the magnificent entertainment given to Louis XIV at Vaux-le-Vicomte by the now disgraced *Surintendant des finances*, Nicolas Foucquet.[46] In fact the day after Foucquet's fall, Louis XIV had proceeded to pillage Vaux, taking statues and young trees from the garden and, in particular, transferring all the orange trees to the orangery he built at Versailles. Perhaps the orange trees of the set served to remind the spectators of the dangers of trying to outdo the King in magnificence, as the *Surintendant* had found to his cost.

However, the perspective was here, so to speak, reversed. The audience no longer looked in from the auditorium through a proscenium arch at a painted perspective scenery. Instead, from the entrance to the grotto where they performed, the actors now gazed into the distance at the perspective of the royal park through Vigarani's elaborate proscenium arch. What they saw was a natural landscape made to look '*comme autant de riches Tableaux, où la Nature elle-mesme represente dans une perspective admirable, le parc & les collines qui l'environnent*' ('like so many rich tableaux, in which Nature itself represents in an admirable perspective the park and surrounding hills'),[47] and dotted with many fountains and marble statues. It too was a constructed theatrical space in which the comedy of court life was played under the gaze of spectators. Moreover the layout of the auditorium, with its spectators seated on the tiers of the amphitheatre and in the parterre, as shown on Le Pautre's engraving (see Figure 9.4), was reminiscent of the set designed by Vigarani for the sixth *intermède* of Molière's *Les Amants magnifiques*, which had been performed for the *Divertissement Royal* at Saint-Germain-en-Laye, on 4 February 1670. According to the *Gazette*, '*La derniére Décoration étoit une vaste Sale, disposée en maniére d'Amphitéatre, enrichie d'une fort belle Architecture. . . . Cette Sale estoit remplie de Spectateurs peints, vestus à la Grecque, de diverses maniéres*' ('The last set represented a large room, set up like an amphitheatre and magnificently decorated. . . . It was filled up with painted spectators, severally dressed in the Greek fashion').[48] The spectators seated in the ballroom of the *château-vieux* at Saint-Germain had been able to see their own mirror-image, albeit in antique garb, reflected back to them in the set. At Versailles, the auditorium itself became part of the natural set placed in front of the actors.

---

[46] The entertainment had included a comedy-ballet by Molière, entitled *Les Fâcheux*, with sets by Torelli. It was performed on an open-air stage built '*au bas de l'allée des sapins*' ('at the far end of the fir-tree walk') and '*sous la grille d'eau*' ('at the foot of the *Grille d'eau*'). See Jean de La Fontaine, 'Lettre à M. de Maucroix', in *Œuvres diverses*, p. 522.

[47] André Félibien, 'Description de la Grotte de Versailles', in *Description de divers Ouvrages de peinture faits pour le Roy* (Paris: Denys Mariette, 1696), p. 346.

[48] 'Les Magnificences du Divertissement qui a esté pris par Leurs Majestez, pendant le Carnaval', *La Gazette*, no. 22, 21 février 1670, p. 177.

Trompe-l'œil gardens

The dramatic productions given for the Versailles festivals of 1664, 1668 and 1674 played on the blurring of distinctions between fictional space and actual space. The natural scenery around the *théâtres de verdure* erected by Vigarani in the palace gardens was not only identical to the one constructed on stage by the decor, it also appeared to extend and even merge with it. As well as being contiguous, both spaces communicated with and alluded to each other, with the result that the spectators not only saw mirror images of themselves in the plays,[49] they also crossed the boundaries between stage and auditorium to perform in the *intermèdes* and could – theoretically at least – catch a glimpse of their fellow courtiers strolling in the real gardens outside, as suggested by Silvestre's engraving for the second day of *Les Plaisirs de l'île enchantée* (Figure 9.1).

Silvestre's engraving also suggests that, like the play they were watching, the gardens were incomplete without an audience. Just as their representation on stage was meant to dazzle the spectators, the real-life gardens were a delight for the eye. The small groups of people represented in the background, strolling or conversing,[50] were a *mise en abyme* of their own experience of the gardens. Like them, the many noble guests who had gathered for the festivals had been called upon to admire the realisations of Le Nôtre and to participate in their theatricality. The gardens at Versailles were manifestly for show, but as Michel Conan remarks,[51] they became an instrument of royal propaganda that created a model of purely visual appreciation of the gardens as the physical expression of their owner's magnificence.

Moreover, the royal gardens turned out to be just as artificial as the ones that were painted on the stage sets devised by Vigarani or Torelli. With their vistas, terraces, *allées* and rows of clipped trees, they employed the rules of geometry, optics and perspective to maximum effect to beguile the eye of the visitor. Like the gardens at Vaux-le-Vicomte, also designed by Le Nôtre, which derived 'much of their strength and originality from an interplay of levels that create[d] shifting perceptions and suddenly reveal[ed] unseen parts',[52] the gardens at Versailles had become a spectacle controlled by artifice, where the visitor's perception of reality was continually transformed by optical illusions, similar to the tricks of the eye in illusionistic theatre. With their sweeping expanses of terrace and monumental

[49] Notably in the first and last *intermèdes* of the *Amants magnifiques* in 1670, as discussed above.

[50] They were represented smaller than life so as to enhance the magnificence of the surroundings by contrast.

[51] Michel Conan, 'Friendship and Imagination in French Baroque Gardens Before 1661', in Michel Conan (ed.), *Baroque Garden Cultures: Emulation, Sublimation, Subversion* (Cambridge, MA: Harvard University Press, 2005), pp. 323–83 (see p. 380).

[52] Ian Thompson, *The Sun King's Gardens: Louis XIV, Le Nôtre and the Creation of the Gardens at Versailles* (New York: Bloomsbury USA, 2006), p. 17.

vistas alternating with enclosed *bosquets* and secluded arbours, their manipulation of the principle of perspective,[53] their well-hidden surprises and sudden revelations, and the variety of their water effects, the natural settings of the festivals were, just like Vigarani's stage, the realm of *trompe-l'œil.* They too were a decor which demonstrated the power of human imagination over appearances and the ability of the human will to shape nature. But they were also an 'enchanted' world where the enchantment precisely 'r[o]se from the illusion that art and nature [could] not be distinguished'.[54]

Bibliography

Primary sources

Benserade, Isaac de, 'Ballet des saisons', in Marie-Claude Canova-Green (ed.), *Benserade : Ballets pour Louis XIV*, 2 vols (Toulouse: SLC/Klincksieck, 1999).

Félibien, André, *Les Divertissemens de Versailles, donnez par le Roy . . . au retour de la conqueste de la Franche-Comté, en l'année MDCLXXIV* (Paris: Imprimerie Royale, par Sébastien Marbre-Cramoisy, 1676).

Félibien, André, *Relation de la Feste de Versailles : Du 18. Juillet mil six cens soixante-huit* (Paris: Imprimerie Royale, 1679).

Félibien, André, 'Description de la Grotte de Versailles', in *Description de divers Ouvrages de peinture faits pour le Roy* (Paris: Denys Mariette, 1696).

Félibien, André, *Les Fêtes de Versailles. Chroniques de 1668 & 1674*, ed. Martin Meade (Paris: Éditions Dédale, Maisonneuve et Larose, 1994).

La Fayette, Marie-Madeleine Pioche de la Vergne, comtesse de, *Histoire de Madame Henriette d'Angleterre* (Amsterdam: M.-C. Le Cène, 1720).

La Fontaine, Jean de, *Œuvres diverses*, ed. Pierre Clarac (Paris: Gallimard, 1978).

'Les Magnificences du Divertissement qui a esté pris par Leurs Majestez, pendant le Carnaval', *La Gazette*, no. 22, 21 February 1670.

'Les Particularitez des Divertissemens pris à Versailles, par leurs Majestez', *La Gazette*, no. 60, 21 May 1664.

Les Plaisirs de l'Isle Enchantée. Course de Bague, Collation ornée de Machines, Comedie meslée de Danse & de Musique, Ballet du Palais d'Alcine, Feu d'Artifice: Et autres Festes galantes & magnifiques; faites par le Roy à Versailles,

[53] To create an illusion of greater depth or distance, Le Nôtre repeatedly used accelerated perspective at Versailles. This exaggeration of perspective was achieved by using *allées* that tapered significantly, thus appearing much longer than they actually were, or by having rows of trees that converged or were trimmed so that they became gradually shorter as they went away from the centre of the gardens or the palace. Conversely, at Vaux, Le Nôtre had used *anamorphosis abscondita* (or hidden distortion) to establish decelerated perspective so as to make elements appear closer than they actually were.

[54] Conan, 'Friendship and Imagination', p. 360.

le 7. May 1664. Et continuées plusieurs autres Jours (Paris: Robert Ballard, 1664).

Les Plaisirs de l'Isle Enchantée. Course de Bague; Collation ornée de Machines; Comedie meslée de Danse et de Musique; Ballet du Palais d'Alcine; Feu d'Artifice: Et autres Festes galantes et magnifiques, faites par le Roy à Versailles, le VII. May M.DC.LXIV. Et continuées plusieurs autres Jours (Paris: Imprimerie Royale, par Sébastien Marbre-Cramoisy, 1673).

Molière, *Œuvres complètes*, ed. Georges Forestier et al., 2 vols (Paris: Éditions Gallimard, 2010).

Montigny, Abbé de, 'La Feste de Versailles. Du 18 juillet 1668. À Monsieur le Marquis de la Füente', in *Recueil de diverses pièces faites par plusieurs personnages* (The Hague: J. & D. Steucker, 1669).

Scudéry, Madeleine de, 'La Feste de Versailles, à M.***', in *La Promenade de Versailles* (Paris: Claude Barbin, 1669).

Villedieu, Marie-Catherine Desjardins, Madame de, 'Description d'une des fêtes que le Roi a faite à Versailles', in *Œuvres de Mme de Villedieu* (Paris: Vve Barbin, 1702).

Secondary sources

Canova-Green, Marie-Claude, *'Ces gens-là se trémoussent bien. . .' Ébats et débats dans les comédies-ballets de Molière* (Tübingen: Gunter Narr, 2007).

Canova-Green, Marie-Claude, 'L'Île comme métaphore politique dans le spectacle de cour au XVIIe siècle', in Christian Zonza (ed.), *L'Île au XVIIe siècle. Jeux et enjeux* (Tübingen: Gunter Narr, 2010), pp. 259–72.

Canova-Green, Marie-Claude, 'Le Jeu du fermé et de l'ouvert dans les comédies-ballets de Molière', in Georges Forestier and Lise Michel (eds), *La Scène et la coulisse dans le théâtre du XVIIe siècle en France* (Paris: PUPS, 2011), pp. 261–77.

Chartier, Roger, 'De la fête de cour au public citadin', in Roger Chartier (ed.), *Culture écrite et société. L'ordre des livres (XIVe–XVIIIe siècle)* (Paris: Albin Michel, 1996), pp. 155–204.

Conan, Michel, 'Friendship and Imagination in French Baroque Gardens Before 1661', in Michel Conan (ed.), *Baroque Garden Cultures: Emulation, Sublimation, Subversion* (Cambridge, MA: Harvard University Press, 2005), pp. 323–83.

Du Crest, Sabine, *Des fêtes à Versailles. Les Divertissements de Louis XIV* (s.l.: Aux Amateurs de livres, 1990).

Fox, Helen M., *André Le Nôtre, Garden Architect to Kings* (London: B.T. Batsford, 1962).

Kapp, Volker, 'Félibien interprète des *Quatre Saisons* de Le Brun. Analyse d'un thème des thuriféraires de Louis XIV et réflexions méthodologiques sur l'étude de la littérature panégyrique', *Cahiers de littérature du XVIIe siècle*, 8 (1986), 179–96.

La Gorce, Jérôme de, *Carlo Vigarani, intendant des plaisirs de Louis XIV* (Paris: Éditions Perrin/Établissement public du musée et du domaine national de Versailles, 2005).

La Gorce, Jérôme de, 'Un lieu de spectacle à Versailles au temps de Louis XIV: la grotte de Thétis', in Charles Mazouer (ed.), *Les Lieux du spectacle dans l'Europe du XVIIe siècle* (Tübingen: Gunter Narr, 2006), pp. 307–18.

Lawrenson, Thomas Edward, *The French Stage in the Seventeenth Century* (Manchester: Manchester University Press, 1957).

Marie, Alfred, *Naissance de Versailles* (Paris: Éditions Vincent, 1968).

Marin, Louis, 'Le Roi magicien ou la fête du prince', in Louis Marin (ed.), *Le Portrait du roi* (Paris: Éditions de Minuit, 1974), pp. 236–50.

Moine, Marie-Christine, *Les Fêtes à la cour du roi Soleil (1653–1715)* (Paris: Éditions Lanore, 1984).

Mukerji, Chandra, *Territorial Ambitions and the Gardens of Versailles* (Cambridge: Cambridge University Press, 1997).

Nolhac, Pierre de, *La Création de Versailles* (Versailles: Librairie L. Bernard, 1901).

Orgel, Stephen, *The Illusion of Power: Political Theater in the Renaissance* (Berkeley, CA: University of California Press, 1975).

Powell, John S., *Music and Theater in France 1600–1680* (Oxford: Oxford University Press, 2000).

Purkis, Helen M.C., 'Le Chant pastoral chez Molière', *Cahiers de l'Association Internationale des Études Françaises*, 28 (May 1976), 133–44.

Purkis, Helen M.C., 'L'Illusion théâtrale', *Studi francesi*, 63 (1977), 407–24.

Smith, Gretchen Elizabeth, *The Performance of Male Nobility in Molière's comédies-ballets* (Aldershot: Ashgate, 2005).

Thompson, Ian, *The Sun King's Gardens: Louis XIV, Le Nôtre and the Creation of the Gardens at Versailles* (New York: Bloomsbury USA, 2006).

Chapter 10
Ephemeral and permanent architecture during the age of Ercole I d'Este in Ferrara (1471–1505)

Francesca Mattei[1]

> *Non fu sposata colà Eleonora per procuratore che il dì I Novembre [1473], e non si pubblicò il maritaggio in Ferrara che il 9 [novembre] a suon di trombe dal poggiuolo del palazzo. Tre giorni di pubbliche feste seguirono il lieto annunzio [. . .]. Il trasporto d'Ercole per gli spettacoli, e la circostanza delle sue nozze, avvegnanché fosse ancor lontana la sposa, avvivarono il carnevale del 1473 oltre l'usato*
>
> [Eleanor was not proclaimed married, by council authority, until the first day of November [1473] and the marriage was not publicly announced in Ferrara until the 9th [of November], to the sound of trumpets from the palace balcony. The happy announcement was followed by three days of public festivities [. . .]. It was Ercole's enthusiasm for celebrations and for his wedding, even though his bride was still far away, that enlivened the Carnival of 1473 more than usual].[2]

Celebrated in November of 1473, the wedding between Ercole I d'Este, Duke of Ferrara, and Eleanor of Aragon, daughter of the King of Naples, constituted an unique opportunity to enhance the Este family's power. The dukedom of Ercole I (1471–1505) was filled with comparable initiatives: sources from that date and later testimonies in fact frequently recall such circumstances as distinct opportunities to legitimise sovereign authority.[3] On such occasions, one can certainly recognise a concentration of political and economic ambition, artistic ideals and

[1] I would like to thank Massimo Bulgarelli and Andrea Marchesi.

List of abbreviations: ASFe: Archivio di Stato di Ferrara; ASMo: Archvio di Stato di Modena; BCA: Biblioteca Comunale Ariostea di Ferrara; BCM: Biblioteca Comunale di Mantova; BEU: Biblioteca Estense Universitaria; BMVe: Biblioteca nazionale Marciana di Venezia; BCR: Biblioteca Casanatense di Roma; BM: London, British Museum; BNF: Bibliothèque nationale de France, Paris.

[2] Antonio Frizzi, *Memorie per la storia di Ferrara*, 5 vols (Ferrara: Domenico Taddei, 1809), vol. 4, pp. 91–2.

[3] Marina Vecchi Calore, 'Rappresentazioni sacre a Ferrara ai tempi di Ercole I', *Atti e Memorie della Deputazione Provinciale Ferrarese di Storia Patria*, 17 (1980), 158–95.

antiquarian aspiration – in exceptional events such as triumphal entrances and weddings, as well as in recurring ones, in the case of carnival celebrations or scheduled theatrical performances.[4]

Predictably, these events also constituted opportunities to reflect upon the city's architectural shortcomings – as demonstrated notably in the entry of Leo X into Florence (1515).[5] It became standard practice for celebrations and commemorations to offer a pretext for the embellishment of the city and the raising of its profile by means of its architecture.[6] Through analysis of written and graphic sources, this chapter will investigate the relationship that ephemeral architecture, designed as a framework for court ceremonies and events, exercised on more established city structures. Furthermore, it will trace such elements through the evolution of Ferrara by observing the city's development from this particular point of view. How was the city transformed on such occasions? What architectural structures became an integral part of the city, and which were conceived as temporary? Was there a relationship between the architecture of the city's ceremonial events and its more established structures? What sources, both ancient and modern, were used to plan and design these spaces?

To answer these questions, the chapter moves from a case-study of the marriage between Ercole I d'Este and Eleanor of Aragon to the examination of other court ceremonies and events.[7]

Eleanor's entry into Ferrara and its festive apparatus

The triumphal journey of Eleanor of Aragon took place between May and July of 1473. While she was travelling to Ferrara accompanied by a '*machina triumphalis*'

---

[4] Bodo Guthmueller, *Mito, poesia, arte. Saggi sulla tradizione ovidiana nel Rinascimento* (Rome: Bulzoni, 1997), pp. 165–86.

[5] Ilaria Ciseri, *L'ingresso trionfale di Leone X in Firenze nel 1515* (Florence: Olschki, 1990). See also Charles M. Rosenberg, 'The Use of Celebrations in Public and Semi-Public Affairs in Fifteenth-Century Ferrara', in Maristella de Panizza Lorch (ed.), *Il teatro italiano del Rinascimento* (Milan: Edizioni di Comunità, 1980), pp. 521–35.

[6] Caroline Elam, 'Il palazzo nel contesto della città: strategie urbanistiche dei Medici nel gonfalone del Leon d'Oro, 1415–1430', in Giovanni Cherubini and Giovanni Fanelli (eds), *Il palazzo Medici Riccardi di Firenze* (Florence: Giunti, 1990), pp. 44–53, esp. p. 52.

[7] Regarding this topic see also Diane Y. Ghirardo, 'Festival Bridal Entries in Renaissance Ferrara', in Sarah Bonnemaison and C. Macy (eds), *Festival Architecture* (London: Routledge, 2008), pp. 43–73; Fabrizio Cruciani, *Teatro nel Rinascimento: Roma 1450–1550* (Rome: Bulzoni, 1983), pp. 151–64; Clelia Falletti, 'Le feste per Eleonora d'Aragona da Napoli a Ferrara (1473)', in *Spettacoli conviviali dall'antichità classica alle corti italiane del '400* (Viterbo: Agnesotti, 1983), pp. 269–89; Clelia Falletti, 'Le feste per Eleonora d'Aragona a Napoli e a Roma (1473)', in *La fête et l'écriture: théâtre de cour, cour-théâtre en Espagne et en Italie: 1450–1530* (Aix-en-Provence: Université de Provence, 1987), pp. 257–76; Thomas Tuohy, *Herculean Ferrara. Ercole d'Este (1471–1505) and the Invention of a Ducal Capital* (Cambridge: Cambridge University Press, 1996), pp. 234–76.

('triumphal cortege'), a procession of the Este family went to receive her.[8] Eleanor had left Naples in May of 1473 and, before reaching Ferrara, had passed through Rome, Florence and Siena. Each stage of this journey was filled with festivities described in many contemporary sources.[9] The Ferrarese humanist Ludovico Carbone, accompanying the bride, gave a detailed account, describing how the spectacle of an itinerant court compared with that of the several cities they visited.[10]

For Eleanor's entry into Ferrara, a '*carroccio*' ('chariot') was decorated by the painters Bartolomeo da Treviso, Giraldo da Costa, Bartolomeo de Benedetto da Venezia and Sperandio da Mantova, as well as by the sculptors Domenico del Caballo and Louis Castellani.[11] An entrance to the city was fashioned for the convenient passage of the bride using a bridge of boats across the River Po. Eleanor, carried under a '*Baldachino de brocado d'oro crimisino cum fraponi*' ('gold-brocade canopy with tassels'), entered across the bridge of San Giorgio.[12] Later ceremonial entrances took place from the area of Castel Tedaldo, such as those of the Duke of Milan, Ludovico il Moro (1493) or another bride, Lucrezia Borgia (1502).[13] The route taken by Eleanor led along the Via Grande (today Ripagrande) and ended at Castelvecchio, the political centre of the city. Here she was greeted by allegorical scenes and by a grand reception prepared in the Palazzo.[14] A mass was then celebrated in the cathedral, and the festivities continued for many days.

For the occasion, a pergola was constructed and covered with vegetation, stretching from the San Giorgio bridge to the Via Grande. No pictorial representations or evidence regarding this event are extant, but we may imagine architectural structures appeared transformed into vegetation, as though an act of metamorphosis were in progress. We can presume that the city, decorated in this fashion, resembled the drawings made by Battista Dossi in collaboration with Camillo Filippi

---

[8] This definition is quoted by Falletti, '*Le feste per Eleonora d'Aragona da Napoli a Ferrara*', p. 151.

[9] For a description of the celebrations in Rome, Florence and Siena see Cruciani, '*Le feste*', pp. 151–64; Falletti, '*Le feste per Eleonora d'Aragona da Napoli a Ferrara*', pp. 275–6; Falletti, '*Le feste per Eleonora d'Aragona a Napoli e a Roma*', pp. 257–76.

[10] For the journey from Naples to Ferrara see Ludovico Carbone, *Ad inclytum et gloriosissimum principem Divum Ferdinandum Siciliae Regem Ludovici Carbonis Dialogus de Neapolitana profectione*, BCR, D.V.8; for the orations read during the travel, see *Ludovici Carbonis Epithalamium Neapoli actum in divam Lianoram Aragonensem et divum Herculem Estensem*, BM, Additional 20.794.

[11] Luigi N. Cittadella, *Notizie relative a Ferrara ricavate da documenti ed illustrate da Luigi Napoleone cav. Cittadella bibliotecario*, 2 vols (Ferrara: Domenico Taddei, 1868), vol. 1, p. 214.

[12] ASMo, Guardaroba, 1473, 98.77, quoted in Tuohy, *Herculean Ferrara*, p. 409. The *frapponi* were painted by Cosimo Tura. See also Ghirardo, 'Festival Bridal Entries', p. 49.

[13] Tuohy, *Herculean Ferrara*, p. 265. For Lucrezia Borgia's entry, see *Lucrezia Borgia in Ferrara sposa a Don Alfonso d'Este. Memorie storiche estratte dalla cronaca ferrarese di Bernardino Zambotto* (Ferrara, 1867), p. 41.

[14] For a reconstruction of the processional sequences of Eleanor of Aragon's bridal entries see Ghirardo, 'Festival Bridal Entries', pp. 43–73.

and Bernardino Bellone for the tapestries woven in wool and silk by Giovanni Karcher (1543–1545), preserved today in the Louvre – even though these represent later events.[15] Among other possible suggestions, we can also include the pergolas painted in the main hall of the Vigna di Belriguardo (1537), much like the room of the Caryatids in the imperial villa of Pesaro (post 1530), also designed by Dosso and Battista Dossi (see Figures 10.1 and 10.2).

The iconography of the tapestries and the Belriguardo room – works designed in part or as a whole by the Dossi brothers – was inspired by Ovid's *Metamorphoses*. The fantastic architecture represented in the tapestries took its inspiration from the *delizie* (court residences) of the Este family. Here we are dealing with indications that serve as a clue to the interweaving of mythology, literature and architecture in vogue at the courts of Ferrara, a theme we shall examine in greater depth later in this chapter.

To celebrate the marriage of Ercole I, the ducal family commissioned the Florentine sculptor Guido de Rizzi to create a statue of Nicolò d'Este. This was completed on 16 August 1473.[16] The streets were paved, the buildings were repainted and furnished with ornaments and other decorations. The most important of the painted images, now lost, appeared on the *Loggia dei Calegari* (loggia of the cobblers), depicting tournament scenes. The *Diario Ferrarese* traces the enhancements made to the city with great precision:

> *Fu dato principio ad essere lavorato intorno al Palazo de la Ragione del Comune, et il palazo de le Banche di Calegari in Piaza, il quale Palazo de la Ragione et torre de hore fu acconzo, cioè dipinti come sono; poi similiter il palazo de le Banche de Calegari ai paladini fu depinto in dicto tempo, cioè de Magio, et Zugno fu fornito ogni cossa [. . .] Girardo Costa fu pagato 240 lire per havere laborado a sbianchezare et a depinser frixi, arme e compassi in la corte dell'Illustrissimo Nostro Signore et altri lavori se fano [. . .] Ove non è mai stato selegado [. . .] fe selegare, tanto se lavora che prede e calzina non se poté havere per dinari*
>
> [Works were begun on the city's Palazzo de la Ragione, and on the Palazzo de le Banche di Calegari in the town's main square. The Palazzo de la Ragione and Clock Tower were decorated, that is painted as they appear today. In a similar fashion, the Palazzo de le Banche de Calegari ai Paladini was painted in the agreed time – that is by May and June everything was provided and completed [. . .] Girardo Costa was paid 240 lire for his work in cleaning and painting

[15] For a history of the Este tapestries, see Felton Gibbons, 'Ferrarese Tapestries of Metamorphosis', *The Art Bulletin*, 48 (1966), 407–11; Nello Forti Grazzini, *L'arazzo ferrarese* (Milan: Electa, 1982); Nello Forti Grazzini, '*Disegni di Giulio Romano per gli arazzi estensi (1537–1543)*', *Arte tessile: rivista-annuario del Centro italiano per lo studio della storia del tessuto*, 1 (1990), 9–21.

[16] Cittadella, *Notizie relative a Ferrara*, vol. 1, p. 215.

Figure 10.1 Sala della Vigna, Villa Belriguardo, Voghiera (Ferrara), post 1530 (photo: Mattei)

Figure 10.2 Sala delle Cariatidi, Villa Imperiale, Pesaro, post 1530 (photo: Mattei)

> friezes, coats of arms and compasses, in addition to other works in the court of our Eminent Lord [. . .] Where work had not been done [. . .] as much as possible was finished with bricks and mortar when money was not available].[17]

The town's citizens living along the processional route were required to hang tapestries and curtains at their windows. This custom, also followed in other cities, remained customary in Ferrara for years to come: for the marriage of Lucrezia Borgia, for example, the Palazzo Bevilacqua, where Isabella d'Este, the Marchioness of Mantua was staying, was sumptuously decorated with precious fabrics of satin.[18] The grandeur of the marriage between Ercole and Eleanor further involved elaborate preparations of an exceptional nature, some of them executed as permanent interventions – such as the paving of roads – and certain aspects of the local environment were enhanced, such as the attention given to paintings adorning the exterior of buildings. The special care taken with decoration of the façades of Ferrara's residential buildings was observed by Sebastiano Serlio and reported in his *Regole generali di architettura*. The Bolognese architect praised the painted façades of Ferrara, comparing them to similar ones in Rome by Baldassarre Peruzzi, Polidoro da Caravaggio and Maturino da Firenze. He particularly recalled the Palazzo Ducale's façade painted by the Dossi brothers and decorated with architectural elements and figures (1536).[19] Even if Serlio's comments are found in a much later source, his words confirm the importance of this local practice in Ferrara.

Eleanor's ceremonial procession was accompanied by seven triumphal chariots, in '*similitudine de li septe pianeti*' ('in the form of the seven planets'), as indicated by the *Diario Ferrarese* and placed in the areas of Santa Maria in Vado, the Gesuiti church and the street of San Francesco.[20] No indication survives however of triumphal arches that were built for this event. By contrast, local sources report that four arches '*facti alla Romana, more antiquo*' ('constructed in Roman

---

[17] Bernardino Zambotti, *Diario ferrarese dall'anno 1476 sino al 1504, Rerum Italicarum Scriptores*, 24, VII, 2, ed. G. Pardi (Bologna: Zanichelli, 1934), 7 April 1473, p. 88 cited in Tuohy, *Herculean Ferrara*, p. 267; Charles M. Rosenberg, *The Este Monuments and Urban Development in Renaissance Ferrara* (Cambridge: Cambridge University Press, 1997), p. 248.

[18] *Lucrezia Borgia in Ferrara*, p. 37. For the pope's procession in Borso's era, see Enea Silvio Piccolomini, *I commentari*, ed. Luigi Totaro (Milan: Adelphi, 1984), p. 409.

[19] Sebastiano Serlio, *Regole generali di architettura sopra le cinque maniere de gli edifici; cioè, thoscano, dorico, ionico, corinthio, e composito; con gli essempi dell'antichità, che per la maggior parte concordano con la dottrina di Vitruvio* (Venice: Francesco Marcolini, 1537), pp. 71v–72r. This quotation is commented upon by Maria Beltramini, '*Un frontespizio estense per le "Regole Generali di Architettura" di Sebastiano Serlio*', in Maria Beltramini and Caroline Elam (eds), *Some degree of happiness: studi di storia dell'architettura in onore di Howard Burns* (Pisa: Edizioni della Normale, 2010), pp. 297–317, 738–41; Michael Bury, 'Serlio on the Painted Decoration of Buildings', in Beltramini and Elam (eds), *Some Degree of Happiness*, pp. 259–72. For the Ferrara wall decorations, see Francesca Mattei, *Eterodossia e vitruvianesimo. Palazzo Naselli a Ferrara (1527–1538)* (Rome: Campisano, 2013), pp. 159–60.

[20] See Falletti, '*Le feste per Eleonora d'Aragona da Napoli a Ferrara*', p. 285.

fashion, in the antique style') were built in February of 1491, when Alfonso I, son of Ercole, married Anna Sforza: the first built in Polesine, depicting Venus on a mountain; the second in Schifanoia with two horses pulling the chariot of the sun; the third at San Francesco, portraying horses pulling the chariot of Cupid; and the fourth between the Duomo and the Palazzo Ducale with a horse and two golden giants.[21] Thanks to payment lists preserved in Modena, it is possible to trace the names of workers involved in these projects: the *marangoni* (wood-working artists) in charge of the arches' construction were Crescimbene, Paolo da Tamara, Francesco Rigone and Bonaventura Novellino, while the master painters Fino Marsigli and Sigismondo di Girardo Costa e Romano dealt with their painted decoration.[22] The two golden giants – perhaps two Herms – were employed also during the celebrations for Lucrezia Borgia where '*davanti alla sala [del palazzo Ducale] eranvi due Giganti grandissimi dorati con le mazze in mano*' ('in front of the Palazzo Ducale were positioned two very large gilded Giants with maces in hand').[23] The arches – as reported in a letter to Ercole I from the architect Biagio Rossetti, who was involved in the project – were dismantled in June of the same year therefore remaining on view for only four months.[24]

In the absence of any pictorial representations, it is difficult to establish the appearance of the triumphal arches created for these celebrations. We can assume however that they were made of wood with metal finishing, as was reported in the payment lists.[25] It is also likely that some decorations were made from the finest of materials – marble and stone – as was customary. We cannot know exactly which contemporary formal style corresponds to Caleffini's description of the arches as being 'antique' or 'Roman'. Nevertheless, when Leonello d'Este, brother of Ercole, commissioned the pedestal of the equestrian statue of Nicolò III (1443), he – probably following the advice of Guarino Veronese and Leon Battista Alberti – opted for a style that made clear reference to imperial Rome (see Figure 10.3).[26]

---

[21] Ugo Caleffini, *Storia della Città di Ferrara dal suo principio al 1471*, 11 February 1491, BNF, cl. XXV, n. 539; Mario Equicola, *Genealogia dei Signori Estensi*, BCA, ms. Cl. II, 349 quoted in Cittadella, *Notizie relative a Ferrara*, vol. 1, pp. 217–18.

[22] For archival documents see also ASMo, Munizioni e Fabbriche, 25, 28–9, quoted in Tuohy, *Herculean Ferrara*, pp. 425, 443. For the triumphal arches of Lucrezia Borgia's entries, see ASFe, Contabilità, fol. 59, cited in Tuohy, *Herculean Ferrara*, p. 267; Richard G. Brown, 'The Politics of Magnificence in Ferrara, 1450–1505: A Study in Socio-Political Implications of Renaissance Spectacle' (PhD dissertation, University of Edinburgh, 1982), pp. 546–50; Richard G. Brown, 'The Reception of Anna Sforza in Ferrara, February 1491', *Renaissance Studies*, 2 (1988), 231–9.

[23] *Lucrezia Borgia in Ferrara*, p. 20.

[24] Letter from Biagio Rossetti to Ercole I d'Este, 13 June 1491, ASMo, Particolari, b. 1239, fol. 13, cited in Ghirardo, 'Festival Bridal Entries', p. 61.

[25] Cittadella, *Notizie relative a Ferrara*, vol. 1, pp. 217–18.

[26] Marco Folin, 'La committenza estense, l'Alberti e il palazzo di corte di Ferrara', in Arturo Calzona et al. (eds), *Leon Battista Alberti. Architetture e committenti* (Florence: Olschki, 2009), pp. 257–304; Maria Teresa Sambin de Norcen, '"Attolli super ceteros mortales". L'arco del Cavallo a Ferrara', in Calzona, *Leon Battista Alberti*, pp. 349–91.

Figure 10.3 Volto del cavallo, Ferrara, 1443–1451 (photo: Mattei)

Going a little further, we can draw on Emanuel Winternitz's proposals and suggestions. Commenting on the paintings of Lorenzo Costa dedicated to celebrating the duchy of Mantua, Winternitz hypothesises that the painter had drawn inspiration from the festivities he had witnessed during his years of working for the Este family.[27] Costa was originally from Ferrara and was summoned to Mantua by Isabella d'Este, daughter of Ercole I and wife of Francesco II Gonzaga; his reference to the Este ceremonies appears to be aimed at highlighting the connection between the Mantuan clients and the Marquis's family. One might think therefore that the triumphal arches adorning Ferrara during the ceremonies were not dissimilar to those represented by Costa in *The Reign of Comus* painting, where the focus of the composition is precisely an arch inspired by Roman models (see Figure 10.4).

Transforming the city: the marriage festival and its enduring legacy

The festivities and triumphal entries organised on the occasion of the ducal weddings of Ercole and Alfonso provide a series of recurring themes. This is further confirmed in the writings of Ludovico Ariosto, where, in the pages of *Orlando Furioso*, he describes an imaginary ceremony which clearly borrows a number of features from the ducal wedding:

> *Con pompa trionfal, con festa grande/ tornaro insieme dentro alla cittade/ che di frondi verdeggia e di ghirlande:/ coperte a panni son tutte le strade;/ nembo d'erbe e di fior d'alto si spande,/ e sopra e intorno ai vincitori cade,/ che da veroni a de finestre amene/ donne e donzelle gittano a man piene./ Al volgersi dei canti in vari lochi/ trovano archi e trofei subito fatti, che di Biserta le ruine e i fochi/ mostran dipinti, et altri degni fatti/ Altrove palchi con diversi giuochi,/ E spettacoli e mimi e scenici atti*
>
> [With pomp triumphal and with festive cheer/ The troop returns within the city-walls:/ With leaves and garlands green the streets appear,/ And tapestried all about with gorgeous palls./ Of herbs and flowers a mingled rain, where'er/ They wend, upon the conquering squadron falls,/ Which with full hands from stand and window throw/ Damsel and dame upon the knights below./ At every turn, in various places are,/ Of sudden structure arch and trophy high,/ Whereon Biserta's sack is painted fair,/ Ruin and fire, and feat of chivalry].[28]

[27] Emanuel Winternitz, 'Instruments de musique étranges chez Filippino Lippi, Piero di Cosimo, et Lorenzo Costa', in Jean Jacquot (ed.), *Les Fêtes de la Renaissance*, 2 vols (Paris: Centre national de la recherche scientifique, 1956), vol. 1, pp. 379–95, esp. p. 394.

[28] Ludovico Ariosto, *Orlando Furioso* (Ferrara: Giovanni Mazzocchi, 1516), canto XLIV, ottave 32–3, trans. William Stewart Rose (London: John Murray, 1910).

Figure 10.4 Lorenzo Costa, *The Reign of Comus*, 1511 (© RMN – Grand Palais/ Thierry Le Mage/Paris, Musée du Louvre)

We cannot determine with any certainty whether Ariosto was thinking about a ceremony which he had himself witnessed, presented in that fashion. It is still however widely accepted by scholars that he drew freely on Ferrarese traditions when describing the events recounted in *Orlando Furioso*; this is evidenced by frequent references to the deeds of Borso, Ercole and Alfonso, as well as other prominent characters of Ferrara's sixteenth century.[29] Ariosto's testimony can, therefore, be accepted as confirmation of the customary rituals staged to accompany the Este ceremonies. These were ceremonies which, despite the absence of ancient monuments to represent contemporary events,[30] almost seem to refer consciously to Roman triumphs – perhaps reflecting the relations of Flavio Biondo, author of *Roma triumphans*, with the Este family.[31]

[29] For the architectural patronage of Borso, Ercole and Alfonso, see in particular Ariosto, *Orlando Furioso*, canto III, ottave 45–8.

[30] For the reuse of ancient monuments see Sandro De Maria, 'L'arco di Rimini nel Rinascimento. Onori effimeri e antichità ritrovata', in Paola Delbianco (ed.), *Culture figurative e materiali tra Emilia e Marche*, 2 vols (Rimini: Maggioli, 1984), vol. 2, pp. 443–61, especially p. 443.

[31] For the relation between Flavio Biondo and Ferrara, see Maria Teresa Sambin de Norcen, *Il cortigiano architetto. Edilizia, politica, umanesimo nel Quattrocento ferrarese* (Venezia: Marsilio, 2012), pp. 64–5; Maria Teresa Sambin de Norcen, 'Gli Este, l'Alberti, Biondo e la nuova villa rinascimentale', *Schifanoia*, 30–31 (2006), 247–64. For the

If ephemeral architecture was designed to represent the magnificence of the ducal family, as the bearer of antiquity's values, the impact of the festivities affected the established permanent architecture of the court as well. In order to increase the citizens' involvement in the celebrations of 1473, the Duke gifted one of the courtyards of the castle to the city as a public space:

> *Ordinò che si selciasse la via di Borgo Leone, e l'altra che dalla via grande conduceva alla Porta di San Pietro, ridusse a pubblica piazza quel cortile ove soleva tener la legna, i cani, e i cavalli barbari verso la Chiesa di San Giuliano, che oggi è detto piazza de' pollaiuoli*
>
> [He ordered that the via di Borgo Leone should be paved, as well as the other main route leading to Porta di San Pietro. He also converted a courtyard near the Church of San Giuliano into a public square. What was once used for wood storage or keeping the Berber horses and the court's dogs is now used as a public plaza, known today as the square of the poultry sellers].[32]

From documentary sources we can learn how the courtyards of Castelvecchio were opened to the public during theatre performances or on other designated occasions.[33] In the *Vita di Ariosto*, for example, Girolamo Baruffaldi describes certain ephemeral structures prepared by the Este family for the construction of theatrical stage sets.[34] For another ceremonial occasion, the Ferrarese scholar, Antonio Frizzi, recounts how the corpse of Alfonso I lay in state in the courtyard of the castle, so that the town's citizens could pay homage to the late Duke.[35] Additionally, starting in 1506, the family hosted the town's Tribunal Courts.[36] The duke therefore made public use of the courtyard official, as had previously occurred on some special occasions only. Moreover, in the absence of suitable premises for theatrical presentations – which were becoming more frequent in

---

description of the ancient ceremonies and for their reenactments during the fifteenth and sixteenth century, see Antonio Pinelli, 'Feste e trionfi: continuità e metamorfosi di un tema', in Salvatore Settis (ed.), *Memorie dell'antico nell'arte italiana*, 3 vols (Turin: Einaudi, 1985), vol. 2, pp. 281–350.

[32] Frizzi, *Memorie per la storia di Ferrara*, vol. 4, p. 92.

[33] Ibid.

[34] Girolamo Baruffaldi, *Vita di Ariosto* (Ferrara: Pe' Soci Bianchi e Negri Stampatori del seminario, 1807), p. 60; Girolamo Tiraboschi, *Storia della letteratura italiana* (Venice: Antonio Fortunato Stella, 1796), p. 182. Other documents in Jadranka Bentini and Luigi Spezzaferro (eds), *L'impresa di Alfonso II: saggi e documenti sulla produzione artistica a Ferrara nel secondo Cinquecento* (Bologna: Nuova Alfa, 1987), p. 50.

[35] Frizzi, *Memorie per la storia di Ferrara*, vol. 4, pp. 318, 327.

[36] Cittadella, *Notizie relative a Ferrara*, vol. 1, p. 716. For the use of the castle's courtyards, see Werner L. Gundersheimer, *Ferrara: The Style of a Renaissance Despotism* (Princeton, NJ: Princeton University Press, 1973), pp. 272–84.

Ferrara during the age of Alfonso I d'Este and Ludovico Ariosto – the courtyard would be the most appropriate location to host performances.[37] In 1486, on the occasion of the presentation of *Menaechmi* – a modern *commedia* whose title acknowledges the text by Plautus – the chronicler Bernardino Zambotti states that a room was prepared in the castle to accommodate the Duke and the court during the play.[38] This was an event attended by many dignitaries of the time: Francesco II Gonzaga was fascinated by theatre performance, so that, imitating his Ferrarese brother-in-law, he staged a number of performances in the loggia of the Palazzo di San Sebastiano in Mantua.[39]

We know from documentary sources that the city's architecture was used to accommodate theatrical sets – as yet another example of the relationship between urban space and the scenic stage. A renowned anonymous stage design, preserved in the State Archives of Modena, portrays a theatre-set that, according to Diane Yvonne Ghirardo, was set up in rural lodges or urban courtyards (see Figure 10.5).[40]

The fact that the set, designed as a backdrop for the theatre performance, portrays a gallery in perspective suggests continuity and conflation between fictitious and permanent structures.

Just as the city, adorned with tapestries and newly-painted decorations, had hosted the passage of Eleanor of Aragon, the space required for festivities also affected ducal residences. Sabadino degli Arienti, author of *De triumphis religionis*, reported that in the Delizia di Belfiore, destroyed by fire in the early sixteenth century, a series of paintings was dedicated to the marriage of Eleanor of Aragon, in order to perpetuate the memory of the historic event.[41] Such circumstances seem to stem from self-referentiality: on the one hand, the festivities constituted an opportunity to beautify the city; on the other, they themselves became a subject for pictorial representation. The hypothesis that the subjects of the Karcher tapestries or the paintings in the Vigna di Belriguardo room echo past celebrations therefore becomes probable.

Ephemeral architecture thus takes on a value comparable to the more permanent architecture of the sovereign courts. In this respect, we may note the impressive

---

[37] Ludovico Zorzi, *Il teatro e la città* (Turin: Einaudi, 1977), especially pp. 5–59.

[38] Zambotti, *Diario ferrarese*, quoted in Cittadella, *Notizie relative a Ferrara*, vol. 1, p. 164.

[39] Rosenberg, 'The Use of Celebrations', pp. 532–3; Molly Bourne, *Francesco II Gonzaga: The Soldier-Prince as Patron* (Rome: Bulzoni, 2008), p. 36.

[40] Anon., *Perspective of the courtyard of a palace, probably for a stage set*. ASMo, Mappario Estense, Fabbriche, 92/34; Ghirardo, 'Festival Bridal Entries', p. 53.

[41] For the description of the decorations in Belfiore, see Sabadino degli Arienti, *De Rriumphis Religionis*, in Werner L. Gundersheimer (ed.), *Art and Life at the Court of Ercole I d'Este: The De Triumphis Religionis of Giovanni Sabadino degli Arienti* (Geneva: Droz, 1972). See also Gundersheimer, *Ferrara*, pp. 263–4; Ghirardo, 'Festival Bridal Entries', pp. 43–73; and Rupert Shepherd, 'Giovanni Sabadino degli Arienti, Ercole I d'Este and the Decoration of the Italian Renaissance Court', *Renaissance Studies*, 9 (1987) 1, 18–57.

Figure 10.5 Anonymous, Perspective of the courtyard of a palace, probably for a stage set, sixteenth century (© Archivio di Stato di Modena, Mappario Estense, Fabbriche, 92/34. Authorization Prot. 1669/ 28.01.02/12.2 / 31.07.19/9)

project for the *loggia grande* in the Piazza del Duomo (1491–1493), commissioned by Ercole to connect the Palazzo Ducale with Castelvecchio. This project, which is part of a broader plan for a rearrangement of the entire ducal residence, radically transformed the structure of the building after the extensive interventions ordered only 20 years previously, on the occasion of Eleanor's entrance to Ferrara.[42] Ercole's intentions remained the same in both instances: in one respect

[42] Folin, 'La committenza estense', pp. 296–304.

to embellish the Palazzo Ducale, and in another, to make it more functional. Commenting on the improvements made during the later part of the century, Sabadino of Arienti stated that Ercole ordered a loggia with 25 new columns of white marble – precious and rare for the city of Ferrara – so as to allow the court to observe the festivals that were held in the square.[43] In the same years the tower of Rigobello was equipped with balconies and, on the side of the same tower, three arches were built to allow access to the *Cortile Nuovo*: such interventions were intended to accommodate '*gran numero di madone a vedere qualche festa o giostra che se facese in piaza*' ('a large number of ladies watching festivals or races organised in the square').[44] Historical sources thus emphasise how the interventions commissioned by Ercole, which aimed to beautify the Palazzo Ducale, had been conceived mainly in terms of their function when used in processions or performances.

The marble portico was eventually destroyed and today only a fragment of a 'waterleaf' capital remains – similar to some of the capitals used for the columns of the loggia in the *Cortile Nuovo* (see Figure 10.6).

A few sixteenth-century depictions that bear testimony to the appearance of the *loggia's* open gallery survive – like the imaginary view of Cathedral's Square (post 1550) or the famous perspective included in the *Imprese dei duchi estensi* (see Figures 10.7 and 10.8).[45]

According to observations by Charles Rosenberg, the space conceived as the square of Ferrara became a huge open-air theatre.[46] The two honorific statues of Nicolò III and Borso d'Este – the latter moved next to the *Volto del Cavallo* by instruction of Ercole in 1472[47] – framed the entrance to the *Cortile Nuovo*, creating a sort of scenographic backdrop, while Ercole's *colonnato* (grand loggia) welcomed the spectators, who watched the stage and its performances intently. In architectural terms, Ercole's idea followed both of Alberti's design principles, which included the use of loggia arcades around the squares, as well as the theories of Pellegrino Prisciani, the Este family's knowledgeable advisor and book keeper. In *Spectacula* (1486–1502) Prisciani had argued that theatre could take place in an open space.[48] It hence appears that Ercole's passion for theatre – proved by the

43 Frizzi, *Memorie per la storia di Ferrara*, p. 92; Gundersheimer, *Ferrara*, pp. 251–2.

44 *Cronica generale di Ferrara*, fol. 213v-214, cited in Rosenberg, *Este Monuments*, p. 246.

45 BCA, Repertorio iconografico, H 5 1. Adriano Franceschini, 'Note sopra un bozzetto scenografico ferrarese del sec. XVI', *Atti e memorie Deputazione Provinciale Ferrarese di Storia Patria*, 4th ser., 17 (2000), pp. 391–410; Folin, 'La committenza estense', pp. 284–96.

46 Rosenberg, *Este Monuments*, p. 116.

47 *Diario Ferrarese*, p. 79; Folin, 'La committenza estense', p. 287.

48 Pellegrino Prisciani, *Spectacula*, ed. D. A. Barbagli (Modena: Panini, 1992); Rosenberg, *Este Monuments*, p. 116; Eugenio Battisti, 'Il manoscritto sugli "spettacoli" di Pellegrino Prisciani', *Necropoli*, 8 (1970), 47–54; Giuliana Ferrari, *Pellegrino Prisciani: Antiche memorie e scena ferrarese* (Rome: Bulzoni, 1990).

Plate 9 Venice, Palazzo Zenobio, central hall, used for music (by kind permission of Luca Sassi, Sassi Editore, San Vito di Leguzzano, Italy)

Plate 10 Venice, Palazzo Zenobio, façade (photo: Martina Frank)

Plate 11 Venice, Palazzo Dolfin, façade (photo: Martina Frank)

Plate 12 Venice, Palazzo Dolfin, 'Magnifica Sala' (by kind permission of Luca Sassi, Sassi Editore)

Plate 13 The Hampton Court Painting of the Field of Cloth of Gold, showing the English procession to the first royal interview, Guisnes Castle, and the English temporary palace and fountains (reproduced by permission of the Royal Collection Trust © Her Majesty Queen Elizabeth II, 2015)

Plate 14 *The Church of the Holy Sepulchre*, woodcut by Erhard Reuwich in Bernhard von Breydenbach, *Peregrinatio in Terram Sanctam* (Mainz, 1486) (public domain)

Plate 15 Scene from *Les plaisirs de l'isle enchantée* in Versailles, 1664. Stage design by Carlo Vigarani, engraving by Israel Silvestre, in *Les plaisirs de l'isle enchantée* . . ., Paris, 1673. Vienna, Theatre Museum, Library 622.229-D.Th.,fol. 58 (© KHM-Museumsverband, Theatermuseum Wien)

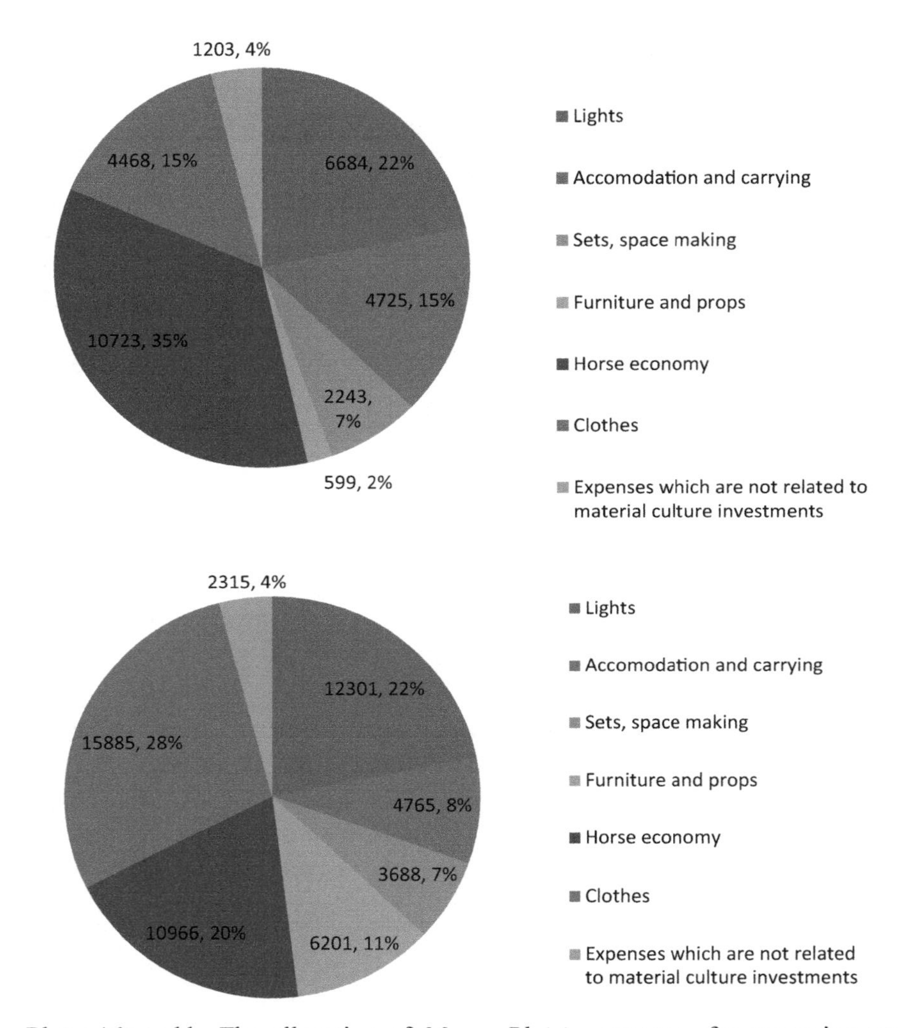

Plates 16a and b The allocation of *Menus Plaisirs* expenses for entertainment and for formal court life in 1698 from the perspective of material culture (*Archives nationales* (Paris), O[1*] 2816–2817 and O[1*] 2830; data presentation by Pauline Lemaigre-Gaffier)

Figure 10.6 Waterleaf capital of the destroyed Great Loggia of Ercole I d'Este, 1492 (photo: Mattei)

frequent performances organised for the court – resulted in his decision to change the structure and arrangement of the Palazzo Ducale as well as Ferrara's main square.[49]

[49] Marco Villoresi, *Da Guarino a Boiardo: La cultura teatrale a Ferrara nel Quattrocento* (Rome: Bulzoni, 1994).

Figure 10.7 Sculptures of Borso and Nicolò III d'Este, Cathedral Square, Ferrara, fifteenth century (photo: Mattei)

Figure 10.8 Anonymous, *Il disegno di Ferrara vecchia*, from *Le memorabili imprese dei Duchi di Ferrara*, fol. 18, late fifteenth century (© Biblioteca Estense Universitaria, it. 429 H.5.3 Prot. 2449/6.7.2013)

The court on public view: the Este and magnificence

The presence of a public audience – even if deliberately separated from the ducal family – was a necessary condition for the completion of the *magnificentia estense* project: many sources describe how the town's citizenry were present at such festive events. On the occasion of the marriage between Lucrezia Borgia and Alfonso I, written sources indicate the building of:

> *un poggiuolo nuovamente fatto per la Torre dell'Orologio che passava la piazza e andava entro il detto palazzo della Ragione ornatissimamente apparato con tribunali, case e castelle di legno finte e dipinte: e lì con feste, canti, giuochi e moresche di gran piacere si rappresentò una comedia di Plauto intitolata Epidico e tutta la brigata sedeva su tribunali altri da dieci gradi in foggia di teatro, coperto di panno di più colori a divisa, che in un tratto da un lato del palazzo si vedeva tutta (la) turba di Madame, e Signori, e Gentiluomini*
>
> [a newly-constructed covered corridor, giving access to the Clock Tower, crossed the square and entered the aforementioned palazzo della Ragione, richly ornamented and adorned with painted figures depicting galleries, apartments and wooden chalets: it was there – amidst festivities, song, sports and delightful Moorish dances – that Plautus's play entitled *Epidicus* was performed. The audience sat in raised galleries, inclined ten degrees as in a theatre, all dressed in costly multi-coloured fabrics, and positioned so that in one perspective view from the side of the palazzo the entire crowd of Ladies, Squires and Gentlemen could be seen simultaneously].[50]

There are also a number of depictions showing courtiers and citizens who attended the celebrations. *Il Salone dei Mesi* in palazzo Schifanoia (1468–1469)[51] is a revealing case in question, built at the time of the dukedom's transition from Ercole I to Borso d'Este. All sections of the pictorial cycle invite consideration: the lower segment devoted to human activities; the astrological section dominated by the signs of the zodiac; and the Olympian segment occupied by the pagan gods riding triumphal chariots. Just below the segment given over to the month of April, there is a balcony with a group of lady on-lookers intently observing a procession of horsemen (see Figure 10.9). The ladies' forms and postures were probably inspired by the figures in the loggia of the Belriguardo residence.[52] The theme of courtiers attending the ducal festivities was also taken up in later written sources.

---

[50] *Lucrezia Borgia in Ferrara*, p. 21.

[51] Salvatore Settis and Walter Cupperi (eds), *Il Palazzo Schifanoia a Ferrara*, 2 vols (Modena: Panini, 2007), vol. 1, pp. 217–309.

[52] Maria Teresa Sambin de Norcen, 'Nuove indagini su Belriguardo e la committenza di villa nel primo Rinascimento', in Francesco Ceccarelli and Marco Folin (eds), *Delizie estensi* (Florence: Olschki, 2009), pp. 145–80; Maria Teresa Sambin de Norcen, '"Ut

Figure 10.9 Processional sequences, April, Palazzo Schifanoia, Ferrara, 1468–1469 (photo: Mattei)

Furthermore, on the ceiling of the *Sala del Tesoro* (1508) painted by Benvenuto Tisi da Garofalo for a Ferrarese nobleman, Antonio Costabili, some figures are depicted on a balcony, constituting an imaginary audience observing the activities of the buyer of the residence itself (Figure 10.10).[53]

In the Schifanoia palace, every section of the painted fresco includes an image of Borso, the undisputed leader of iconographic innovation, in the act of discharging his ducal role surrounded by festival architecture (see Figure 10.11).[54]

The architecture depicted is almost always in the antique style: a coffered ceiling and pilasters supporting an entablature. This *more antiquo* architecture, designed in compliance with the requirements of modern perspective, had already made its appearance in Ferrara, in the aforementioned *Volto del Cavallo*. Another contemporary phenomenon concerns the resolving of the spatial arrangement of the Belriguardo planimetry, modeled on the 'Greek house' of Vitruvius. We can explain how such forms entered Ferrara's traditions of building design – as documentary sources point out – by taking account of the presence of celebrated scholars and practitioners who frequented Ferrara's ducal court including Leon Battista Alberti and Guarino Veronese, the expert in antiquities.

The most significant occasions on which the court showed itself to the people were the banquets.[55] The ducal residences were chosen as the most suitable

apud Plinium": giardino e paesaggio a Belriguardo nel Quattrocento', in Gianni Venturi and Francesco Ceccarelli (eds), *Delizie in villa* (Florence: Olschki, 2008), pp. 65–89.

[53] Alessandra Pattanaro, 'Garofalo e Cesariano in Palazzo Costabili a Ferrara', *Prospettiva*, 73–74 (1994), 97–110.

[54] Luciano Cheles, 'L'immagine del Principe tra informalità e ostentazione', in Ranieri Varese (ed.), *Atlante di Schifanoia* (Modena: Panini, 1989), pp. 57–64. For a discussion of the painted architecture and of the meaning of the Salone dei Mesi, see Zorzi, *Il teatro e la città*, pp. 12–3; and Settis and Cupperi, *Il Palazzo Schifanoia a Ferrara*, vol. 1, pp. 217–309.

[55] Emilio Faccioli, 'Scenicità dei banchetti estensi', in *Il Rinascimento delle corti padane. Società e cultura* (Rome and Bari: Laterza, 1977), pp. 597–606; Jadranka Bentini and Alessandra Chiappini (eds), *A tavola con il principe: materiali per una mostra su alimentazione e cultura nella Ferrara degli Estensi* (Ferrara: Gabriele Corbo, 1988).

Figure 10.10 Benvenuto Tisi da Garofalo and Cesare Cesariano, Sala del Tesoro, Costabili Palace, Ferrara, 1508 (photo: Mattei)

venues for these ceremonies. Both interiors and exteriors, including lodges in the courtyards, were used, as indicated in a number of illustrations and documentary sources. This custom was not, however, a prerogative of the ducal family only. Bartolomeo Pendaglia, a wealthy businessman in the service of Leonello d'Este, celebrated his nuptials with Margherita Costabili, a descendant of a prominent family in Ferrara, at his own residence. The wedding banquet, mentioned in contemporary and later chronicles, was carried out '*in amplissimis porticibus*', that is, in the very spacious portico of Bartolomeo's palazzo (see Figure 10.12).[56]

While following classical tradition, therefore, banquets took on an important civic role. But what sources were used to revive the atmosphere of antiquity? Ludovico Carbone recalls the banquets organised by Caesar, described in the texts of Plutarch and Suetonius, as found in the libraries of the Este family.[57] During the

[56] Quoted in Ludovico Carbone, *Carmina, epistolae, orationes* (BMVe, Lat. XII 137=4451), fol. 130. See also Sambin de Norcen, *Il cortigiano architetto*, p. 51.

[57] Carbone, *Carmina*, fol. 89. See also Sambin de Norcen, *Il cortigiano architetto*, pp. 55–6. For the Estense's library, see Giulio Bertoni, *La biblioteca estense* (Turin: Loescher, 1903); Giulio Bertoni, 'La biblioteca di Borso d'Este', *Atti della R. Accademia delle scienze di Torino*, 61 (1926), 705–28; Andrea Barbieri, 'La biblioteca di Ercole I d'Este in un elenco

Figure 10.11 *Borso d'Este and his court*, April, Palazzo Schifanoia, Ferrara, 1468–1469 (photo: Mattei)

time of Borso, in fact, the library of the Este family is known to have held copy of Suetonius's *The Lives of the Twelve Caesars*. The scholar Battista Guarini, in advising Bartolomeo Pendaglia, makes reference as early as 1452, to Plutarch's *Parallel Lives*. In the following century, Giovanni Battista Giraldi Cinthio in his *Discorso sul comporre de' romanzi* (*Discourse on Composing Romances*) summarised the precepts to be followed in order to stage great theatrical performances inspired by Greek and Latin authors.[58] It is also worth mentioning Apuleius's *Metamorfosi*, of which Ercole I commissioned a vernacular translation by Matteo

inedito', *Atti e memorie della deputazione di storia patria per le antiche provincie modenesi*, 11th ser., 31 (2009), 199–219; and Corinna Mezzetti, 'La biblioteca degli Estensi: inventari dei manoscritti e gestione delle raccolte nel Quattrocento', in Guido Arbizzoni et al. (eds), *Principi e signori, atti del convegno* (Urbino: Accademia Raffaello, 2010), pp. 67–108.

[58] Cittadella, *Notizie relative a Ferrara*, vol. 1, pp. 164–5.

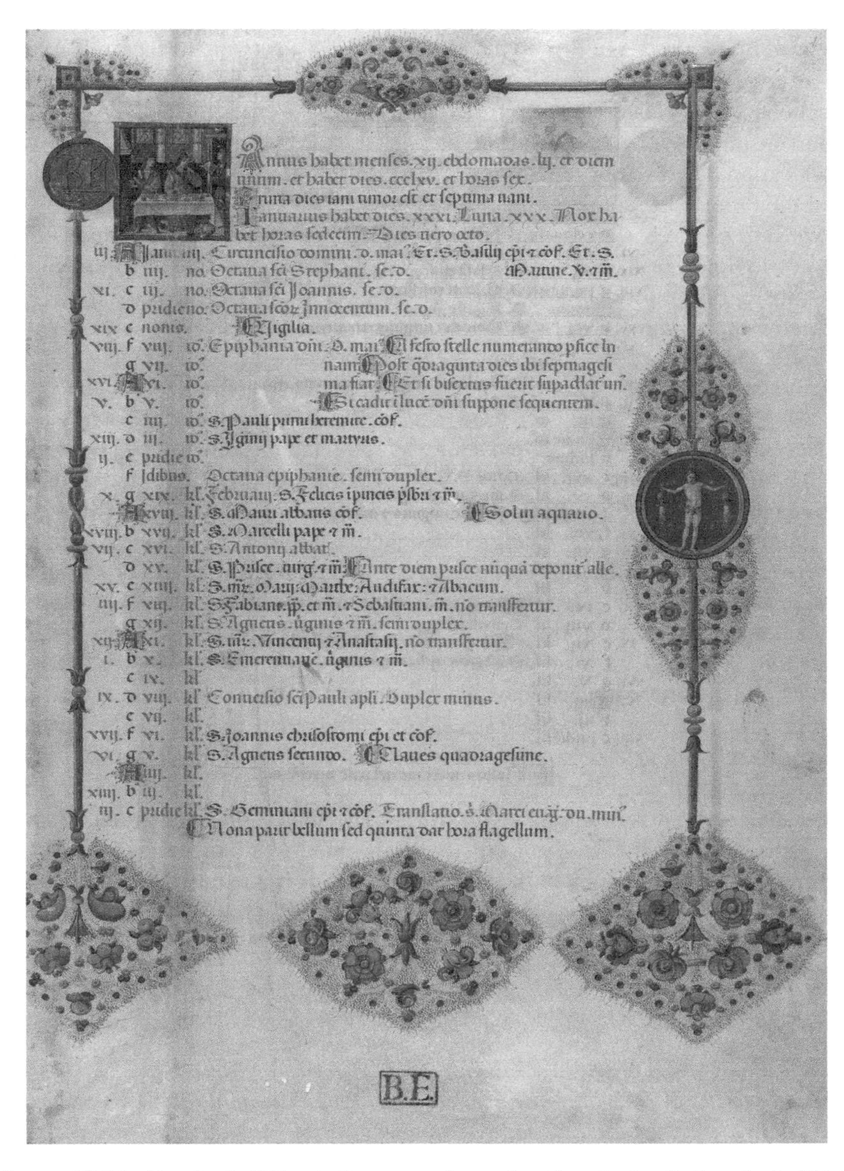

Figure 10.12 *Ercole I d'Este's Banquet*, from the *Breviario di Ercole I d'Este*, fol. 1r, sixteenth century (© Biblioteca Estense Universitaria, Lat. 424=V.G.11 Prot. 2449/6.7.2013)

Maria Boiardo.[59] This great interest in books, nourished initially by Leonello, but later cultivated also by Borso and Ercole, helped to strengthen the antiquarian aspirations of the Este family. Translations and modern editions of the classic texts, entrusted by Ferrara's nobility to the city's humanists, provide further evidence of this attitude and endeavour. Those who belonged to the ducal family, supported by scholars, drew inspiration from literary sources in order to stage an image of a court inspired by the glories of the past. History was invested in this way with an educational and social function, its texts viewed as taking on an active role in promoting the court's self-image.

We do not have a great deal of evidence on this topic, nor, because of the changes to some residences, can we recover the original arrangement of all the fifteenth-century buildings in Ferrara. In addition to Castelvecchio and the Bartolomeo Pendaglia residence, which we have already considered, we know that even the courtyard of the Palazzo dei Diamanti was used for banquets and theatrical performances.[60] A hypothesis is also possible that Palazzo Roverella and Palazzo Costabili may have been used in a similar way, given that they were noble palaces with private courtyards and a loggia running along at least one side – much like the house of Giovanni Romei, where the loggia still bears the remains of decorative painting depicting architectural features (see Figures 10.13 and 10.14).[61]

The organisation of the *all'antica* banquets confirmed the image of *magnificenza* of the hosts and leading figures, while the architecture acted as a theatrical setting. This is a view clearly expressed by Charles Rosenberg when he states that the Este family drew from the ancient texts, and the cultural ethos they communicated, in order to legitimise the family's power. During the age of Ercole I, the classics constituted a fundamental ideal. For example, references to the Roman Empire are evident in both the organisation and display of processional parades (*lustratio*) relating to ceremonies of ancient origin adopted for different types of festivities, as well as in the use of precise architectural forms, such as the arches that signaled triumphal entries (*parousia*).[62] The image of the Este dukes overlaid with images of the Roman Emperors or Roman mythological characters also occurred in the iconography of the family's medals. A prime example of such medals is that made by Ludovico Coradino for Ercole I d'Este (1473), which depicts

---

[59] Sonia Cavicchioli, '"Cose sumptuose, grande et sublime". Ercole I d'Este committente negli ultimi anni del suo ducato', *Civiltà mantovana*, 33 (1998) 106, 87–102, especially 94.

[60] Ghirardo, 'Festival Bridal Entries', p. 51; Barbara di Pascale, *Banchetti Estensi: La spettacolarità del cibo alla corte di Ferrara nel Rinascimento* (Imola: La Mandragora, 1995), p. 13.

[61] Carla di Francesco, 'Casa Romei: Medioevo e Rinascimento nel "400 ferrarese", in *Ferrara, I luoghi del tempo dal domestico al sacro: le dimore* (Ferrara: Comune di Ferrara, 1988), pp. 1–9. For Alfonso II's wedding to Barbara of Austria, his uncle Don Alfonso d'Este organised a banquet in the Palazzo Bevilacqua in Ferrara. However, no sources are left to demonstrate if it was set in the loggia or inside the palace. See Ghirardo, 'Festival Bridal Entries', p. 50.

[62] Ciseri, *L'ingresso trionfale*, pp. 5–6.

Figure 10.13 Loggia of Palazzo dei Diamanti, Ferrara, late fifteenth century (photo: Mattei)

Ercole standing next to three Corinthian columns. Another is that designed by Niccolò Spinelli (1492), in which Alfonso I is shown on a triumphal chariot (see Figures 10.15 and 10.16).[63] In following decades, references deriving from the Carolingian and Breton epic traditions become more prevalent – as evidenced by the literary works of Ariosto.[64]

Conclusion

In Ercole I d'Este's Ferrara a continuous exchange took place between the ephemeral structures created for festivities and the permanent space represented by the

[63] George F. Hill, *A Corpus of Italian Medals of the Renaissance Before Cellini* (London: British Museum, 1930), no. 102, pl. 23 and no. 923, pl. 149. See also Charles M. Rosenberg, 'Money Talks: Numismatic Propaganda Under Alfonso I d'Este', in Gianni Venturi (ed.), *L'età di Alfonso I e la pittura del Dosso* (Modena: Panini, 2004), pp. 145–64.

[64] Charles M. Rosenberg, 'Introduction', in Charles M. Rosenberg (ed.), *Art and Politics in Late Medieval and Early Renaissance Italy: 1200–1500* (Notre Dame, IN: University of Notre Dame Press, 1990), p. 2; Ghirardo, 'Festival Bridal Entries', p. 44.

Figure 10.14 The Loggia of Casa Romei, Ferrara, late fifteenth century (photo: Mattei)

Figure 10.15 Ludovico Coradino da Modena, Ercole I d'Este medal, 1473 (Milan, Gabinetto Numismatico e Medagliere, Raccolte Artistiche del Castello Sforzesco © Comune di Milano. All rights reserved)

Figure 10.16 Niccolò di Forzore Spinelli detto Niccolò Fiorentino, *Alfonso d'Este's triumphal chariot*, 1492 (Museo del Bargello, Inv. Medaglie Bg n. 5998. Su concessione del Ministero dei beni e delle attività culturali e del turismo)

sovereign courts.[65] Architecture and ceremony formed, that is, two complementary aspects of the court's praxis, as demonstrated by cases analysed in this chapter. This is a relationship that can be seen as developed at formal, functional and conceptual levels.

Architecture served in such contexts primarily as a backdrop: the residences of the Este family hosted festivities and banquets and, in parallel, were themselves used as a backdrop for theatre performances. Architecture and festivities were furthermore invested with strongly political meaning: architecture had become a way of exhibiting the power of the patron expressed through the renewal of urban spaces. The same function is assigned to festivities: on one hand, they were inspired by the texts of the classical period to convey a sense of continuity with antiquity, and on the other, they were transformed into pictorial representations that conveyed a powerful image of the prince to the court – as one can see in the painted fresco cycles of the Palazzo Schifanoia and Palazzo Belfiore.

Ercole's guiding principle was the concept of *magnificentia*. According to the Renaissance humanist Mario Equicola, who illustrated this concept for the Marquis of Mantua, the *magnificenza* of architecture consists in '*edificare somptuosamente*'

[65] There is ample bibliography regarding Herculean Ferrara, see first Tuohy, *Herculean Ferrara*; and Rosenberg, *Este Monuments*, with other references.

('building sumptuously').[66] It was this principle that Ercole applied in the design of permanent spaces as well as ephemeral architecture. Ercole was famous for his protracted building schemes, which earned him the title of chief expert in the art of building. Some questions remain however in regard to his personal expertise in the discipline. There are those who claim that he was adept at handling certain architectural principles, and there are those who, more cautiously, suggest that he simply possessed sufficient knowledge to allow for fruitful dialogue with the architects and engineers in his service.[67] The fact of the matter is that, during his reign, in addition to the expansion of Castelvecchio, a series of churches and palaces were completed. This strategy culminated with the *Addizione Erculea* (1492), an expansion plan for the town of Ferrara, which doubled the city's footprint and ensured the memory of the Duke for future generations.[68] In a letter he wrote to the editor Francesco Marcolini, Pietro Aretino memorably describes Ercole's Ferrara with its '*dirittura de le strade larghe*' (geometry of streets, straight and wide), presumably referring to the Strada degli Angeli (now Corso Ercole I d'Este), as the central artery of the *Addizione* (new town).[69] These considerations bear witness to the image of a prince who was engaged in the transformation of a medieval city – made of wood and brick – into a more modern city, supplementing local materials such as brick with stone – a material carrying greater connotations of nobility – as in the façade of the monumental Palazzo dei Diamanti or as in the aforementioned grand loggia of the Piazza del Duomo.

Many of the projects promoted by Ercole were designed to accommodate organised festivities, and particularly theatre presentations.[70] We have already pointed out how the Duke's passion for theatre had influenced some important architectural decisions: the Piazza della Cattedrale, for example, became a huge open-air stage with the city as stage-set on a monumental scale. It was such use of space that influenced how the city was perceived by observers. A perspective drawing, included in the *Imprese dei duchi di Ferrara* cited earlier, gives a glimpse of the town's main square, with the visual image accompanied by a courtly commentary emphasising the beauty of the city.[71] The urban space is designed as a theatrical stage-set, suggesting that the main function of the piazza is to host parades, chariots, triumphal arches and festivities. The urban design of Ferrara in fact recalls

---

66 Mario Equicola, *Cronica di Mantua* (Mantova: unknown publisher, 1521), pp. 154–58v, BCM, Rari 27. For the ephemera of magnificence, see Tuohy, *Herculean Ferrara*, p. 234.

67 For a bibliography about this topic, see Rosenberg, *Este Monuments*, p. 110.

68 Tuohy, *Herculean Ferrara*, p. 483–5; Rosenberg, *Este Monuments*, pp. 110–52.

69 Letter of Pietro Aretino to Francesco Marcolini. The document was published in Serlio, *Regole generali*, p. II, with the date of 10 September 1537.

70 Villoresi, *Da Guarino a Boiardo*, pp. 116–24.

71 BEU, ms. it. 429, *Imprese dei duchi di Ferrara*, XVI sec., fol. 18. Charles Rosenberg attribuited the drawing to Pellegrino Prisciani. Rosenberg, *Este Monuments*, p. 116.

Figure 10.17 View of the Este's Castelvecchio from Strada degli Angeli (now Corso Ercole I d'Este), *Addizione Erculea* of Ferrara, 1492 (photo: Mattei)

certain famous theatrical representations – with both tragic and comic scenes – that Serlio later publishes in a book concerned with the art of perspective.[72]

[72] Sebastiano Serlio, *Il primo e secondo libro d'architettura, di Sebastiano Serlio, bolognese. Le premier liure d'architecture de Sebastian Serlio, bolognois, mis en langue*

Ercole's era marked an important moment of transition. The relationship between urban design and festival and performance architecture – so closely connected during his reign – became less prominent when independent theatre building was revived during the sixteenth century. Their reappearance represented a clear break with previous practices, stimulating new directions in the field of architecture – primarily by Pellegrino Prisciani – which focused more on the design of stage machinery. At the same time, however, theatre influenced the use and perception of urban spaces.[73] We can finally ask whether, and to what degree, the complex use of the city promoted by Ercole I d'Este influenced the design of the city itself. The Strada degli Angeli connects the castle with the Palazzo dei Diamanti and the Porta degli Angeli on the northern edge of the city. By opening a new thoroughfare, Ercole intended to celebrate the Este family: the Strada degli Angeli frames the Castelvecchio and places it at the centre of a notable perspective view.[74] Made of brick and stone – not wood like the ephemeral scenery of a stage set – the Addizione Erculea became equivalent to a theatrical backdrop on an urban scale. This was the last project relating to the design of cityscape during Ercole's era (see Figure 10.17).

Bibliography

Manuscript sources

Biblioteca Casanatense, Rome, D.V.8, Ludovico Carbone, *Ad inclytum et gloriosissimum principem Divum Ferdinandum Siciliae Regem Ludovici Carbonis Dialogus de Neapolitana profectione.*

Biblioteca Comunale Ariostea, Ferrara, ms Cl. I 107, Girolamo Merenda, *Cronache di Ferrara*, sixteenth century. Biblioteca Comunale Ariostea, Ferrara, ms Cl. II, 349, Mario Equicola, *Genealogia dei Signori Estensi.*

Biblioteca Estense Universitaria, Modena, ms it. 429, *Imprese dei duchi di Ferrara*, sixteenth century.

Biblioteca nazionale Marciana, Venice, Lat. XII 137=4451, Ludovico Carbone, *Carmina, epistolae, orationes.*

francoyse, ed. Jean Martin (Paris: Jean Barbel, 1545). For the hypothesis on the city as theatre during the celebrations, see Elam, '*Il palazzo*', pp. 44–57.

[73] Antonio Stäuble, 'Scenografia e architettura teatrale nel Rinascimento', in *Letteratura e critica. Studi in onore di N. Sapegno*, 5 vols (Roma: Bulzoni, 1974–1979), vol. 2, pp. 391–415; Fabrizio Cruciani (ed.), *L'"invenzione del teatro". Studi sullo spettacolo del Cinquecento*, monographic issue of *Biblioteca Teatrale*, 15–16 (1976); Franco Ruffini, *Teatri prima del teatro. Visioni dell'edificio e della scena tra Umanesimo e Rinascimento* (Rome: Bulzoni, 1983).

[74] Ludovico Zorzi defined Ercole's *Addizione* as a combination of perspective order and empiric solutions. Zorzi, *Il teatro e la città*, pp. 5–6.

Bibliothèque nationale de France, Paris, cl. XXV, n. 539, Ugo Caleffini, *Storia della Città di Ferrara dal suo principio al 1471.*

British Museum, London, Additional ms 20.794, *Ludovici Carbonis Epithalamium Neapoli actum in divam Lianoram Aragonensem et divum Herculem Estensem.*

Printed primary sources

Ariosto, Ludovico, *Orlando Furioso* (Ferrara: Giovanni Mazzocchi, 1516).

Baruffaldi, Girolamo, *Vita di Ariosto* (Ferrara: Pe' Soci Bianchi e Negri Stampatori del seminario, 1807).

Cittadella, Luigi N., *Notizie relative a Ferrara ricavate da documenti ed illustrate da Luigi Napoleone cav. Cittadella bibliotecario*, 2 vols (Ferrara: Domenico Taddei, 1868).

Equicola, Mario, *Cronica di Mantua* (Mantua: [unknown], 1521).

Frizzi, Antonio, *Memorie per la storia di Ferrara*, 5 vols (Ferrara: Francesco Pomatelli, 1809).

Lucrezia Borgia in Ferrara sposa a Don Alfonso d'Este. Memorie storiche estratte dalla cronaca ferrarese di Bernardino Zambotto (Ferrara: Domenico Taddei, 1867).

Piccolomini, Enea Silvio [Pope Pius II], *I commentari*, ed. Luigi Totaro (Milan: Adelphi, 1984).

Prisciani, Pellegrino, *Spectacula*, ed. D.A. Barbagli (Modena: Panini, 1992).

Sabadino degli Arienti, Giovanni, 'De triumphis religionis', published in Werner L. (ed.), *Art and Life at the Court of Ercole I D'Este: The De Triumphis Religionis of Giovanni Sabadino degli Arienti* (Geneva: Droz, 1972).

Serlio, Sebastiano, *Regole generali di architettura sopra le cinque maniere de gli edifici; cioè, thoscano, dorico, ionico, corinthio, e composito; con gli essempi dell'antichità, che per la maggior parte concordano con la dottrina di Vitruvio* (Venice: Francesco Marcolini, 1537).

Serlio, Sebastiano, *Il primo e secondo libro d'architettura, di Sebastiano Serlio, bolognese. Le premier liure d'architecture de Sebastian Serlio, bolognois, mis en langue francoyse*, ed. Jean Martin (Paris: Jean Barbel, 1545).

Tiraboschi, Girolamo, *Storia della letteratura italiana* (Venice: Antonio Fortunato Stella, 1796).

Zambotti, Bernardino, *Diario ferrarese dall'anno 1476 sino al 1504, Rerum Italicarum Scriptores*, 24, VII, 2, ed. G. Pardi (Bologna: Zanichelli, 1934).

Secondary sources

Barbieri, Andrea, 'La biblioteca di Ercole I d'Este in un elenco inedito', *Atti e memorie della deputazione di storia patria per le antiche provincie modenesi*, 11th ser., 31 (2009), 199–219.

Battisti, Eugenio, 'Il manoscritto sugli "spettacoli" di Pellegrino Prisciani', *Necropoli*, 8 (1970), 47–54.

Beltramini, Maria, 'Un frontespizio estense per le "Regole Generali di Architettura" di Sebastiano Serlio', in Maria Beltramini and Caroline Elam (eds), *Some Degree of Happiness: studi di storia dell'architettura in onore di Howard Burns* (Pisa: Edizioni della Normale, 2010), pp. 297–317, 738–41.

Bentini, Jadranka and Alessandra Chiappini (eds), *A tavola con il principe: materiali per una mostra su alimentazione e cultura nella Ferrara degli Estensi* (Ferrara: Gabriele Corbo, 1988).

Bentini, Jadranka and Luigi Spezzaferro (eds), *L'impresa di Alfonso II: saggi e documenti sulla produzione artistica a Ferrara nel secondo Cinquecento* (Bologna: Nuova Alfa, 1987).Bertoni, Giulio, 'La biblioteca di Borso d'Este', *Atti della R. Accademia delle scienze di Torino*, 61 (1926), 705–28.

Bertoni, Giulio, *La biblioteca estense* (Turin: Loescher, 1903).

Bourne, Molly, *Francesco II Gonzaga: The Soldier-Prince as Patron* (Rome: Bulzoni, 2008).

Brown, Richard G., 'The Politics of Magnificence in Ferrara, 1450–1505: A Study in Socio-Political Implications of Renaissance Spectacle' (PhD. Dissertation, University of Edinburgh, 1982).

Brown, Richard G., 'The Reception of Anna Sforza in Ferrara, February 1491', *Renaissance Studies*, 2 (1988), 231–9.

Bury, Michael, 'Serlio on the Painted Decoration of Buildings', in Maria Beltramini and Caroline Elam (eds), *Some Degree of Happiness: studi di storia dell'architettura in onore di Howard Burns* (Pisa: Edizioni della Normale, 2010), pp. 259–72.

Cavicchioli, Sonia, ' "Cose sumptuose, grande et sublime": Ercole I d'Este committente negli ultimi anni del suo ducato', *Civiltà mantovana*, 33 (1998) 106, 87–102.

Cheles, Luciano, 'L'immagine del Principe tra informalità e ostentazione', in Ranieri Varese (ed.), *Atlante di Schifanoia* (Modena: Panini, 1989), pp. 57–64.

Ciseri, Ilaria, *L'ingresso trionfale di Leone X in Firenze nel 1515* (Florence: Olschki, 1990).

Cruciani, Fabrizio (ed.), L' "invenzione del teatro". Studi sullo spettacolo del Cinquecento, monographic issue of *Biblioteca Teatrale*, 15–16 (1976).

Cruciani, Fabrizio, *Teatro nel Rinascimento: Roma 1450–1550* (Roma: Bulzoni, 1983).

De Maria, Sandro, 'L'arco di Rimini nel Rinascimento. Onori effimeri e antichità ritrovata', in Paola Delbianco (ed.), *Culture figurative e materiali tra Emilia e Marche* (2 vols, Rimini: Maggioli, 1984), vol. 2, pp. 443–61.

Elam, Caroline, 'Il palazzo nel contesto della città: strategie urbanistiche dei Medici nel gonfalone del Leon d'Oro, 1415–1430', in Giovanni Cherubini and Giovanni Fanelli (eds), *Il palazzo Medici Riccardi di Firenze* (Firenze: Giunti, 1990), pp. 44–53.

Faccioli, Emilio, 'Scenicità dei banchetti estensi', in *Il Rinascimento delle corti padane: Società e cultura* (Rome and Bari: Laterza, 1977), pp. 597–606.

Falletti, Clelia, 'Le feste per Eleonora d'Aragona da Napoli a Ferrara (1473)', in *Spettacoli conviviali dall'antichità classica alle corti italiane del '400* (Viterbo: Agnesotti, 1983), pp. 269–89.

Falletti, Clelia, 'Le feste per Eleonora d'Aragona a Napoli e a Roma (1473)', in *La fête et l'écriture: théâtre de cour, cour-théâtre en Espagne et en Italie: 1450–1530* (Aix-en-Provence: Université de Provence, 1987), pp. 257–76.

Ferrari, Giuliana, *Pellegrino Prisciani: Antiche memorie e scena ferrarese* (Rome: Bulzoni, 1990).

Folin, Marco, 'La committenza estense, l'Alberti e il palazzo di corte di Ferrara', in Arturo Calzona et al. (eds), *Leon Battista Alberti: Architetture e committenti* (Florence: Olschki, 2009), pp. 257–304.

Forti Grazzini, Nello, *L'arazzo ferrarese* (Milan: Electa, 1982).

Forti Grazzini, Nello, 'Disegni di Giulio Romano per gli arazzi estensi (1537–1543)', *Arte tessile: rivista-annuario del Centro italiano per lo studio della storia del tessuto*, 1 (1990), 9–21.

Franceschini, Adriano, 'Note sopra un bozzetto scenografico ferrarese del sec. XVI', *Atti e memorie Deputazione Provinciale Ferrarese di Storia Patria*, 4th ser., 17 (2000), 391–410.

di Francesco, Carla, 'Casa Romei: Medioevo e Rinascimento nel '400 ferrarese', in *Ferrara, I luoghi del tempo dal domestico al sacro: le dimore* (Ferrara: Comune di Ferrara, 1988), pp. 1–9.

Gibbons, Felton, 'Ferrarese Tapestries of Metamorphosis', *The Art Bulletin*, 48 (1966), 407–11.

Ghirardo, Diane Y., 'Festival Bridal Entries in Renaissance Ferrara', in Sarah Bonnemaison and C. Macy (eds), *Festival Architecture* (London: Routledge, 2008), pp. 43–73.

Gundersheimer, Werner L., *Ferrara: The Style of a Renaissance Despotism* (Princeton, NJ: Princeton University Press, 1973).

Guthmuller, Bodo, *Mito, poesia, arte. Saggi sulla tradizione ovidiana nel Rinascimento* (Rome: Bulzoni, 1997).

Hill, George F., *A Corpus of Italian Medals of the Renaissance Before Cellini* (London: British Museum, 1930).

Mattei, Francesca, *Eterodossia e vitruvianesimo. Palazzo Naselli a Ferrara (1527–1538*). (Rome: Campisano, 2013).

Mezzetti, Corinna, 'La biblioteca degli Estensi: inventari dei manoscritti e gestione delle raccolte nel Quattrocento', in Guido Arbizzoni et al. (eds), *Principi e signori, atti del convegno* (Urbino: Accademia Raffaello, 2010), pp. 67–108.

Pascale, Barbara di, *Banchetti Estensi. La spettacolarità del cibo alla corte di Ferrara nel Rinascimento* (Imola: La Mandragora, 1995).

Pattanaro, Alessandra, 'Garofalo e Cesariano in Palazzo Costabili a Ferrara', *Prospettiva*, 73–4 (1994), 97–110.

Pinelli, Antonio, 'Feste e trionfi: continuità e metamorfosi di un tema', in Salvatore Settis (ed.), *Memorie dell'antico nell'arte italiana*, 3 vols (Turin: Einaudi, 1985), vol. 2, pp. 281–350.

Rosenberg, Charles M., 'The Use of Celebrations in Public and Semi-Public Affairs in Fifteenth-Century Ferrara', in Maristella de Panizza Lorch (ed.), *Il teatro italiano del Rinascimento* (Milan: Edizioni di Comunità, 1980), pp. 521–35.

Rosenberg, Charles M. (ed.), *Art and Politics in Late Medieval and Early Renaissance Italy: 1200–1500* (Notre Dame, IN: University of Notre Dame Press, 1990).

Rosenberg, Charles M., *The Este Monuments and Urban Development in Renaissance Ferrara* (Cambridge: Cambridge University Press, 1997).

Rosenberg, Charles M., 'Money Talks: Numismatic Propaganda under Alfonso I d'Este', in Gianni Venturi (ed.), *L'età di Alfonso I e la pittura del Dosso* (Modena: Panini, 2004), pp. 145–64.

Ruffini, Franco, *Teatri prima del teatro. Visioni dell'edificio e della scena tra Umanesimo e Rinascimento* (Rome: Bulzoni 1983).

Sambin de Norcen, Maria Teresa, 'Gli Este, l'Alberti, Biondo e la nuova villa rinascimentale', *Schifanoia*, 30–31 (2006), 247–64.

Sambin de Norcen, Maria Teresa, ' "Ut apud Plinium": giardino e paesaggio a Belriguardo nel Quattrocento', in Gianni Venturi and Francesco Ceccarelli (eds), *Delizie in villa* (Florence: Olschki, 2008), pp. 65–89.

Sambin de Norcen, Maria Teresa, ' "Attolli super ceteros mortales". L'arco del Cavallo a Ferrara', in Arturo Calzona et al. (eds), *Leon Battista Alberti. Architetture e committenti* (Florence: Olschki, 2009), pp. 349–91.

Sambin de Norcen, Maria Teresa, 'Nuove indagini su Belriguardo e la committenza di villa nel primo Rinascimento', in Francesco Ceccarelli and Marco Folin (eds), *Delizie estensi* (Florence: Olschki, 2009), pp. 145–80.

Sambin De Norcen, Maria Teresa, *Il cortigiano architetto: Edilizia, politica, umanesimo nel Quattrocento ferrarese* (Venice: Marsilio, 2012).

Settis, Salvatore and Walter Cupperi (eds), *Il Palazzo Schifanoia a Ferrara*, 2 vols (Modena: Panini, 2007).

Shepherd, Rupert, 'Giovanni Sabadino degli Arienti, Ercole I d'Este and the Decoration of the Italian Renaissance Court', *Renaissance Studies*, 9 (1987) 1, 18–57.

Stäuble, Antonio, 'Scenografia e architettura teatrale nel Rinascimento', in Walter Binni (ed.), *Letteratura e critica. Studi in onore di Natalino Sapegno*, 5 vols (Rome: Bulzoni, 1974–1979), vol. 2, pp. 391–415.

Tuohy, Thomas, *Herculean Ferrara: Ercole d'Este (1471–1505) and the Invention of a Ducal Capital* (Cambridge: Cambridge University Press, 1996).

Vecchi Calore, Marina, 'Rappresentazioni sacre a Ferrara ai tempi di Ercole I', *Atti e Memorie della Deputazione Provinciale Ferrarese di Storia Patria*, 17 (1980), 158–95.

Villoresi, Marco, *Da Guarino a Boiardo. La cultura teatrale a Ferrara nel Quattrocento* (Rome: Bulzoni, 1994).

Winternitz, Emanuel, 'Instruments de musique étranges chez Filippino Lippi, Piero di Cosimo, et Lorenzo Costa', in Jean Jacquot (ed.), *Les Fêtes de la Renaissance*, 2 vols (Paris: Centre national de la recherche scientifique, 1956), vol. 1, pp. 379–95.

Zorzi, Ludovico, *Il teatro e la città* (Turin: Einaudi, 1977).

Chapter 11

'*Ascendendo et descendendo aequaliter*'

Stairs and ceremonies in early modern Venice

Katharina Bedenbender

The early-sixteenth-century poet and satirist Pietro Aretino mentioned in a letter that his friend Giulio Camillo

> used to take a delight in remarking to me that the entrance to my house from the land side, being a dark one with a beastly staircase, was like the terrible name I had acquired by revealing the truth. And then, he would add, that anyone who came to know me would find in my pure, plain and natural friendship the same tranquil contentment that was felt on reaching the portico and coming out on the balconies above.[1]

This letter by the Renaissance writer nicknamed *flagello dei principi* ('scourge of princes') is particularly interesting in that it contains a description of a typical Venetian building in which the main staircase is used as a metaphor for getting to know its owner's character. The dark *androne* staircase is here called a 'scourge'. Normally the ground floor was not inhabited because of the humidity rising from the adjacent canal. The *androne* was used for storing oil, wine, or equipment such as boats. It often had two entrances, one from the land side and another from the waterside. Such a very dark and clammy room also provided space for a staircase, which was anything but convenient or representative of the building as a whole, but nonetheless gave access to the main entrance of the actual living quarters.

Medieval Venice was not the only place where the staircase played a humble role. Across Italy, dark, small and steep spiral stairs were often banished to a distant corner of the palace, whereas open court-stairs leading with a 90-degree-turn to the *piano nobile* were often beautifully decorated, although they remained simple in architectural terms. Alberti, in his architectural treatise completed in 1452, called staircases '*perturbatrices architecturae*' ('the troublemakers of

---

[1] Pietro Aretino, 'Letter LXXX to Messer Domenico Bolani, Description of the House Which He Had Rented of Him', in Samuel Putnam (ed. and trans.), *The Works of Aretino* (Chicago: Pascal Covici, 1926), vol. 2, pp. 180–211 (see p. 181).

architecture').[2] Few problems seemed more complicated than integrating a staircase in a reasonable manner into the structure of a building. Moreover, in the narrow urban confines of a medieval city built on water, few things were more important than living space and natural light. Using these limited resources of space and light in building a beautiful and convenient staircase was considered a waste. This, however, significantly changed in 1483.

The ducal palace as significant location

On 14 September 1483 the east wing of the Ducal Palace in Venice was destroyed by fire. It was rebuilt in the following years by Antonio Rizzo and Pietro Lombardo. On 11 November 1485, meanwhile, the Great Council decided on a notable change in the coronation ceremony of the Doge. The act of coronation, the moment when the youngest and the oldest member of the Great Council crowned the Doge with the *baretta*, was no longer to take place in the Great Council Hall or in the Church of Saint Mark, but instead at the top of a staircase in the courtyard of the Ducal Palace:

> *et in Palatium redierit super scallas illius ad accipiendum juramentum a Dominio, tunc immediate post jusjurandum predictum in capite Serenitatis sue per juniorem Consiliarium ponatur veta et per seniorem Consiliarium ponatur biretum predictum ducale dicentem hec tantum verba: Accipe coronam Ducatus venetiarum*
>
> [and he [the doge] shall return to the palace to receive the coronation oath by way of the said stairs, and to swear the said oath shortly after, and the youngest member of the Great Council shall place the *veta* and the eldest shall place the *baretta* on the doge's head speaking these few words: accept the crown of the Venetian doge].[3]

This decision was made during an interregnum of two weeks: Doge Giovanni Mocenigo died on 4 November 1485, and his successor Marco Barbarigo was crowned on 19 November, at the top of one of the old court-stairs. Probably Marco Barbarigo's coronation, as well as that of his brother and successor Agostino Barbarigo a year later, took place at the top of an open court-staircase which once led to the Great Council Hall. This staircase was demolished during the expansion of the east wing under Scarpagnino between 1533 and 1535. Rizzo not only rebuilt the east wing with the ducal apartments and the new *Sala del Senato*, a separate building unconnected to the

[2] Leon Battista Alberti, *De re aedificatoria*, ed. Max Theuer (Darmstadt: Wissenschaftliche Buchgesellschaft, 1975), book I, chapter 13, p. 62.

[3] Giambattista Lorenzi, *Monumenti per servire alla storia del Palazzo Ducale di Venezia. Serie di atti pubblici dal 1253 al 1797* (Venice: Tip. del commercia di M. Visentini, 1869), vol. 1 (1253–1600), pp. 92–3.

south wing, but also constructed a monumental open staircase composed of a single flight and with remarkably rich relief decoration.[4] It was later called the *Scala dei Giganti*, after Jacopo Sansovino's addition in 1567 of sculptures of Neptune and Mars. Numerous paintings, descriptions of ceremonies and travel reports indicate that more than thirty doges were crowned at the top of these steps. The steps were also used to welcome ambassadors and other important dignitaries. In 1567 the so-called *Scala d'Oro*, erected by Jacopo Sansovino and decorated by Alessandro Vittoria, partly replaced the *Scala dei Giganti* as a ceremonial space for welcoming ambassadors.[5] Depending on their rank, dignitaries were met by the doge halfway up the stairs and accompanied to the upper halls.

The *Scala dei Giganti* evidently fits within a larger tradition of monumental open stairs constructed for town halls in northern Italy, such as that in Cortona. The *Giganti*, however, was executed by Lombard stone masons in the vocabulary of the early Renaissance, with a triumphal arch above the upper landing. The iconography of the bas-reliefs derives from Roman triumphal arches and sarcophagi. But in my view the iconographic programme was inspired more directly by the grand staircase and the *Porta della Guerra* of Federico da Montefeltro's Palazzo Ducale in Urbino, executed prior to 1476 by Luciano Laurana and Ambrogio Barocci.[6] The space under the stairs was used as a prison cell where public enemies were imprisoned, a demonstration of the judicial suzerainty of the doge. The *Scala dei Giganti* served in practice as significant location for the ceremonial and representative opportunities which a staircase could provide. It is no coincidence that only a few months after its construction the *Scuole Grandi* began to erect a series of well-illuminated double-branch and three-branch staircases, which were primarily built for the religious processions of these lay confraternities.

The *Scuole Grandi* of fifteenth-century Venice

The five fifteenth-century *Scuole Grandi* were each dedicated to a saint. Their origins lie in the flagellation movement of the thirteenth century, but their character changed significantly in the course of the fifteenth and sixteenth centuries, becoming exclusive clubs restricted to the wealthy citizenry of Venice. Ostensibly concerned with the welfare of the poor, ill and elderly, the *Scuole Grandi* turned into highly elitist organisations primarily interested in competing with each other and with the nobility. They became a platform for an increasingly rich and

[4] Anne Markham Schulz, *Antonio Rizzo: Sculptor and Architect* (Princeton, NJ: Princeton University Press, 1983), pp. 82–114.

[5] Bruce Boucher, *The Sculpture of Jacopo Sansovino* (New Haven, CT and London: Yale University Press, 1991), pp. 128–59.

[6] Janez Höfler, *Der Palazzo Ducale in Urbino unter den Montefeltre (1376–1508). Neue Forschungen zur Bau- und Ausstattungsgeschichte* (Regensburg: Schnell und Steiner, 2004), pp. 123–238.

powerful citizenry as compensation for the fact that the citizens had no access to the Great Council, which was restricted to the nobility. Francesco Sansovino called the lay confraternities small republics within the great republic of Venice, largely because they tried hard to imitate the *Signoria* in both structure and, particularly, art patronage.[7] The *Scuole Grandi* were not subordinate to the Patriarch, that is to say the Bishop of Venice; they answered instead to the Council of Ten, one of Venice's most powerful magistracies, responsible for internal security.[8] The *Scuole* developed a specific building type, something between a church, a palazzo and a council hall, consisting of three spaces: the *Sala Terrena*, divided by two rows of columns; the *Sala Capitolare* on the first floor, where Mass was celebrated; and the *Albergo*, a kind of council hall for the *Banca*, the *Scuola*'s annually elected board. The *Albergo* also served as an *adytum* where relics were displayed and alms distributed. These powerful lay confraternities played a crucial role in the ceremonial life of the city, especially on the state's great annual feast-days, such as the *Festa della Sensa*, *Giovedi Grasso* or *Corpus Christi*, when they held solemn processions through Saint Mark's square and the city.

The staircase of the *Scuola Grande di San Marco*: the creation of a prototype

On 1 April 1485 the meeting hall of the *Scuola Grande di San Marco*, at the Campo Santi Giovanni e Paolo, was almost completely destroyed by fire. A few days later the *Scuola*'s *Banca* decided to rebuild the structure in the same place, but with an important modification: they bought an additional strip of land from the adjacent friars of Santi Giovanni e Paolo, where the future staircase was to be built. The sales contract from 16 August 1486 describes the arrangement of this new staircase: it has to be constructed '*ascendendo, et descendendo aequaliter, ita quod aleat ascensum ex una parte, et descensum ex alia scala*' ('ascending, and equally descending, in order to facilitate climbing the stairs from one side, and descending them via the other branch').[9] The document also refers to the staircase's bilateral, symmetrical disposition, with two middle landings and one central landing with a pendentive (circular or polygonal) dome and a *bifora* (mullioned) window. The stairs were covered by ascending barrel vaults (see Figures 11.1 and 11.2).

---

[7] Francesco Sansovino, *Venetia, città nobilissima et singolare: con le aggiunte di Giustiniano Martinioni (ristampa dell'edizione del 1663)* (Venice: Filippi, 1968), pp. 281–91.

[8] Brian Pullan, *Rich and Poor in Renaissance Venice: The Social Institutions of a Catholic State to 1620* (Oxford: Blackwell, 1971), pp. 82–134.

[9] Venice, Archivio di Stato, Scuola Grande di San Marco, busta 121, c. 1–4; SS Giovanni e Paolo, busta M, fasc. 22, no. 14. See Philip Sohm, *The Scuola Grande di San Marco (1437–1550). The Architecture of a Venetian lay confraternity* (New York: Garland, 1982), doc. 36.

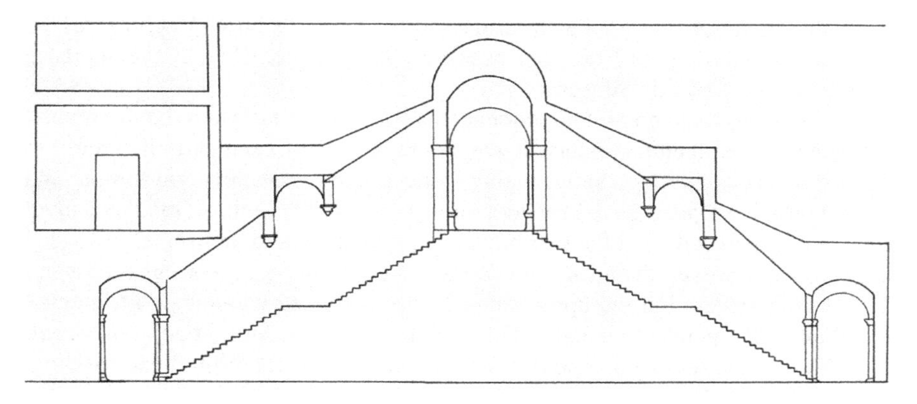

Figure 11.1 The *scalone* of the Scuola Grande di San Marco, transversal section (© Philip Sohm, *Scuola Grande*, ill. 102)

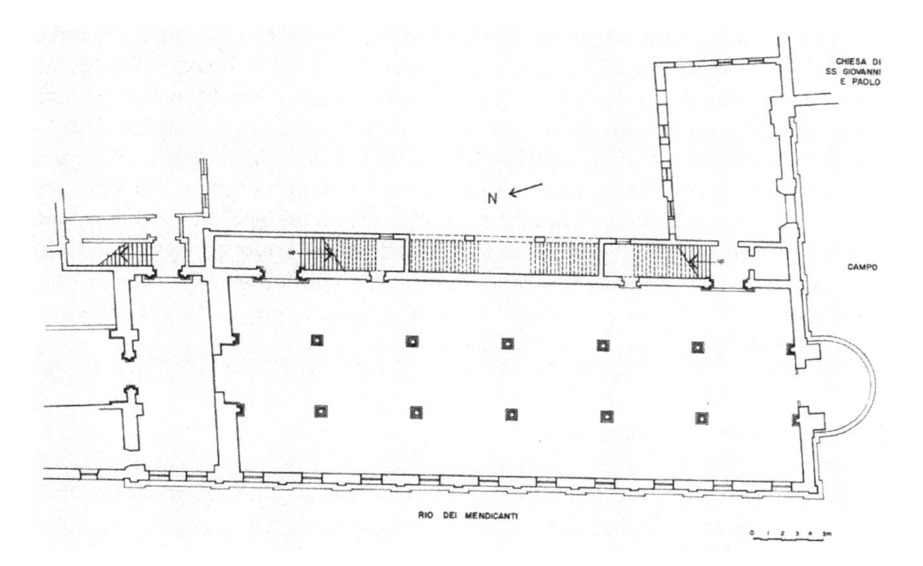

Figure 11.2 The Scuola Grande di San Marco, plan of the ground floor. Drawing by Giuliana Bianco. (© Sohm, *Scuola Grande*, ill. 9)

In view of the fact that Mauro Codussi was only engaged in 1490, four years after this sales contract appeared, his authorship may be doubted, as Philip Sohm has suggested.[10] The staircase, built for the ceremonial requirements of the *Scuola*'s feasts and processions, which took place almost every week, may well have been designed by an expert amongst the members of the *Scuola* who has not yet

[10] See Sohm, *Scuola Grande*, pp. 17–19, 187.

been identified. On the greater feast-days more than a thousand people passed through the building, and on such occasions the two branches of the staircase allowed a regulated flow of traffic.

There seems to be no prototype for such a staircase, but it was to have a crucial influence on architectural history. It was destroyed in 1819 and partially rebuilt in the 1950s. Previous research has mainly concentrated on its bilateral format, and several possible models have been identified, including the stairs of medieval town halls in northern Italy and the two-branch staircase at Rialto, destroyed in 1515.[11] In my view, however, the most remarkable feature of the *Scuola*'s staircase is not the bilateral system but the upper landing with its *bifora* window and triumphal portal under the pendentive dome. This landing marks the highest point of ascent, as well as the cardinal point and threshold of any movement through the building. The pendentive dome is normally restricted to church architecture; it originally derived from Eastern models such as the Hagia Sophia or the Chora Church, mediated by Ravenna and the church of Saint Mark, or *Quattrocento* churches like San Giobbe or Santa Maria dei Miracoli. The use of a dome of this kind emphasises the para-liturgical character of the confraternity's meeting halls and ceremonial activities. Indeed, not only did pilgrims and brethren use the staircase when paying homage to the *Scuola*'s relics, the relics themselves were taken from the building via the staircase on several occasions, when they were carried in splendid reliquaries through the city. The sacralisation of the *Scuola Grande* also becomes apparent in the façade and in the pictorial decoration of the *Albergo*. I assume that an artistic outline, which included the façade, the staircase and the paintings, had been formulated by an artist and member of the confraternity and propose Gentile Bellini as the designer of this programme and, within the programme, of the staircase also. This suggestion cannot be proved definitively, but is supported by circumstantial evidence.

The façade of the *Scuola Grande*

The perspective reliefs of the lower façade, attributed to Tullio Lombardo, show lions, the attribute of Saint Mark, flanking and guarding the *Scuola*'s triumphal main entrance. The reliefs on the right-hand side, flanking the façade's second portal, represent two scenes from the life of Saint Mark, 'the Healing' and 'the Baptism of the cobbler Anianus in Alexandria'. In 1997 Catherina Schmidt-Arcangeli convincingly attributed the design of these reliefs to the Bellini brothers Gentile and Giovanni.[12]

---

[11] Deborah Howard, *The Architectural History of Venice* (New Haven, CT and London: Yale University Press, 2002), p. 143.

[12] Caterina Schmidt-Arcangeli, 'Un tempio aperto. Die Bedeutung der Bellini für den Fassadenentwurf der Scuola Grande di San Marco', in Klaus Bergdolt (ed.), *Kunst und*

The upper storey of the façade was executed by Mauro Codussi and visually connects the *Scuola Grande* with the church of Saint Mark, the sepulchre of the saint and the state church of the republic. The domes of Saint Mark's had been erected in the thirteenth century using a wooden construction covered with lead and allude, according to Deborah Howard, to Egyptian sepulchre churches.[13] They therefore offer an allusion to the provenance of the relics.

The decoration of the *Albergo*

The pictorial decoration of the *Albergo* adopts the façade's programme. In 1492 Gentile Bellini offered to paint the first canvas, *Saint Mark Preaching in Alexandria*, for the most prominent wall directly above the *Banca*.[14] According to surviving documents, Gentile made sure that the decoration would remain in his own hands and those of his brother Giovanni: '*ad algun altro non possi esser dato ditta opera del dito Albergo a far, ne parte ne niente dun modo j diti fradeli*' ('the contract for the decoration of the Albergo cannot be given to anyone else, but to me [Gentile Bellini] and my said brother').[15] Gentile probably had the basic composition of the painting as well as a general idea of the whole cycle in mind. But for several reasons it would take the *Scuola* 14 years after the initial work in 1504 to realise the decorative programme. It may be a coincidence that in Bellini's painting Saint Mark is preaching from a pulpit shaped like a two-branch staircase.[16] The shape of the building in the background, representing the Temple of Serapis in Alexandria is, however, not coincidental. Several authors have commented on the similarities between this fantastic architecture and the church as well as the *Scuola Grande* of Saint Mark.[17] The painting is comparable to Gentile Bellini's *Procession of the Holy Cross in Saint Mark's Square*, completed in 1496 for the *Scuola Grande di San Giovanni Evangelista* as part of the Holy Cross Cycle for

ihre Auftraggeber im 16. Jahrhundert: Venedig und Augsburg im Vergleich (Berlin: Akademie-Velag, 1997), pp. 43–87.

[13] Deborah Howard, *Venice and the East: The Impact of the Islamic World on Venetian Architecture, 1100–1500* (New Haven, CT and London: Yale University Press, 2000), pp. 65–111.

[14] Gentile Bellini, *Saint Mark Preaching in Alexandria*, 1504–7, oil on canvas (347 × 770 cm), Pinacoteca di Brera, Milan.

[15] Venice, Archivio di Stato, Scuola Grande di San Marco, busta 135. See Pietro Paoletti, *L'architettura e scultura del Rinascimento a Venezia* (Venice, 1894), p. 17; Jürg Meyer zur Capellen, *Gentile Bellini* (Stuttgart: Franz Steiner Verlag, 1985), pp. 112–3, doc. 31.

[16] A very similar pulpit still exists in San Lorenzo fuori le Mura in Rome.

[17] Patricia Fortini Brown, *Venetian Narrative Painting in the Age of Carpaccio* (New Haven, CT and London: Yale University Press, 1989), pp. 207–8.

the confraternity's *Oratorio della Croce*.[18] The canvas reveals Gentile's awareness of timing, space, and ceremonial process.

The monuments in the background of *The Preaching of Saint Mark* confirm Alexandria as the place of the miraculous events. Apparently Gentile Bellini had no first-hand knowledge of the Egyptian city, but only information from written travel accounts or pilgrim reports. According to Patricia Fortini Brown, the whole decorative programme is part of the Orientalism fashionable amongst the so-called eyewitness-painters in the second half of the Venetian *Quattrocento*.[19] The visitor to the *Scuola Grande di San Marco* – for example, a pilgrim visiting the monuments and relics of the city while waiting for his passage to the Holy Land – saw a kind of preview of the Holy Places. He did not just visit Venice, but a Venice that saw itself as a second Alexandria. This phenomenon is well known from Holy Sepulchre sites. As replacements of the actual Holy Site, they often became famous and sacred themselves.

The steps and the elevated platform

In my view, the *scalone* fits into this programme very well. I want to suggest that the two-branch staircase of the *Scuola Grande* was designed as an allusion to Calvary, with the Church of the Holy Sepulchre above. In doing so, I am well aware of the inflated use of this analogy in art history in general. The Venetians had been familiar with the shape of the Church of the Holy Sepulchre since 1486, when a credible illustration appeared in Bernhard von Breydenbach's *Peregrinatio in Terram Sanctam* (see Plate 14).[20] The main feature of the church's upper façade is a dome above a *bifora* window. Venetian fifteenth-century painters often used architectural quotations from pictorial and written sources in an eclectic manner. This is illustrated by the so-called sketchbooks of Jacopo Bellini, but can also be seen in the *œuvre* of Vittore Carpaccio, who was greatly influenced by Gentile Bellini. In Carpaccio's *Triumph of Saint George* for the *Scuola di San Giorgio degli Schiavoni*, the fantastic architecture in the background creates an Eastern setting.[21] As Fortini Brown has pointed out, Carpaccio was never satisfied with a simple architectural quotation without transforming it.[22] Here he combined two real buildings, putting the minaret of the mosque of Rama on top of the lower façade of the

---

[18] Gentile Bellini, *Procession of the Holy Cross in Saint Mark's Square*, 1496, oil on canvas (347 × 770 cm), Galleria dell'Accademia, Venice.

[19] Fortini Brown, *Narrative Painting*, p. 73.

[20] Frederike Timm, *Der Palästina-Pilgerbericht des Bernhard von Breidenbach von 1486 und die Holzschnitte Erhard Reuwichs* (Stuttgart: Hauswedell-Verlag, 2006), p. 517.

[21] Vittore Carpaccio, *Triumph of Saint George*, 1502 (tempera on panel, 141 × 360 cm), Scuola San Giorgio degli Schiavoni, Venice.

[22] Fortini Brown, *Narrative Painting*, p. 214.

Church of the Holy Sepulchre. Both buildings were illustrated in Breydenbach's pilgrim report, which served as Carpaccio's main source.

My thesis is that Gentile Bellini acted in a similar manner in designing the staircase of the *Scuola Grande di San Marco* – albeit in the field of architecture rather than painting. Such a design requires certain pre-conditions. Jerusalem's Church of the Holy Sepulchre was built on the site of Calvary, the hill which Christ had climbed with the Cross. After His martyrdom on the Cross, He was buried in the same place, which was where His followers subsequently built the Church of the Holy Sepulchre. In the second half of the fifteenth century the church served as one of the most important pilgrim destinations in the Holy Land, which became increasingly difficult to access. The association of climbing the stairs with the *Via Crucis* is obvious and was employed in the façade of the *Scuola*. The bas-reliefs on the bases of the columns that flank the triumphal portal make use of an iconography that refers to the self-sacrifice of Christ on the Cross. The parallelism of the *scalone* with the *Via Crucis* has a certain tradition within the history of the *Scuola Grande*, as is shown by the earlier pictorial decoration executed by the Vivarini brothers, by Francesco Squarcione, and by Jacopo, Giovanni and Gentile Bellini. These paintings were all destroyed in 1485, but documents show that Squarcione was commissioned in 1465 to paint two canvases for the top and the bottom of the staircase, depicting scenes from the Passion of Christ. The pilgrim, while climbing the steps, was therefore accompanied by paintings depicting the *Via Crucis* with its zenith in the upper hall, where a monumental Crucifixion by Jacopo Bellini adorned the wall between the windows of the *controfacciata*.[23]

There may be a connection between this early programme and the fact that none other than Ambrogio Contarini had donated a relic of the True Cross to the *Scuola Grande*, a souvenir from his last journey to Constantinople.[24] This donation might have been a direct response to the miraculous relic of the Cross of the competing *Scuola Grande di San Giovanni Evangelista*. The competition between the *Scuole Grandi* was legendary. The wooden splinter of the True Cross was locked up in a precious reliquary in the *Tesoro* on the upper floor, directly behind the *Albergo*. On certain feast days it left the *Tesoro* in procession and was carried down and back up the staircase.

Ambrogio Contarini, one of the most remarkable personalities of the Venetian *Quattrocento*, had travelled by order of the Signoria to Russia and the Middle East. An unusually large number of seafaring and travelling men were amongst the *confratelli* of the *Scuola Grande di San Marco* – we might instance Giosaphat Barbaro, Alvise da Mosto, Gaspare da Vedoa and Paolo Valaresso. Each of them made donations of relics and wrote several of the most important travel reports of late-fifteenth-century Venice. Up to 1497, Ambrogio Contarini's brother Agostino

[23] Pietro Paoletti, *La Scuola Grande di San Marco* (Venice: Comune di Venezia, 1929), pp. 80–1.

[24] Fortini Brown, *Narrative Painting*, pp. 74–5.

had the almost exclusive right to organise pilgrimages to the Holy Land. It was on a Contarini galley that the German Dominican Felix Fabri and Bernhard von Breydenbach jointly travelled to Jerusalem in 1483, as the list of passengers indicates. The woodcut in Breydenbach's *Peregrinatio* shows the group in front of the Church of the Holy Sepulchre.[25] According to Fabri, the stream of visitors was greatly in decline and in recent years almost no-one had visited the church because of the Muslim occupying forces.[26] Building a staircase that alludes to Calvary and the Church of the Holy Sepulchre can therefore be seen as a substitute for re-establishing a Christian presence in Jerusalem and a way of acquiring the Holy Places for the city of Venice.

A staircase design by Gentile Bellini?

Research has suggested that Gentile Bellini may have been the artist responsible for the *Albergo*'s pictorial programme as well as designer of the façade reliefs.[27] I want to go one step further and also attribute the design of the staircase to Bellini, thereby suggesting that he designed the entire work, including painting, relief and architecture. Bellini became a member of the confraternity in 1466, while involved in the *Scuola*'s first design studies. From the late 1470s on, after his return from Istanbul, he became one of the most influential *confratelli* of the *Scuola* and was elected to several offices of the *Banca*.[28] He was considered an expert in the field of architecture, and this is confirmed by his paintings, which often comprise architectural *vedute* or cityscapes. A document of 21 July 1476 states that Gentile did not just create paintings for the *Scuola*, but also the designs for the façade reliefs, a pulpit and a staircase, executed by Antonio Rizzo.[29] Gentile was possibly inspired for both staircase designs by the sketchbooks of his father Jacopo Bellini, for example, by the drawings on folios 92 and 93 of the volume now in the British Museum.[30] Folio 93 shows a double-branch staircase in front of the façade of a Venetian palace. This however leads nowhere, since the upper landing lacks an entrance to the building (see Figure 11.3).

---

[25] Timm, *Der Palästina-Pilgerbericht*, p. 517.

[26] Felix Fabri, *Galeere und Karawane. Pilgerreise ins Heilige Land, zum Sinai und nach Ägypten 1483*, ed. Herbert Wiegandt (Stuttgart: K. Thienemanns Verlag, 1996), pp. 27–8, 96–112.

[27] The pictorial decoration of the Albergo was completely destroyed in 1485.

[28] Meyer zur Capellen, *Bellini*, pp. 106–20.

[29] The whole building and its decoration was destroyed in 1485. Venice, Archivio di Stato, Scuola Grande di San Marco, busta 122, fasc. D, c. 15^{r}. See Meyer zur Capellen, *Bellini*, pp. 108–9, doc. 13.

[30] See Colin Eisler, *The Genius of Jacopo Bellini: The Complete Paintings and Drawings* (Ostfildern: Dumont, 1998), pp. 148–9, pl. 52–3.

Figure 11.3 Jacopo Bellini, double-branch staircase in front of a Venetian palace (© The Trustees of the British Museum)

The staircase is a mere monument, a *macchina*; people climb the stairs on the right and descend on the left. Gentile was interested in motion sequences, as can be seen throughout his work. In 1492 he became *Guardian da Matin*, that is, master of ceremonies of the *Scuola Grande*.[31] A few years later he painted the *Procession of the True Cross in Saint Mark's Square* for the *Scuola Grande di San Giovanni Evangelista*, a picture that, as noted, confirms his keen sense of timing, spatial organisation and ceremonial processes.

Gentile was furthermore familiar with the so-called *tribunales*, temporary double-branch staircases, which played an important role in the court ceremonies of the Byzantine emperor. As early as Paoletti in 1894,[32] scholars have mentioned them as a potential source of inspiration, well-known in fifteenth-century Venice, for the double-branch staircases of these *Scuole*.[33] A connection with Gentile Bellini, however, has never to my knowledge been suggested. When Emperor Frederick III visited Venice in 1469, a *scala a tribunale* was erected in his honour in the palace of the Duke of Mantua.[34] On the occasion of the visit, the Emperor bestowed on Gentile Bellini the titles of *Venetus Eques* and *Comes Palatinus*. Another notable patron of the arts and architecture was Sultan Mehmed II, who initiated his own Renaissance in the Ottoman lands. He attempted to replicate the antique empire and revived Byzantine court ceremonies. Gentile Bellini, who stayed about a year at the Ottoman court in 1479, could have seen such a *scala a tribunale* in use on several occasions.

The earliest evidence of a *scala a tribunale* in Venice was identified by Manuela Morresi as a feature of the church of San Zaccaria, which originated from an imperial Byzantine donation. According to Morresi its bilateral staircase explicitly alluded to the Holy Sepulchre complex inside the church.[35] Nearby, at the Riva degli Schiavoni, was the monastery of Santo Sepolcro, which accommodated pilgrims on their journey to the Holy Land and featured a Holy Sepulchre complex created in 1484 by Tullio Lombardo. Morresi argues for a fully formed cult of the Holy Sepulchre established here in the second half of the fifteenth century. The reconstruction of San Zaccaria was finished in the 1490s by Mauro Codussi, who, with his contemporaries, was certainly well aware of the original complex. It is no coincidence that the *Scuola Grande di San Marco* also commissioned Mauro

[31] Venice, Archivio di Stato, Scuola Grande di San Marco, notatorio 16 bis, part II, fol. 62^{v}. See Meyer zur Capellen, *Bellini*, p. 113, doc. 33.

[32] Paoletti, *La Scuola Grande*, pp. 40–53.

[33] See Gianmario Guidarelli, *Una giogia ligata in piombo: La fabbrica della Scuola Grande di San Rocco in Venezia, 1517–1560*, Quaderni della Scuola Grande Arciconfraternita di San Rocco, vol. 8 (Venice: Scuola Grande di San Rocco, 2002), pp. 35–59.

[34] See Pietro Ghinzoni, 'Federico III imperatore a Venezia (7 al 19 Febbrajo 1469)', *Archivio Veneto*, 19 (1889) 7, part I, p. 135.

[35] Manuela Morresi, 'Venezia e la città del Dominio', in Francesco Paolo Fiore (ed.), *Storia dell'architettura italiana. Il Quattrocento* (Milan: Electa, 1998), pp. 200–41, 234–5.

Codussi to finish the upper part of their façade and to build the staircase, as he built the most important pendentive domes in Quattrocento Venice.

It is no surprise that we cannot find any direct evidence of Gentile Bellini in documents concerning the staircase. This is in fact rather typical for the corporate art patronage of the *Scuole Grandi*. The *Scuole* committed themselves openly to the republican ideals of the Serenissima and their own ideology of fraternal co-operation and equality. The *Scuole Grandi* always endeavoured to conceal the identity of important personalities. To engage an artist who was at the same time a member of the confraternity also carried financial advantage for the *Banca*.

The artistic outline of the *Scuola Grande di San Marco* was designed to express the identity of a group of seafaring Venetians, *cittadini* as well as *nobili*, who continued with their attempt to build bridges with the East. A pilgrim could visit the *Scuola Grande di San Marco* as a substitute for the Holy Places in Alexandria and Jerusalem. The pilgrim walked in the footsteps of Saint Mark, who suffered martyrdom because of his devotion to Christ. For the pilgrim climbing its steps, the staircase alluded to Christ's Crucifixion. This allusion became even more explicit on feast days, when the relic of the True Cross was carried in procession via the staircase.

The staircase of the *Scuola Grande di San Giovanni Evangelista*

In 1498, only three years after the completion of the staircase of the *Scuola Grande di San Marco*, the *Scuola Grande di San Giovanni Evangelista* also commissioned Mauro Codussi to construct a bilateral staircase, but with notable modifications (see Figure 11.4).

At the upper landing of the staircase both branches are 70 centimetres wider than at the bottom of the stairs. This difference in width creates an optical illusion, giving the visitor an impression of monumentality.[36] In addition, the stair-head was adorned by four free-standing columns. The great *bifora* window and the windows at the lower landings successfully illuminate the *scalone*, with reflections from the water amplifying the splendid ambiance (see Figure 11.5).

The construction of this staircase was a direct reaction to the building activities at the *Scuola Grande di San Marco* and typical of the constant competition between Venetian lay confraternities.

In the case of the *Scuola Grande di San Giovanni Evangelista* we may again assume a connection between the staircase, the pictorial decoration and a relic. But to understand this connection we must first discuss the historical background. From the early fourteenth century, the confraternity's meeting hall was located in the *sestiere* of San Polo on the terrain of the Badoer family, adjacent to a hospital

---

36 See Chiara Vazzoler, *La Scuola Grande di San Giovanni Evangelista* (Venice: Marsilio, 2005), pp. 30–3.

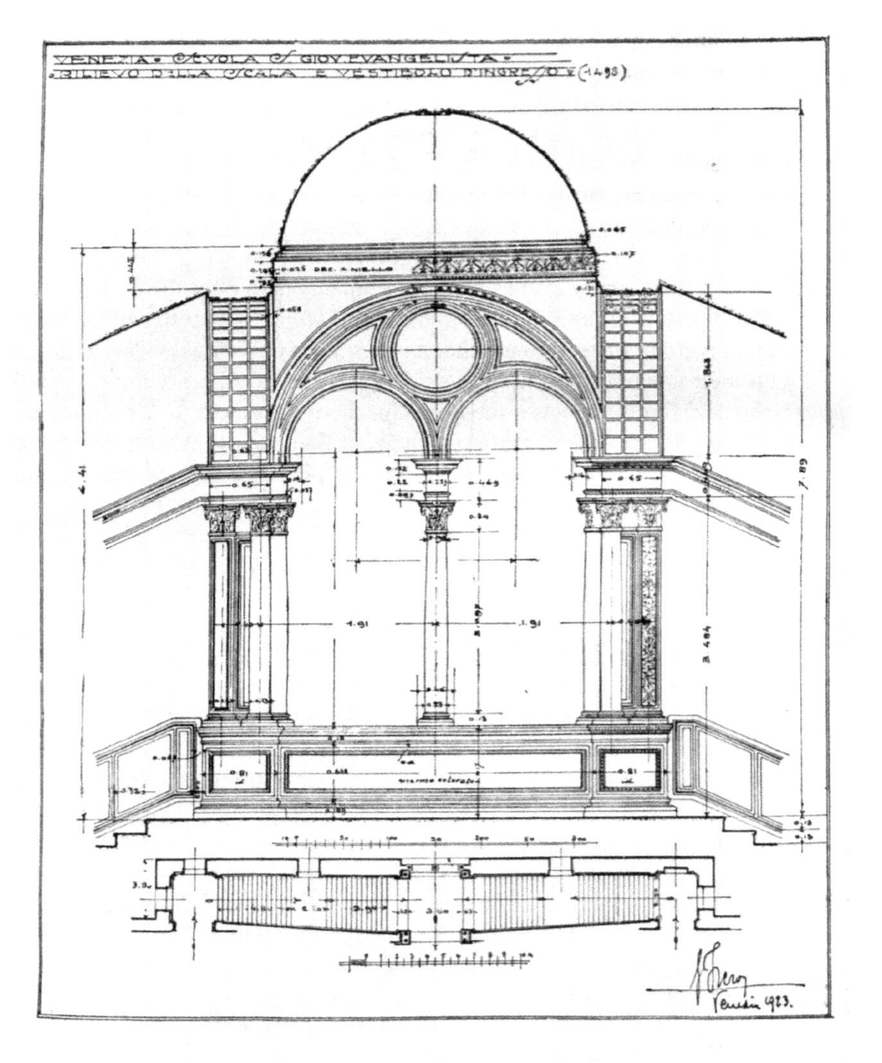

Figure 11.4 *Scuola Grande di San Giovanni Evangelista*, ground plan of the staircase and elevation of the upper landing (© Pietro Paoletti, *La Scuola Grande*, p. 52)

Figure 11.5 *Scuola Grande di San Giovanni Evangelista*, photograph of the upper landing with Mauro Codussi's *bifora* window (© Philip Sohm, *Scuola Grande*, ill. 105)

for the poor and elderly and to the small church of San Giovanni Evangelista, which served as a private chapel of the noble family. In 1369 Philippe de Mézières, chancellor of Cyprus and the kingdom of Jerusalem, donated to the *Scuola* a relic of the True Cross, which immediately began to perform miracles.[37] The relic was kept in the small church, where the *Scuola* celebrated their rites and masses until

[37] Fortini Brown, *Narrative Painting*, p. 135.

the end of the fifteenth century, when the Badoer family instituted legal proceedings against the confraternity to restrict its use of the church. In reaction to that dispute, the *Scuola* decided to construct an oratory on the ground floor of its own building, where the relic was to be kept in future. The location on the ground floor seems to have been important in that it made the relic accessible to old and disabled people. For the Badoer, who asked the Patriarch to intervene, the relocation of the relic would have meant heavy loss of donations. The Patriarch tried to prohibit the erection of the oratory but, as such a decision fell outside his purview, he came into conflict with the Council of Ten. In the end, the *Scuola* was allowed to erect an *Oratorio della Croce*, including an altar, but only on the upper floor of the confraternity's property.[38] At this point it became relevant to commission a convenient and suitably allusive staircase.

It was again Gentile Bellini who was asked to design a concept for the pictorial decoration of the oratory. At the same time, between 1490 and 1506, the *Scuola* published a volume which described at least nine miracles of the relic of the True Cross.[39] Three of the original nine paintings were executed by Gentile Bellini, two by Giovanni Mansueti, four others by Vittore Carpaccio, Pietro Perugino (the lost *Sea Storm*), Benedetto Diana and Lazzaro Bastiani. The style of Bastiani and Mansueti can be described as eclectic; in the oratory of the confraternity's *Scuola Grande* they worked under the formal influence of Gentile Bellini and adapted their style to create a certain unity within the cycle. The paintings depict the nine most famous miracles of the relic of the Cross, which was either carried in procession through the city, or transferred its miracle-working powers via the use of sacred candles. The relic and its movement through urban space correspond to the *Via Crucis* and its several stations, and offer to transform the Serenissima into a second Jerusalem. In this context, it was very appropriate to adopt a staircase design that alluded to Calvary and Jerusalem's Church of the Holy Sepulchre. All we know for certain is that Gentile Bellini and Mauro Codussi were also involved at the same date in the construction and decoration of the *Scuola Grande di San Giovanni Evangelista*, just as we have already seen in the case of the *Scuola Grande di San Marco*.

Taking a closer look at the True Cross cycle, we see that in five of the original nine paintings bridges or staircases play an important role. It seems that the topic of 'staircases' was present in the artists' minds, as the following examples illustrate.

Gentile Bellini's *Miracle of the Cross at the Bridge of San Lorenzo* was completed in 1500,[40] and features a bridge shaped like a double-branch staircase. According to the confraternity's published volume, people stormed the bridge

---

[38] See Alberto Spinazzi, 'Libertà di culto e architettura nella Scuola Grande di San Giovanni Evangelista: Scontro fra poteri a Venezia alla fine del Quattrocento', *Studi Veneziani*, 51 (2006), 145–54.

[39] Fortini Brown, *Narrative Painting*, p. 135.

[40] Tempera on canvas (323 × 430 cm), Galleria dell'Accademia, Venice.

from both sides instead of passing from one side to the other in processional order. As a result the relic fell into the water and could only be retrieved by the *Guardian Grande* of the *Scuola Grande di San Giovanni Evangelista*, who is seen swimming in the foreground of the picture. The actual topic of the painting seems to be the organisation of large crowds during religious processions.

The Miracle of the Bridge of San Lio, executed in 1494 by Giovanni Mansueti,[41] shows the funeral procession of a faithless brother who had several times doubted the relic. Just when the procession tries to cross the bridge of San Lio the relic becomes so heavy that it cannot be carried further and must be replaced by a cross. The lesson seems to be that the weight of a task depends on the faith of its agent.

Mansueti's *Healing of the Daughter of Nicolò Benvegnudo from San Polo*, painted in 1506,[42] shows a three-year-old girl, blind since birth and suffering from epilepsy, being healed in her bed by means of three candles that had touched the relic in the oratory of the *Scuola Grande di San Giovanni Evangelista*. The numerous spectators of the scene can only watch the miracle by crossing over an open court staircase, which also functions as a bridge over a small stream. A similar idea may be found in Carpaccio's Rialto painting.[43]

Candles play an important role in these pictures. They could be acquired from the *confratelli* and after touching the relic were able to transfer its miraculous virtue to a beloved person unable to climb the *Scuola*'s staircase. By the prominent display of candles, staircases and bridges, the concepts of time and space become dominant themes in these paintings. The staircases organise the protagonists' space. Stairs and bridges are thresholds and therefore transitional spaces. A staircase represents a series of thresholds and is, in this respect, a transitional space *par excellence*. This relates to the performed miracles, which transform the condition of a person from sin to grace or from illness to health. Such a transformation could only be achieved by physically or metaphorically climbing the steps of the *Scuola Grande di San Giovanni Evangelista*, where, on the upper floor, the miracle-working relic of the True Cross was kept. The pilgrim, after climbing the staircase that alluded to Calvary, arrived at the *Oratorio della Croce* and saw a panorama of a Venetian Jerusalem, which confirmed the value of taking the painful path to visit the relic, and thus following Christ's example.

A last example of a painted miracle is *The Healing of the Son of Alvise Finetti*, painted between 1505 and 1510 by Benedetto Diana.[44] The son referred to in the title of the painting fell from a rooftop, as implied in the extremely high and narrow

---

[41] Oil on canvas (318 × 458 cm), Galleria dell' Accademia, Venice. In an inscription on the painting Mansueti explicitly identifies himself as a pupil of Bellini, which supports the assumption that Bellini might have been the designer of the whole programme.

[42] Oil on canvas (369 × 296 cm), Galleria dell'Accademia, Venice.

[43] Vittore Carpaccio, *Healing of the Madman*, 1494, tempera on canvas (365 × 389 cm), Galleria dell' Accademia, Venice.

[44] Oil on canvas (365 × 147 cm), Galleria dell' Accademia, Venice.

format of the painting itself. The scene is dominated by a monumental open staircase, similar to the hundreds of staircases that must have stood in the courtyards of Venice's medieval and early Renaissance buildings. Benedetto Diana is better known as a painter of altar screens or pictures of the Virgin Mary. His painting for the *Scuola Grande di San Giovanni Evangelista* is not typical of his *œuvre* and was probably executed under the influence of Gentile Bellini. It is of particular interest that he was asked several years later by the *Scuola Grande di San Rocco* to evaluate its newly constructed staircase, although he had, according to our modern definition, no architectural skills.[45] One could hypothesise that the convincing pictorial representation of a staircase in the painting under discussion was reason enough for the *Scuola Grande di San Rocco* to engage him as an expert in assessing their stone-built *scalone*.

There seems no doubt that artists such as Gentile Bellini and Benedetto Diana, although known as painters, were also closely involved in architectural matters. The profession of 'architect' did not yet exist in the late-fifteenth century – neither in practice nor in theory. 'Architecture' could not be studied in the same way that painters or stonemasons learned their profession. Even Vasari continued using the terms *architectus* and *architectores* in a confusing, heterogeneous manner.[46] The field of activity of the so-called *proto* (master builder) was very flexible and encompassed a variety of jobs and responsibilities, depending on the patron.[47] Our modern distinctions between painting, architecture and sculpture were practically non-existent in the fifteenth century. This constant state of flux among different crafts allowed the artists, the learned *pittori* and *tagliapietri*, to move with ease between the different genres. Similarly, Venice's ceremonies and processions contributed to a change in the conception of staircases in general – not just real, stone-built staircases, but also painted ones.

Bibliography

Printed primary sources

Alberti, Leon Battista, *De re aedificatoria*, ed. Max Theuer (Darmstadt: Wissenschaftliche Buchgesellschaft, 1975).

Aretino, Pietro, 'Letter LXXX to Messer Domenico Bolani, Description of the House Which He Had Rented of Him', in Samuel Putnam (ed.), *The Works of Aretino* (Chicago: Pascal Covici, 1926), vol. 2, pp. 180–211.

---

[45] Schmidt-Arcangeli, 'Un tempio aperto', p. 67, n. 84.

[46] Giorgio Vasari, *Das Leben des Michelangelo*, trans. Victoria Lorini, ed. Caroline Gabbert (Berlin: Wagenbach, 2009), pp. 135–79.

[47] Susan Connell, *The Employment of Sculptors and Stonemasons in Venice in the Fifteenth Century* (London: Warburg Institute, 1976).

Fabri, Felix, *Galeere und Karawane. Pilgerreise ins Heilige Land, zum Sinai und nach Ägypten 1483*, ed. Herbert Wiegandt (Stuttgart: K. Thienemanns Verlag, 1996).

Sansovino, Francesco, *Venetia, città nobilissima et singolare: con le aggiunte di Giustiniano Martinioni (ristampa dell'edizione del 1663), indice analitico a cura di Lino Moretti* (Venice: Filippi, 1968).

Vasari, Giorgio, *Das Leben des Michelangelo*, trans. Victoria Lorini, ed. Caroline Gabbert (Berlin: Wagenbach, 2009).

Secondary sources

Boucher, Bruce, *The Sculpture of Jacopo Sansovino* (New Haven, CT and London: Yale University Press, 1991).

Connell, Susan, *The Employment of Sculptors and Stonemasons in Venice in the Fifteenth Century* (London: Warburg Institute, 1976).

Eisler, Colin, *The Genius of Jacopo Bellini: The Complete Paintings and Drawings* (Ostfildern: Dumont, 1998).

Fortini Brown, Patricia, *Venetian Narrative Painting in the Age of Carpaccio* (New Haven, CT and London: Yale University Press, 1989).

Ghinzoni, Pietro, 'Federico III imperatore a Venezia (7 al 19 Febbrajo 1469)', *Archivio Veneto*, 19 (1889) 7, part I, p. 135.

Good, Robert, 'Double Staircases and the Vertical Distribution of Housing in Venice 1450–1600: An Examination of the Evolution of the Double Staircases in Palatial Residences, and Its Incorporation Into Renaissance Multi-Family Architecture in Venice', *Architectural Research Quarterly*, 13 (2009), 73–85.

Goy, Richard, *Building Renaissance Venice: Patrons, Architects and Builders, 1430–1500* (New Haven, CT and London: Yale University Press, 2006).

Guidarelli, Gianmario, *Una giogia ligata in piombo: La fabbrica della Scuola Grande di San Rocco in Venezia, 1517–1560*, Quaderni della Scuola Grande Arciconfraternita di San Rocco, vol. 8 (Venice: Scuola Grande di San Rocco, 2002).

Höfler, Janez, *Der Palazzo Ducale in Urbino unter den Montefeltre (1376–1508). Neue Forschungen zur Bau- und Ausstattungsgeschichte* (Regensburg: Schnell und Steiner, 2004).

Howard, Deborah, *Venice and the East. The Impact of the Islamic World on Venetian Architecture, 1100–1500* (New Haven, CT and London: Yale University Press, 2000).

Howard, Deborah, *The Architectural History of Venice* (New Haven, CT and London: Yale University Press, 2002).

Lorenzi, Giambattista, *Monumenti per servire alla storia del Palazzo Ducale di Venezia. Serie di atti pubblici dal 1253 al 1797* (Venice: Tip. del commercia di M. Visentini, 1869).

Meyer zur Capellen, Jürg, *Gentile Bellini* (Stuttgart: Franz Steiner Verlag, 1985).

Morresi, Manuela, 'Venezia e la città del Dominio', in Francesco Paolo Fiore (ed.), *Storia dell'architettura italiana. Il Quattrocento* (Milan: Electa, 1998), pp. 200–241.

Paoletti, Pietro, *L'architettura e scultura del Rinascimento a Venezia* (Venice: Ongania-Naya, 1894).

Paoletti, Pietro, *La Scuola Grande di San Marco* (Venice: Comune di Venezia, 1929).

Pullan, Brian, *Rich and Poor in Renaissance Venice: The Social Institutions of a Catholic State, to 1620* (Oxford: Blackwell, 1971).

Schmidt-Arcangeli, Caterina, 'Un tempio aperto. Die Bedeutung der Bellini für den Fassadenentwurf der Scuola Grande di San Marco', in Klaus Bergdolt (ed.), *Kunst und ihre Auftraggeber im 16. Jahrhundert: Venedig und Augsburg im Vergleich* (Berlin: Akademie-Velag, 1997), pp. 43–87.

Schulz, Anne Markham, *Antonio Rizzo: Sculptor and Architect* (Princeton, NJ: Princeton University Press, 1983).

Sohm, Philip, 'The Staircase of the Venetian Scuole Grandi and Mauro Codussi', *Architectura*, 8 (1978), 125–49.

Sohm, Philip, *The Scuola Grande di San Marco (1437–1550): The Architecture of a Venetian Lay Confraternity* (New York: Garland, 1982).

Spinazzi, Alberto, 'Libertà di culto e architettura nella Scuola Grande di San Giovanni Evangelista: Scontro fra poteri a Venezia alla fine del Quattrocento', *Studi Veneziani*, 51 (2006), 145–54.

Timm, Frederike, *Der Palästina-Pilgerbericht des Bernhard von Breidenbach von 1486 und die Holzschnitte Erhard Reuwichs* (Stuttgart: Hauswedell-Verlag, 2006).

Vazzoler, Chiara, *La Scuola Grande di San Giovanni Evangelista* (Venice: Marsilio, 2005).

Chapter 12

Permanent places for festivals at the Habsburg court in Innsbruck

The 'comedy houses' of 1628 and 1654

Veronika Sandbichler

The two figures most closely associated with festivals at the Habsburg Court in Innsbruck flourished in the early and later parts of the sixteenth century: Emperor Maximilian I (1459–1519) and his great-grandson Archduke Ferdinand II (1529–1595). Both were fascinated by chivalry and thus strongly drawn to the tournament, a type of theatrical performance closely connected with chivalry since the end of the twelfth century. Both made use of tournament as a form of princely representation in their festivals, and developed it in accordance with their own purposes. In the case of Maximilian I, tournaments inspired by the refined court of Burgundy were turned into tournaments featuring costume and masquerades known as 'Verkleidungsturniere'.[1] Archduke Ferdinand II continued this tradition when he staged tournaments replete with allusions to the Habsburg dynasty.[2] Although these were ephemeral in character, many of them are documented through such forms of source material as printed and manuscript books or coloured etchings.[3] In addition, objects and parts of the original equipment have been preserved, notably

---

[1] See Dirk Breiding, 'Rennen, Stechen und Turnier zur Zeit Maximilians I', in *Vor Halbtausend Jahren [. . .]. Festschrift zur Erinnerung an den Besuch des Kaisers Maximilian I. in St. Wendel* (St. Wendel: Stadtmusem 2012), pp. 51–82; Eric Bousmar, 'Pasos de armas, justas y torneos en la corte de Borgoña (siglo XV y principios del XVI). Imaginario callabresco, rituales e implicaciones socio-políticas', in Krista de Jonge, Bernardo J. García García and Alicia Esteban Estríngana (eds), *El legado de Borgoña. Fiesta y ceremonia cortesana en la Europa de los Austrias* (Madrid: Marcial Pons Ediciones de Historia, 2004), pp. 561–605.

[2] Veronika Sandbichler, 'Torneos y fiestas de corte de los Habsburgo en los siglos XV y XVII', in ibid., pp. 607–24.

[3] For example Maximilian's tournament book *Freydal*, 1512–1515 (Kunsthistorisches Museum Wien, Inv. No. KK 5073), the *Kolowrat-Wedding*, 1580 (Schloss Ambras Innsbruck, Inv. No. KK 5269) and the *Wedding Festival Book of Archduke Ferdinand II*, 1582 (Schloss Ambras Innsbruck, Inv. No. KK 5270); cf. Elisabeth Scheicher, 'Ein Fest am Hofe Erzherzog Ferdinands II', *Jahrbuch der Kunsthistorischen Sammlungen in Wien*, 77 (1981), 119–54; Veronika Sandbichler, 'Der Hochzeitskodex Erzherzog Ferdinands II', *Jahrbuch des Kunsthistorischen Museums Wien*, 6/7 (2006), 47–89.

in the collections of the castle of Ambras and of the Kunsthistorisches Museum in Vienna.[4] However, the courtyards, streets and squares where the tournaments were actually staged have changed. Only rarely do we find that tournaments took place indoors.

The seventeenth century saw substantial changes in festival culture. The elaborate plots of the 'theatrical' tournament – the 'tournoi à thème' – developed into the sumptuously-staged horse-ballet or *caroussel*. Interludes became more important, leading to the creation of a new genre. Both developments stemmed from contemporary and earlier theatrical forms at courts in Italy. Around 1600, Florentine intellectuals, artists and musicians with a love of Greek drama revived what they thought to be the style of recitation practised in classical Greece. Their manner of composing was completely new, introducing recitative, monody and the vocal concerto, together with the forms which they named 'spettacolo' (Cavalieri, 1600) or 'favola in musica' (Monteverdi, 1607). These last told whole stories, not just a variety of different epic images as the former interludes had. Monteverdi wrote his *Orfeo* to be performed at the Academia degl'Invaghiti. Later it was repeated at the important court of Mantua and in other cities such as Cremona and Turin. In today's terms the performance venues were tiny, with the number of spectators barely exceeding the number of performers.[5]

Archduke Leopold V (1586–1632) and his son Archduke Ferdinand Karl (1628–1662), of the so-called 'younger' Tyrolean line of the Habsburgs, were among the first to cultivate this new style north of the Alps and to establish permanent venues for the staging of ballets and operas. These were the Innsbruck '*Comedihäuser*' ('play houses'), which survive to the present day in more or less altered form.

In this chapter I focus not only on these buildings and on their function but also on the artistic influences that came to Innsbruck from Italy and their transfer from Innsbruck, a growing centre of Baroque music, to the court of Emperor Leopold I in Vienna.

Innsbruck 1626

In 1626 Archduke Leopold (1586–1632), brother of Emperor Ferdinand II and ruler of the county of Tyrol, married Claudia de' Medici (1604–1648) in Innsbruck.[6] The marriage revived and reinforced conjugal ties between the House of Austria (and thus the Holy Roman Empire) and the Grand Duchy of Florence going back

---

[4] See Wilfried Seipel (ed.), *Wir sind Helden: Habsburgische Feste in der Renaissance* (Innsbruck: Kunsthistorisches Museum Sammlungen Schloss Ambras, 2005).

[5] Cf. Nikolaus Harnoncourt, *Der musikalische Dialog: Gedanken zu Monteverdi, Bach und Mozart* (Salzburg and Vienna: Residenzverlag, 1984), pp. 165–7.

[6] Sabine Weiss, *Claudia de'Medici: Eine italienische Prinzessin als Landesfürstin von Tirol, 1604–1648* (Innsbruck and Vienna: Tyrolia, 2004), pp. 63–81.

to 1565 and the marriage of Archduchess Johanna of Austria, daughter of Emperor Ferdinand I, to Franceso I de' Medici. While, for the Habsburgs, these marriages were a means of consolidating their hegemony in northern Italy, the Medici, whose loyalty to the Emperor had resulted in their elevation to princely rank, used them to confirm their new political position by securing strong allies. As well as helping to cement political relations, the marriages also promoted a free flow of cultural influence.[7] In the context of the wedding of 1626 it should be noted that in 1608 relations between the Habsburgs and the Medici had been revived through the marriage of Archduchess Maria Magdalena, sister of both Archduke Leopold V and Emperor Ferdinand II, to Grand Duke Cosimo II de' Medici, who in his turn was the brother of Leopold's future bride Claudia de' Medici. In the event, Maria Magdalena emerged as the influential figure behind the marriage between her elder brother and younger sister-in-law.[8]

The central goal of the wedding festivities, lasting from 19 April to 1 May 1626, was to glorify the relations between the Habsburgs and the Medici. Maria Magdalena sent Alfonso Parigi, son and later successor of the famous Medici court architect Giuglio Parigi, to Innsbruck to collaborate on the festival decor with the local architect Adam Lucchese.[9] A splendid triumphal entry into Innsbruck was obligatory. The three temporary triumphal arches were designed by Parigi, one of them depicting the rich produce of the Tyrol: silver, salt and wine.[10] The celebrations also included tournaments and hunts. In the context of the present chapter it is particularly noteworthy that the celebrations, in the 'Golden Hall' of the Innsbruck court residence, saw the first-ever performance of a ballet on a curtained stage. Along with the 'Paradeis Stube', the 'Goldener Saal' had originally been built as a banqueting hall in the era of Maximilian I.[11] Archduke Ferdinand II converted it in 1565 into a festival hall '*so zugerichtet, wie in Italia gebreuchig*'[12] ('set out in the Italian fashion') clearly meaning that a curtain divided the audience from the performers.

---

[7] Sabine Haag (ed.), *Nozze italiane. Österreichische Erzherzoginnen im Italien des 16. Jahrhunderts* (Vienna, 2010).

[8] Weiss, *Claudia de' Medici*, p. 63.

[9] Arcivio di Stato di Firenze, *Mediceo del Principato* 6379, fol. 108r; Arcivio di Stato di Firenze, *Miscellanea Medicea* 5/2, fols 197v, 201r.

[10] Cf. the copperplate engraving of Andreas Spängler *Die Schätze Tirols* (1626) in the Tiroler Landesmuseum Ferdinandeum, Bibliothek, FB 6500.

[11] Ricarda Oettinger, 'Hofburg', in *Österreichische Kunsttopographie*, vol. XLVII. *Die Kunstdenkmäler der Stadt Innsbruck. Die Hofbauten* (Vienna: Anton Schroll & Co, 1986), p. 64.

[12] Josef Hirn, *Erzherzog Ferdinand II. von Tirol. Geschichte seiner Regierung und seiner Länder*, 2 vols (Innsbruck:Wagner'sche Universitätsbuchhandlung, 1885), vol. 1, p. 385; Walter Senn, *Musik und Theater am Hof zu Innsbruck. Geschichte der Hofkapelle von 15. Jhdt. bis zu deren Auflösung im Jahre 1748* (Innsbruck: Österreichische Verlagsanstalt, 1954), p. 69.

A contemporary festival account describes the ballet in detail.[13] The bride, bridegroom and visitors from Florence were entertained by dancers emerging from artificial mountains – among them the mountain of Venus, in allusion to the nature of the occasion – and singing and reciting poems '*ganz lieblich und anmutig in welscher Sprach*' ('sweet and charming in the Italian tongue'). The highlight of the ballet was the choreographic representation of the letters of the alphabet 'C' and 'L', for Claudia and Leopold. As usual, the dancers and singers were members of the court, directed by a French dancing master. The music between the acts – the *intermezzi* – was performed by the '*kayser- und erzherzogische Musici*' ('imperial and archducal musicians').

Innsbruck 1628

Two years after the wedding of Archduke Leopold and Claudia de' Medici, the birth of their son Archduke Ferdinand Karl on 17 May 1628 provided another occasion for great festivities in Innsbruck. To celebrate the baptism of Ferdinand Karl his Florentine relatives – among them Grand Duke Ferdinand II of Tuscany, who acted as proxy godfather, standing in for Emperor Ferdinand II – visited Innsbruck, where they will have heard the words of a *canzonetta*, dedicated to the newborn prince, that echoed programmatically the values of an era frequently described as the age of Absolutism: '*Hoggi è nato il vero sole*' ('today the true sun in born').[14]

This occasion was also celebrated with a ballet, performed at the *'Ballspielhaus'* ('a hall for playing the ball game *jeu de paume')* in the castle of Ambras. According to a manuscript festival report,[15] the Ballspielhaus had been lavishly equipped and transformed into a space resembling a theatre venue. As well as a

---

[13] Hans Jakob Leonhardt von Ferklehen, *Hochzeitsfeierlichkeiten bei der Vermählung von Erzherzog Leopold V. mit Claudia von Medici im Jahr 1626* (manuscript, 1626), np (Tiroler Landesmuseum Ferdinandeum, Bibliothek, Dip. 803); cf. Anonymous, *Wahrhaffte und Gründtliche Relation Deren Solennitäten Welche sich bey der Hochfürstli: Durchl: Ertzhertzog Leopoldi zu Oesterreich [et]c. mit Durchl: Fürstlichen Claudia Großhertzogin von Florentz Im Monat April diß 1626 Jars. Zu Ynsprugg gehaltener Hochfürstlichen Hochzeit zuegetragen haben* (Augsburg, 1626), np; cf. Archivio di Stato di Firenze, *Miscellanea Medicea*, 5/2, fols 196–201r; cf. Senn, *Musik und Theater*, p. 224.

[14] Claudio Panta, *Aurea Corona al potentiss.o et seren.mo Arcduica Leopoldo, et ser. ma Clavdia Arciduchessa d'Austria, nel glorioso giorno del Battesimo del Sere.ma Clavdia Arciduchessa d'Austria, nel serenissimo Ferdinando Carlo loro figlio. [. . .] Ispruch di 18 Giugnio 1628*, fols 18v–20v.

[15] Hans Jakob Leopardt von Ferklehen, *Erzherzog Ferdinandt Carl zu Österreich etc. und angebornen Grafen zu Tyrol, fürstliche Tauff verlauff beschreibung* (Innsbruck, 1628), Manuscript, Tiroler Landesarchiv Hs. 3069; Ignaz Philipp Dengel, 'Reisen Mediceischer Fürsten durch Tirol in den Jahren 1628 und 1667/68', in *Veröffentlichungen des Museums Ferdinandeum in Innsbruck*, vol. VIII (1928), pp. 1–45, here pp. 10–17.

stage fitted with a black curtain there were special seating arrangements for the spectators, made of wood, shaped like ascending steps and covered with red textile fabrics. In front of them, additional chairs, also covered in red, were reserved for guests of princely rank so that they would have the best view of the show. As the performance started in the afternoon, the windows were darkened and the players given lanterns to hold. As in the ballet staged for the wedding of 1626, members of the court danced in elaborate costumes, singing in Italian. Scene settings depicted Heaven, Earth and Sea, with the narrative taking place in the worlds of the respective gods. Mock battles alluded to the defence of the Catholic faith already being undertaken in the name of the newborn prince, with the letters 'C' and 'L' being complemented with an 'F' for the infant Ferdinand Karl. An Italian report mentions that every guest received a printed text of the play,[16] which unfortunately has not survived, so that we do not know the author or composer. The report describes the spectacle as a *'comedia con mutazione di prospettive, con macchine e con altre galanterie'* ('a play with changes of scene, with stage devices and with other courtly effects').[17] This implies that the building was already equipped with basic forms of stage machinery, although not to a sufficient extent for us to call it a theatre in the full sense. It was still just a Ballspielhaus, but one that happened to possess dimensions allowing it to be used for spectacles that required space for a large number of spectators and actors: to be more specific, the hall was about 36 metres long and about 12 metres wide; a ratio of 3:1 (see Figure 12.1).[18]

The first Innsbruck 'Comedihaus' (1628)

Located in the north of the court palace in Innsbruck was a second *Ballspielhaus* dating from the seventeenth century. As neither the building in Ambras nor the one in Innsbruck matched the standards of contemporary Italian models, they could not possibly fulfil Archduke Leopold V's high ambitions. Plans were already circulating concerning the forthcoming reception of the Spanish princess Maria Anna as she passed through Innsbruck on her way to Vienna to marry the emperor-to-be King Ferdinand III. Leopold will doubtless have been eager to impress the imperial bride with the newest entertainments, including horse ballets and performances of musical dramas. In order to compensate for the lack of a court theatre it was decided to convert the existing *Ballspielhaus* into a *Comedihaus*. Given the rather short period of time available, a remodelling seemed a practicable solution,

---

[16] 'Questa Commedia si stampò, ed á chiunque andò alla Commedia, sene dette una stampa': *Istoria del viaggio d'Alemagna del Serenissimo Gran Duca di toscana Ferdinando Secondo [. . .]* (Venice [1630]), p. 322 (Tiroler Landesmuseum Ferdinandeum, Bibliothek W 869).

[17] Ibid., p. 322.

[18] Cf. the 'Ballhaus' in Vienna measured 32 by 12 meters; for the dimensions in general cf. Antonio Scaino, *Trattato del Givocco della Palla* (Venice, 1555), pp. 158–77.

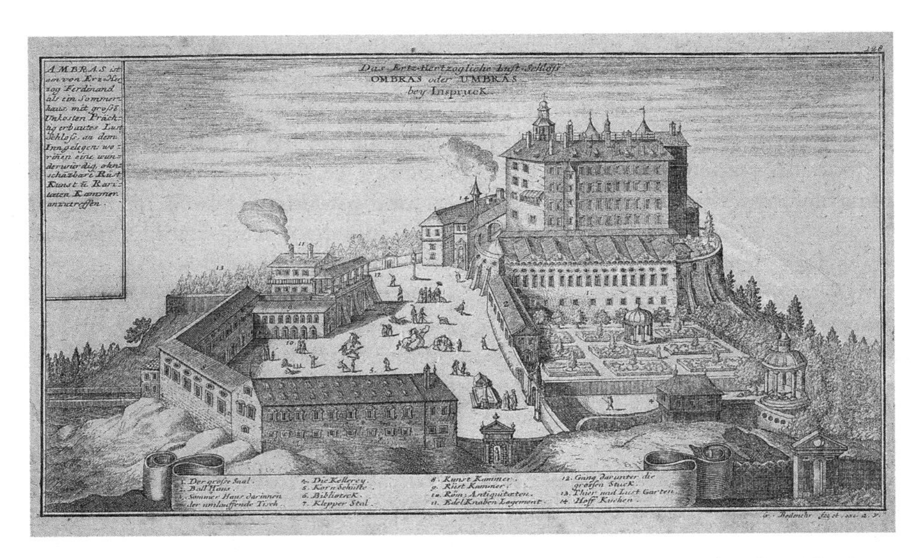

Figure 12.1 The Castle of Ambras and the 'Ball Haus' ('no. 2'), after Matthäus Merian, 1649 (© Kunsthistorisches Museum, Vienna)

not to mention a financial saving. In the end, however, the bridal itinerary was changed and the performance of a horse ballet with the archducal couple as participants had to be transferred to Vienna. Another work originally intended for the occasion, a *commedia in musica*, also had to be postponed and was not performed until June 1631, when Archduke Leopold's second son, Archduke Sigmund Franz, was baptised. Once again Alfonso Parigi, who stayed in Innsbruck for two years in order to prepare the performances, was responsible for the text, scenery and staging of this piece of musical theatre.[19]

The creation of the *Comedihaus* was carried out under the direction of Leopold's court architect Christoph Gumpp, who was sent to Italy in the summer of 1628 in order to study the theatres there. From letters he wrote to Leopold during his stay in Italy we know that he studied theatres in Parma, Florence and Rome in detail, produced sketches of them, and had a preference for the theatre in Parma.[20]

---

19 Sabine Weiss, 'Der Innsbrucker Hof unter Leopold V. und Claudia de' Medici', in Heinz Noflatscher and Jan Paul Niederkorn (eds), *Der Innsbrucker Hof. Residenz und höfische Gesellschaft in Tirol vom 15. bis 19. Jahrhundert* (Wien: Verlag der Österreichischen Akademie der Wissenschaften, 2005), pp. 241–348, 338.

20 About his favorite theatre in Parma Gumpp wrote from Florence that he intended to come back again to Parma: '*weil mir selbige infentionen besser als hiegische gefallen*' ('because I prefer their inventions [i.e. Parma] much more than the local ones [i.e. Florence]'), 18 July 1628, Gumpp to Archduke Leopold, Tiroler Landesarchiv, *Kunstsachen* I,

The new building in Innsbruck, therefore, may well have been modelled on the Teatro Farnese in Parma, which Roy Strong has classified as a 'prototype' of the Baroque theatre:

> With the official inauguration of Giovanni Aleotti's Teatro Farnese (1618–1619) in Parma in 1628 the *tournoi à theme* can be said to have entered its Baroque phase. This prototype Baroque theatre framed the tournament in a permanent court *salle des fêtes* which combined elements from a *sbarra* in the *cortile* of a palazzo, the curved horseshoe of the *gradini* and arcading from the auditorium of the theatre of the academies, with the proscenium arch and machinery of the Teatro Mediceo.[21]

According to the account books, the construction works in Innsbruck started in spring 1629 and lasted two years.[22] One hundred metres in length, 30 metres wide and 12 metres high, the *'neuerpaute Comedj Hauß'* ('newly-built comedy house')[23] was of similar dimensions to Italian hall or tournament theatres including Parma's Teatro Farnese (87 by 32 metres).[24] Unlike the Italian theatres, however, which were at the time still integrated into existing buildings,[25] the Innsbruck *Comedihaus* was free-standing. Although it appears to have been the first free-standing theatre, this was certainly no deliberate revolutionary innovation in architecture,[26] but resulted from re-use of the existing – free-standing – *Ballspielhaus*. The interior was fitted with balconies for spectators and the building also incorporated a smaller, north-facing section housing stage sets and technical equipment for machines. The *Comedihaus* had room for audiences of several hundred.

The only surviving depiction of the *Comedihaus* is a watercolour drawing from 1800 showing it at a time when it had long since been split into two parts, the *riding school* and the *theatre*, as a result of alterations made by Archduke Ferdinand Karl in 1653 (see Figure 12.2).[27] Clearly visible inside the building as drawn,

---

1556. Another letter dates from 8 August 1628, Gumpp to Archduke Leopold, Tiroler Landesarchiv, *Kunstsachen* I, 1556.

[21] 'The Spectacles of State', in Roy Strong, *Art and Power: Renaissance Festivals 1450–1650* (Woodbridge: The Boydell Press, 1984), pp. 42–62, 55.

[22] Weiss, *Claudia de' Medici*, p. 304.

[23] Ibid., p. 304.

[24] Ursula Quecke, 'Aspekte des oberitalienischen Theaterbaus vom 16. bis 19. Jahrhundert', in Österreichisches Theatermuseum Wien (ed.), *Teatro. Eine Reise zu den oberitalienischen Theatern des 16. -19. Jahrhunderts* (Vienna, 2001), pp. 14–27, p. 18.

[25] Cf. *Teatro Olimpico* in Vicenza (1580/1585), *Teatro Mediceo* in Florence (1589), *Teatro Olimpico* in Sabbioneta (1590) and *Teatro Farnese* in Parma (1618/1628).

[26] Michael Krapf, *Die Baumeister Gumpp* (Vienna and Munich: Herold, 1979), p. 71.

[27] Cf. '*Hofbauamtsliste*' ('listing of the constructions of the court', author's translation) of 1667; Johanna Felmayer, 'Liste der Innsbrucker Hofbauten 1667', in *Österreichische*

Figure 12.2 View of the former *Comedihaus,* watercolour and pen drawing, Josef Strickner, 1800 (© Tiroler Landesmuseum Ferdinandeum, Innsbruck)

Figure 12.3 Present-day view into the former *Comedihaus* showing how it was used for performances (© Congress Innsbruck)

however, are Ionic columns wound around with foliage. These formed part of Baroque wall painting dating from the era of Archduke Leopold.

Apart from the above-mentioned *commedia in musica* of 1631 staged on the occasion of the baptism of Sigmund Franz, no archival records or references tell us which works were performed at the *Comedihaus*, although extant scores and an inventory of 1634 itemizing the court costumes indicate that the works included pieces of musical theatre and ballets (see Figure 12.3).[28]

The 'new' or 'archducal' *Comedihaus*

Italian-inspired theatre once again became an area of interest during the reign of Leopold's son and successor Archduke Ferdinand Karl (b. 1628, r. 1646–1662). Following in his father's footsteps, Ferdinand Karl was ambitious to have a modern theatre of his own and was married to a Medici princess, his cousin Anna de' Medici, daughter of Grand Duke Cosimo II and Archduchess Maria Magdalena, who in their turn were brother and sister of Archduke Leopold V and Claudia de' Medici.

'*Mala educatio, maschere, comedie, balli praetereaque nihil*' ('Bad education, disguisings, plays, balls and nothing else').[29] This contemporary verdict sums up the poor reputation that Ferdinand Karl gained for his extravagant spending, especially on entertainments such as ballets, music and plays. Between 1652 and 1654, Archduke Ferdinand Karl built the so-called 'New' or 'Archducal' *Comedihaus* in emulation of the innovative Italian Baroque theatre of the seventeenth century.[30] Unlike his father's, which was a conversion or reconstruction of the *Ballspielhaus*, Ferdinand Karl's *Comedihaus* was a brand new building that was built, decorated and fitted with a stage by artists and craftsmen from Italy (see Figure 12.4). The account books mention the woodworkers Pellegrin Letterini and Fantino Fantinelli from Venice and Hieronimo Tamara and Camillo Muscai from Ferrara. Among the painters the Venetians Domenico Cerusi (Cerù) and Pietro Negro are mentioned several times; in 1657, for example, Cerusi is listed as a permanently-employed court painter '*so bey dem* Comedihaus *gebraucht*' ('being

---

Kunsttopographie, vol. XLVII. *Die Kunstdenkmäler der Stadt Innsbruck. Die Hofbauten* (Vienna: Anton Schroll & Co, 1986), pp. 645–9, 645.

[28] Senn, *Musik und Theater*, p. 232; Peter Tschmuck, *Die höfische Musikpflege in Tirol im 16. und 17. Jahrhundert. Eine sozioökonomische Untersuchung* (Innsbruck and Vienna: Studienverlag, 2001), p. 282; Innsbruck, Universitäts- und Landesbibliothek Tirol, Ms 966.

[29] Compare Josef Hirn, *Kanzler Bienner und sein Prozess: Quellen und Forschungen zur Geschichte, Literatur und Sprache Österreichs und seiner Kronländer*, 5 vols (Innsbruck: Wagner'sche Universitätsbuchhandlung, 1898), vol. 5, p. 157.

[30] Veronika Sandbichler, 'Die Bühne des Fürsten: Festkultur am Hof Erzherzog Ferdinand Karls', in Sabine Haag (ed.), *Ferdinand Karl: Ein Sonnenkönig in Tirol* (Innsbruck: Kunsthistorisches Museum Sammlungen Schloss Ambras, 2009), pp. 171–8.

Figure 12.4 View of the former *Comedihaus* of Archduke Ferdinand Karl, watercolour and ink drawing, Josef Strickner, 1800 (© Tiroler Landesmuseum Ferdinandeum, Innsbruck)

employed on the *Comedihaus*').[31] At this time Venice had the largest number of theatres in Italy, having been a leading centre of early-seventeenth-century theatre architecture. In 1659 the Italian envoy Nani described the theatre in Innsbruck as '*veramente bello d'Architetura e pitura, presa la forma da quelli, che sono in Venetia, ma diversificato molto nella qualità de i lavori*' ('its architecture and décor truly beautiful, in appearance like those now in Venice, but with a greatly differing quality of workmanship').[32]

The drawing (Figure 12.5) shows the front of the theatre in 1773, from the west. In 1844 the dilapidated theatre was demolished and a new municipal theatre built in its place, later transformed into the present-day Tiroler Landestheater.

The longitudinal section through the *Comedihaus* (Figure 12.5) gives an impression of its interior: it was a simple construction in wood, equipped with boxes and provision for stage machinery. In what was still an innovative technical feature, the floor sloped downward slightly towards the stage to provide all the spectators with a good view. A system of stairs on various levels allowed access to the technical devices. Stage sets and scenographic 'machines' could be moved synchronously along runners, using a technique featuring counterweights invented by the Venetian Giacomo Torelli, who first deployed it in the Teatro Novissimo in Venice (built 1641).[33] The original U-shaped auditorium, the two proscenium

---

[31] Senn, *Musik und Theater*, p. 273.

[32] *Descrizione del viaggio, fatto dall'Eccell. Nani eletto ambasciatore estraordinario a Vienna 1659*, np.

[33] Vana Greisenegger-Georgila, 'Aspekte der Bühnendekoration im 17. Jahrhundert', in *Teatrum Mundi: Die Welt als Bühne* (Munich: Edition Minerva, 2003), pp. 25–9, 26.

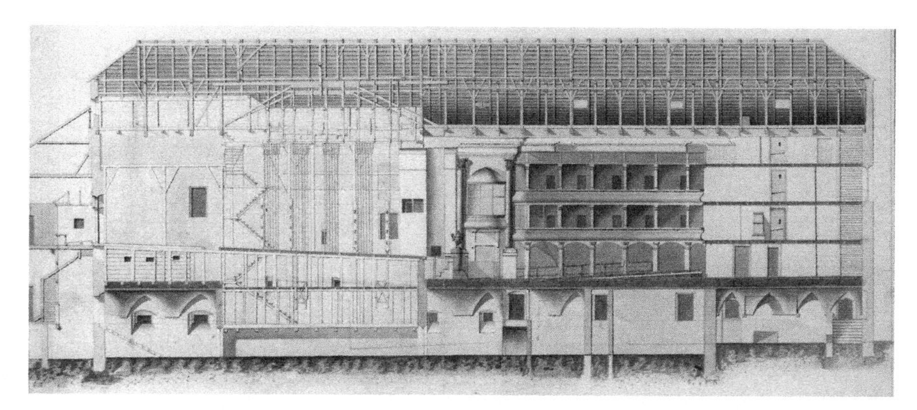

Figure 12.5 Longitudinal section through the former *Comedihaus* of Archduke Ferdinand Karl, watercolour and ink drawing, 1818 (© Tiroler Landesmuseum Ferdinandeum, Innsbruck)

boxes and the square stage can still be identified on a 1771 floor plan of what was then the Innsbruck court theatre of Empress Maria Theresa.[34] The plan suggests that the stage was 20 metres square and the auditorium approximately 25 metres deep and 18 metres wide. In 1776 Joseph Ceschi mentions that the theatre '*[konnte] gegen 1000 Personen in sich fassen*' ('[can] accommodate about 1000 persons').[35]

Six grand operas were performed in this theatre during the reign of Archduke Ferdinand Karl, all composed by Antonio Cesti, who had become court composer at Innsbruck in 1652: *La Cleopatra* (1654), *L'Argia* (1655), *L'Orontea* (1656), *La Dori* (1657), *La Venere Cacciatrice* (1659) and *La Magnanimità d' Alessandro* (1662).

L'Argia was staged on 4 November 1655 on the occasion of the visit of Queen Christina of Sweden, who abdicated in order to convert to Catholicism and made her first public confession of faith in Innsbruck. A prologue praises the Queen's virtues, a woman who was to become an important patron of the arts and opera in Italy, turning the production into a pageant in her honour. The plot of the fast-moving libretto by Giovanni Filippo Apolloni features a variety of complications, male characters disguised as female or vice versa, amorous intrigues and unlikely circumstances, all deftly interwoven with comedy.[36] Valerio Spada made copperplate engravings of the eight scenes and the proscenium arch (Figure 12.6 shows one of these). The stage was equipped with a complex system of machinery consisting

---

[34] Innsbruck, Tiroler Landesarchiv, *Karten und Pläne* 487/2.

[35] Joseph Freiherr von Ceschi, *Beschreibung der kaiserlich-königl. Stadt Innsbruck* (Innsbruck, 1776), p. 30.

[36] *L'Argia: dramma musicale rappresentato in Ispruch alla maesta della serenissima Christina, regina di Svetia &c.* (Innsbruck, 1655).

Figure 12.6 Scene from *L'Argia*, copperplate engraving, Valerio Spada, 1655 (© Tiroler Landesmuseum Ferdinandeum, Innsbruck)

of an overhead pulley device and carriages running on rails beneath the stage, enabling scenery to be moved synchronously in the manner invented by Giacomo Torelli in the 1640s. While the settings used in *L'Argia* – seashores, gardens, halls, courtyards and caves – were typical of contemporary Italian operas, there were also carriages that flew through the clouds, and colonnades, squares and streets that seemed to extend to infinity.

Christina was highly impressed by the opera:

> *so sehr gefiel dieses szenische Schauspiel ihrer Majestät und der Adelsgesellschaft, die das ganze Stück mit begeisterten Jubelrufen feierten, dass sie bekannten, niemals etwas Ähnliches gesehen zu haben*
>
> [The queen and the noble courtiers, who cheered and shouted during the performance, were so impressed by the whole play that they acknowledged they had never seen anything comparable previously].[37]

[37] Christine Pertoll, 'Diego Tafuri de Leguile OFM (SO), Festivus Adventus Virgines Christinae Suetorum, Gothorum Vandalorum Reginae oder Festliche Ankunft der Jungfrau Christina Königin der Schweden, Goten und Vandalen', in *Einleitung, Text, Übersetzung und Kommentar* (Diplomarbeit Universtät Innsbruck, 2003), p. 84; Diego Tafuri de Leguile,

As the Queen wanted to see the work once again, it was repeated a few days later.

Cultural transfer

As we have observed, the seventeenth century saw intensive cultural transfer from Italy to Austria, with the musical *stile nuovo* and the rise of a new theatrical medium, the opera, being foremost amongst the cultural goods that came to Austria from beyond its southern borders. This is not surprising, given the close conjugal ties between the Habsburgs and the Medici over two successive generations. What is more remarkable is that personal experience provided Archduke Ferdinand Karl such a large measure of inspiration in these fields. In 1652 he and his wife Anna de' Medici undertook a six-month tour of Italian courts, attending tournaments, spectacles and operas in such cities as Mantua, Florence, Ferrara, Modena and Venice. The tour is documented in a manuscript travel-diary that gives a vivid picture of the ceremonies and receptions held in honour of the princely guests.[38] In addition, the diary focuses especially on the music, opera and horse ballets performed, and describes in detail the structure and the technical features of certain theatres. In some parts it reads like a handbook on 'how to perform an opera' and 'how to build an opera house'.[39]

Although Innsbruck was not the only city to benefit from cultural transfer of the 'Italian style', it was a pioneer in this respect and performed an active intermediary role in the transfer by imparting its knowledge to other courts. For example, the first known Italian-style horse ballet, *Il sole e dodici segni del zodiac*, which was performed at the imperial court in Vienna in 1631, had originally come from Innsbruck.[40] It was one of the spectacles that, as mentioned above, should have been performed for Princess Maria Anna of Spain, who eventually did not stop in Innsbruck on her way to Vienna for her marriage to King Ferdinand III. The horse ballet, in which Archduke Leopold V and his wife Claudia de' Medici

---

Erfreuliche Erzehlung Was gestalten Christina, Die Durchleuchtigste Königin auß Schweden, als sie Anno 1655. nachher Rom gereißt, Von dem Durchleuchtigsten Fürsten und Herrn, Herrn Ferdinand Carl Ertzhertzogen zu Oesterreich [et]c. in Tyrol emfangen [. . .] (Innsbruck, 1665), p. 19.

[38] Innsbruck, Tiroler Landesmuseum Ferdinandeum, Bibliothek, Dip. 905; Thomas Kuster and Veronika Sandbichler, 'Erz Füst.etc.Raiss nacher Welsch Landt [. . .] de anno 1652. Das Reisetagebuch Erzherzog Ferdinand Karls', in Wolfgang Meighörner (ed.), *Wissenschaftliches Jahrbuch der Tiroler Landesmuseen* (Innsbruck: Studienverlag, 2010), pp. 195–385.

[39] Innsbruck, Tiroler Landesmuseum Ferdinandeum, Bibliothek, Dip. 905, pp. 86–92, 102–32, 264–83, 426–40, 475–80.

[40] 'The sun and the twelve signs of the zodiac' (author's translation); Weiss, *Innsbrucker Hof*, pp. 331, 336.

themselves participated, was inspired by the Florentine horse ballet *La guerra de Bellezza* ('Beauty's War') of 1616. Based on an allegorical plot about the zodiac, it achieved great success in Vienna.[41]

Conclusion

The era of operas and horse ballets finally reached its zenith in Vienna under Emperor Leopold I (b. 1640, reg. 1658–1705). He and his second cousin Archduke Ferdinand Karl corresponded on their common interest in music and opera, as is shown by a series of four unpublished letters written by Leopold to Ferdinand Karl in 1659 and 1660.[42]

During the reign of Emperor Leopold I the court of Innsbruck once again played an important role in the transfer of the Italian style to the imperial capital. While Innsbruck already had its own purpose-built theatre, the 'Archducal' *Comedihaus* of 1652–1654, it was not until 1668, more than 10 years later, that Vienna acquired its first opera house, the theatre at the *Cortina* designed by Ludovico Ottavio Burnacini.[43] It was here that one of the greatest operas of the time, *Il pomo doro* (*The Golden Apple*) by Antonio Cesti, was performed. Significantly, Cesti was a former court composer at the Innsbruck court who along with his librettist Francesco Sbarra had moved to the imperial court of Vienna after the death of Archduke Ferdinand Karl.[44]

Bibliography

Primary sources

Anonymous, *Wahrhaffte und Gründtliche Relation Deren Solennitäten Welche sich bey der Hochfürstli: Durchl: Ertzhertzog Leopoldi zu Oesterreich [et]c. mit Durchl: Fürstlichen Claudia Großhertzogin von Florentz Im Monat April diß 1626 Jars. Zu Ynsprugg gehaltener Hochfürstlichen Hochzeit zuegetragen haben* (Augsburg: Georg Wellhöffer 1626).

---

[41] Franz Christoph Khevenhüller, *Annales Ferdinandei: oder Wahrhaffte Beschreibung Käysers Ferdinandi des andern, mildesten Gedächtniss, geburth, Aufferziehung und bisshero in Krieg und Friedens-Zeiten Vollbrachten thaten, geführten Kriegen und Vollzogenen hochwightigen geschäfften [. . .]*, vol. 11 (Leipzig, 1726), pp. 1513–14.

[42] Innsbruck, Tiroler Landesarchiv, *Kunstsachen* II/551 (6 Februray 1659, 26 February 1659, 31 December 1659, 14 September 1660).

[43] Cf. the chapter by Andrea Sommer-Mathis in this volume; Herbert Seifert, *Der Sig-prangende Hochzeit-Gott: Hochzeitsfeste am Wiener Kaiserhof 1622–1699* (Vienna: Musikwissenschaftlicher Verlag, 1988), pp. 13–18.

[44] Senn, *Musik und Theater*, p. 293.

Ceschi, Joseph Freiherr von, *Beschreibung der kaiserlich-königl: Stadt Innsbruck* (Innsbruck: Wagner, 1776).

Khevenhüller, Franz Christoph, *Annales Ferdinandei: oder Wahrhaffte Beschreibung Käysers Ferdinandi des andern, mildesten Gedächtniss, geburth, Aufferziehung und bisshero in Krieg und Friedens-Zeiten Vollbrachten thaten, geführten Kriegen und Vollzogenen hochwightigen geschäffte [. . .]*, vol. 11 (Leipzig: Weidmann, 1726).

Leonhardt von Ferklehen, Hans Jakob, *Hochzeitsfeierlichkeiten bei der Vermählung von Erzherzog Leopold V. mit Claudia von Medici im Jahr 1626*, Tiroler Landesmuseum Ferdinandeum, Dip. 803 (ms, n.d.).

Leopardt von Ferklehen, Hans Jakob, *Erzherzog Ferdinandt Carl zu Österreich etc. und angebornen Grafen zu Tyrol, fürstliche Tauff verlauff beschreibung* (ms, Innsbruck 1628), Tiroler Landesarchiv Hs. 3069.

Panta, Claudio, *Aurea Corona alpotentiss.o et seren.mo Arcicica Leopoldo, et ser. ma Clavdia Arciduchessa d'Austria, nel glorioso giorno del Battesimo del Sere.ma Clavdia Arciduchessa d'Austria, nel nissimo Ferdinando Carlo loro figlio. [. . .] Ispruch di 18 Giugnio 1628.*

Scaino, Antonio, *Trattato del Givocco della Palla* (Venice: Gabriel Giolito de' Ferrari et Fratelli, 1555).

Tafuri de Leguile, Diego, *Erfreuliche Erzehlung Was gestalten Christina, Die Durchleuchtigste Königin auß Schweden, als sie Anno 1655. nachher Rom gereißt, Von dem Durchleuchtigsten Fürsten und Herrn, Herrn Ferdinand Carl Ertzhertzogen zu Oesterreich [et]c. in Tyrol emfangen [. . .]* (Innsbruck: Wagner, 1665).

Secondary sources

Bousmar, Eric, *Pasos de armas, justas y torneos en la corte de Borgoña (siglo XV y principios del XVI). Imaginario callabresco, rituales e implicaciones socio-políticas*, in Krista de Jonge, Bernardo J. García García and Alicia Esteban Estríngana (eds), *El legado de Borgoña. Fiesta y ceremonia cortesana en la Europa de los Austrias* (Madrid: Marcial Pons Ediciones de Historia, 2004), pp. 561–605.

Breiding, Dirk, *Rennen, Stechen und Turnier zur Zeit Maximilians I.*, in *Vor Halbtausend Jahren* [. . .] *Festschrift zur Erinnerung an den Besuch des Kaisers Maximilian I. in St. Wendel* (St. Wendel: Stadtmuseum, 2012), pp. 51–82.

Dengel, Ignaz Philipp, 'Reisen Mediceischer Fürsten durch Tirol in den Jahren 1628 und 1667/68', *Veröffentlichungen des Museums Ferdinandeum in Innsbruck*, 8 (1928), 1–45.

Felmayer, Johanna, 'Liste der Innsbrucker Hofbauten 1667', in *Österreichische Kunsttopographie*, 47. Die Kunstdenkmäler der Stadt Innsbruck. Die Hofbauten 645–9.

Greisenegger-Georgila, Vana, 'Aspekte der Bühnendekoration im 17. Jahrhundert', in *Teatrum Mundi. Die Welt als Bühne* (München: Edition Minerva, 2003), pp. 25–9.

Harnoncourt, Nikolaus, *Der musikalische Dialog. Gedanken zu Monteverdi, Bach und Mozart* (Salzburg and Vienna: Residenzverlag, 1984), pp. 165–7.

Hirn, Josef, *Erzherzog Ferdinand II. von Tirol. Geschichte seiner Regierung und seiner Länder*, 2 vols (Innsbruck: Wagner'sche Universitätsbuchhandlung, 1885/1888).

Hirn, Josef, 'Kanzler Bienner und sein Prozess', in *Quellen und Forschungen zur Geschichte, Literatur und Sprache Österreichs und seiner Kronländer*, 5 vols (Innsbruck: Wagner'sche Universitätsbuchhandlung, 1898).

Krapf, Michael, *Die Baumeister Gumpp* (Vienna and Munich: Herold, 1979).

Kuster, Thomas and Veronika Sandbichler, Erz Füst.etc.Raiss nacher Welsch Landt [. . .] de anno 1652. Das Reisetagebuch Erzherzog Ferdinand Karls, in Meighörner Wolfgang (ed.), *Wissenschaftliches Jahrbuch der Tiroler Landesmusee* (Innsbruck: Studienverlag, 2010), pp. 195–385.

Oettinger, Ricarda, 'Hofburg', in *Österreichische Kunsttopographie*, vol. 47, *Die Kunstdenkmäler der Stadt Innsbruck. Die Hofbauten* (Vienna: Anton Schroll & Co, 1986), pp. 55–207.

Pertoll, Christine, 'Diego Tafuri de Leguile OFM (SO), Festivus Adventus Virgines Christinae Suetorum, Gothorum Vandalorum Reginae oder Festliche Ankunft der Jungfrau Christina Königin der Scweden, Goten und Vandalen', in *Einleitung Text, Übersetzung und Kommentar* (Diplomarbeit, Universtät Innsbruck, 2003).

Quecke, Ursula, 'Aspekte des oberitalienischen Theaterbaus vom 16. bis 19. Jahrhundert', in *Teatro. Eine Reise zu den oberitalienischen Theatern des 16.–19. Jahrhunderts* (Vienna: Österreichisches Theatermuseum, 2001), pp. 14–27.

Sandbichler, Veronika, 'Torneos y fiestas de corte de los Habsburgo en los siglos XV y XVII', in Krista de Jonge, Bernardo J. García García and Alicia Esteban Estríngana (eds), *El legado de Borgoña. Fiesta y ceremonia cortesana en la Europa de los Austrias* (Madrid: Marcial Pons Ediciones de Historia, 2004), pp. 607–624.

Sandbichler, Veronika, 'Der Hochzeitskodex Erzherzog Ferdinands II', *Jahrbuch des Kunsthistorischen Museums Wien*, 6/7 (2006), 47–89.

Sandbichler, Veronika, 'Die Bühne des Fürsten: Festkultur am Hof Erzherzog Ferdinand Karls', in Sabine Haag (ed.), *Ferdinand Karl. Ein Sönnenkönig in Tirol* (Innsbruck: Kunsthistorisches Museum Sammlungen Schloss Ambras, 2009), pp. 171–8.

Scheicher, Elisabteh, 'Ein Fest am Hofe Erzherzog Ferdinands II', *Jahrbuch der Kunsthistorischen Sammlungen in Wien*, 77 (1981), 119–54.

Seifert, Herbert, *Der Sig-prangende Hochzeit-Gott: Hochzeitsfeste am Wiener Kaiserhof 1622–1699* (Vienna: Musikwissenschaftlicher Verlag, 1988).

Seipel, Wilfried (ed.), *Wir sind Helden. Habsburgische Feste in der Renaissance* (Innsbruck: Kunsthistorisches Museum Sammlungen Schloss Ambras, 2005).

Senn, Walter, *Musik und Theater am Hof zu Innsbruck. Geschichte der Hofkapelle vom 15. Jhdt. bis zu deren Auflösung im Jahre 1748* (Innsbruck: Österreichische Verlagsanstalt, 1954).

Strong, Roy, *Art and Power: Renaissance Festivals 1450–1650* (Woodbridge: The Boydell Press, 1984).

Tschmuck, Peter, *Die höfische Musikpflege in Tirol im 16. und 17. Jahrhundert. Eine sozioökonomische Untersuchung* (Insbruck: Studienverlag, 2011).

Weiss, Sabine, *Claudia de'Medici. Eine italienische Prinzessin als Landesfürstin von Tirol (1604–1648)* (Innsbruck and Vienna: Tyrolia, 2004).

Weiss, Sabine, 'Der Innsbrucker Hof unter Leopold V. und Claudia de' Medici', in Heinz Noflatscher and Jan Paul Niederkorn (eds), *Der Innsbrucker Hof. Residenz und höfische Gesellschaft in Tirol vom 15. bis 19. Jahrhundert* (Vienna: Verlag der Österreichischen Akademie der Wissenschaften, 2005), pp. 241–348.

Chapter 13
La Favorita festeggiante
The imperial summer residence of the Habsburgs as festive venue

Andrea Sommer-Mathis

Most festivities and opera or theatre performances at the imperial court of the Habsburgs did not take place in a designated free-standing theatre building, but in a ceremonial hall, a ballroom, a gallery, the imperial apartments, or in the courtyards and gardens of one of the residences in or near Vienna.[1] The scenic adaptation of all these indoor and outdoor spaces ranged from building simple platforms to the construction of real stages, which increasingly became technically equipped with elaborate scenery and machinery. One of the most important festive venues of the Austrian Habsburgs during the seventeenth and the first half of the eighteenth century was their main summer residence, the so-called *Favorita*. Its history dates back to the fourteenth century, when ancient *cadastral* (regional) registers refer to a dairy farm located outside the city walls of Vienna in the midst of meadows,

[1] For an overview of the festive and theatrical venues at the imperial court in Vienna from the late sixteenth to the eighteenth century see: Herbert Seifert, *Die Oper am Wiener Kaiserhof im 17. Jahrhundert* (Tutzing: Hans Schneider, 1985), pp. 387–427; Andrea Sommer-Mathis, 'Luoghi teatrali alla corte imperiale di Vienna nel Seicento. Dalla sala all'edificio teatrale', in Laura Sannita Nowé et al. (eds), *Sentir e meditar: Omaggio a Elena Sala Di Felice* (Rome: Aracne, 2005), pp. 75–84 [French version: 'Lieux de representation théâtrale à la cour impériale de Vienne au XVIIe siècle: de la salle à l'édifice', in Charles Mazouer (ed.), *Les Lieux du spectacle dans l'Europe du XVIIe siècle* (Tübingen: Gunter Narr Verlag, 2006), pp. 355–75]; Susanne Rode-Breymann, 'Raum: eine Kategorie musikalischer Gattungshistoriographie?', in Christine Siegert et al. (eds), *Gattungsgeschichte als Kulturgeschichte: Festschrift Arnfried Edler* (Hildesheim, Zurich and New York: Georg Olms Verlag, 2008), pp. 189–204; Susanne Rode-Breymann, *Musiktheater eines Kaiserpaars. Wien 1677 bis 1705* (Hildesheim, Zurich and New York: Georg Olms Verlag, 2010), pp. 368–407; Andrea Sommer-Mathis, 'VI.3. Musik, Theater und Tanz: Die Wiener Hofburg als Schauplatz von szenischen Aufführungen' and 'VI.4. Residenz und öffentlicher Raum. Höfisches Fest in Wien im Wandel vom 16. zum 17. Jahrhundert', in Herbert Karner (ed.), *Die Wiener Hofburg im 16. und 17. Jahrhundert. Baugeschichte, Funktion und Etablierung als Kaiserresidenz (1521–1705)*, Veröffentlichungen zur Kunstgeschichte, 13; Veröffentlichungen zur Bau- und Funktionsgeschichte der Wiener Hofburg, 2 (Vienna: Verlag der Österreichischen Akademie der Wissenschaften, 2014), pp. 470–508.

fields and vineyards. Today the former suburban area is part of Vienna occupying the fourth district called *Wieden*. The building located on the site of the former farmyard is the *Theresianum*, which houses both a famous private grammar school and the diplomatic academy.[2]

From the middle of the sixteenth century the estate changed hands and names frequently, and the original simple farmyard metamorphosed into a mighty castle-like complex. In 1614 Emperor Matthias acquired the property for his wife Anna of Tirol with the intention of establishing a *villa suburbana* or *villeggiatura* there, as a summer residence for the imperial family. Unfortunately, we do not possess any information about the architect responsible for the construction, or rather reconstruction, of the palace, which was built on the foundations of the former farm building. The use of a Venetian scale of measurement in the surviving documents, however, points in the direction of an Italian architect.[3]

The first phase of construction under Emperor Matthias and his wife Anna seems to have advanced rather slowly. After the early deaths of the two monarchs, in 1618 and 1619 respectively, construction works came to a temporary halt, but they were quickly resumed under Emperor Ferdinand II, especially after his second marriage, with Eleonora of Gonzaga, in 1622.[4] Eleonora, a daughter of Duke Vincenzo I of Mantua, became the new owner of the estate and in a letter from 20 August 1622, proudly reported to her brother, Duke Ferdinando, that she now had a *Favorita* of her own in a very beautiful place outside Vienna.[5] She described her villa as a '*nipote*' ('niece') of Ferdinando's summer residence, the

---

[2] On the history of the *Favorita* see Johann Schwarz, *Die kaiserliche Sommerresidenz Favorita auf der Wieden in Wien, 1615–1746* (Vienna and Prague: Tempsky, 1898); Erich Schlöss, *Das Theresianum. Ein Beitrag zur Bezirksgeschichte der Wieden* (Vienna: Verein für Geschichte der Stadt Wien, 1979); Géza Hajós, 'Theresianische Akademie', in *Österreichische Kunsttopographie*, vol. 44: *Die Kunstdenkmäler Wiens. Die Profanbauten des III., IV. und V. Bezirks* (Vienna: Verlag Anton Schroll & Co., 1980), pp. 235–44; Karl Krejci, 'Angerfelderhof, Schaumburgerhof, Favorita. Ein Beitrag zur Geschichte des Theresianums und des Schaumburgergrundes', *Wiener Geschichtsblätter*, 2 (1981), 87–94; Erich Schlöss, 'Die Favorita auf der Wieden um 1700', *Wiener Geschichtsblätter*, 46 (1991), 162–70; Christian Benedik, 'Zeremonielle Abläufe in habsburgischen Residenzen um 1700: Die Wiener Hofburg und die Favorita auf der Wieden', *Wiener Geschichtsblätter*, 46 (1991), 171–8; Eugen Guglia, *Das Theresianum in Wien. Vergangenheit und Gegenwart* (Vienna, Cologne and Weimar: Böhlau Verlag, 1996); Erich Schlöss, *Baugeschichte des Theresianums in Wien* (Vienna, Cologne and Weimar: Böhlau Verlag, 1998); Otto G. Schindler, 'Von Favorita zu Favoriten. Ein Lustschloss in Mantua als Namenspatron eines Wiener Arbeiterbezirks', *Sonderbeilage zur Wiener Zeitung*, 24/25 September 1999.

[3] See Schlöss, *Das Theresianum*, p. 11; Schlöss, *Baugeschichte*, p. 31.

[4] On the wedding see Herbert Seifert, *Der Sig-prangende Hochzeits-Gott. Hochzeitsfeste am Wiener Hof der Habsburger und ihre Allegorik 1622–1699* (Vienna: Musikwissenschaftlicher Verlag, 1988), pp. 9–12.

[5] Archivio di Stato di Mantova (ASMn), Archivio Gonzaga (AG), E.II.2, busta (b.) 434: letter from Empress Eleonora to Duke Ferdinando, 20 August 1622.

Villa La Favorita on the outskirts of Mantua, at that time still under construction (1615–1624). The Lombardian architect Nicolò Sebregondi had planned it not just as a *villeggiatura*, but as a second residence of the Dukes of Gonzaga. The Mantuan villa was a spacious building complex with a two-branched external staircase leading to the gardens with their ponds, fountains, ornamental flowerbeds, boscages and artificial hills.[6] Eleonora of Gonzaga must have been very impressed by her brother's villa, since she asked him to send her the plans of the *Favorita* in order to model her own summer residence according to the Mantuan pattern. Thus the imperial *Favorita* developed from a 'niece' into a 'daughter' of the ducal 'maternal' model.[7]

The naming of the Viennese villa *Favorita* can be interpreted as a conscious act of Eleonora and is significant as a factor in her role as an agent in the process of cultural transfer of an Italian – and specifically a Mantuan – style to Vienna, not only in the field of architecture, but, from the very start, also in the fields of theatre, music and ballet.[8] In the same summer of 1622, Eleonora arranged a dance performance or, as she described it to her brother, '*una piccola inuencione*

---

[6] See Dino Nicolini, 'Una piccola Versailles gonzaghesca. La Favorita', in Ercolano Marani (ed.), *Corti e dimore del Contado Mantovano* (Florence: Vallecchi, 1969), pp. 65–80; Pamela Askew, 'Ferdinando Gonzaga's Patronage of the Pictorial Arts: The Villa Favorita', *The Art Bulletin*, 60 (1978), 274–95; Peter Fidler, 'Loggia mit Aussicht. Prolegomena zu einer Typologie', *Wiener Jahrbuch für Kunstgeschichte*, 40 (1987), 84–9.

[7] See Schindler, 'Von Favorita zu Favoriten'; Friedrich Polleroß, 'Les femmes des Habsbourg dans le mécenat architectural', in Sabine Frommel, Juliette Dumas and Raphaël Tassin (eds), *Bâtir au feminine? Traditions et strategies en Europe et dans l'Empire ottoman* (Paris: Picard, 2013), pp. 37–8.

[8] On the beginnings of Italian opera and ballet at the imperial court see Herbert Seifert, *Die Oper*, pp. 26–7; Herbert Seifert, 'Frühes italienisches Musikdrama nördlich der Alpen: Salzburg, Prag, Wien, Regensburg und Innsbruck', in Markus Engelhardt (ed.), *In Teutschland noch gantz ohnbekandt. Monteverdi-Rezeption und frühes Musiktheater im deutschsprachigen Raum* (Frankfurt am Main and Vienna: Lang, 1996), pp. 29–44; Seifert, 'Rapporti musicali tra i Gonzaga e le corti asburgiche', in Umberto Artioli and Cristina Grazioli (eds), *I Gonzaga e l'Impero. Itinerari dello spettacolo. Con una selezione di materiali dall'Archivio informatico Herla (1560–1630)* (Florence: Casa Editrice Le Lettere, 2005), pp. 219–29; Otto G. Schindler, 'Von Mantua nach Ödenburg. Die ungarische Krönung Eleonoras I. Gonzaga (1622) und die erste Oper am Kaiserhof. Ein unbekannter Bericht aus der Széchényi-Nationalbibliothek', *Biblos*, 46 (1997) 2, 243–93; Schindler, '"Mio compadre Imperatore". Comici dell'arte an den Höfen der Habsburger', *Maske und Kothurn*, 38 (1997), 2–4, see pp. 46–9, 130–2 (notes 111–15); Schindler, 'L'incoronazione ungherese di Eleonora I Gonzaga (1622) e gli inizi del teatro musicale alla corte degli Asburgo', *Quaderni di Palazzo Te*, 5 (1999), 70–93; Schindler, '"Sonst ist es lustig alhie". Italienisches Theater am Habsburgerhof zwischen Weißem Berg und Sacco di Mantova', in Andreas Weigl (ed.), *Wien im Dreißigjährigen Krieg. Bevölkerung, Gesellschaft, Kultur, Konfession* (Vienna, Cologne and Weimar: Böhlau Verlag, 2001), pp. 565–654; Schindler, 'Viaggi teatrali tra l'Inquisizione e il Sacco. Comici dell'Arte di Mantova alle corti degli Asburgo d'Austria', in Artioli and Grazioli (eds), *I Gonzaga e l'Impero*, pp. 107–60.

in Musicha con un baletto' ('a little musical composition with a ballet'),[9] which she performed together with her ladies-in-waiting in her new summer residence.[10] Eleonora was not only the inventor and choreographer of this ballet, but also the instructor of her ladies-in-waiting, particularly the Austrian ones, who were not yet familiar with this new genre.[11]

From 1622 on, Eleonora regularly staged dance performances and other theatrical events, which soon became an integral part of the festivities at the imperial court in Vienna. By 1624, the gardens of the *Favorita* must have been nearly completed as we know that special 'pleasure boats' ('*Lustschiffl*') were ordered for trips on the pond.[12] These early performances by courtiers were designed for an intimate circle of aristocratic spectators only. The stage still consisted of a simple scaffold with a single set for the entire play – with, in addition, some flying machines as entry vehicles for allegorical figures. Although the Habsburgs were already familiar at the time with some of the more sophisticated inventions of Italian scenography – witness a performance in Prague in 1617[13] – it would take a few more years before these new techniques were also used in Vienna. When that happened, the *Favorita* once again played an important role in the cultural life of the Imperial court.

Eleonora of Gonzaga patronised not only the ballet, but also introduced Italian opera to Vienna. Opera was performed by professional singers and used complex stage arrangements with frequent changes of settings and many special effects. Given these requirements, simply adapting one of the existing residential or ceremonial chambers in the imperial residences would no longer do. That is why, during the late 1620s, special festival halls or complete theatre spaces were added to both the imperial *Hofburg* palace[14] and the *Favorita* summer residence.

---

[9] ASMn, AG, E.II.2, busta 434: letter from Empress Eleonora to Duke Ferdinando, 20 August 1622; quoted in Seifert, *Die Oper*, p. 589.

[10] This performance is also described in a letter of Federico Gonzaga to Ercole Marliani from 24 August 1622, in ASMn, AG, b. 493, fol. II, c. 316, quoted in Elena Venturini, *Le collezioni Gonzaga. Il carteggio tra la Corte Cesarea e Mantova (1559–1636). Fonti, repertori e studi per la storia di Mantova* (Milan: Silvana, 2002), pp. 671–2.

[11] See Andrea Sommer-Mathis, *Die Tänzer am Wiener Hofe im Spiegel der Obersthofmeisteramtsakten und Hofparteienprotokolle bis 1740* (Vienna: Berger, 1992), pp. 8–10.

[12] See the archival documents from the Austrian State Archives quoted in Schlöss, *Das Theresianum*, p. 71 (n. 3, n. 4).

[13] *Breve relatione del balletto fatto avanti le M.Mta dell'Imperatore et Imperatrice a di 5 di Febr: 1617* (n.p., n.d.). See among others Marc Niubò, 'Phasma Dionysiacum Pragense', in Alena Jakubcová and Matthias J. Pernerstorfer (eds), *Theater in Böhmen, Mähren und Schlesien. Von den Anfängen bis zum Ausgang des 18. Jahrhunderts. Ein Lexikon* (Vienna: Österreichischen Akademie der Wissenschaften, 2013), pp. 512–15.

[14] See Herbert Karner, 'IV.13. Vom Tanzaal zum Saaltheater (Redoutensaaltrakt)', in Karner, *Die Wiener Hofburg*, pp. 361–76 and Sommer-Mathis, VI.3. Musik, Theater und Tanz', in Karner, *Die Wiener Hofburg*, pp. 474–6.

As far as the *Hofburg* is concerned, we know that in 1629 Eleonora commissioned the imperial architect Giovanni Battista Carlone to build a huge new hall that would allow more space for a better-equipped stage and for a bigger audience. This so-called *Großer Tanzsaal* (Great Dance Hall) or *Comoedi Saal* (Drama Hall) was opened with two ballets on the occasion of the wedding festivities in 1631 of Ferdinand III and his Spanish bride Maria Anna.[15] Soon after, this hall was regularly used for opera and ballet performances, and also for masques and tournaments.

A similar hall specifically designed for ballets and other theatrical events must already have existed at the *Favorita* also, because a play that included several changes of scenery was performed there in 1633.[16] It is unknown whether Giovanni Battista Carlone had also been entrusted with designing that hall or whether he was even involved in the contemporary enlargement of the *Favorita*, but this possibility cannot be ruled out. The first proof of his collaboration in the *Favorita*, however, dates only from 1642, when he repaired the pond and built a new grotto in the gardens.[17]

The play performed in the *Favorita* in 1633 was Lope de Vega's mythological drama *El vellocino de oro*, when the actresses were Maria Anna's Spanish ladies-in-waiting. This is the first recorded use of different stage sets for one play in Vienna. Archival sources indicate that Giuseppe Mattei, who would become court architect of Emperor Ferdinand III in 1637,[18] had been asked to prepare a small wooden model of a stage that would allow for frequent changes of scenery, from a seascape with a rock that could be opened, to a lovely garden, and would feature the temple of Mars, with doors that could open and close as needed, a forest and a celestial scene. The stage machines included two flying horses, a dolphin and a golden ram, as well as two bulls and a dragon designed to act as 'spitfires'. The stage was lit by 400 small lamps wrapped in iron sheets, each of them holding one to four candles, their light being reflected by 250 mirrors. The auditorium, in contrast, was lit by four huge brass chandeliers and wooden torches on the side-walls.[19] When Lope de Vega's play was first staged in Spain in 1622, it was

---

[15] On the wedding of 1631 see Seifert, *Die Oper*, pp. 30–33; Seifert, *Der Sig-prangende Hochzeit-Gott*, pp. 14–17.

[16] Andrea Sommer-Mathis and Mercedes Reyes Peña, 'Una fiesta teatral en la corte de Viena (1633): *El vellocino de oro* de Lope de Vega', in Maria Grazia Profeti (ed.), *"... Otro Lope no ha de haber ..."*, 3 vols (Florence: Alinea, 2000), vol. 2, pp. 201–51; Andrea Sommer-Mathis, 'Ein *pícaro* und spanisches Theater am Wiener Hof zur Zeit des Dreißigjährigen Krieges', in Weigl, *Wien im Dreißigjährigen Krieg*, pp. 674–80; Maria Grazia Profeti (ed.), *Lope de Vega, El vellocino de oro* (Kassel: Edition Reichenberger, 2007), pp. 30–34.

[17] See Schlöss, *Das Theresianum*, pp. 71–2 (notes 5–6).

[18] HHStA, OMeA SR 186: *Hoff Statts Buech Ferd: III*, fol. 35v. See Peter Fidler, *Architekten des Seicento. Baumeister, Architekten und Bauten des Wiener Hofkreises* (habilitation diss., University of Innsbruck, 1990), p. 62.

[19] HHStA, OMeA SR 75, nr. 4, fol. 55r–56v. See Sommer-Mathis and Reyes Peña, 'Una fiesta', pp. 233–5.

presented as an open-air performance in the gardens of Aranjuez.[20] The organiser of this performance, the Spanish Infanta Maria Anna, later took over as the owner of the *Favorita* after her father-in-law, Emperor Ferdinand II, died in 1637. After the Infanta's death in 1646 the *villeggiatura* reverted to Eleonora, who as Empress-Dowager continued to play an influential part in the cultural life of the imperial court. When she died in 1655, the *Favorita* went to another Eleonora of Gonzaga, her niece and Ferdinand III's third wife.[21]

Due to the committed initiatives of the three empresses, the *Favorita* palace and gardens were transformed into extremely popular (literally 'favourite') locations for festivities and theatre performances. These were designed by the Italian architects and stage designers Giovanni and Lodovico Ottavio Burnacini, who from 1651 on were responsible for the decor of all the operatic and festive productions at the imperial court, including those at the *Favorita*.[22] For nearly five decades the Burnacinis designed almost all the stage sets, machines and costumes for the theatrical performances, as well as the religious *sacre rappresentazioni*, the masquerades and memorial ceremonies of the Viennese court. They also carried out a great deal of architectural work, including the construction of the court theatre, the so-called *Teatro sulla Cortina*.[23]

---

[20] See José María Díez Borque, 'Sobre el teatro cortesano de Lope de Vega: El vellocino de oro, comedia mitológica', in Jean Canavaggio (ed.), *La comedia* (Madrid: Casa de Velázquez, 1995), pp. 155–77; Teresa Ferrer Valls, '*El vellocino de oro* y *El amor enamorado*', in José Juan Berbel Rodríguez (ed.), *En torno al teatro del Siglo de Oro* (Almería: Instituto de Estudios Almerienses, 1996), pp. 49–63; Profeti, *Lope de Vega*, pp. 25–30; Sommer-Mathis, 'Ein *pícaro*', pp. 673–5.

[21] On the two empresses and their cultural influence at the imperial court see Giovanni Battista Intra, 'Le due Eleonore Gonzaga imperatrici', *Archivio Storico Lombardo*, 18 (1891), 342–63, 629–57; Herbert Seifert, 'Die Musiker der beiden Kaiserinnen Eleonora Gonzaga', in Manfred Angerer et al. (eds), *Festschrift Othmar Wessely zum 60. Geburtstag* (Tutzing: Hans Schneider, 1982), pp. 527–54; Linda Maria Koldau, *Frauen, Musik, Kultur: Ein Handbuch zum deutschen Sprachgebiet* (Köln: Böhlau Verlag, 2005), pp. 82–102.

[22] On Giovanni and Lodovico Ottavio Burnacini see Flora Biach-Schiffmann, *Giovanni und Ludovico Burnacini* (Vienna and Berlin: Krystall, 1931); Sabine Solf, *Festdekoration und Groteske. Der Wiener Bühnenbildner Lodovico Ottavio Burnacini. Inszenierung barocker Kunstvorstellung* (Baden-Baden: Koerner, 1975); Hans Tintelnot, *Barocktheater und barocke Kunst. Die Entwicklungsgeschichte der Fest- und Theater-Dekoration in ihrem Verhältnis zur barocken Kunst* (Berlin: Verlag Gebr. Mann, 1939), pp. 56–9, 274–6; Manfred Boetzke, 'Giovanni Burnacini', in Stanley Sadie (ed.), *The New Grove Dictionary of Opera*, 4 vols (London and New York: Macmillan Press Limited, 1994), vol. 1, p. 649; Andrea Sommer-Mathis, 'Lodovico Ottavio Burnacini scenografo e costumista di Antonio Draghi', in Emilio Sala and Davide Daolmi (eds), *'Quel novo Cario, quel divin Orfeo'. Antonio Draghi da Rimini a Vienna* (Lucca: LIM, 2000), pp. 387–410.

[23] On the *Teatro sulla Cortina* see Peter Fleischacker, *Rekonstruktionsversuch des Opernhauses und des Bühnenapparates in dem Theater des Ludovico Ottavio Burnacini* (doctoral thesis, University of Vienna, 1962); Seifert, *Die Oper*, pp. 400–5; Franz

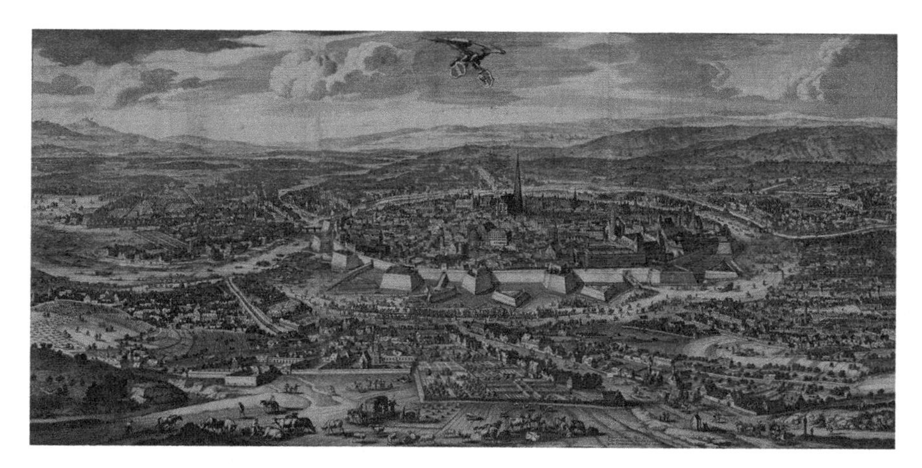

Figure 13.1 The *Hofburg* and the *Favorita* before the siege of Vienna, 1683. Design by Folbert van Ouden-Allen, engraving by Joseph Mulder, 1686. (© Vienna, Austrian National Library, Map Department, Z115113402)

These festive activities were suddenly interrupted by war with the Ottomans and the siege of Vienna in 1683. In fact, the Viennese authorities did not even wait for the Turks before putting a torch to the *Teatro sulla Cortina* and the imperial *Villa La Favorita* (see Figure 13.1).

The military commander of Vienna, Count Ernst Rüdiger Starhemberg, ordered the wooden theatre and all the houses in the suburbs to be burned down in order to have a clear field of fire, with no shelter for the besieging army. The court theatre (*Teatro sulla Cortina*), located at the bastions near the *Hofburg* palace, was not rebuilt, but the *Favorita* was soon reconstructed by Emperor Leopold I (1687–90), who had become its new owner after the death of his step-mother Eleonora II of Gonzaga in 1686.

What the *Favorita* looked like before the siege of Vienna can be seen in an engraving by Georg Matthäus Vischer published in 1672 (see Figure 13.2).

This shows the whole complex of the villa which, in a second construction phase after 1660, had been enlarged with new wings and a second large courtyard. A three-storey wing contained the theatre (*Comœdi Haus*, N° 5 in the engraving)

Hadamowsky, *Wien. Theatergeschichte. Von den Anfängen bis zum Ende des Ersten Weltkriegs* (Vienna and Munich: Jugend & Volk, 1988, 2nd ed., 1994), pp. 142–3; Andrea Sommer-Mathis, 'Fest und Festung. Die Wiener Burgbefestigung als Bauplatz von Tanzsälen und Opernhäusern im 16. und 17. Jahrhundert', *Österreichische Zeitschrift für Kunst und Denkmalpflege*, 64 (2010), 83–92; Sommer-Mathis, IV.15 ('Das Komödienhaus auf der Kurtine'), in Karner, *Die Wiener Hofburg*, pp. 422–7.

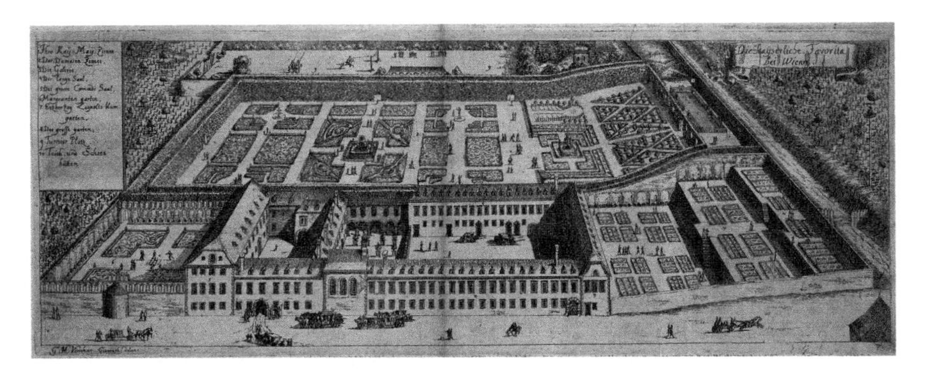

Figure 13.2 The palace and gardens of the imperial *Favorita* before the siege of Vienna, 1672. Design by Georg Mathaeus Vischer, in *Topographia Archiducatus Austriae Inferioris Modernae* (Vienna, 1672; reprint Graz: Akademische Druck- und Verlagsanstalt, 1976). (© Vienna, Austrian State Archives, Blau 763a)

and the spacious gardens consisted of several separate parts including formal gardens (N°s 6, 7, 8), a huge courtyard for tournaments (N° 9), and a large pond (N° 10). It is interesting to note that there is still almost no relationship between the architecture of the palace and the gardens. The co-existence of various different areas is also documented in a detailed description of the gardens from 1660 by Johann Sebastian Müller, who on his journey through Europe had the chance to visit Vienna and the *Favorita*.[24] Müller was especially impressed by the triangular form of the vineyards, the high Spanish trellis, the stone-built pond, and the grottoes with their marble statues. His description largely corresponds to the view of the *Favorita* in Vischer's engraving and also to that in a drawing by Wolfgang Wilhelm Prämer from about 1676 (see Figure 13.3).[25]

---

[24] Cf. Johann Sebastian Müller, 'Reiße-Diarium bey kayserlicher Belehnung des Chur- und Fürstl. Hauses Sachsen', in Johann Joachim Müller (ed.), *Entdecktes Staats-Cabinet* . . . (Jena, 1714), p. 178 [new edition: Katrin Keller, Martin Scheutz and Harald Tersch (eds), *Einmal Weimar. Wien und retour. Johann Sebastian Müller und sein Wienbericht aus dem Jahr 1660*, Veröffentlichungen des Instituts für Österreichische Geschichtsforschung, 42 (Vienna and Munich: Oldenbourg, 2005), pp. 66–7]; see also the description of the *Favorita* in the diary of the French traveller Gouveau from 1661 [manuscript in ÖNB, Cod. 6942, quoted in 'Reisetagebuch eines Franzosen durch Niederösterreich im Jahre 1661', *Monatsblatt des Alterthums-Vereines zu Wien*, 18 (1901), p. 81.]

[25] See Friedrich Polleroß, 'Der Wiener und sein Gartenhaus: Wolfgang Wilhelm Prämer (um 1637–1716)', in Martin Scheutz and Vlasta Valeš (eds), *Wien und seine WienerInnen. Ein historischer Streifzug durch Wien über die Jahrhunderte* (Vienna, Cologne and Weimar: Böhlau Verlag, 2008), pp. 99–124. Prämer published a volume of designs on

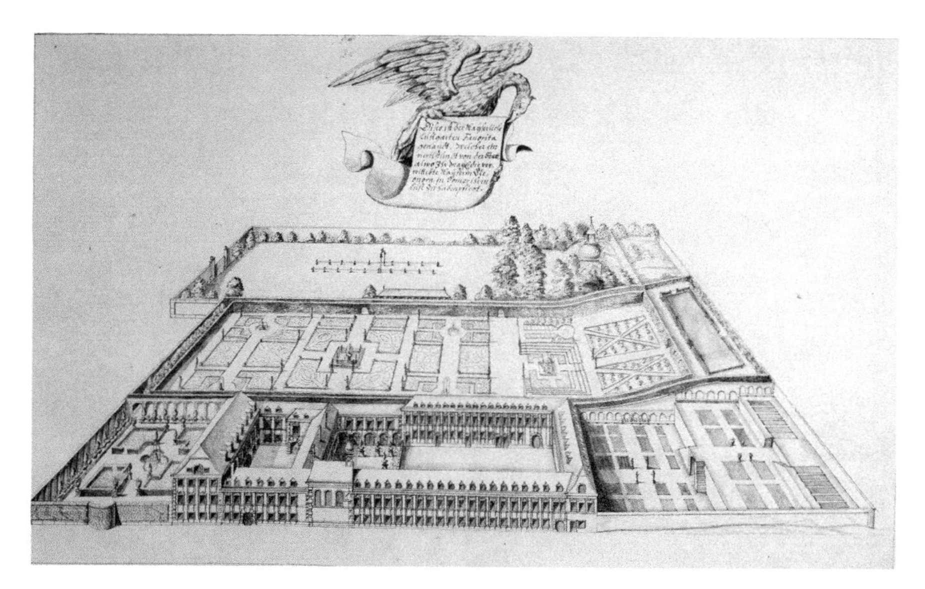

Figure 13.3 Design of the palace and gardens of the *Favorita*, ca. 1676. Drawing by Wolfgang Wilhelm Praemer in *Architecturischer Schauplatz, benenend die tugendsame Verwändnus, worinen sechs mathematische Hauptpuncten bei den architecturn zu ersehen.* (© Vienna, Austrian National Library, Department of Manuscripts and Rare Books, Cod. Ser. nov. 365, fol. 216r. Photo: Bildarchiv NB9869C)

This last might have been an early project for the modification of the façade of the *Favorita*,[26] although such a modification was only realised after the demolition of the complex in 1683[27] and then in a different way.

After the expulsion of the Ottomans from Vienna and following the death of Eleonora II of Gonzaga, the new owner of the *Favorita*, Emperor Leopold I, ordered that the original late-Renaissance building should be rebuilt as a Baroque palace with uniform three-storey wings and a stylistically-consistent façade, depicted in an engraving of the early eighteenth century by Salomon Kleiner (see Figure 13.4).

---

contemporary architecture and building praxis (*Architecturischer Schauplatz* . . .) and dedicated one part of his book (*Architettura practica*) to early Baroque façades.

[26] See also Erich Schlöss, 'Hofburg und Favorita in Praemers Architekturwerk', *Wiener Geschichtsblätter*, 46 (1991), 179–83.

[27] See also the information about the *Favorita* after its destruction provided by the Swedish architect Nicodemus Tessin the Younger in his travel diary from the years 1687–1688, quoted in Merit Laine and Börje Magnusson (eds), *Nicodemus Tessin the Younger. Sources, Works, Collections. Travel Notes 1673–77 and 1687–88* (Stockholm: Nationalmuseum, 2002), p. 411.

Figure 13.4 The façade of the *Favorita*, 1725. Design by Salomon Kleiner, engraving by G.D. Heumann, in Salomon Kleiner and Johann Andreas Pfeffel, *Vera et accurata delineatio tam residentiae et secessuum Caesareorum*, vol. 2 (Vienna, 1725). (© Vienna, Austrian Academy of Sciences, Sammlung Woldan, AW-V: OE/Vie 102: Kleiner II-004)

It was long believed that Lodovico Ottavio Burnacini was responsible for the *Favorita*'s rebuilding after 1683, but it is much more likely that the architect entrusted with the new project was Giovanni Pietro Tencalla. One piece of evidence might be the shape of the façade, which is very similar to that of the *Hofburg*'s so-called Leopoldinian Wing (*Leopoldinischer Trakt*), designed by Tencalla around the same time (see Figure 13.5).[28]

By 1690 the original palace of the *Favorita* had metamorphosed into an impressive Baroque structure which nonetheless was criticised by some visitors as not grand enough for an emperor.[29] What really counted as an impressive development, however, was the park with its fountains, grottoes, the large pond and a new natural theatre (see Figure 13.6).

---

[28] See also Karner, *Die Wiener Hofburg*, V.13 ('Leopoldinischer Trakt').

[29] See also [Casimir Freschot], *Memoires de la Cour de Vienne, contenant les remarques d'un voyageur sur l'etat present de cette Cour, & sur ses interêts . . .* (Cologne: Guillaume Etienne, 1705), pp. 33–4.

Figure 13.5 The façade of the Leopoldinian wing of the imperial palace, 1725. Design by Salomon Kleiner, engraving by I. A. Corvinus, in Kleiner and Pfeffel, *Vera et accurata delineatio tam residentiae et secessuum Caesareorum*, vol. 2 (Vienna, 1725). (© Vienna, Austrian Academy of Sciences, Sammlung Woldan, AW-V: OE/Vie 102: Kleiner II-003)[30]

The person chosen for the installation of the new gardens and also for the design of the open-air theatre was the French landscape designer Jean Trehet (Johann Trechet).[31] He had originally been summoned to Vienna as a specialist in tapestry, but soon showed his talent in landscape gardening and was entrusted with several garden projects, both by the imperial court (*Favorita, Schönbrunn, Augarten*) and by a number of aristocratic families. In 1706 Emperor Joseph I appointed

[30] See Herbert Karner, 'IV.14, Der Leopoldinische Trakt', in Karner, *Die Wiener Hofburg*, pp. 377–421.

[31] On Jean Trehet see Walter Pillich, 'Jean Trehet. Ein französischer Künstler im Dienst des Wiener Hofes 1686–1740', *Jahrbuch des Vereins für Geschichte der Stadt Wien*, 12 (1955/56), 130–44; Eva Berger, *Historische Gärten Österreichs, Garten- und Parkanlagen von der Renaissance bis um 1930*, vol. 3: *Wien* (Vienna, Cologne and Weimar: Böhlau Verlag, 2004), pp. 97, 115, 147–9, 207–9; Beatrix Hajós, 'Schönbrunn: The Garden Designer Jean Trehet Around 1700 and the Modernization of the Gardens by the "Colonie Lorraine" Around 1750', in *Habsburg: The House of Habsburg and Garden Art* (Die Gartenkunst, 20) (Worms: Wernersche Verlagsgesellschaft, 2008), pp. 41–8.

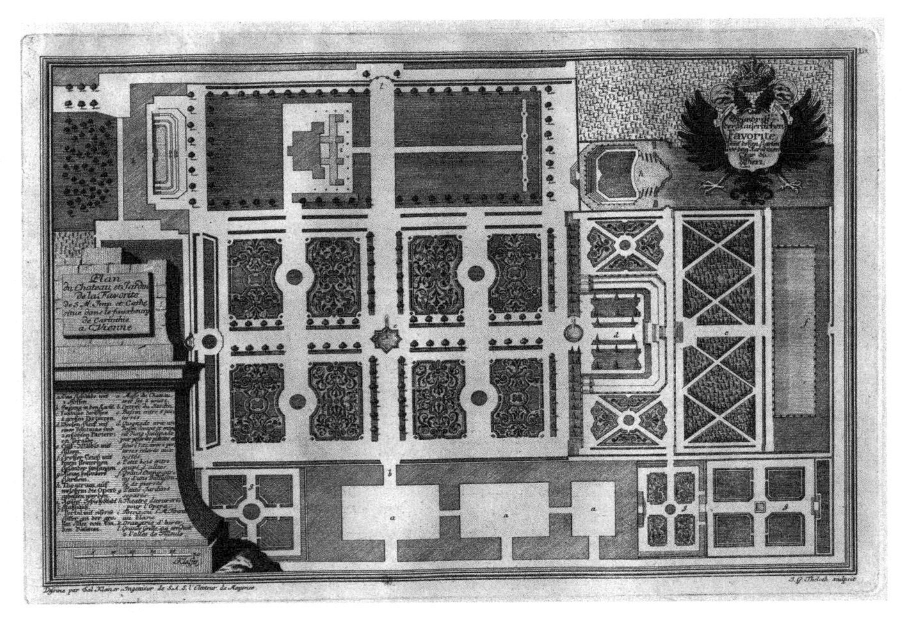

Figure 13.6 Plan of the palace and gardens of the *Favorita*, 1735. Design by Salomon Kleiner, engraving by J.G. Theloth (*Plan du Chateau et Jardin de la Favorite de S.M. Imp. et Cath. Situé dans le Fauxbourg de Carinthie à Vienne*), in Salomon Kleiner and Johann Andreas Pfeffel, *Viererley Vorstellungen* [. . .], first part (Vienna, 1735). (© Vienna, Austrian Academy of Sciences, Sammlung Woldan, AW-V: OE/Vie 102: Kleiner V-001)

him as imperial garden designer and he also remained in charge of the gardens during the reign of Charles VI. In the first half of the eighteenth century the imperial gardens, especially those of the *Favorita*, were even admiringly described as a tourist destination.

The construction of the new palace and gardens of the *Favorita* had been completed by 1690, and from this year onwards it was used again as the 'favourite' summer residence of the imperial family. Some important political and dynastic events were also celebrated there, among them the visit of the Russian Tsar Peter the Great in 1698,[32] the reception one year later of the bride of Joseph I, Amalia

---

[32] On the reception of Tsar Peter the Great and the festivities (opera performance, masquerade and banquet) in the *Favorita* in 1698, see HHStA, Ält. ZA 18 and ZA Prot. 5, fol. 411r–452v; Erich Schlöss, 'Über die Begegnungen des Zaren Peter I. mit Kaiser Leopold I', *Wiener Geschichtsblätter* 49 (1994), 149–62; Schlöss, 'Zar Peter der Große in Wien. Übertragung der Blätter 411 bis 452 der Ceremonialprotokolle 1698 [ZA Prot. 5] in die Schrift

Wilhelmine of Brunswick-Lüneburg,[33] and the proclamation of Archduke Charles as King of Spain in 1703. In addition, the birthdays and name days of the principal members of the imperial family were again regularly commemorated with theatrical productions.[34] Almost every year, the Emperor's birthday on 9 June was greeted by the performance of a major opera with six to eight stage sets in the rebuilt theatre hall. The name day of the Empress Eleonora Magdalena Theresia on 25 June and the birthday of the heir to the throne, the future Joseph I, on 26 July were both celebrated in the gardens with smaller performances, employing at most one or two stage designs, where use could be made of natural landscape features such as the pond and the grotto. There was a certain hierarchy both of the persons to whom the festivities were dedicated – with the Emperor at the summit – and of the theatrical genres, from major operas to one-act serenades and their corresponding locations. In the case of indoor performances, apart from the large theatre hall, smaller pieces were every now and then also presented in the gallery, the so-called *Lange Halle* (Long Hall), or the second *Antecamera*.[35]

Two spectacular outdoor performances in the *Favorita*'s gardens are documented in engravings which provide at least a broad indication of the way these open-air events were staged at the end of the seventeenth century. The engraving of the serenade *L'Euleo festeggiante nel ritorno d'Alessandro Magno dall'Indie*, performed on the occasion of the birthday of Joseph I in 1699, depicts the audience and the illuminated scenery, which included the pond (see Figure 13.7).[36] A second engraving derives from a performance of the one-act opera *La costanza d'Ulisse* in honour of Leopold I in 1700 (see Figure 13.8).[37]

The first two of these engravings (Figures 13.7 and 13.8) show an undeniable influence of the famous French open-air festivities in Versailles during the 1660s (see Plate 15).[38]

At the *Favorita*, the Viennese stage designer Lodovico Ottavio Burnacini clearly knew very well how to make best possible use of the natural features of the gardens. He took advantage of the reflection of light on water – from both the

unserer Zeit wort- und zeilengetreu', *Mitteilungen des Österreichischen Staatsarchivs* 51 (2004), 375–546.

[33] On the wedding of Joseph I in 1699 see Seifert, *Der Sig-prangende Hochzeit-Gott*, pp. 67–72.

[34] See the repertory from 1690–1705 in Seifert, *Die Oper*, pp. 530–82.

[35] See also Rode-Breymann, *Musiktheater*, pp. 380–6.

[36] *L'Euleo festeggiante nel ritorno d'Alessandro Magno dall'Indie. Serenata . . .* (Vienna: Susanna Christina Cosmerovio, 1699).

[37] [Donato Cupeda], *La costanza d'Ulisse. Drama per Musica . . .* (Vienna: Susanna Christina Cosmerovio, 1700). See also the stage directions in the librettos of *L'Euleo festeggiante* and *La costanza d'Ulisse* and their illustrations.

[38] For the Versailles festivities see Marie-Claude Canova-Green's chapter in this volume, 'Transformed Gardens. The Trompe-l'œil Scenery of the Versailles Festivals (1664–1674).

Figure 13.7 Performance of *L'Euleo festeggiante nel ritorno d'Alessandro Magno dall'Indie* (Vienna, 1699) in the gardens of the *Favorita*, 1699. Design by L.O. Burnacini, engraving by I. Krausen, in the libretto of *L'Euleo festeggiante* (Vienna, 1699). (Vienna, Austrian National Library, Department of Music, 406.744-B.Mus.5)

Figure 13.8 Performance of *La costanza d'Ulisse* on the pond of the *Favorita*, 1700. Design by L.O. Burnacini, engraving by Johann Ulrich Krauß, in the libretto of *La costanza d'Ulisse* (Vienna, 1700). Vienna, Theatre Museum, GS_GSU2471. (© KHM-Museumsverband, Theatermuseum Wien)

torches and the stars – as well as of the illusionistic effects of the central perspective. Even when taking into account the idealizing tendencies of the engravings that also served as a public relations exercise, one still gets a good idea of the potential of Baroque stagecraft.[39]

The large pond of the *Favorita*, about 95 metres long and 19 metres wide, remained in its original position and would be used as a swimming pool until 1963, whereas the former courtyard for tournaments made room for a shooting gallery and a new garden theatre built into a gently-inclined slope. The stage was slightly elevated with a space for musicians in front of it. The audience, with the imperial couple in the centre, was placed opposite to, and at a distance from, the stage. The central section of the stone-built rear-stage wall lay a little lower than the side sections of the stage and was accentuated with a grotto. This grotto could

[39] See Andrea Sommer-Mathis, 'Das Wiener Theatralfest *Angelica vincitrice di Alcina* im europäischen Kontext', in Andrea Sommer-Mathis, Daniela Franke and Rudi Risatti (eds), *Spettacolo barocco! Triumph des Theaters* (Petersberg: Michael Imhof, 2016), pp. 170–1.

Figure 13.9 Stage design for a pastoral opera to be performed in the gardens of the *Favorita*, 1710. Drawing by Francesco Galli Bibiena. Vienna, Theatre Museum, HZ_III_43. (© KHM-Museumsverband, Theatermuseum Wien)

be completely integrated into the stage design, as can be seen in a drawing by Francesco Galli Bibiena designed for a pastoral opera in 1710 (see Figure 13.9).[40]

The most spectacular open-air performance ever to be staged in the *Favorita* was the 'festa teatrale' *Angelica vincitrice d'Alcina* (see Figure 13.10),[41] performed in 1716 to celebrate both the birth of a long-desired heir to Emperor Charles VI, and Prince Eugene's victory over the Ottomans at Peterwardein in what proved to be the final phase of Austrian expansion into the Balkans.

[40] See Martina Frank, cat. n. 8.11 in *Spettacolo barocco!*, p. 317.

[41] Pietro Pariati, *Angelica vincitrice di Alcina. Festa teatrale* . . . (Vienna: Van Ghelen, 1716). See also Hilde Haider-Pregler, 'Höfisches und nicht-höfisches Theater in Paris und Wien', in Rudolf Flotzinger (ed.), *J.J. Fux-Symposium Graz '91. Bericht* (Graz: Akademische Druck- und Verlagsanstalt, 1992), pp. 49–54; Ulrike Dembski-Riss, 'Bühnenarchitektur und Bühnendekoration in Opernaufführungen zur Zeit von Johann Joseph Fux. Anmerkungen zu den Szenenbildern der Opern *Angelica vincitrice di Alcina* und *Costanza e Fortezza*', in Arnfried Edler and Friedrich W. Riedel (eds), *Johann Joseph Fux und seine Zeit* (Laaber: Laaber Verlag, 1996), pp. 187–202; Ulrike Dembski, 'Theateraufführungen in Wien 1716', in Ulf Küster (ed.), *Theatrum Mundi. Die Welt als Bühne* (Munich: Edition Minerva, 2003), pp. 34–7; Deanna Lenzi and Jadranka Bentini (eds), *I Bibiena. Una famiglia europea* (Venice: Marsilio, 2000), pp. 254–7; Sommer-Mathis, 'Wiener Theatralfest', pp. 168–79.

Figure 13.10 Performance of *Angelica vincitrice di Alcina* in the gardens of the *Favorita*, 1716. Design by Giuseppe Galli Bibiena, engraving by Franz Dietell, in the libretto of *Angelica vincitrice di Alcina* (Vienna, 1716). (Vienna, Austrian National Library, Departent of Music, BE.12.Q.18.Mus.6)

During the first half of the eighteenth century, some further important dynastic events took place in the *Favorita*, especially the wedding ceremonies for the two daughters of Emperor Joseph I in 1719 and 1722 respectively,[42] and also many imperial and royal birthdays and name days which occurred during the summer months.

The end of the *Favorita*, not only as festive venue but also as a summer residence of the Habsburgs, is connected with a very sad event for the dynasty: the death of Emperor Charles VI, who died on the night of 19 to 20 October 1740 during his stay in the *Favorita*. His daughter and heiress, Maria Theresia, preferred Schönbrunn as her summer residence and abandoned the *Favorita*. She finally sold the palace to the Jesuits in 1746 with a proviso that they install a seminary for the nobility there. This marked the beginning of the Theresian Academy, an institution which survives to this day.

---

[42] On the wedding festivities of 1719 and 1722 see among others Andrea Sommer-Mathis, *Tu felix Austria nube. Hochzeitsfeste der Habsburger im 18. Jahrhundert* (Vienna: Musikwissenschaftlicher Verlag, 1994), pp. 31–67.

Note on this chapter

This article has been published in an edited Spanish version under the title 'Visiones del poder en un ambiente pastoral. La residencia estival de la Favorita como lugar festivo de los Habsburgo', in Inmaculada Rodriguez Moya and Victor Minguez Cornelles (eds), *Visiones de un imperio en fiesta* (Serie Leo Belgicus 4) (Madrid, 2016), pp. 339–58.

Bibliography

Manuscript Sources

Ältere Zeremonialakten (Ält. ZA) 17–20 (1691–1705)

Mantua, Archivio di Stato di Mantova (ASMn), Archivio Gonzaga (AG), busta 434, 493.

Obersthofmeisteramt Sonderreihe (OMeA SR) 75, 186 (*Hoff Statts Buech Ferd: III.*)Vienna, Österreichische Nationalbibliothek (ÖNB), Sammlung von Handschriften und alten Drucken, Cod. Ser. Nov. 365: Wolfgang Wilhelm Praemer, *Architecturischer Schauplatz.*

Vienna, Österreichisches Staatsarchiv (ÖStA), Haus-, Hof- und Staatsarchiv (HHStA)

Zeremonialprotokolle (ZA Prot.) 4–6 (1681–1709)

Printed primary sources

Breve relatione del balletto fatto avanti le M.Mta dell'Imperatore et Imperatrice a di 5 di Febr: 1617 (n.p., n.d.) [Stuttgart, Württembergische Landesbibliothek, Alte und wertvolle Drucke, MC Fr.D.]

[Cupeda, Donato], *La costanza d'Ulisse. Drama per Musica nel felicissimo dì natalizio della S.C.R. M.tà dell'Imperatore Leopoldo I . . . .* (Vienna: Susanna Christina Cosmerovio, 1700).

[Freschot, Casimir], *Memoires de la Cour de Vienne, contenant les remarques d'un voyageur sur l'etat present de cette Cour, & sur ses interêts . . .* (Cologne: Guillaume Etienne, 1705).

[Gouveau], 'Reisetagebuch eines Franzosen durch Niederösterreich im Jahre 1661', *Monatsblatt des Alterthums-Vereines zu Wien*, 18 (1901), 79–86 [Original in ÖNB, Sammlung von Handschriften und alten Drucken, Cod. 6942].

Kleiner, Salomon and Johann Andreas Pfeffel, *Vera et accurata delineatio tam residentiæ et secessuum Cæsareorum quam variorum ad principes et comites spectantium, vel aliorum amœnorum et memorabilium Palatiorum et Prospectuum, qui partim in Cæsarea sede Vienna, partim in adjacentibus suburbijs et proximis territorijs oculis occurrunt . . .*, part II (Augsburg, 1725).

Kleiner, Salomon and Johann Andreas Pfeffel, *Viererley Vorstellungen angenehm- und zierlicher Grundriße folgender Lustgärten und Prospecten, so ausser der Residenz-Stadt Wienn zu finden, nemlich/ 1. Der Kayserl. Favorite. . . .*, part I (Augsburg, 1735).

L'Euleo festeggiante nel ritorno d'Alessandro Magno dall'Indie. Serenata nella sera del felicissimo giorno natalizio della Sacra Real Maestà di Giuseppe I. Re de'Romani . . . (Vienna: Susanna Christina Cosmerovio, 1699).

Müller, Johann Sebastian, 'Reiße-Diarium bey kayserlicher Belehnung des Chur- und Fürstl. Hauses Sachsen', in Johann Joachim Müller (ed.), *Entdecktes Staats-Cabinet* . . . (Jena, 1714), pp. 83–314 [new edition: Katrin Keller, Martin Scheutz and Harald Tersch (eds), *Einmal Weimar. Wien und retour. Johann Sebastian Müller und sein Wienbericht aus dem Jahr 1660*, Veröffentlichungen des Instituts für Österreichische Geschichtsforschung, 42 (Vienna and Munich: Oldenbourg, 2005)].

Laine, Merit and Börje Magnusson (eds), *Nicodemus Tessin the Younger. Sources, Works, Collections. Travel Notes 1673–77 and 1687–88* (Stockholm: National-museum, 2002).

Pariati, Pietro, *Angelica vincitrice di Alcina. Festa teatrale da rappresentarsi sopra la grande peschiera dell'Imperiale Favorita solennizzandosi la felicissima, e gloriosa nascita di Leopoldo Arciduca d'Austria e Real Principe de las Asturias*, . . . (Vienna: Van Ghelen, 1716).

Venturini, Elena, *Le collezioni Gonzaga. Il carteggio tra la Corte Cesarea e Mantova (1559–1636). Fonti, repertori e studi per la storia di Mantova*, Collana del Centro Internazionale d'Arte e di Cultura di Palazzo Te (Milan: Silvana, 2002).

Secondary sources

Artioli, Umberto and Cristina Grazioli (eds), *I Gonzaga e l'Impero. Itinerari dello spettacolo. Con una selezione di materiali dall'Archivio informatico Herla (1560–1630)*, Storia dello spettacolo. Fonti, 4 (Florence: Casa Editrice Le Lettere, 2005).

Askew, Pamela, 'Ferdinando Gonzaga's Patronage of the Pictorial Arts: The Villa Favorita', *The Art Bulletin*, 60 (1978), 274–95.

Benedik, Christian, 'Zeremonielle Abläufe in habsburgischen Residenzen um 1700. Die Wiener Hofburg und die Favorita auf der Wieden', *Wiener Geschichtsblätter*, 46 (1991), 171–8.

Berger, Eva, *Historische Gärten Österreichs, Garten- und Parkanlagen von der Renaissance bis um 1930*, vol. 3: *Wien* (Vienna, Cologne and Weimar: Böhlau Verlag, 2004).

Biach-Schiffmann, Flora, *Giovanni und Ludovico Burnacini* (Vienna and Berlin: Krystall, 1931).

Boetzke, Manfred, 'Giovanni Burnacini', in Stanley Sadie (ed.), *The New Grove Dictionary of Opera*, 4 vols (London and New York: Macmillan Press Limited, 1994), vol. 1, p. 649.

Dembski-Riss, Ulrike, 'Bühnenarchitektur und Bühnendekoration in Opernaufführungen zur Zeit von Johann Joseph Fux. Anmerkungen zu den Szenenbildern der Opern *Angelica vincitrice di Alcina* und *Costanza e Fortezza*', in Arnfried Edler and Friedrich W. Riedel (eds), *Johann Joseph Fux und seine Zeit* (Laaber: Laaber Verlag, 1996), pp. 187–202.

Dembski-Riss, Ulrike, 'Theateraufführungen in Wien 1716', in Ulf Küster (ed.), *Theatrum Mundi: Die Welt als Bühne* (Munich: Edition Minerva, 2003), pp. 34–7.

Díez Borque, José María, 'Sobre el teatro cortesano de Lope de Vega: El vellocino de oro, comedia mitológica', in Jean Canavaggio (ed.), *La comedia* (Madrid: Casa de Velázquez, 1995), pp. 155–77.

Ferrer Valls, Teresa, '*El vellocino de oro* y *El amor enamorado*', in José Juan Berbel Rodríguez (ed.), *En torno al teatro del Siglo de Oro* (Almería: Instituto de Estudios Almerienses, 1996), pp. 49–63.

Fidler, Peter, 'Loggia mit Aussicht: Prologemena zu einer Typologie', *Wiener Jahrbuch für Kunstgeschichte*, 40 (1987), 83–101.

Fidler, Petr, *Architekten des Seicento: Baumeister, Architekten und Bauten des Wiener Hofkreises* (thesis, University of Innsbruck, 1990).

Fleischacker, Peter, *Rekonstruktionsversuch des Opernhauses und des Bühnenapparates in dem Theater des Ludovico Ottavio Burnacini* (doctoral thesis, University of Vienna, 1962).

Guglia, Eugen, *Das Theresianum in Wien: Vergangenheit und Gegenwart* (Vienna, Cologne and Weimar: Böhlau Verlag, 1996).

Hadamowsky, Franz, 'Barocktheater am Wiener Kaiserhof', *Jahrbuch der Gesellschaft für Wiener Theaterforschung*, 1951/52 (1955), 7–117.

Hadamowsky, Franz (ed.), *Die Familie Galli-Bibiena in Wien. Leben und Werk für das Theater* (Vienna: Prachner, 1962).

Hadamowsky, Franz, *Wien. Theatergeschichte. Von den Anfängen bis zum Ende des Ersten Weltkriegs*, Geschichte der Stadt, 3. (Vienna and Munich: Jugend & Volk, 1988; 2nd ed., 1994).

Haider-Pregler, Hilde, 'Höfisches und nicht-höfisches Theater in Paris und Wien', in Rudolf Flotzinger (ed.), *J.J. Fux-Symposium Graz '91. Bericht*, Grazer musikwissenschaftliche Arbeiten, 9 (Graz: Akademische Druck- und Verlagsanstalt, 1992), pp. 43–56.

Hajós, Beatrix, 'Schönbrunn: The Garden Designer Jean Trehet Around 1700 and the Modernization of the Gardens by the "Colonie Lorraine" Around 1750', in *Habsburg. The House of Habsburg and Garden Art*, Die Gartenkunst 20 (Worms: Wernersche Verlagsgesellschaft, 2008), pp. 41–8.

Hajós, Géza, 'Theresianische Akademie', in *Österreichische Kunsttopographie*, vol. 44: *Die Kunstdenkmäler Wiens. Die Profanbauten des III., IV. und V. Bezirks* (Vienna: Verlag Anton Schroll & Co., 1980), pp. 235–44.

Intra, Giovanni Battista, 'Le due Eleonore Gonzaga imperatrici', *Archivio Storico Lombardo*, 18 (1891), 342–63, 629–57.

Karner, Herbert (ed.), *Die Wiener Hofburg 1521–1705. Baugeschichte, Funktion und Etablierung als Kaiserresidenz*, Veröffentlichungen zur Kunstgeschichte, 13; Veröffentlichungen zur Bau- und Funktionsgeschichte der Wiener Hofburg, 2 (Vienna: Verlag der Österreichischen Akademie der Wissenschaften, 2014).

Karner, Herbert, 'IV.13. Vom Tanzsaal zum Saaltheater (Redoutensaaltrakt)', in Herbert Karner (ed.), *Die Wiener Hofburg*, pp. 361–76.

Karner, Herbert, 'IV.14. Der Leopoldinische Trakt', in Herbert Karner (ed.), *Die Wiener Hofburg*, pp. 377–421.

Koldau, Linda Maria, *Frauen, Musik, Kultur. Ein Handbuch zum deutschen Sprachgebiet* (Cologne: Böhlau Verlag, 2005).

Krejci, Karl, 'Angerfelderhof, Schaumburgerhof, Favorita. Ein Beitrag zur Geschichte des Theresianums und des Schaumburgergrundes', *Wiener Geschichtsblätter*, 2 (1981), 87–94.

Lenzi, Deanna and Jadranka Bentini (eds), *I Bibiena. Una famiglia europea* (Venice: Marsilio, 2000).

Nicolini, Dino, 'Una piccola Versailles gonzaghesca. La Favorita', in Ercolano Marani (ed.), *Corti e dimore del Contado Mantovano* (Florence: Vallecchi, 1969), pp. 65–80.

Njubò, Marc, 'Phasma Dionysiacum pragense', in Alena Jakubcová and Matthias J. Pernerstorfer (eds), *Theater in Böhmen, Mähren und Schlesien. Von den Anfängen bis zum Ausgang des 18. Jahrhunderts. Ein Lexikon*, Theatergeschichte Österreichs, X/6, (Vienna: Verlag Österreichischen Akademie der Wissenschaften, 2013), pp. 512–15.

Pillich, Walter, 'Jean Trehet. Ein französischer Künstler im Dienst des Wiener Hofes 1686–1740', *Jahrbuch des Vereins für Geschichte der Stadt Wien*, 12 (1955/56), 130–44.

Polleroß, Friedrich, 'Tradition und Recreation. Die Residenzen der österreichischen Habsburger in der frühen Neuzeit (1490–1780)', *Majestas*, 6 (1998), 91–148.

Polleroß, Friedrich, 'Der Wiener und sein Gartenhaus: Wolfgang Wilhelm Prämer (um 1637–1716)', in Martin Scheutz and Vlasta Valeš (eds), *Wien und seine WienerInnen. Ein historischer Streifzug durch Wien über die Jahrhunderte* (Vienna-Cologne-Weimar: Böhlau Verlag, 2008), pp. 99–124.

Polleroß, Friedrich, 'Les femmes des Habsbourg dans le mécenat architectural', in Sabine Frommel, Juliette Dumas and Raphaël Tassin (eds), *Bâtir au feminin? Traditions et stratégies en Europe et dans l'Empire ottoman* (Paris: Picard, 2013), pp. 35–46.

Profeti, Maria Grazia (ed.), *Lope de Vega, El vellocino de oro*, Teatro del Siglo de oro. Ediciones críticas, 18 (Kassel: Edition Reichenberger, 2007).

Rode-Breymann, Susanne, 'Die beiden Kaiserinnen Eleonora oder: Über den Import der italienischen Oper an den Habsburger Hof in der zweiten Hälfte des 17. Jahrhunderts', in Norbert Bolin et al. (eds), *Aspetti musicali. Musikhistorische Dimensionen Italiens 1600 bis 2000. Festschrift für Dietrich Kämper zum 65. Geburtstag* (Cologne and Rheinkassel: Dohr, 2001), pp. 197–204.

Rode-Breymann, Susanne, 'Raum: eine Kategorie musikalischer Gattungshistoriographie?', in Christine Siegert et al. (eds), *Gattungsgeschichte als Kulturgeschichte. Festschrift Arnfried Edler*, Ligaturen, 3 (Hildesheim, Zurich and New York: Georg Olms Verlag, 2008), pp. 189–204.

Rode-Breymann, Susanne, *Musiktheater eines Kaiserpaars. Wien 1677 bis 1705* (Hildesheim, Zurich and New York: Georg Olms Verlag, 2010).

Schindler, Otto G., '"Mio compadre Imperatore". Comici dell'arte an den Höfen der Habsburger', *Maske und Kothurn*, 38 (1997) 2–4, 25–154.

Schindler, Otto G., 'Von Mantua nach Ödenburg. Die ungarische Krönung Eleonoras I. Gonzaga (1622) und die erste Oper am Kaiserhof. Ein unbekannter Bericht aus der Széchényi-Nationalbibliothek', *Biblos*, 46 (1997) 2, 243–93.

Schindler, Otto G., 'L'incoronazione ungherese di Eleonora I Gonzaga (1622) e gli inizi del teatro musicale alla corte degli Asburgo', *Quaderni di Palazzo Te*, 5 (1999), 70–93.

Schindler, Otto G., 'Von Favorita zu Favoriten. Ein Lustschloss in Mantua als Namenspatron eines Wiener Arbeiterbezirks', *Sonderbeilage zur Wiener Zeitung*, 24/25 September 1999.

Schindler, Otto G., '"Sonst ist es lustig alhie". Italienisches Theater am Habsburgerhof zwischen Weißem Berg und Sacco di Mantova', in Andreas Weigl (ed.), *Wien im Dreißigjährigen Krieg. Bevölkerung, Gesellschaft, Kultur, Konfession*, Kulturstudien, 32 (Vienna, Cologne and Weimar: Böhlau Verlag, 2001), pp. 565–654.

Schindler, Otto G., 'Viaggi teatrali tra l'Inquisizione e il Sacco. Comici dell'Arte di Mantova alle corti degli Asburgo d'Austria', in Umberto Artioli and Cristina Grazioli (eds), *I Gonzaga e l'Impero. Itinerari dello spettacolo. Con una selezione di materiali dall'Archivio informatico Herla (1560–1630)*, Storia dello spettacolo. Fonti, 4 (Florence: Casa Editrice Le Lettere, 2005), pp. 107–60.

Schlöss, Erich, *Das Theresianum. Ein Beitrag zur Bezirksgeschichte der Wieden*, Forschungen und Beiträge zur Wiener Stadtgeschichte, 5 (Vienna: Verein für Geschichte der Stadt Wien, 1979).

Schlöss, Erich, 'Die Favorita auf der Wieden um 1700', *Wiener Geschichtsblätter*, 46 (1991), 162–70.

Schlöss, Erich, 'Hofburg und Favorita in Praemers Architekturwerk', *Wiener Geschichtsblätter*, 46 (1991), 179–83.

Schlöss, Erich, 'Über die Begegnungen des Zaren Peter I. mit Kaiser Leopold I', *Wiener Geschichtsblätter*, 49 (1994), 149–62.

Schlöss, Erich, *Baugeschichte des Theresianums in Wien* (Vienna, Cologne and Weimar: Böhlau Verlag, 1998).

Schlöss, Erich, 'Zar Peter der Große in Wien. Übertragung der Blätter 411 bis 452 der Ceremonialprotokolle 1698 [ZA Prot. 5] in die Schrift unserer Zeit wort- und zeilengetreu', *Mitteilungen des Österreichischen Staatsarchivs*, 51 (2004), 375–546.

Schwarz, Johann, *Die kaiserliche Sommerresidenz Favorita auf der Wieden in Wien, 1615–1746* (Vienna and Prague: Tempsky, 1898).

Seifert, Herbert, 'Die Musiker der beiden Kaiserinnen Eleonora Gonzaga', in Manfred Angerer et al. (eds), *Festschrift Othmar Wessely zum 60. Geburtstag* (Tutzing: Hans Schneider, 1982), pp. 527–54.

Seifert, Herbert, *Die Oper am Wiener Kaiserhof im 17. Jahrhundert*, Wiener Veröffentlichungen zur Musikgeschichte, 25 (Tutzing: Hans Schneider, 1985).

Seifert, Herbert, *Der Sig-prangende Hochzeits-Gott. Hochzeitsfeste am Wiener Hof der Habsburger und ihre Allegorik 1622–1699*, dramma per musica, 2 (Vienna: Musikwissenschaftlicher Verlag, 1988).

Seifert, Herbert, 'Frühes italienisches Musikdrama nördlich der Alpen: Salzburg, Prag, Wien, Regensburg und Innsbruck', in Markus Engelhardt (ed.), *In Teutschland noch gantz ohnbekandt. Monteverdi-Rezeption und frühes Musiktheater im deutschsprachigen Raum*, Perspektiven der Opernforschung, 3 (Frankfurt am Main and Vienna: Lang, 1996), pp. 29–44.

Seifert, Herbert, 'Rapporti musicali tra i Gonzaga e le corti asburgiche', in Umberto Artioli and Cristina Grazioli (eds), *I Gonzaga e l'Impero. Itinerari dello spettacolo. Con una selezione di materiali dall'Archivio informatico Herla (1560–1630)*, Storia dello spettacolo. Fonti, 4 (Florence: Casa Editrice Le Lettere, 2005), pp. 219–29.

Solf, Sabine, *Festdekoration und Groteske. Der Wiener Bühnenbildner Lodovico Ottavio Burnacini. Inszenierung barocker Kunstvorstellung*, Studien zur deutschen Kunstgeschichte, 355 (Baden-Baden: Koerner, 1975).

Sommer-Mathis, Andrea, *Die Tänzer am Wiener Hofe im Spiegel der Obersthofmeisteramtsakten und Hofparteienprotokolle bis 1740*, Mitteilungen des Österreichischen Staatsarchivs. Ergänzungsband, 11 (Vienna: Berger, 1992).

Sommer-Mathis, Andrea, *Tu felix Austria nube. Hochzeitsfeste der Habsburger im 18. Jahrhundert*, dramma per musica, 4 (Vienna: Musikwissenschaftlicher Verlag, 1994).

Sommer-Mathis, Andrea, 'Lodovico Ottavio Burnacini scenografo e costumista di Antonio Draghi', in Emilio Sala and Davide Daolmi (eds), '*Quel novo Cario, quel divin Orfeo'. Antonio Draghi da Rimini a Vienna*, ConNotazioni, 7 (Lucca: LIM, 2000), pp. 387–410.

Sommer-Mathis, Andrea and Mercedes Reyes Peña, 'Una fiesta teatral en la corte de Viena (1633): *El vellocino de oro* de Lope de Vega', in Maria Grazia Profeti (ed.), "*. . .Otro Lope no ha de haber. . .*", 3 vols, Secoli d'oro, 15 (Florence: Alinea, 2000), vol. 2, pp. 201–51.

Sommer-Mathis, Andrea, 'Ein *pícaro* und spanisches Theater am Wiener Hof zur Zeit des Dreißigjährigen Krieges', in Andreas Weigl (ed.), *Wien im Dreißigjährigen Krieg. Bevölkerung, Gesellschaft, Kultur, Konfession*, Kulturstudien, 32 (Vienna, Cologne and Weimar: Böhlau Verlag, 2001), pp. 655–94.

Sommer-Mathis, Andrea, 'Luoghi teatrali alla corte imperiale di Vienna nel Seicento. Dalla sala all'edificio teatrale', in Laura Sannita Nowé et al. (eds), *Sentir e meditar. Omaggio a Elena Sala Di Felice*, AIO, 108 (Rome: Aracne, 2005), pp. 75–84.

Sommer-Mathis, Andrea, 'Lieux de representation théâtrale à la cour impériale de Vienne au XVIIe siècle: de la salle à l'édifice', in Charles Mazouer (ed.), *Les*

Lieux du spectacle dans l'Europe du XVIIe siècle, Biblio, 17/165 (Tübingen: Gunter Narr Verlag, 2006), pp. 355–75.

Sommer-Mathis, Andrea, 'Fest und Festung. Die Wiener Burgbefestigung als Bauplatz von Tanzsälen und Opernhäusern im 16. und 17. Jahrhundert', *Österreichische Zeitschrift für Kunst und Denkmalpflege* 64 (2010), 83–92.

Sommer-Mathis, Andrea, 'VI.3. Musik, Theater und Tanz: Die Wiener Hofburg als Schauplatz von szenischen Aufführungen', in Karner, *Die Wiener Hofburg*, pp. 470–93.

Sommer-Mathis, Andrea, 'VI. 4. Residenz und öffentlicher Raum. Höfisches Fest in Wien im Wandel vom 16. zum 17. Jahrhundert', in Karner, *Die Wiener Hofburg*, pp. 494–508.

Sommer-Mathis, Andrea, 'IV.15. Das Komödienhaus auf der Kurtine', in Karner, *Die Wiener Hofburg*, pp. 422–7.

Sommer-Mathis, Andrea, 'Das Wiener Theatralfest "Angelica vincitrice di Alcina" im europäischen Kontext', in *Spettacolo barocco!* pp. 168–79.

Sommer-Mathis, Andrea, Daniela Franke and Rudi Risatti (eds.), *Spettacolo barocco! Triumph des Theaters* (Petersberg: Michael Imhof, 2016).

Tietze, Hans, 'Wolfgang Wilhem Praemers Architekturwerk und der Wiener Palastbau des 17. Jahrhunderts', *Jahrbuch der kunsthistorischen Sammlungen des allerhöchsten Kaiserhauses*, 32 (1915), 343–402.

Tintelnot, Hans, *Barocktheater und barocke Kunst: Die Entwicklungsgeschichte der Fest- und Theater-Dekoration in ihrem Verhältnis zur barocken Kunst* (Berlin: Verlag Gebr. Mann, 1939).

Weigl, Andreas (ed.), *Wien im Dreißigjährigen Krieg. Bevölkerung, Gesellschaft, Kultur, Konfession*, Kulturstudien, 32 (Vienna, Cologne and Weimar: Böhlau Verlag, 2001).

Chapter 14

Between props and sets

The *Menus Plaisirs* administration and space conversions in the French court, 1660–1700

Pauline Lemaigre-Gaffier

The *Menus Plaisirs du roi* administration served in the later seventeenth century as a distinctive institution in charge of organizing practical arrangements for royal ceremonies and court festivals. In spite of its frivolous reputation – the expression '*les Menus Plaisirs*', still familiar to French ears, evokes charming insignificance – analysis of its sophisticated functions and organisation throws light on links between royal institutions and civic government, that is to say between the court and state-centred political processes – since public representation of the court was one royal means of governing.[1]

From the end of the seventeenth century to the end of the Old Regime, it appears that the *Menus Plaisirs* served not only to organise festivities but also to stimulate a festival spirit across court life. As Ralph Giesey and Frédérique Leferme-Falguières have shown,[2] from the second part of Louis XIV's reign, an organised and formally-established court ceremonial tended to replace former state rituals and festivities that took place routinely during each reign. In such a context, the *Menus Plaisirs* administration grew into a typical bureaucratic organisation.[3] If this institution developed its new practices at the very time when large festivals were in decline, this is precisely because both festival and its administration were concerned with integrating public display into a royal ceremonial which ritualised the entire life of the court and highlighted its key moments. Just as the words 'festival' or 'festivity' imply multiple dimensions – summed up in performances embracing both sacred and profane features[4] – so the role of the *Menus Plaisirs* administration provided the king with the material means to present a

---

1 Pauline Lemaigre-Gaffier, *Du cœur de la Maison du Roi à l'esprit des institutions. L'Administration des Menus Plaisirs du Roi au xviiie* siècle, 3 vols (Diss., Université Paris 1, 2011).

2 Ralph Giesey, *Cérémonial et puissance souveraine. France xive-xviie* siècles (Paris: Cahier des Annales, 41, 1987); Frédérique Leferme-Falguières, *Les Courtisans. Une société de spectacle sous l'Ancien Régime* (Paris: Presses Universitaires de France, 2007).

3 Lemaigre-Gaffier, *L'Administration des Menus Plaisirs*, vol. 2, pp. 2–207.

4 On French festival historiography see Mona Ozouf, 'La fête sous la Révolution française', in Jacques Le Goff and Pierre Nora (eds), *Faire de l'histoire*, 3 vols (Paris: Gallimard, 1974), vol. 3, *Nouveaux Objets*, pp. 256–77.

series of court occasions, from the king's *levée* to preparations for his own funeral, without neglecting either routine or occasional spectacle. Thus, the *Menus Plaisirs* strengthened their position in the King's Household, enabling the monarch's role so far as this was concerned with entertainment and celebration.[5]

Creating props and sets, organizing entertainments and festivals, the *Menus Plaisirs* repeatedly staged the royal body, associating the king's physical and symbolic body with the royal palace and its spaces. From the beginning to the end of the reign of Louis XIV, we can observe how making space for festival reinforced the administration's increasing responsibility for creating a comprehensive royal ceremonial.

This chapter analyses the entertainment expenses the *Menus Plaisirs* paid in 1669 and 1698 under the direction of the First Gentleman of the Bedchamber, in order to demonstrate how material and financial expenses evolved throughout Louis XIV's reign. It also shows how the *Menus Plaisirs* contributed to the institutionalisation of monarchical celebrations and their political effect.

The king's body and court space: the responsibilities of the *Menus Plaisirs* administration

The *Menus Plaisirs* administration, the full name of which was '*Argenterie, Menus Plaisirs et Affaires de la Chambre du Roi*', was closely linked to the development of the King's Household and within it of his Chamber, ever since the *Argenterie* (Treasurer's office) had been created at the beginning of the fourteenth century, when Household institutions were allocated their own funds.[6] In the early period, the *Argenterie* was in charge of personal clothing and furniture for the king. The office of the *Menus Plaisirs* Treasurer came into being in the fifteenth century in order to meet entertainment and scenery expenses. Subsequently, the creation of an office of Controller common to the two treasuries of *Argenterie* and *Menus Plaisirs* provided a basis for the development of a new Household department.[7] By the end of the seventeenth century, *Menus Plaisirs* had become an institution with wide responsibilities, whose distinctive identity would be confirmed during the Enlightenment. Under the authority of the First Gentleman of the Bedchamber, the *Menus Plaisirs* acted as an accounting and administrative structure for the whole of the King's Chamber, as one of its specialised departments, and as a regulatory authority in charge of French and Italian players settled in Paris. In fact, the *Menus Plaisirs* became an institutional monster, whose history and creative outputs help to explain its nature and activities.

---

[5] Alain Viala, *La France galante. Essai historique sur une catégorie culturelle de ses origines jusqu'à la Révolution* (Paris: Presses Universitaires de France, 2008).

[6] Lemaigre-Gaffier, *L'Administration des Menus Plaisirs*, vol. 1, pp. 49–60.

[7] Ibid., pp. 61–84.

As a treasury and administrative structure, the *Menus Plaisirs* paid all the wages of the Chamber officers – including *valets de chambre*, physicians and musicians – and kept till the very end of the Old Regime close links with the Wardrobe and the *Garde-Meuble*.[8] Even if these departments had been formally separated from the Chamber at the beginning of the seventeenth century,[9] the *Argenterie* Treasurer still controlled them and paid most of their expenses.

The *Menus Plaisirs* continued, moreover, to play a part in supplying the king with clothes and furniture in specific circumstances, such as ceremonies or travel. It could replace the Wardrobe or *Garde-Meuble* in creating the king's robes for his coronation and the special furniture for his apartments on the occasions of royal mourning.[10] It also supplied toilet articles, linen, clocks or portable furniture for the valets who watched over the king's bed and royal wardrobe. Thus, as a specialised department, it had specific responsibility for the material organisation of court theatre, including the making of scenery for state and dynastic ceremonies, as well as providing supplies for the king's and the royal family's day-to-day lives.[11]

In addition to inherited duties, the responsibilities shared between the Household departments reveal both material court culture and the king's specific needs. In fact, the parallels between common needs – to eat, get dressed, be entertained – and the existence of formal Household departments, suggest the possibility of constructing an organisational chart – but such a chart would be unable to represent adequately such a complex, detailed and changing reality. However, one can begin to perceive an orderly structure based on inherited practices and the relationship between officers and control of the material reality for which they were responsible.[12]

The *Argenterie, Menus Plaisirs et Affaires de la Chambre du Roi* became an active administrative department when its role was separated from the Wardrobe – in charge of clothing – where expenses were considered as the principal expenditure *en la personne du roy*, and also from the *Garde-Meuble*, in charge of furniture,

---

8 It was a specific institution in charge of furniture (supplying, depository and maintenance).

9 William Richtey Newton, *La Petite Cour. Domestiques et serviteurs à Versailles au xviii*^e^ *siècle* (Paris: Perrin, 2003); Stéphane Castelluccio, *Le Garde-Meuble de la Couronne et ses intendants du xvi*^e^ *au* XVIIIe *siècles* (Paris: Comité des Travaux Historiques et Scientifiques, 2004).

10 Known as the *grand deuil*, this was a specific mourning ceremonial for the most important members of the royal family.

11 On such objects see Raphaël Mariani, *Les Menus Plaisirs dans la vie quotidienne du Roi et des princes. 1715–1774* (Paris: Université Paris 4, Sorbonne, 2000); *Les Menus Plaisirs dans la vie quotidienne de la famille royale. 1770–1792* (Paris: Université Paris 4, Sorbonne, 2001).

12 Lemaigre-Gaffier, *L'Administration des Menus Plaisirs*, vol. 1, pp. 146–60.

with its expenditure seen as *hors la personne du roy*.[13] As for the *Menus Plaisirs*, it was in charge of supplying the king with all the necessary coffers, chests, trunks and bags to keep and carry his clothes as well as with all his own *portable* furniture – *meubles brisés* – that could be conveniently carried and *meubles de campagne* to be taken on military campaigns. Such possessions constituted a specific material category, a halfway house between expenses 'in' and 'out of' the royal body – thus helping to explain how this institution can be regarded as linking the royal body to court space.

Many conflicts occurred between the *Menus Plaisirs* and the *Garde-Meuble*, but also between the *Menus Plaisirs* and the *Bâtiments du Roi*, due to the complexity of sharing their overlapping responsibilities. For instance, in 1669, the *Bâtiments du Roi* built several boats for use on the Grand Canal, with furniture provided by *Garde-Meuble* suppliers and paid for by the *Argenterie* Treasurer.[14] However, *Bâtiments*, *Garde-Meuble* and *Menus Plaisirs* also shared the triple category of *immeuble*, *meuble* and *portatif*: a division which covers buildings, which are *immovable*, furniture which is *movable*, and, finally, *portable* objects which were particular to the *Menus Plaisirs*. Thus, the *Menus Plaisirs* could be seen as the institution in charge of ensuring the spectacular, solemn and ritual character of the king's life, drawing on a specific material culture and skills. For instance, the *Menus Plaisirs* claimed the right to supply the royal canopy for the 1789 *États-Généraux*, in opposition to the *Garde-Meuble*, drawing attention to its right to supply covers not only for the clothes in the king's wardrobe but also for his throne in Reims cathedral or his coffin in Saint-Denis abbey.[15] The *Menus Plaisirs* argued that their craftsmen and administrators possessed skills which *Bâtiments* and *Garde-Meuble* lacked, such as their ready adaptability to changed circumstances and requirements.[16] This perspective may explain why in the eighteenth century the division of responsibilities between *Menus Plaisirs* and *Bâtiments* was not based on the distinction between *dedans* and *dehors*,[17] but according to the distinction between ephemeral and permanent.[18] From the end of the seventeenth century to

---

[13] 'In' and 'out of the king's body', as regular publications such as *Etats de la France* and other almanacs told them from the seventeenth century, according to medieval regulations (see for instance, *Etats de la France* (Paris: David, 1749, p. 291)).

[14] *Archives nationales* (Paris), O[1] 2130 (Bâtiments du Roi, Recette et dépense, 1669); O[1] 2816 ('Registre des Ordonnances du Roy de toute la despence extraordinaire qui a esté faicte en son Argenterie pendant l'année 1669').

[15] Pierre Pinon, Patrick Brasart and Claude Malécot, *Des Menus Plaisirs aux droits de l'homme. La salle des États-généraux à Versailles* (Paris: Caisse Nationale des Monuments Historiques et des Sites, 1989), pp. 31–64; Lemaigre-Gaffier, *L'Administration des Menus Plaisirs*, vol. 1, pp. 159–60.

[16] It is a recurrent argument in the memoirs that were written in defense of the *Menus Plaisirs* administration (*Archives nationales* (Paris), O[1] 2809 and 2810).

[17] 'Inside' and 'outside'.

[18] 'Reglement entre Les Premiers Gentilshommes de la Chambre du Roy; les Capitaines et Gouverneurs des Maisons Royales et le Directeur General des Bâtimens, Jardins,

the first part of the eighteenth, many regulations made official these material distinctions and clarified the specific responsibilities falling to the *Menus Plaisirs*.

Transforming court space: costs and logistics

The transformation of court space entailed the drawing up of accounts which throw light on the evolution of the economy of the royal household and the way in which changes in material court culture interacted with political and ceremonial practices. Using the *Argenterie* and *Menus Plaisirs* account books allows the enquirer to assess the different kinds of expenses according to their uses and their users at court after 1682 and the court's establishment in Versailles.[19] In this chapter, analysis of these expenses is set alongside analysis of accounts from the period when the French court had not yet settled in Versailles. Even if there is some continuity, changing places meant a change in the symbolic and economic background of royal ceremonial: in this perspective, material court culture turns out to be not only a result but also a mainspring of ceremonial evolution.

The beginning of Louis XIV's personal reign remained vivid in contemporary memory because of the major festivals which took place in the gardens at Versailles.[20] The king had commissioned several festival books[21] so as to enable a large audience to become aware of the detail of these festivals. For its part, the Household administration – Ceremonies and *Menus Plaisirs* officers – kept official, if not public, record of these festivities so as to be able to repeat them.[22]

However, this chapter avoids focusing on 1664, 1668 or 1674 – years when the *Plaisirs de l'île enchantée*, the *Grand divertissement de Versailles* and celebrations referring to the Dutch war took place – but will instead concentrate on two 'ordinary' years in the life of the court, *before* and *after* the king settled in Versailles and decided to create a more permanent stage for his own glory. A comparison of this

Arts et Manufactures de Sa Majesté' (*Archives nationales* (Paris), O[1] 194, f° 357 r°-359 r° or O[1] 820, n° 8). I have edited this 1745 regulation in Lemaigre-Gaffier, *L'Administration des Menus Plaisirs*, vol. 3, pp. 58–61. Jérôme de La Gorce, 'Quand les Menus Plaisirs et les Bâtiments du Roi s'associent pour servir la monarchie', in Jérôme de La Gorce and Pierre Jugie (eds), *Les Menus Plaisirs du Roi. xviie-xviiie* siècle (Paris: Presses de l'Université Paris-Sorbonne, 2013).

[19] Lemaigre-Gaffier, *L'Administration des Menus Plaisirs*, vol. 2, pp. 210–83.

[20] Marie-Christine Moine, *Les Fêtes à la Cour du Roi-Soleil. 1653–1715* (Paris: F. Sorlot and F. Lanore, 1984); Philippe Beaussant and Patricia Bouchenot-Déchin, *Les Plaisirs de Versailles. Théâtre et Musique* (Paris: Fayard, 1996); Michel Jeanneret, *Versailles. Ordre et Chaos* (Paris: Gallimard, 2012).

[21] André Félibien, *Les Fêtes de Versailles*, ed. Michel Jeanneret (Paris: Le Promeneur, 2012).

[22] Marie-Lan Nguyen, *Les Grands-Maîtres des Cérémonies et le service des Cérémonies à l'époque moderne. 1585–1792* (Paris: Université Paris 4, Sorbonne, 1999); Lemaigre-Gaffier, *L'Administration des Menus Plaisirs*, vol. 1, pp. 319–41.

kind offers an effective way to look at economic and accountancy evidence of the role festive celebration played daily in court life and royal representation during the reign of Louis XIV. With this in mind, 1669 – for which payment orders to both *Argenterie* and *Menus Plaisirs* survive[23] – is compared with 1698.

1669: an 'ordinary' year before the court settled in Versailles

As Table 14.1 shows, several routine kinds of entertainment[24] – some lasting hours, days or even weeks – punctuated each year of court life, in addition to the large-scale festivals and the most famous celebrations, which have been fully documented by contemporary observers as well as modern historians.

I focus here on the economic and political significance of the 1669 entertainment expenses.[25] The peculiar administrative framework of the *Argenterie* and *Menus Plaisirs* accounts, and their apportioning of responsibility and reward, reveal material investment in the practical aspects of celebration.

According to the account books, 7 payment orders were delivered to the *Argenterie* Treasurer and 42 to the Treasurer of the *Menus Plaisirs*.[26] These payment orders represent the huge amount of 222,105 *livres tournois*,[27] exclusive of expenses for past and future entertainments,[28] and for the funeral of Queen Henrietta Maria of England. Since currency values were stable during this period, these

---

[23] *Archives nationales* (Paris), O[1] 2816 (*Argenterie*) et 2817 (*Menus Plaisirs*).

[24] Several words such as 'fêtes' or 'divertissements' are used to qualify these events.

[25] For further discussion of different aspects of these festivals see Marie-Françoise Christout, *Le Ballet de Cour de Louis XIV: 1643–1712* (Paris: Picard, 2005 [1967]); Pierre Béhar and Helen Watanabe-O'Kelly (eds), *Spectaculum Europeum: Theatre and Spectacle in Europe/Histoire du Spectacle en Europe (1580–1750)* (Wiesbaden: Harrassowitz Verlag, 1999); Jérôme de La Gorce and Pierre Jugie, *Dans l'atelier des Menus Plaisirs du Roi. Spectacles, fêtes et cérémonies aux xviie et xviiie* siècles (Paris: Archives Nationales/Artlys, 2011). See also Marie-Claude Canova-Green's chapter in this volume.

[26] This logic is as much material as symbolical: in every kind of circumstance (profane or sacred), the *Argenterie* Treasurer paid for clothes, whereas the *Menus Plaisirs* Treasurer paid for ephemeral buildings and arrangements. However, the *Menus Plaisirs* Treasurer was the one who paid all the musicians' and comedians' wages and benefits. See also Lemaigre-Gaffier, *L'Administration des Menus Plaisirs*, vol. 1, pp. 65–9, 81–2.

[27] However, entertainment expenses never represented the major part of State expenses, nor even the major part of King's Household expenses: see Jeroen Duindam, *Vienna and Versailles: The Court of Europe's Dynastic Rivals. 1550–1780* (Cambridge: Cambridge University Press, 2003).

[28] These books (*Archives nationales* (Paris), O[1] 2816 and 2817) are not organised according to a financial-year logic and compiled all the payment orders delivered in 1669: even if most of them are relevant to events which took place in 1669, some of them are relevant to a 1667 ballet or 1670 spectacles (especially to a January performance of *Les Amants magnifiques*, Molière's *comédie-ballet*).

Table 14.1 Entertainment programme in 1669

Date	Place	Events
16 February	Tuileries[29]	*Ballet de Flore*
3, 5 and 6 March	Tuileries (antechamber)	Masquerades
July and August	Saint-Germain-en-Laye (*château neuf* gallery)	Three comedies (*Le Baron d'Albikrach, L'Avare, Tartuffe)*, for which a natural setting was created
11 August	Versailles (Orangery)	A tragedy (*Nicomède)*, a ball and a 'collation'[30]
26 August	Saint-Germain-en-Laye	Molière's *comédie-ballet, La Princesse d'Élide*
Autumn	Residence in Chambord	15 comedies represented: the most striking being Molière's *comédie-ballet, Monsieur de Pourceaugnac.*
December	Saint-Germain-en-Laye castle	An ephemeral gallery constructed for the winter festivities

very high expenses represent more than the costs of the 1668 *Grand Divertissement* and three times more than the cost of the 1674 festival.[31] Thus, the figures endorse the claim that entertainments and *ad hoc* performances were intended to extend the effect festivals conferred on court life as a whole.

Such an amount is all the more striking since it does not include any outdoor festivities. This kind of work was under the control of the *Bâtiments du Roi*. According to its 1669 account book, however, it seems not to have undertaken that year any activities in royal parks and courtyards, apart from fireworks.[32] By contrast the

---

[29] Jérôme de La Gorce, *Carlo Vigarani intendant des plaisirs de Louis XIV* (Paris/Versailles: Perrin, 2005), p. 95, indicates that an ephemeral theatre was built up in the Grand Salon.

[30] Light meal.

[31] According to Florence Sorkine, *Propagande et mécénat royal: les fêtes louis-quatorziennes à Versailles et leurs représentations. 1661–1682* (Diss. Paris: Université Paris 3, Sorbonne Nouvelle, 1993), pp. 110–29, they cost 161,181 *livres tournois* 16 *sous* 9 *deniers*. [Marie-Christine Moine (*Les Fêtes à la Cour du Roi-Soleil*, p. 207) indicates 149,543 *livres tournois* and 63,713*lt* 8*s* 9*d*.] Moreover, these figures include data from several King's Household departments.

[32] *Archives nationales* (Paris), O[1] 2130 (*Bâtiments du Roi, Recette et dépense*, 1669).

Menus Plaisirs' artists, craftsmen and officers, who worked only under the direction of the duke of Saint-Aignan, first Gentleman of the Bedchamber, appear to have compensated for the lack of spectacular events in the gardens. Expenses connected with indoor occasional theatres are indeed among the most considerable in the books analyzed. Even if it is impossible to give a precise figure, as the accounts may conflate different sets of expenses, from material and chronological points of view, payments for indoor activity may be estimated at 25,078 *livres tournois* at least. Moreover, it is known from regulations and from previous and later registers that expenses related to buildings and space conversions were paid by the *Menus Plaisirs* Treasurer and allocated to his coffer, whereas expenses for clothes and costumes – for ceremonies, *ballets* and masquerades – were recorded in the *Argenterie* register, even if not individually listed. Therefore, the imbalance between the amounts recorded in the two registers (see Table 14.2) confirms that expenses for scenery, scaffolding and timber framework were among the largest amounts.

To give an example, Carlo Vigarani – *gentilhomme modenois inventeur de machines* – who had been working for both the *Bâtiments du Roi* and the *Menus Plaisirs* during the 1660s, built a *theâtre de feuillées*[33] for the Versailles Orangery. For the year 1669, Vigarani, who had been granted 6,000 *livres tournois* a year paid by the *Menus Plaisirs* Treasurer, was given a new title: *intendant des Plaisirs, Ballets, Théâtres et Comédies du Roi*.[34] This range of responsibilities shows that the organisation of court entertainment was not yet a unified task allocated to a specific administration, while underlining also the growing part played by the *Menus Plaisirs*. Their officers, employees and craftsmen still had to compete and cooperate with the *Bâtiments du Roi*; Vigarani himself worked under Charles Perrault's command[35] for the *Grand Divertissement* fireworks in 1674. However, when Vigarani began, from the end of the 1660s, to engage more and more in the design of permanent architecture, in spite of his commitment also to the largest court festivities, he tended to leave smaller-scale ephemeral occasions (such as funerals) to Henri Gissey,[36] *dessinateur de la Chambre du Roi*. Significantly, this office was to be linked with the *Menus Plaisirs* from that period up to the end of the Old Regime.

Apart from the costs of constuction and lighting, there are other expenses which art historians often neglect, even though they represent substantial sums. For example, several acting companies[37] were paid 48,600 *livres tournois* a year according to the 1669 accounts. Payments to actors were granted in accordance with existing payments to musicians,[38] which means that some festival expenses had become *permanent*. In addition, transporting and accommodating actors,

---

[33] Set consisting of foliage.

[34] Jérôme de La Gorce, *Carlo Vigarani*, p. 96.

[35] Charles Perrault was *contrôleur des Bâtiments du Roi*.

[36] Jérôme de La Gorce, *Carlo Vigarani*, pp. 118–19.

[37] *Comédiens Espagnols*, *Comédiens Italiens* and *Comédiens du Palais-Royal*.

[38] Even if actors from the *Comédie Française* and the *Comédie Italienne* would never have been granted the same status as musicians from the *Musique de la Chambre* or *Musique de la Chapelle du Roi*.

Table 14.2 1669 entertainment expenses in *livres tournois* (French currency unit under the Old Regime), according to payment orders delivered to the *Argenterie* Treasurer and the *Menus Plaisirs'* Treasurer[39]

Argenterie: 55,177lt 14s 6d	Paid by *Argenterie* to the *Garde-Meuble* suppliers for the 'Grand Canal' boats: 18,096*lt* 14*s*	*Menus Plaisirs*: 151, 830*lt* 17*s* 10*d*

musicians and every kind of artist and craftsman also represented significant expense. Some work was necessary in Chambord, for instance, as an item from the 1669 *Menus Plaisirs* book clearly shows.[40] Indeed, festival requirements transformed not only the gallery, orangery or room where a ball or play took place, but in fact the whole palace, since it was necessary to accommodate extra people in addition to the audience. Making space for festival implied many alterations to the palace fabric, because magnificence had to be overt and ostentatious.

Towards the integration of festival into court ceremonial

The settling of the Court at Versailles in 1682 seems to mean the end of festival culture in every respect. There were no more magnificent festivals lasting several days, and the overall historical account insists on the dullness and contentiousness of court life after the death of Queen Marie-Thérèse. In and after 1691, the *Menus Plaisirs* kept records which listed all the payment orders for each financial year. These *États de la dépense* are much more complete and coherent than the books of payment orders that survive for previous periods,[41] a consideration which must be kept in mind when comparing 1669 data with those of following years. However, as Table 14.3 shows, the documents enable us to produce some striking figures which may be used to illustrate court life in decline, but should nevertheless be put into perspective.

---

[39] *Archives nationales* (Paris), O[1] 2816 and 2817. Jérôme de La Gorce (*Carlo Vigarani*, pp. 95–102) allocates very specific amounts to the *Ballet de Flore* stage machines (79,622 *livres tournois*) and the Chambord ephemeral theatre (30, 972 *livres tournois* 18 *sous* 6 *deniers*). By contrast, Marie-Christine Moine (*Les Fêtes à la cour du Roi-Soleil*, p. 202) gives annual amounts from data established by the *Menus Plaisirs* administration in the eighteenth century – see below – but without distinguishing entertainment expenses from others.

[40] *Archives nationales* (Paris), O[1] 2817, no. 33: '*paiement de la despence qui a esté faicte tant pour la construction de plusieurs cloisonnages de planches pour des logemens aux musiciens, danceurs, comediens que j'ay fait venir à Chambord [. . .]*'.

[41] Lemaigre-Gaffier, *L'Administration des Menus Plaisirs*, vol. 1, pp. 218–52.

Table 14.3 Comparison between the 1669 *Argenterie* and *Menus Plaisirs* expenses and the 1698 expenses (in *livres tournois* and gold marks)[42]

	Entertainment expenses	**Expenses for main elements of court life**[43]
1669	222,105*lt* (593 gold marks)	276,569*lt*[44] (623 gold marks)
1698	30,645*lt* (60 gold marks)	56,121*lt* (111 gold marks)

Even if the 1698 accounts are the first *États de la dépense* outside war time, expenses for every kind of festivity turn out to have dwindled drastically. Even after the Ryswick Treaty, they remained very low compared to expenses in the 1660s. However, we can choose to allocate to festival spirit not only entertainment but also spectacle. In this perspective, if we add in all the expenses for every kind of circumstance which made court life a performance, the gap is much less wide.

The allocation of these expenses is of interest. In the case of entertainment expenses, it appears that investment in settings had become minor and that the *Menus Plaisirs* used mainly props, rather than sets, in staging palace events. Plate 16a shows that lights, costumes and stage properties took up 56% of entertainment expenses: 4,401 *livres tournois* were paid to a wax seller and 2,012 *livres tournois* to two tailors. These payments, added to the huge amount of 10,367 *livres tournois* paid to three carriers, represent the major payments to suppliers in 1698.

This division of expenses reveals how the administration henceforth supplied Versailles by contrast with other palaces. As a matter of fact, it is necessary to emphasise that 80% of entertainment expenses were devoted to the court's habitual autumn residence in Fontainebleau. In Versailles, *appartement* evenings alternated with comedies to entertain courtiers.[44] In this way different kinds of entertainment, including festivals, followed each other over an extended period, but these exceptional occurrences were replaced with subtle changes of emphasis under the *Menus Plaisirs* administration. Just as the *grand appartement* constituted a magnificent setting for the *appartement* evenings, ephemeral indoor and outdoor theatres were replaced by a new theatre, still ephemeral but located permanently

[42] For the 1698 expenses, see *Archives nationales* (Paris), O[1] 2830. According to Marcel Marion, in *Dictionnaire des institutions de la France aux xvii*[e] et *xviii*[e] siècles (Paris: Picard,1993 [1923]), p. 384, 1 *marc d'or* (gold mark) was worth 444 *livres tournois* at the beginning of the reign of Louis XIV, whereas 507 *livres tournois* were worth only one *marc d'or* in 1693, after monetary changes had begun.

[43] I only exclude daily supplies (clothes and furniture).

[44] On court theatre in Versailles after 1682, see Beaussant and Bouchenot-Déchin, *Les Plaisirs de Versailles*, pp. 67–75; Leferme-Falguières, *Les Courtisans*, pp. 259–70; Lemaigre-Gaffier, *L'Administration des Menus Plaisirs*, vol. 2, pp. 285–306.

in the Princes' Courtyard.[45] Fontainebleau's *theâtre de l'aile de la Belle Cheminée* was however bigger than the *théâtre de la Cour des Princes* at Versailles and could be used for *comédies-ballets* and operas.[46] While the *Menus Plaisirs* presented comedies three times a week in Versailles – so as to integrate festival into ceremonial's daily rhythms – they also helped to make Fontainebleau, both outdoors and indoors, a location additional to the artificial gardens of the palace of Versailles – a location where both hunting and *grand spectacle* could come together each year to create spectacular festivals. These practical arrangements for court theatre in Versailles and Fontainebleau reveal the role *Menus Plaisirs* played in reviving, in the new circumstances, the memory of a former court life, itinerant and dependent on ephemeral settings.

Versailles became a permanent setting devoted to the glory of the king: the palace was no longer merely an *image* but also an *extension* of the king's body,[47] a circumstance to which the *Menus Plaisirs* contributed by sometimes taking on the responsibilities of other departments and supplying specific clothes, props and furniture up to the end of the Old Regime. In spite of a huge decline in expenditure, the administration remained active everywhere, as Plate 16b suggests. Whereas their main expenditure on court theatre was related to transporting and accommodating the *Comédiens du Roi*, who came from Paris, the *Menus Plaisirs* spent proportionately more for clothes, furniture and portable items provided to the king, the royal family and the Household officers to be used in court ritual – for example, a religious procession or the presentation of a *Te Deum*.

Moreover, the end of the seventeenth century is the moment when liturgy developed to glorify the dynasty through baptisms, weddings and funerals, which were also integrated into royal ceremonial.[48] For instance, members of the royal family were buried with great solemnity and magnificence during a series of ceremonies in Versailles, Saint-Denis and Notre-Dame, implying detailed organisation in these places. In 1683, the *Menus Plaisirs* Treasurer paid 89,654 *livres tournois* for the funeral of Queen Marie-Thérèse, representing 46% of his annual outlay.[49] These costs totaled more than all 1685's entertainment expenses.[50] The *Menus Plaisirs* artists, such as Henri Gissey, were charged with adopting an Italian style

[45] Vincent Pruchnicki, 'Un théâtre au château de Versailles: la comédie de la cour des Princes', *Bulletin du Centre de recherche du château de Versailles*, 2009, www.crcv.revues.org/10139.

[46] *Théâtre de Cour: Les spectacles à Fontainebleau au xviiie* siècle (Paris: Réunion des Musées Nationaux, 2005).

[47] Edouard Pommier, 'Versailles, l'image du souverain', in Pierre Nora (ed.), *Les Lieux de mémoire*, 3 vols (Paris: Gallimard, 1997), vol. 1, 2 *La Nation*, pp. 1253–81; Gérard Sabatier, *Versailles ou la figure du roi* (Paris: Albin Michel, 1999).

[48] Leferme-Falguières, *Les Courtisans*, pp. 81–221.

[49] *Archives nationales* (Paris), O^1 2820.

[50] Almost 58,000 *livres tournois* according to *Archives nationales* (Paris), O^1 2822.

of funeral decoration; the growing part played by dynastic *pompes funèbres* in royal ceremonial stimulated the organisational process which transformed the whole institution. Thus, the *Menus Plaisirs* administration began to create its own stores in Paris (*magasins* or *hôtels*) and at every royal residence after Queen Marie-Thérèse's funeral – as the *Bâtiments du Roi* had already done.[51] They provided themselves with places to store and even re-use more and more props and sets. In the eighteenth century, they kept on developing these facilities and were therefore able to achieve recognition as festival craftsmen, even in outdoor locations. They would devise innovative stage designs in order to create a specifically royal mode of theatrical presentation, which associated dramatic performance with material luxury, thus embracing ordinary spectacles as well as dynastic liturgy, in the way that the largest festivals in the eighteenth century brought together theatre with princely weddings.[52]

Louis XIV's reign and the reputation of the *Menus Plaisirs* in the eighteenth century

From the 1690s on, the *Menus Plaisirs* administration grew and became a fully-developed organisation, making use of its own stores and developing its own staff. In this process, archives played a crucial role, both as legal backing and management tool. First of all, the administrators devised rules in order to create an official framework in which accounts, inventories and registers could be produced and kept. Besides, they tried to collect as many ancient documents as possible, so as to have available long-term information from the beginning of Henri IV's reign – that is to say, not only an historical perspective but a dynastic one.

The *Menus Plaisirs* archives[53]

The accounts system formed part of a documentary practice whose first aim was to secure legal protection within the general framework of the audit of public finances. Documents were submitted to the Chamber of Accounts, in charge of checking payment authorisation and even inventories from the mid-eighteenth century on. However, they could also be used by their compilers in legal cases, such as disputes with their creditors or within the State and Household administration.

From the seventeenth century to the beginning of the eighteenth century the regulations governing the financial dealings of the *Menus Plaisirs*, together with

[51] Lemaigre-Gaffier, *L'Administration des Menus Plaisirs*, vol. 2, pp. 105–6.

[52] Ibid., pp. 265–83.

[53] On the 'archivistic turn' in early modern history see Filippo de Vivo, 'Cœur de l'Etat, lieu de tension. Le tournant archivistique vu de Venise (XVe–XVIIe siècles)', *Annales. HSS*, 2013/3, 699–728.

the Wardrobe, *Garde-Meuble* or *Bâtiments du Roi*, enabled the administration to monitor the rights and practices of each of them within the king's Household. In 1716, the first Gentleman of the Bedchamber claimed authority over the *Grande Écurie*,[54] basing his case on accounting records for the funerals of Henri IV, Louis XIII and Ann of Austria. After giving evidence and getting recognition of his right to provide royal clothes and insignia, he was also authorised to revise and alter existing accounts.[55] Clothes and insignia ought to be items in the *Argenterie* accounts, whereas the *Argenterie* Treasurer had not in fact provided these clothes and insignia under his own authority nor had he paid for them. These accounts could be used in future as evidence of the rights of the first Gentlemen of the Bedchamber.

The accounts provided the *Menus Plaisirs*' officers, artists and employees with model documents which it was possible to produce as circumstances warranted. From this perspective, records management enabled them to establish ceremonial standards and to become keepers of the monarchy's history and status, just as the Ceremonies' Officers were.[56]

In the second part of the eighteenth century, financial and central administration regarded *Menus Plaisirs* as a Household department under public scrutiny and in need of reform. As stated by Papillon de La Ferté, the intendant of the *Menus Plaisirs* from 1756 to the end of the Old Regime, most of the *Contrôleurs généraux des Finances* did not understand why spectacles were necessary for the king's glory[57] and even less why an administration could make such unsubstantiated claims. From the 1750s, the *Menus Plaisirs* administrators continued to keep their accounts and documents, representing information they could use in the many *memoirs* they circulated within the royal administration when seeking to under-prop the legitimacy of their own department. These archives also constituted material evidence, similar to the objects stored in their *hôtels*, which they could call on publicly to testify to their political and symbolic role.[58]

A double collection of documents

At the beginning of the 1760s the *Menus Plaisirs* administrators built up a double collection of archival documents which they kept in the library they created in the new *hôtel* in Paris. As a detailed inventory proves, the *Etats de la dépense*, established in 1691, were stored in these archives and could therefore provide administrators and creative personnel with consistently tabulated information,

---

[54] The department of the Master of the Horse.

[55] *Archives nationales* (Paris), O[1] 1042, n° 138.

[56] Lemaigre-Gaffier, *L'Administration des Menus Plaisirs*, vol. 1, pp. 305–18.

[57] Denis Pierre Jean Papillon de La Ferté, *Journal des Menus Plaisirs du Roi. 1756–1780* (Clermont-Ferrand: Paléo, 2002), p. 8.

[58] Lemaigre-Gaffier, *L'Administration des Menus Plaisirs*, vol. 1, pp. 232–52.

since the classification of items in the accounts did not change significantly from the beginning to the end of the eighteenth century.[59] On the one hand, the *Etats de la dépense* were integrated into a very sophisticated accountancy system offering more accurate financial control and also easier access to information, thanks to the provision of *indices* and tables. On the other hand, the *Menus Plaisirs* tried to make up for a lack of standard records before 1691 by collecting every book of accounts they could find since the beginning of Henri IV's reign. In this way, they compiled a history of the Bourbon festivals through administrative and accountancy evidence.

Similarly, Papillon de La Ferté had various historical files made.[60] Each file corresponded to one of the responsibilities of the *Menus Plaisirs* – an object or event they were in charge of – and contained extracts of accounts, administrative rolls, newspapers such as the *Mercure de France*, or festival books. One of the files is devoted to outdoor festivals, in spite of the fact that during the seventeenth century this kind of event was in part under the authority of the *Bâtiments du Roi* administration. The *Menus Plaisirs* intendant used these files to write up a full record of the large festivals which took place in the 1660s and the 1670s. There is a copy of a *Recueil gravé des fêtes du Roy Louis Quatorze* which is annotated to explain the responsibilities the *Menus Plaisirs* shared during these festivals with other organisations in the king's Household (see Figures 14.1a and 14.1b). There are also many extracts from accounts, administrative correspondence and suppliers' invoices. Thus, the administrators of the *Menus Plaisirs* provided themselves with material and artistic information which demonstrated how they discharged their responsibilities.

Finally, two very distinct types of document produced by officers of the *Menus Plaisirs* show us precisely how seventeenth century performances and data could be used during the Enlightenment. For his own private office, but also for the conduct of the administration, the *Garde-Magasin* Lévêque created books in which he gathered works by various *dessinateurs de la Chambre* such as Henri Gissey or Berain.[61] Among them, there is a project Vigarani drew up for a puppet theatre (see Figure 14.2) that may have been that created for the 'entertainment' for which the famous Briocher was rewarded in 1669.[62]

Lévêque's books were integrated into the *Menus Plaisirs* archive; one of them was even copied so as to incorporate changes that made it perfectly appropriate for the second half of the eighteenth century.[63] The reign of Louis XIV served as a model, but an ambiguous one, which explains why the *Menus Plaisirs* administrators dared to draw on their archives to establish tables of comparison between

---

[59] *Archives nationales* (Paris), O[1] 2807.

[60] *Archives nationales* (Paris), O[1] 3259–3266.

[61] La Gorce and Jugie (eds), *Dans l'atelier des Menus Plaisirs du Roi.*

[62] *Archives nationales* (Paris), O[1] 2817, order no. 37.

[63] *Bibliothèque de l'Institut* (Paris), mss. no. 1003: "Habillements de Théâtre', par Denis-Pierre-Jean Papillon de La Ferté, intendant des Menus-Plaisirs (1777). Provient de la Bibliothèque des Menus-Plaisirs du Roy'. For instance, costumes from equestrian performances were not copied.

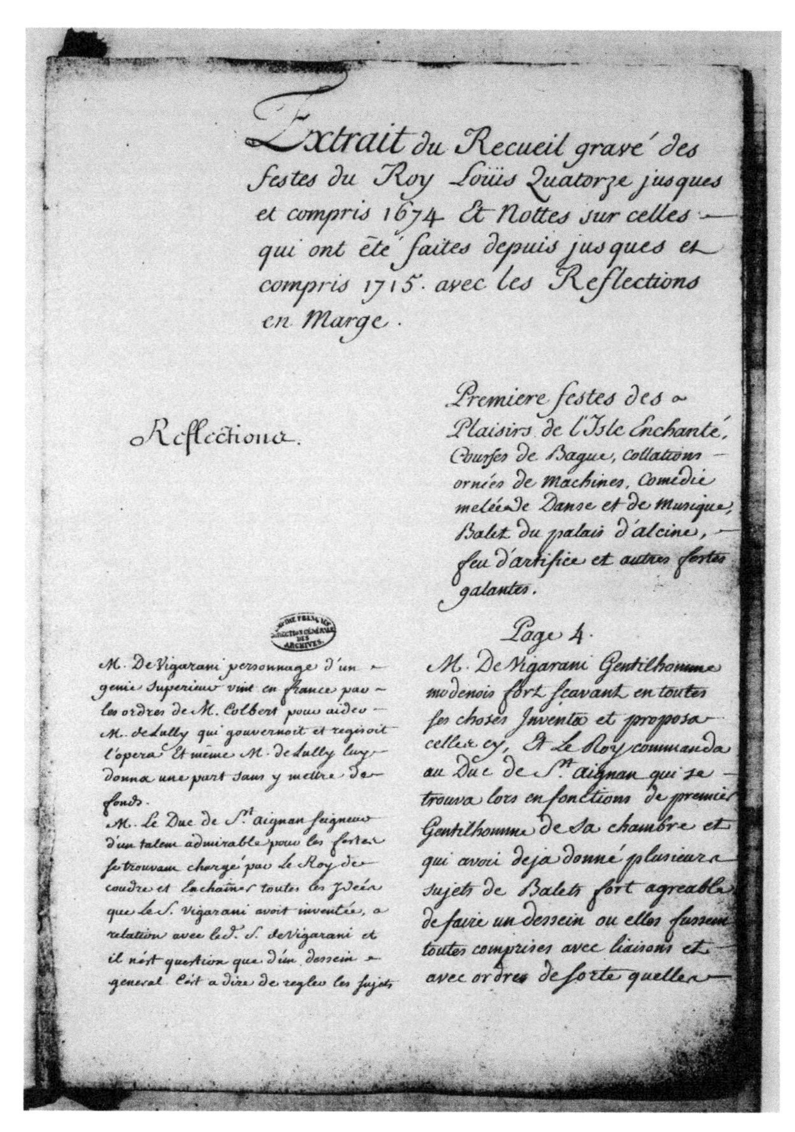

Extrait du Recueil gravé des festes du Roy Loüis Quatorze jusques et compris 1674 Et Nottes sur celles qui ont été faites depuis jusques et compris 1715. avec les Reflections en Marge.

Reflections.

Premiere festes des Plaisirs de l'Isle Enchanté, Courses de Bague, Collations ornées de machines, Comédie melée de Danse et de Musique, Balet du palais d'alcine, feu d'artifice et autres sortes galantes.

Page 4.

M. De Vigarani Gentilhomme modenois fort sçavant en toutes ses choses Invента et proposa celles cy, Et Le Roy commanda au Duc de St. aignan qui se trouva lors en fonctions de premier Gentilhomme de sa chambre et qui avoit deja donné plusieurs sujets de Balets fort agreables de faire un dessein ou elles fussent toutes comprises avec liaisons et avec ordres de sorte quelles

M. De Vigarani personnage d'un genie superieur vint en france par les ordres de M. Colbert pour aider M. de Lully qui gouvernoit et regissoit l'opera Et même M. de Lully luy donna une part sans y mettre de fonds.

M. Le Duc de St. aignan seigneur d'un talent admirable pour les fetes se trouvant chargé par Le Roy de coudre et Enchainer toutes les Idées que le S. Vigarani avoit inventées, a relation avec led. S. de Vigarani et il n'est question que d'un dessein general C'est a dire de regler les sujets

Figures 14.1a and 14.1b Examples of documents compiled in the *Menus Plaisirs* file devoted to outdoor festivals (*Archives nationales* (Paris), O[1] 3263, n° 2 and 3) (© With permission of the *Archives nationales* (*Centre de recherche du Château de Versailles*))

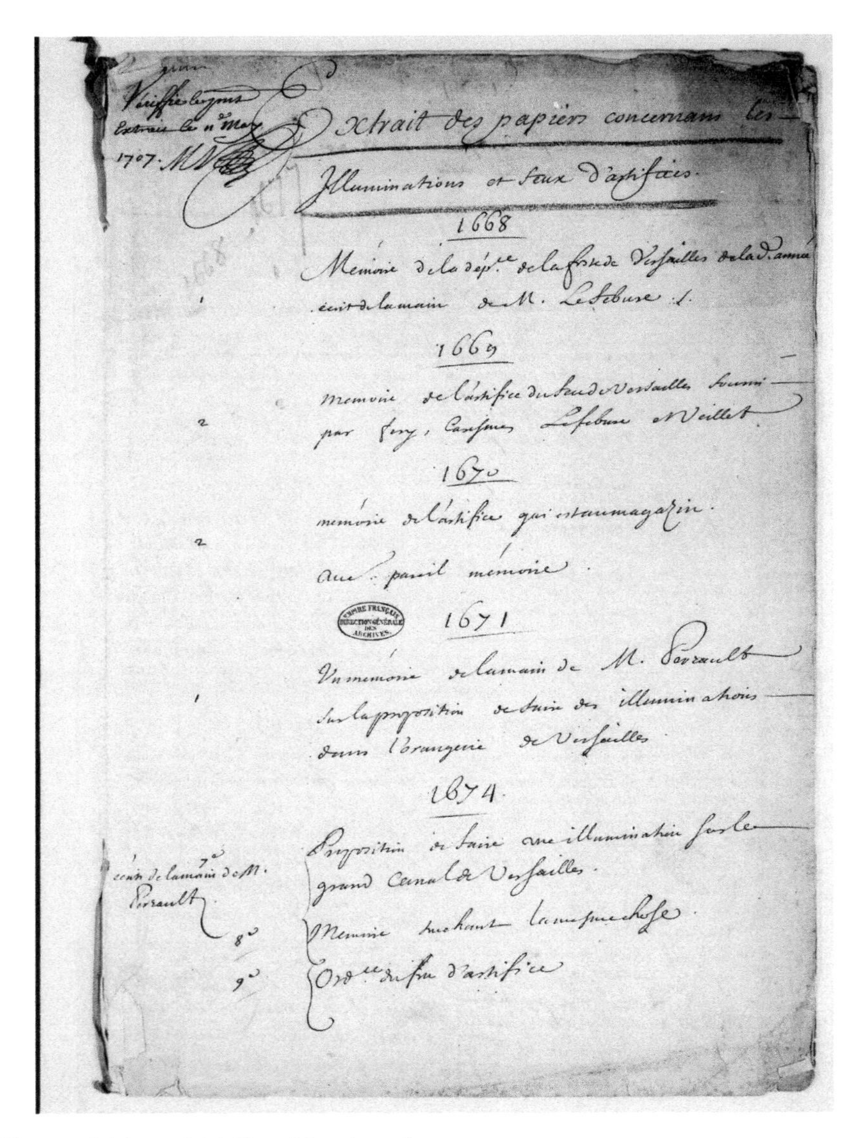
Extrait des papiers concernant les
Illuminations et feux d'artifices.

1668

Memoire de la dep.ce de la feste de Versailles de lad. année
escrit de la main de M. Le Febure 1.

1669

memoire de l'artifice du feu de Versailles fourni
par Jory, Caresmes Lefebure et Veillet.

1670

memoire de l'artifice qui est au magazin.

autre pareil memoire.

1671

Un memoire de la main de M. Perrault
sur la proposition de faire des illuminations
dans l'orangerie de Versailles.

1674

7° Proposition de faire une illumination sur le grand Canal de Versailles.
8° Memoire touchant la mesme chose.
9° Ord.ce du feu d'artifice

escrit de la main de M. Perrault

Figures 14.1a and 14.1b (Continued)

expenses in the 1760s and those incurred in the 1660s.[64] The administrators used these figures in an attempt to prove that the *Menus Plaisirs* had become a fully-fledged organisation, whose administrators were good managers, succeeding in spending less than in the *Grand Siècle*.

---

[64] *Archives nationales* (Paris), O^1 3095.

Figure 14.2 Carlo Vigarani, Puppet theatre for Saint-Germain-en-Laye (1669) (© With permission of the *Archives nationales* (Paris), O^1 3238^A)

Despite the figures, festival and entertainment expenses in the Enlightenment were at least as high as they had been in the first part of Louis XIV's reign,[65] since the *Menus Plaisirs* strengthened their institutional position in court life by heavy expenditure on the staging of festivals. Thus, an organisation specializing in ephemeral performances can be viewed as comparable to those which created permanent settings, both in Versailles and Paris, locations where the *Menus Plaisirs* produced more and more props and settings for court theatre and royal ceremonies.

[65] In 1762, court theatre expenses represented 489,484 *livres tournois* (661 gold marks), without considering other performances and ceremonies, nor what the maintenance of stores cost where lots of props and sets were produced. See Pauline Lemaigre-Gaffier, 'Les Menus Plaisirs, gestionnaires de la vie théâtrale des Lumières', *European Performance and Drama Studies*, 1 (2013), 49–75.

Bibliography

Primary sources

L'Etat de la France (Paris: David père, 1749).

Papillon de La Ferté, Denis Pierre Jean, *Journal des Menus Plaisirs du Roi. 1756–1780* (Clermont-Ferrand: Paléo, 2002).

Secondary sources

Beaussant, Philippe and Patricia Bouchenot-Déchin, *Les Plaisirs de Versailles. Théâtre et Musique* (Paris: Fayard, 1996).

Béhar, Pierre and Helen Watanabe-O'Kelly (eds), *Spectaculum Europaeum: Theatre and Spectacle in Europe/Histoire du Spectacle en Europe (1580–1750)* (Wiesbaden: Harrassowitz Verlag, 1999).

Castelluccio, Stéphane, *Le Garde-Meuble de la Couronne et ses intendants du XVIe au XVIIIe siècles* (Paris: Comité des Travaux Historiques et Scientifiques, 2004).

Christout, Marie-Françoise, *Le Ballet de Cour de Louis XIV: 1643–1712* (Paris: Picard, 2005 [1967]).

Duindam, Jeroen, *Vienna and Versailles. The Court of Europe's Dynastic Rivals. 1550–1780* (Cambridge: Cambridge University Press, 2003).

Félibien, André, *Les Fêtes de Versailles*, ed. Michel Jeanneret (Paris: Le Promeneur, 2012).

Giesey, Ralph, *Cérémonial et puissance souveraine. France XIVe–XVIIe siècles* (Paris: Cahier des Annales, no. 41, 1987).

Jeanneret, Michel, *Versailles. Ordre et Chaos* (Paris: Gallimard, 2012).

La Gorce, Jérôme de, *Carlo Vigarani intendant des plaisirs de Louis XIV* (Paris/Versailles: Perrin, 2005).

La Gorce, Jérôme de and Pierre Jugie (eds), *Les Menus Plaisirs du Roi. XVIIe–XVIIIe siècle* (Paris: Presses de l'Université Paris-Sorbonne, 2013).

La Gorce, Jérôme de and Pierre Jugie, *Dans l'atelier des Menus Plaisirs du Roi. Spectacles, fêtes et cérémonies aux XVIIe et XVIIIe siècles* (Paris: Archives nationales/Artlys, 2011).

Leferme-Falguières, Frédérique, *Les Courtisans: Une société de spectacle sous l'Ancien Régime* (Paris: Presses Universitaires de France, 2007).

Lemaigre-Gaffier, Pauline, *Du cœur de la Maison du Roi à l'esprit des institutions. L'Administration des Menus Plaisirs du Roi au XVIIIe siècle*, 3 vols. (Diss., Université Paris 1, 2011).

Lemaigre-Gaffier, Pauline, 'Les Menus Plaisirs, gestionnaires de la vie théâtrale des Lumières', *European Performance and Drama Studies*, 1 (2013), 49–75.

Mariani, Raphaël, *Les Menus Plaisirs dans la vie quotidienne du Roi et des princes. 1715–1774* (Paris: Université Paris 4, Sorbonne, 2000).

Mariani, Raphaël, *Les Menus Plaisirs dans la vie quotidienne de la famille royale. 1770–1792* (Paris: Université Paris 4, Sorbonne, 2001).

Moine, Marie-Christine, *Les Fêtes à la Cour du Roi-Soleil. 1653–1715* (Paris: F. Sorlot and F. Lanore, 1984).

Newton, William Richtey, *La Petite Cour. Domestiques et serviteurs à Versailles au XVIIIe siècle* (Paris: Perrin, 2003).

Nguyen, Marie-Lan, *Les Grands-Maîtres des Cérémonies et le service des Cérémonies à l'époque moderne. 1585–1792* (Paris: Université Paris 4, Sorbonne, 1999).

Ozouf, Mona, 'La fête sous la Révolution française', in Jacques Le Goff and Pierre Nora (eds), *Faire de l'histoire*, 3 vols (Paris: Gallimard, 1974), vol. 3, *Nouveaux Objets*.

Pinon, Pierre, Patrick Brasart and Claude Malécot, *Des Menus Plaisirs aux droits de l'homme. La salle des États-généraux à Versailles* (Paris: Caisse nationale des Monuments historiques et des sites, 1989).

Pommier, Edouard, 'Versailles, l'image du souverain', in Pierre Nora (ed.), *Les Lieux de mémoire*, 3 vols (Paris: Gallimard, 1997), vol. 1, pp. 1253–81.

Pruchnicki, Vincent, 'Un théâtre au château de Versailles: la comédie de la cour des Princes', *Bulletin du Centre de recherche du château de Versailles*, 2009, www.crcv.revues.org/10139

Sabatier, Gérard, *Versailles ou la figure du roi* (Paris: Albin Michel, 1999).

Sorkine, Florence, *Propagande et mécénat royal: les fêtes louis-quatorziennes à Versailles et leurs représentations. 1661–1682* (Diss., Paris: Université Paris 3, Sorbonne Nouvelle, 1993).

Théâtre de Cour: Les spectacles à Fontainebleau au XVIIIe siècle, Exhibition Catalogue (Paris: Réunion des Musées nationaux, 2005).

Viala, Alain, *La France galante. Essai historique sur une catégorie culturelle de ses origines jusqu'à la Révolution* (Paris: Presses Universitaires de France, 2008).

Vivo, Filippo de, 'Cœur de l'Etat, lieu de tension. Le tournant archivistique vu de Venise (XVe–XVIIe siècles)', *Annales. HSS* (2013/3), 699–728.

Index

This index includes the personal names and brief descriptions of those architects, landscape designers, urban planners, artists, performers, scenographers and composers who created or were principal participants in Festivals, and those who commissioned these events or were otherwise important historical or cultural figures. It also lists the sites where performances were held and other named locations. Names mentioned in footnote references and bibliographies are not included. The names of twentieth- and twenty-first century scholars and commentators are also omitted; these names can be found in the extensive bibliographies which follow each chapter. Figures and plates illustrating the various Festivals are indicated by ***bold*** *numerals.*